CONVECTION OVEN COOKBOOK

© Copyright 2021 - All rights reserved.

This document is geared towards providing exact and reliable information in regard to the topic and issue covered.

- From a Declaration of Principles which was accepted and approved equally by a Committee of the American Bar Association and a Committee of Publishers and Associations.

In no way is it legal to reproduce, duplicate, or transmit any part of this document in either electronic means or in printed format. All rights reserved.

The information provided herein is stated to be truthful and consistent, in that any liability, in terms of inattention or otherwise, by any usage or abuse of any policies, processes, or directions contained within is the solitary and utter responsibility of the recipient reader. Under no circumstances will any legal responsibility or blame be held against the publisher for any reparation, damages, or monetary loss due to the information herein, either directly or indirectly.

Respective authors own all copyrights not held by the publisher.

The information herein is offered for informational purposes solely and is universal as so. The presentation of the information is without contract or any type of guarantee assurance.

The trademarks that are used are without any consent, and the publication of the trademark is without permission or backing by the trademark owner. All trademarks and brands within this book are for clarifying purposes only and are owned by the owners themselves, not affiliated with this document.

Table of Contents

8

Introduction

If you are looking for a way to cook that is both healthier and faster than your traditional oven, then the convection oven might be the cooking solution for you. A convection oven cooks food by circulating hot air inside of it. This circulation ensures that food will be cooked at a quicker rate without sacrificing its flavor or texture.

The latest models also include automatic temperature adjustment, delayed timer start, and rapid preheating, where they can reach high temperatures within minutes. With these features, you can prepare your dishes at a fraction of the time it would take on the traditional stovetop.

The first step to cooking with a convection oven is familiarizing yourself with its operation. There are many different models available in the marketplace. Each model has different speeds and speeds that you need to match your recipe with.

There are three primary areas when buying a convection oven: size, warranty, and accessories. Most convection ovens can be adjusted to fit into any size kitchen. The materials that the machine is made of also vary depending on which model you choose. Most units are made of stainless steel, but some models are made with aluminum. Most come with a warranty for the product's life, but some models offer one-year warranties instead. Finally, most units feature accessories like cooking racks, fan covers, and shelves with clips for keeping dishes straight while cooking.

There are many different types, but there are three main categories: microwave ovens, conventional ovens, and convection or big-bake cooktops. Microwaves cook using electromagnetic radiation, which heats the food from outside in instead of from inside out like conventional ovens do. Conventional ovens work by circulating hot air within the kitchen to cook food directly. Convective cooking is a combination of both heating methods. This cooking method is more efficient than warm air since a fan circulates hot air over the dish.

It is important to note that each has different features for convection ovens and may have all the possible settings mentioned below. Here is a list of all the possible settings found in a convection oven:

- **Main settings:** the temperature range is the first set to be considered. The convection oven can vary from a lower temperature of about 200° F for a grill to as high as 450° F for a pizza oven or broiler. Most of these types of ovens have lower end ranging from 250° F to 350° F whereas higher-end ranges from 400° F to 450° F. Depending on the type of food you are cooking in an oven; a different amount of heat is required to achieve the best result. For instance, a pizza might require a higher temperature to achieve a crispy crust or browning, while a roasted chicken or pork might require a lower temperature. These kinds of ovens usually have an extensive range from 250° F to 450° F.

- **Compressor:** this setting determines if there is a compressor or not. The convection ovens with a compressor run on a higher temperature range of 525° F to 550° F. If the oven doesn't have a compressor, it will run at 325° F to 375° F.

- **Fan speed:** this setting determines if the fan will be on or off. The fan will work hard and churn out as much as 1900 cm of airflow for convection results if it is set at high. If the fan is turned off, the airflow will be considerably less.

- **Settings for baking:** in many cases, there are settings to bake bread, cookies, and cake along with various levels of browning for your recipes. One example is when baking bread at lower temperatures of about 250° F, you would need the light setting for browning to avoid over-browning. This feature is useful when using convection cooking in combination with other cooking such as rotisserie. You can also get a crispy exterior by using the convection bake setting.

- **Settings for cooking pizza, meat, poultry, and more:** you can choose specific settings for cooking these types of food, including broil, roast, microwave, and convection cook. Broil is typically used for chicken or roast. Microwave is commonly used for cooking fast food items like chicken wings, burgers, or sandwiches. The convection cook setting usually helps to achieve browning and maintain a steady temperature level during the entire cooking process. A larger oven has many settings to help accomplish specific tasks for larger meals, such as roasts, casseroles, or even cheesecakes.

There are other exciting settings that you might come across, such as defrost, pastry, and pizza. Defrost is used to thaw meat and poultry to grill/roast it in a higher temperature setting. A pizza setting is used to brown the top before putting the pizza in the oven for an even baking effect. Pastry setting can be used to raise yeast dough and cook steaks and salmon quickly.

- **Settings for slow cooking:** typically, these types of convection ovens cook food with a combination of steam and radiant heat at lower temperatures that range from 170° F to 350° F. There is an automatic timer that shuts the oven off once the food has cooked. This setting is best used for cooking pot roast, slow-cooked ribs, or, furthermore, lasagna.

- **Settings for broiling:** usually, this is done using a rack in the uppermost position of the oven. There are mainly three settings helpful for this task: high broil, express broil and finish broil. The high broil option cooks the food quickly to obtain a good browning over it while having an even temperature across the surface to obtain that perfect finish. Combining this with convection bake is recommended to achieve browning in meat, particularly chicken pieces. The express broil option immediately starts broiling after you initiate it using a control knob. The finish broil option usually combines the broiling process's finish with the oven's primary function to provide a better result.

- **Warming settings:** this feature has a temperature range from about 150° F to 200° F and keeps food warm after cooking, especially when guests are waiting to be served. This setting helps food retain its flavor and texture without becoming burdensome or dry. You can also use this setting if you want to keep your food warm until it is served immediately without reheating.

- **Settings for grilling:** you will need to use a fireproof surround or broil rack in this type of oven. This serves the purpose of searing the food before placing it in the oven. The temperature level is relatively lower so that the food isn't cooked above the well-done range. The broiling effect can be achieved by using this setting with roast, grill, and roast again settings.

The oven's settings are critical in helping to create healthy meals with nutrient-rich foods. One can use their choice of timer styles to set the desired times for cooking their food. Some models have a signal to let you know when the food is fully cooked. The convection oven is also much better for meat dishes since heat circulates them much more uniformly instead of just building up in one spot.

The convection oven is already being used in commercial kitchens across the country. By cooking with this method, you are getting cooked meals much faster than before. You can use it at any time of your choosing to make your meals taste great while cutting out the excess fat and calories that come with traditional cooking methods. This machine will change how you think about healthy eating and make preparing your family's favorite foods even more accessible.

With the convection oven, you can create your favorite foods just like you would if you were cooking on your stovetop. Even better than that, it does it in less time than using traditional cooking techniques. By using this machine, you can quickly cook anything suitable for the stovetop and many baking dishes that might not be cooked in a conventional oven.

The convection oven uses a technology that circulates air within its chamber for faster and more uniform heating throughout the entire machine. When cooked food is put inside this oven, air blown from underneath creates a whirlwind effect to help circulate the air around your food. This ensures that the food will be cooked at a much faster rate without losing any of its natural juices or flavor that you expect from it.

The convection oven allows you to create all of your favorite foods in a fraction of the time it would typically take. The great thing about this machine is it can work on any cooking surface, so you can cook your food on a baking sheet if you want to. This is because the convection oven does not require anything beneath it to cook properly, unlike other types of ovens. Be sure to keep an eye on your dishes though because the results can vary by model and other factors such as altitude and weather conditions.

The convection oven can be used to cook your favorite foods in many different settings. Some models even come with features like voice activation and automatic temperature adjust, so you just have to set it and forget it as the oven does all the work for you. These settings make it easier than ever to create delicious meals without all of the hassles that usually come along with cooking.

From the Static Oven to the Convection Oven

FOOD	CONVENTIONAL OVEN		CONVECTION OVEN	
	Temp (°F)	Time	Temp (°F)	Time
CHICKEN				
Whole (5 lbs)	350	2 hrs to 2 hrs 15 mins	330	1 hr 30 mins to 1 hr 41 mins
Boneless Breast	350	20 to 30 mins	330	15 – 22 mins
Legs/Thighs (4-8 oz)	350	40 to 50 mins	330	30 – 37 mins
FISH				
Whole (3-5 lbs)	350	30 mins	330	22 mins
Fillet (3-5 lbs)	350	30 mins	330	22 mins
Steaks (3-5 lbs)	350	40 mins	330	30 mins
BEEF				
Rib Roast, Bone-In (4 lbs)	325	1 hr 30 mins to 1 hr 45 mins	305	1 hr 7 mins to 1 hr 18 mins
Rib Roast, Boneless (4 lbs)	325	1 hr 50 min to 2 hr 15 mins	305	1 hr 22 mins to 1 hr 41 mins
Round or Rump Roast (4 lbs)	325	2 hrs to 2 hrs 30 mins	305	1 hr 30 mins to 1 hr 52 mins
Tenderloin (4 lbs)	425	45 to 60 minutes	405	33-45 mins
PORK				
Loin Roast (2 lbs)	325	40 to 60 mins	305	30 – 45 mins
Crown Roast (4 lbs)	325	1 hr 20 mins to 2 hrs	305	1 hr to 1 hr 30 mins
Tenderloin (1 ½ lbs)	425	20 to 30 mins	405	15 – 22 mins
BAKED FOOD				
Pie Crust	350	10 mins	350	10 mins
Cake	350	40 to 45 mins	300	40 – 45 mins
Fruit Cobbler	400	25 to 30 mins	350	25 – 30 mins
Baked Potato	325	1 hr 30 mins	275	1 hr 30 mins

15 Minutes
Breakfast
1. Baked Oatmeal

Preparation Time: 10 minutes
Cooking Time: 15 minutes
Servings: 6
Ingredients:

- 1 egg
- 2 cups old fashioned oats
- 1 ½ tsp. baking powder
- ¼ cup maple syrup
- 1 ½ cups almond milk
- 1 cup strawberries, sliced
- 1 cup blueberries
- ½ tsp. salt
- 1/8 tsp. vanilla

Directions:
1. Preheat the oven to 375° F.
2. In a bowl, mix oats, salt, and baking powder.
3. Add egg, vanilla, maple syrup, and almond milk and stir well.
4. Add strawberries and blueberries and stir well.
5. Fill the oiled baking dish halfway with the mixture.
6. Place a baking dish onto the oven rack and bake for 20 minutes.
7. Serve and enjoy.
Nutrition: Calories: 413. **Fat:** 18.7 g. **Carbs:** 53.9 g. **Sugar:** 14.9 g. **Protein:** 9.3 g. **Cholesterol:** 27 mg.

2. Healthy Oat Muffins
Preparation Time: 10 minutes
Cooking Time: 15 minutes
Servings: 12
Ingredients:

- 2 eggs
- 1 cup oats
- ½ cup plain yogurt
- ½ cup maple syrup
- 1 tbsp. pumpkin pie spice
- 2 tsp. baking powder
- 1 cup butternut squash puree
- 1 cup flour
- 1 tsp. vanilla
- ⅓ cup olive oil
- ½ tsp. sea salt

Directions:
1. Preheat the oven to 390° F.
2. Spray 12-cups muffin tray with cooking spray and set aside.
3. Whisk eggs with vanilla, oil, yogurt, butternut squash puree, and maple syrup in a large bowl.
4. In a separate bowl, mix flour, pumpkin pie spice, oats, and salt.
5. Add flour mixture into the egg mixture and stir to combine.
6. Spoon the batter to the prepared muffin tray.
7. Place muffin tray onto the oven rack and bake for 20 minutes.
8. Serve and enjoy.
Nutrition: Calories: 167. **Fat:** 7.1 g. **Carbs:** 22.9 g. **Sugar:** 8.8 g. **Protein:** 3.5 g. **Cholesterol:** 28 mg.

3. Toasty Quinoa Chunky Bites
Preparation Time: 10 minutes
Cooking Time: 15 minutes
Servings: 4
Ingredients:

- 8 oz. walnuts
- ½ cup uncooked quinoa
- 1 tsp. salt
- 1 tbsp. olive oil
- 1 tsp. ground onion powder
- 1 tsp. paprika powder

Directions:
1. Preheat your oven to 400° F in "Air Fry" mode.
2. Take a bowl and mix everything.
3. Transfer mixture to a cooking basket lined with parchment paper.
4. Bake for 10 minutes.
5. Break into pieces and serve.
6. Enjoy!
Nutrition: Calories: 180. **Protein:** 5 g. **Fat:** 3 g. **Carbs:** 6 g.

4. Mexican Quinoa Lime
Preparation Time: 10 minutes
Cooking Time: 15 minutes
Servings: 4
Ingredients:

- 2 tbsp. avocado oil
- ¼ white onion, chopped
- Pinch of salt
- 2 garlic cloves, minced

- 1 cup quinoa
- ½ lime, juiced
- 1 tbsp. onion powder
- 1 tsp. chili powder
- ¼ tsp. paprika
- 2 cups vegetable stock

Directions:
1. Preheat your oven to 300° F in "Air Fry" mode.
2. Take a pan and place it over medium heat.
3. Add onion and salt. Sauté for 3 minutes.
4. Add garlic, quinoa, lime, cumin, chili, paprika, and sauté for 2 minutes.
5. Transfer mix to a cooking basket.
6. Add stock and cook for 20 to 25 minutes.
7. Serve and enjoy!

Nutrition: Calories: 266. **Protein:** 9 g. **Fat:** 8 g. **Carbs:** 8 g.

5. Morning Candied Walnut and Strawberry

Preparation Time: 10 minutes
Cooking Time: 15 minutes
Servings: 4
Ingredients:
- ½ cup walnuts, chopped
- 1 tbsp. raw agave nectar
- ¼ tsp. salt

Dressing:
- ½ cup strawberries, sliced
- 2 tbsp. shallots
- ½ cup grapeseed oil
- 2 tsp. raw agave nectar
- 1 tsp. onion powder
- 1 and ½ tsp. lime juice
- ½ tsp. ginger
- ¼ tsp. dill
- ¼ tsp. salt

Directions:
1. Coat walnuts with agave and salt.
2. Transfer to a cooking basket lined with parchment.
3. Preheat oven to 300° F in "Air Fry" mode, roast for 6 to 8 minutes.
4. Let them cool.
5. Add dressing ingredients to a bowl, blend for half a minute.
6. Add walnuts.
7. Mix and enjoy!

Nutrition: Calories: 260. **Protein:** 4value peg. **Fat:** 16 g. **Carbs:** 28 g.

6. Blueberry Pancake

Preparation Time: 10 minutes
Cooking Time: 15 minutes
Servings: 4
Ingredients:
- 2 cups all-purpose flour
- 1 cup hemp milk
- ½ cup spring water
- 2 tbsp. grapeseed
- ½ cup agave
- ½ cup blueberries
- ¼ tsp. sea moss
- 2 tbsp. hemp seeds
- Grapeseed oil

Directions:
1. Place moss, agave, hemp seeds, grapeseed oil, flour in a large bowl.
2. Mix well.
3. Add milk and water, mix until you have your desired consistency.
4. Toss in blueberries and toss well.
5. Preheat your oven to 325° F in "Air Fry" mode.
6. Transfer batter to the basket lined with parchment paper.
7. Cook for 3 to 4 minutes, flip and cook for 3 minutes more until golden on both side
8. Serve and enjoy!

Nutrition: Calories: 279. **Protein:** 9 g. **Fat:** 11 g. **Carbs:** 36 g.

7. Bacon, Egg, and Cheese Breakfast Hash

Preparation Time: 15 minutes
Cooking Time: 15 minutes
Servings: 4
Ingredients:
- 2 slices bacon
- 4 tiny potatoes
- ¼ tomato
- 1 egg
- ¼ cup shredded cheese

Directions:
1. Preheat the oven to 200° C or 400° F on bake mode. Set bits of bacon on a double-layer tin foil.
2. Cut the vegetables to put over the bacon. Crack an egg over it.
3. Shape the tin foil into a bowl and cook it in the oven at 177° C or 350° F for 15 to 20 minutes. Put some shredded cheese on top.

Nutrition: Calories: 150.5. **Carbs:** 18 g. **Protein:** 6 g. **Fat:** 6 g.

8. Southwestern Hash With Eggs

Preparation Time: 55 minutes
Cooking Time: 15 minutes
Servings: 4
Ingredients:

- 1-½ lbs. pork steak
- 1 tsp. vegetable oil
- 1 large potato, peeled and cubed
- 1 medium-sized onion, chopped
- 1 garlic clove, minced
- ½ cup green pepper, chopped
- 1 can diced tomatoes and green chilies
- 1 beef bouillon cube
- ½ tsp. ground cumin
- ½ tsp. salt
- ¼ tsp. pepper
- ⅛ tsp. cayenne pepper
- 4 eggs
- ¾ cup shredded cheddar cheese
- 4 corn tortillas (six inches)

Directions:

1. Cook pork in oil until brown and add potato, onion, garlic, green pepper. Cook for 4 minutes.
2. Stir in tomatoes, bouillon, cumin, salt, pepper, and cayenne. Cook with low heat until potatoes become tender.
3. Create four wells inside the hash and crack eggs into them.
4. Bake it in the oven uncovered for 10 to 12 minutes at 177° C or 350° F and scatter some cheese over it.
5. Serve over tortillas.

Nutrition: Calories: 520. **Carbs:** 29 g. **Protein:** 49 g. **Fat:** 23 g.

9. Maple-Glazed Sausages and Figs

Preparation Time: 20 minutes.
Cooking Time: 15 minutes.
Servings: 2
Ingredients:

- 2 tbsp. maple syrup
- 2 tbsp. balsamic vinegar
- 2 packages (12 oz. each) fully cooked chicken, cooked garlic sausages
- 8 fully ripe fresh figs, cut lengthwise
- ½ large sweet onion, minced
- 1-½ lbs. Swiss chard, with sliced stems, minced leaves
- 2 tsp. olive oil
- Salt and pepper

Directions:

1. Preheat the oven to 232° C or 450° F, mix syrup with 1 tbsp. of vinegar in a tiny bowl. Put sausages with figs on a one-layer foil-lined oven tray.
2. Roast for 8 to 10 minutes by grazing the syrup mix throughout the cooking.
3. Cook the onions in the oven in a bowl with plastic wrap for 9 minutes.
4. Mix oil and seasoning with 1 tsp. of vinegar. Serve the chards with figs and sausages.

Nutrition: Calories: 450. **Carbs:** 42 g. **Protein:** 34 g. **Fat:** 17 g.

10. Watching Over the Bay Sunday Brunch Benedict

Preparation Time: 10 minutes
Cooking Time: 15 minutes
Servings: 4
Ingredients:

- 4 bays English Muffins cut and toasted
- 4 eggs
- 1 lb. pancetta, chopped
- Smoky paprika
- Fresh cilantro
- Hollandaise sauce

Directions:

1. Put a muffin in the oven on both sides of the plates.
2. Make crisp pancetta in a small pan, cook eggs over easy, and prepare hollandaise sauce on the side.
3. Put pancetta evenly on top of muffins and eggs above the pancetta.
4. Put hollandaise sauce on top and sprinkle smoky paprika and freshly minced cilantro.

Nutrition: Calories: 560. **Carbs:** 39 g. **Protein:** 43 g. **Fat:** 29 g.

Brunch

11. Roasted Brussels Sprouts

Preparation Time: 30 minutes
Cooking Time: 15 minutes
Servings: 4
Ingredients:

- 2 lbs. brussels sprouts, cut
- ¼ cup olive oil
- Fresh lemon juice
- 1 tsp. minced fresh sage
- 2 tbsp. mixed seasonal herbs
- Salt and pepper
- ¼ cup Pine nuts
- ¼ cup freshly minced parmesan-Reggiano

Directions:

1. Preheat the oven to 204° F (200° C).
2. Coat the brussels sprouts with all the ingredients evenly in a plastic bag.
3. Put the brussels sprouts inside a huge sheet pan.
4. Roast for 10 minutes inside the oven. Put cheese, pine nuts, and some lemon juice afterward.

Nutrition: Calories: 135 **Carbs:** 11 g. **Protein:** 3.9 g. **Fat:** 9.8 g.

12. Grilled Cheese Sandwich

Preparation Time: 5 minutes
Cooking Time: 15 minutes
Servings: 2
Ingredients:

- 4 slices of sourdough bread
- 2 slices of cheddar cheese
- 2 tbsp. butter, unsalted, softened
- 2 slices of Havarti cheese

Directions:

1. Select the oven cooking technique after turning on the oven and setting the temperature to 375° F.
2. Meanwhile, spread the butter on one side of each bread slice and then place two bread slices butter-side-down on the oven tray.
3. Top the bread slices with 1 slice of Havarti and cheddar cheese, and then arrange the remaining bread slices on top of the cheese, butter-side up.
4. Place the oven tray into the oven and then cook for 7 minutes.
5. Flip the sandwiches, continue cooking them for 3 minutes until toasted on all sides, and then serve.

Nutrition: Calories: 334. **Fat:** 23 g. **Carbs:** 20 g. **Protein:** 13 g. **Fiber:** 2 g.

13. Hard-Boiled Eggs

Preparation Time: 5 minutes
Cooking Time: 15 minutes
Servings: 4
Ingredients:

- 4 eggs

Directions:

1. Select the oven cooking technique after turning on the oven and setting the temperature to 270° F.
2. Meanwhile, place the eggs in the oven basket.
3. Then place the oven basket into the oven and cook for 15 minutes or more until hard-boiled.
4. When done, transfer the eggs into the bowl containing chilled water and let them soak for 10 minutes.
5. Serve the eggs after peeling and slicing them.

Nutrition: Calories: 155. **Fat:** 11 g. **Carbs:** 1.1 g. **Protein:** 13 g. **Fiber:** 0 g.

14. Baked Eggs

Preparation Time: 5 minutes
Cooking Time: 15 minutes
Servings: 6
Ingredients:

- 6 slices of deli ham
- ¼ tsp. salt
- ¼ tsp. ground black pepper
- 6 eggs
- 3 tbsp. shredded cheddar cheese

Directions:

1. Select the oven cooking technique after turning on the oven and setting the temperature to 400° F.
2. Meanwhile, take 6 muffins cups, place a ham slice in it, and then crack an egg into each cup.
3. Sprinkle salt, black pepper, and cheese on top of each egg and then bake for 13 to 18 minutes until done.
4. Then switch on the broiler, continue cooking the eggs for 2 minutes, and then serve.

Nutrition: Calories: 213. **Fat:** 17 g. **Carbs:** 1 g. **Protein:** 14 g. **Fiber:** 0 g.

15. Sausage Patties

Preparation Time: 5 minutes
Cooking Time: 15 minutes
Servings: 8
Ingredients:

- 1 lb. breakfast sausage
- 1 tsp. salt
- ½ tsp. ground black pepper

Directions:

1. Select the oven cooking technique after turning on the oven and setting the temperature to 400° F.
2. Meanwhile, place sausage in a bowl, add salt and black pepper, and then stir until well combined.
3. Shape the mixture into patties, arrange patties on a parchment-lined baking pan and then bake for 10 minutes per side until cooked.
4. Then switch on the broiler, cook the patties for 2 minutes per side until browned, and serve.

Nutrition: Calories: 182. **Fat:** 15 g. **Carbs:** 1 g. **Protein:** 10 g. **Fiber:** 0 g.

16. Bacon

Preparation Time: 5 minutes
Cooking Time: 15 minutes
Servings: 12
Ingredients:

- 1 pound bacon

Directions:

1. Select the oven cooking technique after turning on the oven and setting the temperature to 350° F.
2. Meanwhile, arrange bacon on an oven basket in a single layer and then cook for 5 minutes per side until crispy.
3. Place the cooked bacon on a plate lined with paper towels to cool.
4. Serve straight away.

Nutrition: Calories: 46. **Fat:** 3.6 g. **Carbs:** 0.1 g. **Protein:** 3.1 g. **Fiber:** 0 g.

17. Baked Zucchini Chips

Preparation Time: 15 minutes
Cooking Time: 15 minutes
Servings: 4
Ingredients:

- 2 tbsp. extra virgin olive oil (extra virgin)
- 3 small zucchini rounds, cut into ¼-inch-thick slices
- 12 ½ cup seasoned Italian bread crumbs
- 2 tbsp. Parmesan ham, grated
- 2 tsp. oregano, virgin

Directions:

1. Preheat the oven at 350° F.
2. Zucchini should be put in a tub. Drizzle olive oil over zucchini and toss to cover; toss in bread crumbs to coat. On a baking sheet, spread out the zucchini that has been sprayed. Over the zucchini, sprinkle Parmesan cheese and oregano.
3. In a preheated oven, bake for 15 minutes, or until zucchini is soft and cheese is browned.

Nutrition: Calories: 143. **Protein:** 4.2 g. **Carbs:** 13.4 g. **Fat:** 8.5 g. **Cholesterol:** 2.4 mg. **Sodium:** 311.1mg.

18. Crispy Keto Onion Rings Recipe

Preparation Time: 5 minutes
Cooking Time: 15 minutes
Servings: 2
Ingredients:

- 59 g. / 2.1 oz. pork rinds (or make your own)
- 7 g. coconut flour
- 1 large egg (44 g.), beaten oil, deep-frying
- 1 big peeled and cut into rings onion (110 g.) salt and freshly ground black pepper chopped parsley

Directions:

1. Place the pork rinds in a bowl and blitz them into crumbs.

2. In a separate dish, combine the coconut flour and the beaten egg.
3. In a grill, heat enough oil to deep fry the onions. With batches, coat the onion rings in coconut flour and brush off the excess. Then dunk them in the egg and let the excess run out. Finally, press the onion rings onto the pork crumbs until they are fully covered.
4. Cook the rings for 4 to 5 minutes in the heated oil, rotating them carefully with a slotted spoon. Remove the item and thoroughly drain it.
5. Until serving, season with salt and freshly ground black pepper, and garnish with chopped parsley.

Nutrition: Calories: 219. **Sugar:** 3 g. **Fat:** 18 g. **Carbs:** 6 g. **Fiber:** 2 g. **Protein:** 7 g.

19. Air Fryer Cauliflower Fried Rice

Preparation Time: 5 minutes
Cooking Time: 15 minutes
Servings: 2
Ingredients:

- 1 frozen cauliflower rice bag (12 oz.)
- 2 slices daily sliced ham (approximately 11 percent fat)
- 2 large chickens
- 14 cups of green onions, chopped
- 2 tbsp. soy sauce (optional)

Directions:

1. Microwave the cauliflower rice for 5 to 6 minutes. Allow 1 minute to pass before carefully opening the package.
2. Preheat the air fryer to 400° F (200° C) before using. Aluminum foil can be used to cover the bottom and ½ inch of the basket ends.
3. In a mixing dish, combine the cauliflower rice, eggs, ham, green onions, and soy sauce.
4. 5 minutes in the air fryer. Remove the basket from the cauliflower mixture and stir it around. Cook for an extra 5 minutes in the air fryer.

Nutrition: Calories: 170. **Protein:** 16.2 g. **Carbs:** 11.6 g. **Fat:** 7.4 g. **Cholesterol:** 202 mg. **Sodium:** 1379 mg.

20. Winter Vegetable Frittata

Preparation Time: 5 minutes
Cooking Time: 15 minutes
Servings: 8
Ingredients:

- 2 carrots
- 1 pound parsnip
- ½ (small) (about 350 g.) celeriac is a kind of celeriac
- Garlic-infused gear oil blended from olive oil or a store-bought substitute
- 1 oz. (30 g.) butter that has not been salted
- 2 thyme sprigs, with the leaves removed

- A big handful of shredded kale leaves with the stalks cut
- 6 big beaten eggs 5 ¼ oz. (150 g.) crumbled Stilton or goat's cheese

Directions:

1. Preheat the grill to medium-high temperatures. Peel and dice carrots, parsnips, and celeriac into long, thin matchsticks.

2. In a big nonstick frying pan, heat a splash of garlic-infused olive oil over medium-high heat. After the butter has foamed, add the vegetable matchsticks and fry for 5 to 6 minutes, stirring often, until softened. Connect the thyme and cook, stirring occasionally, for a few minutes, until fragrant. Raise the heat to high and add the greens, cooking for 2 to 3 minutes, until softened. Switch off the heat in the tub.

3. Make sure the vegetables are uniformly spread around the bottom of the pan before pouring the beaten eggs on top. Return the pan to the stovetop over low heat and sprinkle the cheese on top. Cook for a few minutes until the eggs are gently set with a gentle wobble in the center of the plate, then slip the pan under the grill (protect the handle from the heat if it isn't Cook for a few minutes, or until the eggs are lightly set with a soft wobble in the middle (heatproof). Before turning it out and slicing it, remove the pan from the grill and set it aside for 2 to 3 minutes. Serve warm or at room temperature, as desired.

4. Tips:

5. We strongly advise you to try celeriac if you haven't already. It has an imposing appearance, with its knobs and nooks and crannies, and it is typically filthy. The good news is that it simply peels very quickly after a short shower, revealing its creamy-colored skin.

Nutrition: Calories: 169. **Carbs:** 7 g. **Protein:** 8 g. **Fat:** 11 g. **Saturated Fat:** 1 g. **Sodium:** 47 mg. **Potassium:** 73 mg. **Fiber:** 2 g. **Sugar:** 2 g. **Vitamin C:** 3.3 mg. **Calcium:** 7 mg. **Iron:** 0.1 mg.

21. Crispy Honey Garlic Chicken Wings

Preparation Time: 15 minutes
Cooking Time: 15 minutes
Servings: 6
Ingredients:

- 2 tbsp. extra virgin olive oil
- 4 garlic cloves, minced
- 1 cup honey
- ¼ cup soy sauce
- 1 tsp. black pepper
- 2 cups of flour
- 3 tbsp. ginger powder, to taste
- 1 tsp. cayenne pepper, or to taste
- 1 ½ tbsp. salt
- 2 tsp. cayenne pepper

- 3 lb. chicken wings
- 2 eggs
- 1 ½ cup rice
- 3 tbsp. water (cold)

Directions:

1. Heat the olive oil and garlic in a small saucepan over medium heat. Sauté the garlic until it softens but does not brown.

2. Combine the honey, soy sauce, and 1 tsp. black pepper in a mixing bowl.

3. Cook for 5 to 10 minutes, then remove from the heat and cool completely. As it simmers, keep an eye on it because it will quickly foam over the pot.

4. Combine the rice, ginger, cayenne pepper, salt, and 1 tbsp. black pepper in a mixing bowl.

5. Whisk together the eggs and water to produce an egg wash.

6. Wash the wings, pat them off, shorten the tips, and segment them.

7. Toss the wing parts in the flour mixture after dipping them in the egg wash. Place the coated wings in a deep fryer filled with canola, peanut, or soy oil that has been preheated to 350° F.

8. Depending on the size of the wing bits, fry until golden brown, around 15 to 20 minutes. Toss the wing pieces in a big mixing bowl with some of the honey garlic sauce while they're still hot out of the grease. Serve right away.

Nutrition: Calories: 540. **Saturated Fat:** 6 g. **Cholesterol:** 148 mg. **Sodium:** 2397 mg. **Carbs:** 50 g. **Fiber:** 1 g. **Sugar:** 35 g. **Protein:** 27 g.

Appetizers, Snacks, and Bun

22.   Potato Flakes Fish Fillets

Preparation Time: 20 minutes
Cooking Time: 15 minutes
Servings: 4
Ingredients:

- 1 egg
- 1 ½ cups instant potato flakes (mashed)
- ¼ cup frying oil
- 2 tbsp. yellow mustard (prepared)
- 6-oz. 4 fillets sole
- ½ tsp. salt
- Tomato sauce

Directions:

1.   Take one shallow dish and whisk salt, mustard, and egg together. Keep it aside. Put your potato flakes in a separate shallow dish.
2.   Preheat your convection oven to 375° F.
3.   Dip your fish fillets in whisked egg mixture and dredge them into potato flakes. Make sure to coat each fillet thoroughly.
4.   If you want extra crispy flavor, dip in the egg mixture and potato flakes again.
5.   Fry these fillets in the convection oven for almost 3 to 4 minutes on every side to make them golden brown. Serve warm with tomato sauce.

Nutrition: Calories: 368. **Protein:** 24.65 g. **Fat:** 19.63 g. **Carbs:** 22.88 g.

23.   Delicious Chicken Meatballs

Preparation Time: 30 minutes
Cooking Time: 15 minutes
Servings: 6
Ingredients:

- 1 lb. ground chicken
- 1 tbsp. Italian seasoning
- 1 tbsp. garlic powder
- 2 beaten eggs
- 1 ½ tbsp. vegetable oil
- ¼ cup cream cheese (light and roasted)
- 1 tsp. salt
- ¼ cup parmesan cheese (grated)
- 1 tsp. black pepper (ground)
- 1 tbsp. bread crumbs (dry)
- 1 tsp. crushed pepper flakes (red)

Directions:

1.   Preheat your convection oven to almost 450° F. Line one rimmed baking pan (to adjust in a convection oven) with an aluminum foil and grease with a cooking spray.
2.   Combine pepper, salt, vegetable oil, garlic powder, Italian seasoning, pepper flakes, bread crumbs, parmesan cheese, cream cheese, eggs, and chicken in one bowl.
3.   Form almost 20 meatballs with this mixture and put in one greased pan.
4.   Bake in your preheated convection oven for almost 17 to 18 minutes to clear all juice. Turn twice while cooking.

Nutrition: Calories: 470. **Protein:** 34.01 g. **Fat:** 33.07 g. **Carbs:** 7.34 g.

24.   Cauliflower Bites

Preparation Time: 10 minutes
Cooking Time: 15 minutes
Servings: 4
Ingredients:

- 1 head cauliflower, cut into small florets
- 1 tsp. garlic powder
- pinch of salt and pepper
- 1 tbsp. butter, melted
- ½ cup chili sauce
- Olive oil

Directions:

1.   Place cauliflower into a bowl and pour oil over florets to lightly cover.
2.   Season florets with salt, pepper, and garlic powder and toss well.
3.   Place florets into the air fryer oven at 350° for 14 minutes.
4.   Remove cauliflower from the Air Fryer.
5.   Combine the melted butter with the chili sauce.
6.   Pour over the florets so that they are well coated.
7.   Return to the air fryer oven and cook for an additional 3 to 4 minutes.
8.   Serve as a side or with ranch or cheese dip as a snack.

Nutrition: Calories: 75. **Protein:** 2.41 g. **Fat:** 2.25 g. **Carbs:** 11.16 g.

25.   Fried Pickles

Preparation Time: 5 minutes
Cooking Time: 15 minutes
Servings: 32
Ingredients:

- 32 slices of dill pickles
- ½ cup all-purpose flour

- ½ tsp. garlic powder
- ½ tsp. salt
- ½ tsp. cayenne pepper
- 2 cups panko breadcrumbs
- 2 tbsp. chopped dill
- 2 tbsp. dill pickle juice
- 3 eggs

Directions:

1.	Select the oven cooking technique after turning on the oven and setting the temperature to 400° F.

2.	Meanwhile, in a medium mixing basin, combine flour and salt.

3.	In a medium mixing bowl, crack the eggs, add the garlic powder, cayenne pepper, and pickle juice, and whisk to blend.

4.	Place panko breadcrumbs in a shallow dish, add dill and then stir until combined.

5.	Working on one slice of dill pickle, dredge it in flour mixture, dip into the egg mixture, coat in crumb mixture, and place in the oven basket.

6.	Spray oil over the pickle slices and then cook for 7 to 10 minutes per side until crisp and golden.

7.	Serve straight away.

Nutrition: Calories: 26. **Fat:** 1 g. **Carbs:** 1 g. **Protein:** 1 g. **Fiber:** 0 g.

## 26.	Smoky Potato Chips

Preparation Time: 5 minutes
Cooking Time: 15 minutes
Servings: 6
Ingredients:

- 1 ½ lb. potatoes
- ¾ tsp. salt, divided
- ¼ tsp. ground black pepper
- 1 tbsp. smoked paprika
- 2 tbsp. olive oil

Directions:

1.	Select the oven cooking technique after turning on the oven and setting the temperature to 400° F.

2.	Meanwhile, slice the potatoes into rounds, about ⅛-inch thick, and then pat dry with paper towels.

3.	Take a large bowl, place the potato slices into the bowl, add ½ tsp. salt, paprika, oil, and black pepper and then toss until coated.

4.	Spread the potato rounds in a single layer on the baking pan and then bake for 20 minutes until nicely browned.

5.	When done, sprinkle salt over the potato chips, cool completely, and then serve.

Nutrition: Calories: 130. **Fat:** 4.7 g. **Carbs:** 20 g. **Protein:** 2 g. **Fiber:** 2 g.

## 27.	Buffalo Cauliflower

Preparation Time: 15 minutes
Cooking Time: 15 minutes

Servings: 4
Ingredients:

- 1 cup panko breadcrumbs mixed with 1 tsp. salt
- 4 cups cauliflower florets
- ¼ cup butter, melted
- ¼ cup buffalo sauce
- Mayo

Directions:

1.	Add butter to a mug and microwave to melt it. Whisk in the buffalo sauce. Dip each floret into the above mixture and coat well. Dredge it in the panko/salt mixture and add to the oven basket.

2.	Place on top of the baking pan and position it in rack position 2. Set the temperature to 350° F and the time to 17 minutes. Serve with mayo.

Nutrition: Calories: 305. **Fat:** 19 g. **Carbs:** 28 g. **Protein:** 7 g.

## 28.	Chicken Nuggets

Preparation Time: 15 minutes
Cooking Time: 15 minutes
Servings: 4
Ingredients:

- ½ cup breadcrumbs
- ½ cup unsalted butter, melted
- 1 boneless, skinless chicken breast
- 2 tbsp. Parmesan, grated
- ¼ tsp. salt
- ⅛ tsp. black pepper

Directions:

1.	Trim fat from chicken and slice into ½ "thick slices. Cut each into 2 nuggets. Season with salt and pepper. Melt the butter in one bowl and mix the breadcrumbs and parmesan cheese in another.

2.	Dip each chicken piece in butter, then the breadcrumbs/cheese mixture. Add to the oven basket in a single layer.

3.	Place on top of the baking pan and position it in rack position 2. Set the temperature to 390° F and the time to 4 minutes.

Nutrition: Calories: 364. **Fat:** 15 g. **Carbs:** 5 g. **Protein:** 14 g.

## 29.	Mozzarella Sticks

Preparation Time: 15 minutes
Cooking Time: 15 minutes
Servings: 6
Ingredients:

- 1 egg
- ¼ cup mayonnaise
- ¼ cup breadcrumbs, fine and dry
- 12 oz. pack mozzarella cheese stick, each stick cut in half
- ¼ cup all-purpose flour

- ½ tsp. garlic powder
- ½ tsp. onion powder
- 1 cup marinara sauce

Directions:

1. Place the halved cheese sticks on a baking pan lined with parchment paper. Freeze for 30 minutes. Whisk egg and mayo in a bowl. Add breadcrumbs, flour, onion, and garlic powder to a bowl and mix to combine.

2. Roll the frozen cheese stick in the mayo-egg mixture to coat and then in flour mixture. Add the coated cheese sticks to the parchment-lined baking pan. Repeat with remaining cheese sticks. Freeze for 10 minutes.

3. Add the sticks to the oven basket. Place on top of the baking pan and position it in rack position 2. Set the temperature to 370° F and the time to 5 minutes. Serve with marinara sauce.

Nutrition: Calories: 273. **Fat:** 22 g. **Carbs:** 28 g. **Protein:** 22 g.

30. Jalapeno Poppers

Preparation Time: 15 minutes
Cooking Time: 15 minutes
Servings: 4

Ingredients:

- 4 oz. goat cheese
- 5 medium jalapenos
- 1 scoop salsa
- Salt, to taste
- Onion
- Cilantro
- Garlic

Directions:

1. Deseed the jalapenos and cut them in half. Add salsa and salt to goat cheese and mix well. Stuff the jalapenos halves with goat cheese mixture and add to the oven basket.

2. Place on top of the baking pan and position it in rack position 2. Set the temperature to 350° F and the time to 8 minutes. Serve.

Nutrition: Calories: 425. **Fat:** 17 g. **Carbs:** 37 g. **Protein:** 31 g.

31. Onion Rings

Preparation Time: 15 minutes
Cooking Time: 15 minutes
Servings: 2

Ingredients:

- 2 tbsp. olive oil
- ½ cup all-purpose flour
- 1 tsp. paprika
- 1 cup panko breadcrumbs
- 1 egg
- ½ cup buttermilk
- 1 sweet yellow onion, sliced

- 1 tsp. salt
- Cooking spray

Directions:

1. Mix paprika, flour, and ½ tsp. salt in a bowl. Mix buttermilk and egg in another bowl. Add ¼ cup flour mixture to this bowl.

2. Mix breadcrumbs, olive oil, and ½ tsp. salt in the third bowl and mix well. Dredge the onion rings in flour, buttermilk, and panko mixture in that order.

3. Add onion rings in a single layer into the oven basket. Place on top of the baking pan and position it in rack position 2. Set the temperature to 400° F and the time to 15 minutes. Serve.

Nutrition: Calories: 193. **Fat:** 8 g. **Carbs:** 26 g. **Protein:** 4 g.

32. Mozzarella Balls

Preparation Time: 20 minutes
Cooking Time: 15 minutes
Servings: 12

Ingredients:

- 1 egg
- 3 tbsp. cornstarch
- 2 cups mozzarella, grated
- 1 tbsp. oregano
- 1 cup Italian seasoned breadcrumbs
- 1 ½ tbsp. parmesan
- 1 ½ tsp. garlic powder
- 1 tsp. salt

Directions:

1. Add parmesan and cornstarch to shredded cheese and mix well. Roll the cheese into bite-sized balls and freeze for 1 hour.

2. Beat egg in a bowl; mix the garlic powder, salt, and breadcrumbs in another bowl. Dip cheese balls into the egg and coat well. Roll these balls in the breadcrumbs and place them on the baking pan.

3. Freeze for 20 minutes. Add the balls to the oven basket.

4. Place on top of the baking pan and position it in rack position 2. Set the temperature to 400° F and the time to 10 minutes. Let rest for 2 minutes. Serve.

Nutrition: Calories: 317. **Fat:** 13 g. **Carbs:** 37 g. **Protein:** 14 g.

Vegetables

33. Almond Flour Battered and Crisped Onion Rings

Preparation Time: 5 minutes
Cooking Time: 15 minutes
Servings: 4
Ingredients:

- ½ cup almond flour
- ¾ cup coconut milk
- 1 big white onion, sliced into rings
- 1 egg, beaten
- 1 tbsp. baking powder
- 1 tbsp. smoked paprika
- Salt and pepper to taste

Directions:
1. Preheat the air fryer oven for 5 minutes.
2. Combine the almond flour, baking powder, smoked paprika, salt, and pepper in a mixing bowl.
3. In another bowl, combine the eggs and coconut milk.
4. Soak the onion slices into the egg mixture.
5. Dredge the onion slices in the almond flour mixture.
6. Pour into the oven rack/basket. Set temperature to 325° F, and set time to 15 minutes. Select start/stop to begin. Shake the fryer basket for even cooking.

Nutrition: Calories: 217. **Fat:** 17.9 g. **Protein:** 5.3 g. **Carbs:** 6.52 g.

34. Asparagus Strata

Preparation Time: 12 minutes
Cooking Time: 15 minutes
Servings: 4
Ingredients:

- 6 asparagus spears, cut into 2-inch pieces
- 2 slices whole-wheat bread, cut into ½-inch cubes
- 4 eggs
- 3 tbsp. whole milk
- ½ cup grated Havarti or Swiss cheese
- 2 tbsp. chopped flat-leaf parsley
- Pinch salt
- Freshly ground black pepper

Directions:
1. Place the asparagus spears and 1 tbsp. of water in a 6-inch baking pan and place in the Air fryer basket oven.
2. Drain the asparagus after removing it from the pan. Spray the pan with nonstick cooking spray. Arrange the bread cubes and asparagus into the pan and set them aside. In a medium mixing basin, whisk together the eggs and milk until smooth. Add the cheese, parsley, salt, and pepper. Pour into the baking pan. Set temperature to 360° F, and set time to 14 minutes or until the eggs are set and the top starts to brown. Select START/STOP to begin.

Nutrition: Calories: 166. **Fat:** 49 g. **Protein:** 12 g. **Fiber:** 2 g.

35. Jalapeño Poppers

Preparation Time: 10 minutes
Cooking Time: 15 minutes
Servings: 4
Ingredients:

- 12-18 whole fresh jalapeño
- 1 cup refried beans (nonfat)
- 1 cup Monterey Jack or extra-sharp cheddar cheese, shredded
- 1 scallion, sliced
- 1 tsp. salt, divided
- ¼ cup all-purpose flour
- 2 large eggs
- ½ cup fine cornmeal
- Olive oil or canola oil cooking spray

Directions:
1. Start by slicing each jalapeño lengthwise on one side. Place the jalapeños side by side in a microwave-safe bowl and microwave them until they are slightly soft; usually around 5 minutes.
2. While your jalapeños cook; mix refried beans, scallions, ½ tsp. of salt, and cheese in a bowl.
3. Once your jalapeños are softened you can scoop out the seeds and add 1 tbsp. of your refried bean mixture (It can be a little less if the pepper is smaller.) Press the jalapeño closed around the filling.
4. In a small dish, whisk together your eggs and flour in a separate basin. In a third bowl mix your cornmeal and the remaining salt.
5. Each pepper should be rolled in flour, then dipped in egg, and then rolled in cornmeal, being careful to cover the entire pepper.
6. Spray the peppers with a cooking spray, such as olive oil cooking spray, and place them on a flat surface.
7. Pour into the oven rack/basket. Place the rack on the middle shelf of the Air fryer oven. Set temperature to 400° F, and set time to 5 minutes. Select Start/Stop to begin. Turn each pepper, and then cook for another 5 minutes; serve hot.

Nutrition: Calories: 244. **Fat:** 12 g. **Protein:** 12 g. **Fiber:** 2.4 g.

36. Parmesan Breaded Zucchini Chips

Preparation Time: 15 minutes
Cooking Time: 15 minutes
Servings: 5
Ingredients:
Zucchini chips:

- 2 medium zucchinis
- 2 eggs
- ⅓ cup bread crumbs

- $1/3$ cup grated Parmesan cheese
- Salt
- Pepper
- Cooking oil

Lemon aioli:
- $1/2$ cup mayonnaise
- $1/2$ tbsp. olive oil
- Juice of $1/2$ lemon
- 1 tsp. minced garlic
- Salt
- Pepper

Directions:

To make the zucchini chips:

1. Slice the zucchini into thin chips (about $1/8$ inch thick) using a knife or mandoline.
2. Beat the eggs in a small bowl. Combine the bread crumbs, Parmesan cheese, and salt & pepper to taste in a separate small bowl.
3. Cooking oil should be sprayed into the air fryer basket.
4. Dip the zucchini slices one at a time in the eggs and then the bread crumb mixture. You can also sprinkle the bread crumbs onto the zucchini slices with a spoon.
5. Place the zucchini chips in the air fryer basket, but do not stack.
6. Pour into the oven rack/basket. Place the rack on the middle shelf of the Air fryer oven. Cook in batches. Spray the chips with cooking oil from a distance (otherwise, the breading may fly off). Cook for 10 minutes.
7. Remove the cooked zucchini chips from the air fryer oven, then repeat with the remaining zucchini.

To make the lemon aioli:

8. While the zucchini is cooking, combine the mayonnaise, olive oil, lemon juice, and garlic in a small bowl, adjusting to taste with salt and pepper. Mix well until fully combined.
9. Cool the zucchini and serve alongside the aioli.

Nutrition: Calories: 192. **Fat:** 13 g. **Protein:** 6 g. **Fiber:** 4 g.

37. Bell Pepper-Corn Wrapped in Tortilla

Preparation Time: 5 minutes
Cooking Time: 15 minutes
Servings: 4
Ingredients:
- 1 small red bell pepper, chopped
- 1 small yellow onion, diced
- 1 tbsp. water
- 2 cobs grilled corn kernels
- 4 large tortillas
- 4 pieces commercial vegan nuggets, chopped
- Mixed greens for garnish

Directions:
1. Preheat the air fryer oven to 400° F.
2. In a skillet heated over medium heat, sauté the vegan nuggets together with the onions, bell peppers, and corn kernels. Set aside.
3. Place filling inside the corn tortillas.
4. Pour the tortillas into the oven rack/basket. Place the rack on the middle shelf of the Air fryer oven. Set temperature to 400° F, and set time to 15 minutes until the tortilla wraps are crispy.
5. Serve with mixed greens on top.

Nutrition: Calories: 548. **Fat:** 20.7 g. **Protein:** 46 g. **Carbs:** 43.54 g.

38. Creamy Spinach Quiche

Preparation Time: 10 minutes
Cooking Time: 15 minutes
Servings: 4
Ingredients:
- Premade quiche crust, chilled and rolled flat to a 7-inch round
- 2 eggs
- $1/4$ cup milk
- Pinch of salt and pepper
- 1 garlic clove, peeled and coarsely minced
- $1/2$ cup cooked spinach, drained and coarsely chopped
- $1/4$ cup shredded mozzarella cheese
- $1/4$ cup shredded cheddar cheese

Directions:
1. Preheat the air fryer oven to 360° F.
2. Press the premade crust into a 7-inch pie tin, or any appropriately sized glass or ceramic heat-safe dish. Press and trim at the edges if necessary. With a fork, pierce several holes in the dough to allow air circulation and prevent cracking of the crust while cooking.
3. Beat the eggs in a mixing dish until frothy and the yolks and whites are equally mixed.
4. Add milk, garlic, spinach, salt and pepper, and half the cheddar and mozzarella cheese to the eggs. Set the rest of the cheese aside for now, and stir the mixture until completely blended. Make sure the spinach is not clumped together but rather spread among the other ingredients.
5. Pour the mixture into the pie crust, slowly and carefully to avoid splashing. The mixture should almost fill the crust, but not completely, leaving a $1/4$ inch of crust at the edges.
6. Place the baking dish in the Air fryer oven cooking basket. Set the air fryer oven timer for 15 minutes. After 15 minutes, the air fryer will shut off, and the quiche will already be firm and the crust begins to brown. On top of the quiche filling, sprinkle the

remaining cheddar and mozzarella cheeses. Reset the air fryer oven at 360° F for 5 minutes. After 5 minutes, when the air fryer shuts off, the cheese will have formed an exquisite crust on top and the quiche will be golden brown and perfect. With oven gloves or tongs, remove the air fryer from the heat and set it on a heat-safe surface to cool for a few minutes before cutting.

Nutrition: Calories: 299. **Protein:** 15.34 g. **Fat:** 8.18 g. **Carbs:** 40.55 g.

39. Air Fryer Cauliflower Rice

Preparation Time: 5 minutes
Cooking Time: 20 minutes
Servings: 4
Ingredients:
Round 1:
- 1 tsp. turmeric
- 1 cup diced carrot
- ½ cup diced onion
- 2 tbsp. low-sodium soy sauce
- ½ block of extra firm tofu

Round 2:
- ½ cup frozen peas
- 2 minced garlic cloves
- ½ cup chopped broccoli
- 1 tbsp. minced ginger
- 1 tbsp. rice vinegar
- 1 ½ tsp. toasted sesame oil
- 2 tbsp. reduced-sodium soy sauce
- 3 cups of riced cauliflower

Directions:
1. Crumble tofu in a large bowl and toss with all the round 1 ingredients.
2. Preheat the air fryer oven to 370° F, place the baking dish in the Air fryer oven cooking basket, set the temperature to 370° F, and set the time to 10 minutes and cook 10 minutes, making sure to shake once.
3. In another bowl, toss ingredients from Round 2 together.
4. Add Round 2 mixture to air fryer and cook another 10 minutes, ensuring to shake 5 minutes in.
5. Enjoy!

Nutrition: Calories: 67. **Fat:** 8 g. **Protein:** 3 g. **Carbs:** 51.36 g.

40. Brussels Sprouts With Balsamic Oil

Preparation Time: 5 minutes
Cooking Time: 15 minutes
Servings: 4
Ingredients:
- ¼ tsp. salt
- 1 tbsp. balsamic vinegar
- 2 cups Brussels sprouts, halved

- 1 Tbsp. olive oil

Directions:
1. Preheat the air fryer oven for 5 minutes.
2. Mix all ingredients in a bowl until the zucchini fries are well coated.
3. Place in the air fryer oven basket.
4. Close and cook for 15 minutes at 350° F.

Nutrition: Calories: 82. **Fat:** 6.8 g. **Protein:** 1.5 g. **Carbs:** 4.62 g.

41. Air Fried Kale Chips

Preparation Time: 5 minutes
Cooking Time: 15 minutes
Servings: 6
Ingredients:
- ¼ tsp. Himalayan salt
- 3 tbsp. yeast
- Avocado oil
- 1 bunch of kale

Directions:
1. Clean the kale by rinsing it and patting it dry with paper towels.
2. Tear the leaves of the kale into big chunks. Remember that they will shrink as they cook, so use large portions.
3. Place kale pieces in a bowl and spritz with avocado oil till shiny. Sprinkle with salt and yeast.
4. With your hands, toss kale leaves well to combine.
5. Pour half of the kale mixture into the air fryer oven basket, set the temperature to 350° F, and set the time to 5 minutes. Remove and repeat with another half of kale.

Nutrition: Calories: 55. **Fat:** 10 g. **Protein:** 1 g. **Sugar:** 0 g.

42. Zucchini Omelet

Preparation Time: 10 minutes
Cooking Time: 15 minutes
Servings: 2
Ingredients:
- 1 tsp. butter
- 1 zucchini, julienned
- 4 eggs
- ¼ tsp. fresh basil, chopped
- ¼ tsp. red pepper flakes, crushed
- Season with salt and freshly ground black pepper, to taste

Directions:
1. Preheat the air fryer oven to 355° F.
2. In a medium saucepan, melt the butter.
3. Add zucchini and cook for about 3 to 4 minutes.
4. In a bowl, add the eggs, basil, red pepper flakes, salt, and black pepper and beat well.
5. Add cooked zucchini and gently, stir to combine.

6. Transfer the mixture into the air fryer oven pan.

7. Cook for about 10 minutes, or until totally cooked.

Nutrition: Calories: 279. **Protein:** 18.24 g. **Fat:** 21.22 g. **Carbs:** 2.78 g.

43. Cheesy Cauliflower Fritters

Preparation Time: 10 minutes

Cooking Time: 15 minutes

Servings: 8

Ingredients:

- ½ cup chopped parsley
- 1 cup Italian breadcrumbs
- ⅓ cup shredded mozzarella cheese
- ⅓ cup shredded sharp cheddar cheese
- 1 egg
- 2 minced garlic cloves
- 3 chopped scallions
- 1 head of cauliflower
- Salt and pepper

Directions:

1. Cut the cauliflower up into florets. Wash well and pat dry. Place into a food processor and pulse 20 to 30 seconds till it looks like rice.

2. Place the cauliflower rice in a bowl and mix with pepper, salt, egg, cheeses, breadcrumbs, garlic, and scallions.

3. With hands, form 15 patties of the mixture. Add more breadcrumbs if needed.

4. With olive oil, spritz patties, and place into your air fryer oven basket in a single layer. Set temperature to 390° F, and set time to 7 minutes, flipping after 7 minutes.

Nutrition: Calories: 209. **Fat:** 17 g. **Protein:** 6 g. **Sugar:** 0.5 g.

Poultry

44. Almond Flour Coco-Milk Battered Chicken

Preparation Time: 5 minutes
Cooking Time: 15 minutes
Servings: 4
Ingredients:

- ¼ cup coconut milk
- ½ cup almond flour
- 1 ½ tbsp. old bay Cajun seasoning
- 1 egg beaten
- 4 small chicken thighs
- Salt and pepper to taste

Directions:
1. Preheat the oven for 5 minutes.
2. Mix the egg and coconut milk in a bowl.
3. Soak the chicken thighs in the beaten egg mixture.
4. In a mixing bowl, combine the almond flour, Cajun seasoning salt, and pepper.
5. Dredge the chicken thighs in the almond flour mixture.
6. Place in the oven basket.
7. Cook for 30 minutes at 350° F.

Nutrition: Calories: 590. **Fat:** 38 g. **Protein:** 32.5 g. **Carbs:** 3.2 g.

45. Basil-Garlic Breaded Chicken Bake

Preparation Time: 5 minutes
Cooking Time: 15 minutes
Servings: 2
Ingredients:

- 2 boneless skinless chicken breast halves (4 oz. each)
- 1 tbsp. butter, melted
- 1 large tomato, seeded and chopped
- 2 garlic cloves, minced
- 1 ½ tbsp. minced fresh basil
- ½ tbsp. olive oil
- ½ tsp. salt
- ¼ cup all-purpose flour
- ¼ cup egg substitute
- ¼ cup grated Parmesan cheese
- ¼ cup dry bread crumbs
- ¼ tsp. pepper

Directions:
1. In a shallow bowl, whisk well egg substitute and place flour in a separate bowl. Dip chicken in flour, then egg, and then flour. In a small bowl whisk well butter, bread crumbs, and cheese. Sprinkle over chicken.

2. Lightly grease the baking pan of the oven with cooking spray. Place breaded chicken on the bottom of the pan. Cover with foil.
3. For 20 minutes, cook at 390° F.
4. Meanwhile, in a bowl, whisk well-remaining ingredients.
5. Remove foil from pan and then pour over chicken the remaining ingredients.
6. Cook for 8 minutes.
7. Serve and enjoy.

Nutrition: Calories: 311. **Fat:** 11 g. **Protein:** 31 g. **Carbs:** 22 g.

46. Buffalo Chicken Wings

Preparation Time: 5 minutes
Cooking Time: 15 minutes
Servings: 8
Ingredients:

- 1 tsp. salt
- 1 to 2 tbsp. brown sugar
- 1 tbsp. Worcestershire sauce
- ½ cup vegan butter
- ½ cup cayenne pepper sauce
- 4 lb. chicken wings

Directions:
1. Whisk salt, brown sugar, Worcestershire sauce, butter, and hot sauce together and set to the side.
2. Dry wings and add to oven basket.
3. Set temperature to 380° F, and set time to 25 minutes. Cook tossing halfway through.
4. When the timer sounds, shake wings and bump up the temperature to 400° F and cook for another 5 minutes.
5. Take out wings and place them into a big bowl. Add sauce and toss well.
6. Serve alongside celery sticks.

Nutrition: Calories: 402. **Fat:** 16 g. **Protein:** 17 g. **Sugar:** 4 g.

47. Honey and Wine Chicken Breasts

Preparation Time: 5 minutes
Cooking Time: 15 minutes
Servings: 4
Ingredients:

- 2 chicken breasts, rinsed and halved
- 1 tbsp. melted butter
- ½ tsp. freshly ground pepper, or to taste
- ¾ tsp. sea salt, or to taste
- 1 tsp. paprika
- 1 tsp. dried rosemary
- 2 tbsp. dry white wine
- 1 tbsp. honey

Directions:

1. Firstly, pat the chicken breasts dry. Lightly coat them with melted butter.
2. Then, add the remaining ingredients.
3. Transfer them to the oven basket; bake for about 15 minutes at 330° F. Serve warm and enjoy!

Nutrition: Calories: 189. **Fat:** 14 g. **Protein:** 11 g. **Sugar:** 1 g.

48. Orange Curried Chicken Stir-Fry

Preparation Time: 10 minutes
Cooking Time: 15 minutes
Servings: 4
Ingredients:

- ¾-pound boneless, skinless chicken thighs, cut into 1-inch pieces
- 1 yellow bell pepper, cut into 1 ½-inch piece
- 1 small red onion, sliced
- Olive oil for misting
- ¼ cup chicken stock
- 2 tbsp. honey
- ¼ cup orange juice
- 1 tbsp. cornstarch
- 3 tsp. curry powder

Directions:
1. Put the chicken thighs, pepper, and red onion in the oven basket and mist with olive oil.
2. Cook for 12 to 14 minutes or until the chicken is cooked to 165° F, shaking the basket halfway through cooking time.
3. Remove the chicken and vegetables from the oven basket and set them aside.
4. In a 6-inch metal bowl, combine the stock, honey, orange juice, cornstarch, and curry powder, and mix well. Add the chicken and vegetables, stir, and put the bowl in the basket.
5. Return the basket to the oven and cook for 2 minutes. Remove and stir, then cook for 2 to 3 minutes or until the sauce is thickened and bubbly.

Nutrition: Calories: 230. **Fat:** 7 g. **Protein:** 26 g. **Fiber:** 2 g.

49. Fried Chicken

Preparation Time: 5 minutes
Cooking Time: 15 minutes
Servings: 4
Ingredients:

- 4 chicken thighs, with skin and bones
- ½ tsp. salt
- ½ tsp. ground black pepper

Directions:
1. Turn on the oven, set the temperature to 350° F, and then select the oven cooking method.
2. Meanwhile, season the chicken with salt and black pepper and then arrange them in the oven basket.

3. Then insert the fryer basket into the oven and bake the chicken for 10 minutes per side until cooked.
4. Serve straight away.

Nutrition: Calories: 248. **Fat:** 18 g. **Carbs:** 2 g. **Protein:** 18 g. **Fiber:** 0 g.

50. Southern Fried Chicken

Preparation Time: 20 minutes
Cooking Time: 15 minutes
Servings: 6
Ingredients:

- 6 chicken legs
- 1 cup self-rising flour
- ¼ cup cornstarch
- 2 eggs
- 1 tbsp. hot sauce
- 2 tbsp. buttermilk
- ¼ cup water

Spice mix:

- 1 ½ tsp. garlic powder
- 2 tsp. sea salt
- 1 ½ tsp. ground black pepper
- 1 ½ tsp. paprika
- 1 tsp. onion powder
- 1 tsp. Italian seasoning

Directions:
1. Turn on the oven, set the temperature to 350° F, and then select the oven cooking method.
2. Meanwhile, take a small bowl, place the spice mix in it, and then stir until mixed.
3. Then sprinkle some of the spice mix on chicken legs and set aside until required.
4. Place flour in a large plastic bag add remaining spice mix and cornstarch and then stir until mixed.
5. Crack eggs in a large bowl, add hot sauce, pour water and milk, and then whisk until combined.
6. Place chicken legs in the flour mixture, seal the bag and then shake well until coated.
7. Arrange the chicken legs on a plate, let them rest for 5 minutes, coat each chicken leg in the egg mixture, and then coat in the flour mixture.
8. Let the coated chicken legs rest for 15 minutes, and then sprinkle with oil.

9. Arrange the chicken thighs on the oven basket and then cook for 9 minutes per side until golden brown.
10. When done, let the chicken rest for 5 minutes and then serve.

Nutrition: Calories: 164. **Fat:** 9 g. **Carbs:** 12 g. **Protein:** 20 g. **Fiber:** 3 g.

51. Chicken Tenders

Preparation Time: 10 minutes
Cooking Time: 15 minutes
Servings: 4
Ingredients:

- 1 ½-pound chicken breast tenders
- ¼ cup flour
- ½ tsp. seasoned salt
- 1 cup cornflake crumbs
- 1 cup breadcrumbs
- ½ tsp. garlic powder
- 1 tsp. paprika
- 1 tsp. salt
- ½ tsp. ground black pepper
- 2 eggs
- 2 tbsp. water

Directions:
1. Turn on the oven, set the temperature to 425° F, and then select the oven cooking method.
2. Meanwhile, cut the chicken tender into ¾-inch pieces. Then season with salt and black pepper.
3. Place flour in a medium bowl, add salt and then stir until mixed.
4. Place crumbs in a shallow dish, add salt, black pepper, garlic powder, and paprika, and then stir until mixed.
5. Crack the eggs in a bowl and then whisk until blended.
6. Working on one chicken piece at a time, dredge it in flour, dip into eggs and then coat in breadcrumb mixture.
7. Place the coated chicken pieces on the baking pan, spray with oil and then bake for 18 to 22 minutes until thoroughly cooked.
8. Serve straight away.

Nutrition: Calories: 527. **Fat:** 8 g. **Carbs:** 67 g. **Protein:** 46 g. **Fiber:** 3 g.

52. Baked Chicken Tenders

Preparation Time: 25 minutes
Cooking Time: 15 minutes
Servings: 6 to 8
Ingredients:

- 1 to ½ lb. boneless chicken tenders
- 2 eggs
- 2 tsp. butter, melted
- ⅔ cup graham crackers
- ⅔ cup breadcrumbs
- Salt and pepper for seasoning

Directions:
1. Preheat the oven to 232° C or 450° F and spray some oil on the baking pan
2. Combine the crackers, breadcrumbs, and butter until smooth.
3. Beat the eggs in another bowl with salt and pepper.
4. Dip the chicken pieces in the eggs first and then the breadcrumbs.
5. Bake for 15 to 18 minutes.

Nutrition: Calories: 362. **Carbs:** 16.5 g. **Protein:** 58 g. **Fat:** 5.8 g.

53. Apple-Stuffed Chicken Breast

Preparation Time: 10 minutes
Cooking Time: 15 minutes
Servings: 2
Ingredients:

- 2 chicken breasts
- 1 large apple
- ¼ cup cheddar cheese, shredded
- 2 tbsp. panko breadcrumbs
- 2 tbsp. chopped pecans
- 2 tbsp. light brown sugar
- 1 tsp. cinnamon
- 1 tsp. curry powder

Directions:
1. In a large bowl, add chopped apple, cheese, breadcrumbs, pecans, brown sugar, cinnamon, and curry powder. Stir to combine well.
2. Pound chicken breasts between waxed paper sheets till thick.
3. Spread half the apple mixture on every chicken breast. Roll the chicken up and secure it with toothpicks.
4. Place chicken on the 4-inch rack and cook on high power for 12 minutes. Flip over and cook for another 10 to 12 minutes.
5. Serve hot.

Nutrition: Calories: 268. **Carbs:** 18 g. **Fat:** 15 g. **Protein:** 25 g.

54. Easy Chicken Fajitas

Preparation Time: 10 minutes
Cooking Time: 15 minutes
Servings: 4
Ingredients:

- 3 breasts of chicken
- 1 onion, medium
- A single lime
- 3 red, black, green, or orange bell peppers
- 3 tbsp. extra virgin olive oil, split
- 1 tsp. cayenne pepper

- ½ tsp. paprika (smoked)
- ½ tsp. onion powder
- ½ tsp. black pepper
- ½ tsp. cumin, plus salt to taste
- ½ tsp. cinnamon
- ½ tsp. chili powder

Directions:

1. Break onion and peppers into slivers.
2. Combine 1 tbsp. of olive oil, 12 lime juice, chili powder, paprika, onion powder, cinnamon, cumin, and salt in a separate dish. Toss the chicken with the spice mixture after it has been cut into strips.
3. 1 tbsp. olive oil, heated over medium-high heat. Cook for 3 to 5 minutes, or until 12 of the chicken is just fried. Remove the pan from the fire and set it aside. Rep with the rest of the chicken.
4. Remove the chicken from the pan and apply 1 tbsp. of oil. Cook for 2 minutes after draining onions well. Cook for an additional 2 minutes, or until the peppers are hot. Return the chicken to the pan and whisk to mix it.
5. Serve with a squeeze of lime on top and tortillas.

Nutrition: Calories: 334. **Carbs:** 10 g. **Protein:** 37 g. **Fat:** 15 g. **Saturated Fat:** 2 g. **Cholesterol:** 108 mg. **Sodium:** 210 mg. **Potassium:** 882 mg. **Fiber:** 3 g. **Sugar:** 5 g. **Vitamin A:** 3115IU. **Vitamin C:** 122.9 mg. **Calcium:** 27 mg. **Iron:** 1.5 mg.

Beef

55. Cheeseburger Egg Rolls

Preparation Time: 10 minutes
Cooking Time: 15 minutes
Servings: 6
Ingredients:

- 6 egg roll wrappers
- 6 chopped dill pickle chips
- 1 tbsp. yellow mustard
- 3 tbsp. cream cheese
- 3 tbsp. shredded cheddar cheese
- ½ cup chopped onion
- ½ cup chopped bell pepper
- ¼ tsp. onion powder
- ¼ tsp. garlic powder
- 8 oz. raw lean ground beef

Directions:

1. In a skillet, add seasonings, beef, onion, and bell pepper. Stir and crumble beef till fully cooked, and vegetables are soft.
2. Take the skillet off the heat and add cream cheese, mustard, and cheddar cheese, stirring till melted.
3. Pour beef mixture into a bowl and fold in pickles.
4. Lay out egg wrappers and place ⅙ of beef mixture into each one. Moisten egg roll wrapper edges with water. Fold sides to the middle and seal with water.
5. Repeat with all other egg rolls.
6. Place rolls into the air fryer, one batch at a time.
7. Pour into the oven rack/basket. Place the rack on the middle shelf of the Air fryer oven. Set temperature to 392° F, and set time to 7 minutes.

Nutrition: Calories: 153. **Fat:** 4 g. **Protein:** 12 g. **Sugar:** 3 g.

56. Juicy Cheeseburgers

Preparation Time: 5 minutes
Cooking Time: 15 minutes
Servings: 4
Ingredients:

- 1 lb. 93% lean ground beef
- 1 tsp. Worcestershire sauce
- 1 tbsp. burger seasoning
- Salt
- Pepper
- Cooking oil
- 4 slices cheese
- Buns

Directions:

1. In a large bowl, mix the ground beef, Worcestershire, burger seasoning, and salt and pepper to taste until well blended. Spray the air fryer basket with cooking oil. You will need only a quick spritz. The burgers will produce oil as they cook. Shape the mixture into 4 patties. Place the burgers in the air fryer. The burgers should fit without the need to stack, but stacking is okay if necessary.
2. Pour into the oven rack/basket. Place the rack on the middle shelf of the Air fryer oven. Set temperature to 375° F, and set time to 8 minutes. Cook for 8 minutes. Open the air fryer and flip the burgers. Cook for an additional 3 to 4 minutes. Check the inside of the burgers to determine if they have finished cooking. You can stick a knife or fork in the center to examine the color.
3. Top each burger with a slice of cheese. Cook for an additional minute, or until the cheese has melted. Serve on buns with any additional toppings of your choice.

Nutrition: Calories: 566. **Fat:** 39 g. **Protein:** 29 g. **Fiber:** 1 g.

57. Spicy Thai Beef Stir-Fry

Preparation Time: 15 minutes
Cooking Time: 15 minutes
Servings: 4
Ingredients:

- 1 lb. sirloin steaks, thinly sliced
- 2 tbsp. lime juice, divided
- ⅓ cup crunchy peanut butter
- ½ cup beef broth
- 1 tbsp. olive oil
- 1 ½ cups broccoli florets
- 2 cloves garlic, sliced
- 1 to 2 red chili peppers, sliced

Directions:

1. In a medium bowl, combine the steak with 1 tbsp. of the lime juice. Set aside.
2. Combine the peanut butter and beef broth in a small bowl and mix well. Drain the beef and add the juice from the bowl into the peanut butter mixture.
3. In a 6-inch metal bowl, combine the olive oil, steak, and broccoli.
4. Pour into the oven rack/basket. Place the rack on the middle shelf of the Air fryer oven. Set temperature to 375° F, and set time to 4 minutes. Cook for 3 to 4 minutes or until the steak is almost cooked and the broccoli is crisp and tender, shaking the basket once during cooking time.
5. Add the garlic, chili peppers, and the peanut butter mixture and stir.
6. Cook for 3 to 5 minutes or until the sauce is bubbling and the broccoli is tender.
7. Serve over hot rice.

Nutrition: Calories: 387. **Fat:** 22 g. **Protein:** 42 g. **Fiber:** 2 g.

58. Steak and Mushroom Gravy

Preparation Time: 15 minutes
Cooking Time: 15 minutes
Servings: 4

Ingredients:

- 4 cubed steaks
- 2 large eggs
- ½ dozen mushrooms
- 4 tbsp. unsalted butter
- 4 tbsp. black pepper
- 2 tbsp. salt
- ½ tsp. onion powder
- ½ tsp. garlic powder
- ¼ tsp. cayenne powder
- 1 ¼ tsp. paprika
- 1 ½ cups whole milk
- ⅓ cup flour
- 2 tbsp. vegetable oil

Directions:

1. Mix ½ flour and a pinch of black pepper in a shallow bowl or on a plate.
2. Beat 2 eggs in a bowl and mix in a pinch of salt and pepper.
3. In another shallow bowl mix together the other half of the flour with pepper to taste, garlic powder, paprika, cayenne, and onion powder.
4. Chop mushrooms and set them aside.
5. Press your steak into the first flour bowl, then dip in egg, then press the steak into the second-floor bowl until covered completely.
6. Pour into the oven rack/basket. Place the rack on the middle shelf of the Air fryer oven. Set temperature to 360° F, and set time to 15 minutes flipping halfway through.
7. While the steak cooks, warm the butter over medium heat and add mushrooms to sauté.
8. Add 4 tablespoons of the flour and pepper mix to the pan and mix until there are no clumps of flour.
9. Mix in whole milk and simmer.
10. Serve over steak for breakfast, lunch, or dinner.

Nutrition: Calories: 442. **Fat:** 27 g. **Protein:** 32 g. **Fiber:** 2.3 g.

59. Chimichurri Skirt Steak

Preparation Time: 10 minutes
Cooking Time: 15 minutes
Servings: 2
Ingredients:

- 2 x 8 oz. skirt steak
- 1 cup finely chopped parsley
- ¼ cup finely chopped mint
- 2 tbsp. fresh oregano (washed & finely chopped)
- 3 finely chopped cloves of garlic
- 1 tsp. red pepper flakes (crushed)
- 1 tbsp. ground cumin
- 1 tsp. cayenne pepper
- 2 tsp. smoked paprika

- 1 tsp. salt
- ¼ tsp. pepper
- ¾ cup oil
- 3 tbsp. red wine vinegar

Directions:

1. Throw all the ingredients in a bowl (besides the steak) and mix well.
2. Put ¼ cup of the mixture in a plastic baggie with the steak and leave it in the fridge overnight.
3. Leave the bag out at room temperature for at least 30 min before popping it into the air fryer. Preheat for a minute or two to 390° F before cooking until med-rare (8 to 10 min). Pour into the oven rack/basket. Place the rack on the middle shelf of the Air fryer oven. Set temperature to 390° F, and set time to 10 minutes.
4. Put 2 tbsp. of the chimichurri mix on top of each steak before serving.

Nutrition: Calories: 880. **Protein:** 15.16 g. **Fat:** 88.78 g. **Carbs:** 9.19 g.

60. Country Fried Steak

Preparation Time: 5 minutes
Cooking Time: 15 minutes
Servings: 2
Ingredients:

- 1 tsp. pepper
- 2 cups of almond milk
- 2 tbsp. almond flour
- 6 oz. ground sausage meat
- 1 tsp. pepper
- 1 tsp. salt
- 1 tsp. garlic powder
- 1 tsp. onion powder
- 1 cup panko breadcrumbs
- 1 cup almond flour
- 3 beaten eggs
- 6 oz. sirloin steak pounded till thin

Directions:

1. Season panko breadcrumbs with spices.
2. Dredge steak in flour, then egg, and then seasoned panko mixture.
3. Place into air fryer basket.
4. Set temperature to 370° F, and set time to 12 minutes.
5. To make sausage gravy, cook sausage and drain off fat, but reserve 2 tbsp.
6. Add flour to sausage and mix until incorporated. Gradually mix in milk over medium to high heat till it becomes thick.
7. Season mixture with pepper and cook 3 minutes longer.
8. Serve steak topped with gravy and enjoy.

Nutrition: Calories: 395. **Fat:** 11 g. **Protein:** 39 g. **Sugar:** 5 g.

61. Warming Winter Beef with Celery

Preparation Time: 5 minutes
Cooking Time: 15 minutes
Servings: 4
Ingredients:

- 9 oz. tender beef, chopped
- ½ cup leeks, chopped
- ½ cup celery stalks, chopped
- 2 cloves garlic, smashed
- 2 tbsp. red cooking wine
- ¾ cup cream of celery soup
- 2 sprigs rosemary, chopped
- ¼ tsp. smoked paprika
- ¾ tsp. salt
- ¼ tsp. black pepper, or to taste

Directions:

1. Add the beef, leeks, celery, and garlic to the baking dish; cook for about 5 minutes at 390° F.
2. Once the meat is starting to tender, pour in the wine and soup. Season with rosemary, smoked paprika, salt, and black pepper. Now, cook an additional 7 minutes.

Nutrition: Calories: 105. **Protein:** 14.3 g. **Fat:** 3.42 g. **Carbs:** 4.71 g.

62. Beef & Veggie Spring Rolls

Preparation Time: 5 minutes
Cooking Time: 15 minutes
Servings: 10
Ingredients:

- 2-oz. Asian rice noodles
- 1 tbsp. sesame oil
- 7-oz. ground beef
- 1 small onion, chopped
- 3 garlic cloves, crushed
- 1 cup fresh mixed vegetables
- 1 tsp. soy sauce
- 1 packet spring roll skins
- 2 tbsp. water
- Olive oil, as required

Directions:

1. Soak the noodles in warm water till soft.
2. Drain and cut into small lengths. In a pan heat the oil and add the onion and garlic and sauté for about 4 to 5 minutes.
3. Add beef and cook for about 4 to 5 minutes.
4. Add vegetables and cook for about 5 to 7 minutes or till cooked through.
5. Stir in soy sauce and remove from the heat.
6. Immediately, stir in the noodles and keep them aside till all the juices have been absorbed.
7. Preheat the air fryer oven to 350° F.
8. Place the spring rolls skin onto a smooth surface.
9. Add a line of the filling diagonally across.
10. Fold the top point over the filling and then fold in both sides.
11. On the final point brush, it with water before rolling to seal.
12. Brush the spring rolls with oil.
13. Arrange the rolls in batches in the air fryer and cook for about 8 minutes.
14. Repeat with remaining rolls. Now, place spring rolls onto a baking sheet.
15. Bake for about 6 minutes per side.

Nutrition: Calories: 289. **Protein:** 3.54 g. **Fat:** 29.39 g. **Carbs:** 4.55 g.

63. Beef Stroganoff

Preparation Time: 10 minutes
Cooking Time: 15 minutes
Servings: 4
Ingredients:

- 9 oz tender beef
- 1 onion, chopped
- 1 tbsp. paprika
- ¾ cup sour cream
- Salt and pepper to taste
- Baking dish

Directions:

1. Preheat the air fryer oven to 390° F.
2. Chop the beef and marinate it with paprika.
3. Add the chopped onions into the baking dish and heat for about 2 minutes in the air fryer oven.
4. When the onions are transparent, add the beef into the dish and cook for 5 minutes.
5. Once the beef is starting to tender, pour in the sour cream and cook for another 7 minutes.
6. At this point, the liquid should have been reduced. Season with salt and pepper and serve.

Nutrition: Calories: 79. **Protein:** 2.28 g. **Fat:** 4.84 g. **Carbs:** 7.61 g.

64. Beef Korma

Preparation Time: 10 minutes
Cooking Time: 15 minutes
Servings: 6
Ingredients:

- ½ cup yogurt
- 1 lb. beef
- 1 tbsp. curry powder
- 1 tbsp. olive oil
- 1 onion, chopped
- 2 cloves garlic, minced
- 1 tomato, diced
- ½ cup frozen baby peas, thawed

Directions:

1.   In a medium bowl, combine the beef, yogurt, and curry powder. Stir and set aside.
2.   In a 6-inch metal bowl, combine the olive oil, onion, and garlic.
3.   Cook for 3 to 4 minutes or until crisp and tender.
4.   Add the steak along with the yogurt and the diced tomato. Cook for 12 to 13 minutes or until steak is almost tender.
5.   Stir in the peas and cook for 2 to 3 minutes or until hot.

Nutrition: Calories: 289. **Fat:** 11 g. **Protein:** 38 g. **Fiber:** 2 g.

65. Crispy Mongolian Beef

Preparation Time: 5 minutes
Cooking Time: 15 minutes
Servings: 6
Ingredients:

- Olive oil
- ½ cup almond flour
- 2 pounds beef tenderloin or beef chuck, sliced into strips

Sauce:

- ½ cup chopped green onion
- 1 tsp. red chili flakes
- 1 tsp. almond flour
- ½ cup brown sugar
- 1 tsp. hoisin sauce
- ½ cup water
- ½ cup rice vinegar
- ½ cup low-sodium soy sauce
- 1 tbsp. chopped garlic
- 1 tbsp. finely chopped ginger
- 2 tbsp. olive oil

Directions:
1.   Toss strips of beef in almond flour, ensuring they are coated well. Add to the air fryer oven.
2.   Pour into the oven rack/basket. Place the rack on the middle shelf of the Air fryer oven. Set temperature to 300° F, and set time to 10 minutes, and cook 10 minutes.
3.   Meanwhile, add all sauce ingredients to the pan and bring to a boil. Mix well.
4.   Add beef strips to the sauce and cook for 2 minutes.
5.   Serve over cauliflower rice!

Nutrition: Calories: 290. **Fat:** 14 g. **Protein:** 22 g. **Sugar:** 1 g.

Lamb

66. Roast Lamb

Preparation Time: 5 minutes
Cooking Time: 15 minutes
Servings: 2
Ingredients:

- 10 oz. lamb leg roast, butterflied
- 1 tsp. dried rosemary
- 1 tsp. dried thyme
- 1 tbsp. olive oil

Directions:

1. Select the oven cooking method after turning on the oven and setting the temperature to 360° F.
2. Meanwhile, stir together thyme, rosemary, and oil until combined, and then brush this mixture generously over the lamb until coated.
3. Place the lamb leg into the oven basket and then cook for 15 to 20 minutes until cooked to desire doneness.
4. When done, cover the lamb leg with foil, let it rest for 5 minutes, and then cut it into slices.
5. Serve straight away.

Nutrition: Calories: 181. **Fat:** 11 g. **Carbs:** 1 g. **Protein:** 18 g. **Fiber:** 0 g.

67. Leg of Lamb

Preparation Time: 5 minutes
Cooking Time: 15 minutes
Servings: 4
Ingredients:

- 1-lb. lamb sirloin steaks, boneless
- ½ of a medium white onion, peeled
- 4 slices of ginger
- 5 cloves of garlic, peeled
- 1 tsp. salt
- 1 tsp. ground fennel
- 1 tsp. garam masala
- 1 tsp. ground cinnamon
- 1 tsp. cayenne pepper
- ½ tsp. ground cardamom

Directions:

1. Place all the ingredients in a blender except for steaks, and then pulse until well blended.
2. Make cuts in lamb chops, place them in a large bowl, add the blended mixture, toss until coated, and then let it marinate for 30 minutes.
3. Then preheat the oven to 330° F and pick the oven cooking technique.
4. Arrange the lamb steaks in a single layer in the oven basket and then cook for 15 minutes until cooked, flipping halfway.
5. Serve straight away.

Nutrition: Calories: 182. **Fat:** 7 g. **Carbs:** 3 g. **Protein:** 24 g. **Fiber:** 1 g.

68. Herbed Rack of Lamb

Preparation Time: 5 minutes
Cooking Time: 15 minutes
Servings: 4
Ingredients:

- 1 rack of lamb

Marinade:

- 2 tsp. minced garlic
- 1 tsp. salt
- 2 tbsp. dried rosemary
- 1 tsp. ground black pepper
- 1 tbsp. dried thyme
- 4 tbsp. olive oil

Directions:

1. Select the oven cooking method after turning on the oven and setting the temperature to 360° F.
2. Meanwhile, take a small bowl, place all the ingredients for the marinade, and then stir until combined.
3. Rub the marinade on all sides of the rack of lamb, place it in the oven basket, and then 10 to 12 minutes until done.
4. When done, slice the rack of lamb into pieces and then serve.

Nutrition: Calories: 293. **Fat:** 15 g. **Carbs:** 4 g. **Protein:** 32 g. **Fiber:** 1 g.

69. Lamb Chops

Preparation Time: 5 minutes
Cooking Time: 15 minutes
Servings: 4
Ingredients:

- 4 lamb chops, about 1-inch
- 2 tsp. salt
- 2 tsp. ground black pepper

Marinade:

- 1 tbsp. chopped parsley
- 2 tbsp. Dijon mustard
- 1 tbsp. chopped thyme
- 1 tbsp. chopped rosemary
- 1 tbsp. chopped mint
- 2 tbsp. olive oil

Directions:

1. Select the oven cooking technique after turning on the oven and setting the temperature to 375° F.
2. Meanwhile, prepare the marinade and for this, place all of its ingredients in a small bowl and then stir until mixed.
3. Season the lamb chops with salt and black pepper and then brush the prepared marinade on both sides of the lamb chops.

4.   Arrange the lamb chops on the oven basket and then cook them for 5 minutes per side until done.
5.   Serve straight away.
Nutrition: Calories: 295. **Fat:** 17 g. **Carbs:** 1 g. **Protein:** 34 g. **Fiber:** 0 g.

Pork

70. Pork Taquitos

Preparation Time: 10 minutes
Cooking Time: 15 minutes
Servings: 8
Ingredients:

- 1 juiced lime
- 10 whole-wheat tortillas
- 2 ½ cups shredded mozzarella cheese
- 30 oz. cooked and shredded pork tenderloin

Directions:

1. Ensure your air fryer oven is preheated to 380° F.
2. Drizzle pork with lime juice and gently mix.
3. Heat up tortillas in the microwave with a dampened paper towel to soften.
4. Add about 3 oz. of pork and ¼ cup of shredded cheese to each tortilla. Tightly roll them up.
5. Spray the air fryer basket with a bit of olive oil.
6. Set temperature to 380° F, and set time to 10 minutes. Air fry taquitos for 7 to 10 minutes till tortillas turn a slight golden color, making sure to flip halfway through the cooking process.

Nutrition: Calories: 309. **Fat:** 11 g. **Protein:** 21 g. **Sugar:** 2 g

71. Panko-Breaded Pork Chops

Preparation Time: 5 minutes
Cooking Time: 15 minutes
Servings: 6
Ingredients:

- 5 (3 ½- to 5-oz.) pork chops (bone-in or boneless)
- Seasoning salt
- Pepper
- ¼ cup all-purpose flour
- 2 tbsp. panko bread crumbs
- Cooking oil

Directions:

1. Season the pork chops with the seasoning salt and pepper to taste.
2. Sprinkle the flour on both sides of the pork chops, then coat both sides with panko bread crumbs.
3. Place the pork chops in the air fryer. Stacking them is okay.
4. Spray the pork chops with cooking oil. Pour into the oven rack/basket. Place the rack on the middle shelf of the Air fryer oven. Set temperature to 375° F, and set time to 6 minutes. Cook for 6 minutes.
5. Open the air fryer oven and flip the pork chops. Cook for an additional 6 minutes
6. Cool before serving.
7. Typically, bone-in pork chops are juicier than boneless. If you prefer really juicy pork chops, use bone-in.

Nutrition: Calories: 246. **Fat:** 13 g. **Protein:** 26 g. **Fiber:** 0 g.

72. Barbecue Flavored Pork Ribs

Preparation Time: 5 minutes
Cooking Time: 15 minutes
Servings: 6
Ingredients:

- ¼ cup honey, divided
- ¾ cup BBQ sauce
- 2 tbsp. tomato ketchup
- 1 tbsp. Worcestershire sauce
- 1 tbsp. soy sauce
- ½ tsp. garlic powder
- Freshly ground white pepper, to taste
- 1 ¾ pound pork ribs

Directions:

1. In a large bowl, mix together 3 tbsp. of honey and remaining ingredients except for pork ribs.
2. Refrigerate to marinate for about 20 minutes.
3. Preheat the air fryer oven to 355° F.
4. Place the ribs in an Air fryer basket.
5. Cook for about 13 minutes.
6. Remove the ribs from the air fryer oven and coat them with the remaining honey.
7. Serve hot.

Nutrition: Calories: 251. **Protein:** 28.4 g. **Fat:** 8.03 g. **Carbs:** 15.87 g.

73. Rustic Pork Ribs

Preparation Time: 5 minutes
Cooking Time: 15 minutes
Servings: 4
Ingredients:

- 1 rack of pork ribs
- 3 tbsp. dry red wine
- 1 tbsp. soy sauce
- ½ tsp. dried thyme
- ½ tsp. onion powder
- ½ tsp. garlic powder
- ½ tsp. ground black pepper
- 1 tsp. smoke salt
- 1 tbsp. cornstarch
- ½ tsp. olive oil

Directions:

1. Begin by preheating your air fryer oven to 390° F. Place all ingredients in a mixing bowl and let them marinate for at least 1 hour.
2. Pour into the oven rack/basket. Place the rack on the middle shelf of the Air fryer oven. Set temperature to 390° F, and set time to 25 minutes. Cook the marinated ribs for approximately 25 minutes.
3. Serve hot.

Nutrition: Calories: 100. **Protein:** 10.73 g. **Fat:** 4.09 g. **Carbs:** 3.93 g.

74. Keto Parmesan Crusted Pork Chops

Preparation Time: 10 minutes
Cooking Time: 15 minutes
Servings: 8
Ingredients:

- 3 tbsp. grated parmesan cheese
- 1 cup pork rind crumbs
- 2 beaten eggs
- ¼ tsp. chili powder
- ½ tsp. onion powder
- 1 tsp. smoked paprika
- ¼ tsp. pepper
- ½ tsp. salt
- 4 to 6 thick boneless pork chops

Directions:
1. Ensure your air fryer oven is preheated to 400° F.
2. With pepper and salt, season both sides of pork chops.
3. In a food processor, pulse pork rinds into crumbs. Mix crumbs with other seasonings.
4. Beat eggs and add to another bowl.
5. Dip pork chops into eggs then into pork rind crumb mixture.
6. Spray down the air fryer with olive oil and add pork chops to the basket. Set temperature to 400° F, and set time to 15 minutes.

Nutrition: Calories: 422. **Fat:** 19 g. **Protein:** 38 g. **Sugar:** 2 g.

75. Fried Pork Quesadilla

Preparation Time: 10 minutes
Cooking Time: 15 minutes
Servings: 2
Ingredients:

- Two 6-inch corn or flour tortilla shells
- 1 medium-sized pork shoulder, approximately 4 oz., sliced
- ½ medium-sized white onion, sliced
- ½ medium-sized red pepper, sliced
- ½ medium-sized green pepper, sliced
- ½ medium-sized yellow pepper, sliced
- ¼ cup shredded pepper-jack cheese
- ¼ cup shredded mozzarella cheese

Directions:
1. Preheat the air fryer oven to 350° F.
2. In the oven on high heat for 20 minutes, grill the pork, onion, and peppers in foil in the same pan, allowing the moisture from the vegetables and the juice from the pork to mingle together. Remove pork and vegetables in foil from the oven. While they're cooling, sprinkle half the

shredded cheese over one of the tortillas, then cover with the pieces of pork, onions, and peppers, and then layer on the rest of the shredded cheese. Top with the second tortilla. Place directly on the hot surface of the air fryer basket.
3. Set the air fryer timer for 6 minutes. After 6 minutes, when the air fryer shuts off, flip the tortillas onto the other side with a spatula; the cheese should be melted enough that it won't fall apart, but be careful anyway not to spill any toppings!
4. Reset the air fryer to 350° F for another 6 minutes.
5. After 6 minutes, when the air fryer shuts off, the tortillas should be browned and crisp, and the pork, onion, peppers, and cheese will be crispy and hot, and delicious. Remove with tongs and let sit on a serving plate to cool for a few minutes before slicing.

Nutrition: Calories: 146. **Protein:** 13.07 g. **Fat:** 7.72 g. **Carbs:** 6.4 g.

76. Cilantro-Mint Pork BBQ Thai Style

Preparation Time: 5 minutes
Cooking Time: 15 minutes
Servings: 4
Ingredients:

- 1 minced hot chili
- 1 minced shallot
- 1-lb. ground pork
- 2 tbsp. fish sauce
- 2 tbsp. lime juice
- 3 tbsp. basil
- 1 Tbsp. chopped mint
- 3 tbsp. cilantro

Directions:
1. In a shallow dish, mix well all ingredients with your hands. Form into 1-inch ovals.
2. Thread ovals in skewers. Place on skewer rack in the air fryer.
3. For 15 minutes, cook on 360° F. Halfway through cooking time, turnover skewers. If needed, cook in batches.
4. Serve and enjoy.

Nutrition: Calories: 455. **Fat:** 31.5 g. **Protein:** 40.4 g.

77. Tuscan Pork Chops

Preparation Time: 10 minutes
Cooking Time: 15 minutes
Servings: 4
Ingredients:

- ¼ cup all-purpose flour
- 1 tsp. salt
- ¾ tsp. seasoned pepper
- 4 (1-inch-thick) boneless pork chops
- 1 tbsp. olive oil

- 3 to 4 garlic cloves
- $1/3$ cup balsamic vinegar
- $1/3$ cup chicken broth
- 3 plum tomatoes, seeded and diced
- 2 tbsp. capers

Directions:
1. Combine flour, salt, and pepper
2. Press pork chops into flour mixture on both sides until evenly covered.
3. Cook in your air fryer oven at 360° F for 14 minutes, flipping halfway through.
4. While the pork chops cook, warm olive oil in a medium skillet.
5. Add garlic and sauté for 1 minute; then mix in vinegar and chicken broth.
6. Add capers and tomatoes and turn to high heat.
7. Bring the sauce to a boil, stirring regularly, then add pork chops, cooking for one minute.
8. Remove from heat and cover for about 5 minutes to allow the pork to absorb some of the sauce; serve hot.

Nutrition: Calories: 349. **Fat:** 23 g. **Protein:** 20 g. **Fiber:** 1.5 g.

78. Peanut Satay Pork

Preparation Time: 5 minutes
Cooking Time: 15 minutes
Servings: 6
Ingredients:
- 11 oz pork fillet, sliced into bite-sized strips
- 4 cloves garlic, crushed
- 1 tsp. ginger powder
- 2 tsp. chili paste
- 2 tbsp. sweet soy sauce (kecap manis)
- 2 tbsp. vegetable oil
- 1 shallot, finely chopped
- 1 tsp. ground coriander
- ¾ cup coconut milk
- $1/3$ cup peanuts, ground

Directions:
1. Mix half of the garlic in a dish with the ginger, a tbsp. of sweet soy sauce, and a tbsp. of the oil. Combine the meat into the mixture and leave to marinate for 15 minutes
2. Preheat the air fryer oven to 390° F.
3. Place the marinated meat into the air fryer oven basket. Set the timer to 12 minutes and roast the meat until brown and done. Turn once while roasting
4. In the meantime, make the peanut sauce by heating the remaining tbsp. of oil in a saucepan and gently sauté the shallot with the garlic. Add the coriander and fry until fragrant
5. Mix the coconut milk and the peanuts with the chili paste and remaining soy sauce with the shallot mixture and gently boil for 5 minutes, while stirring

6. Drizzle over the cooked meat and serve with rice.

Nutrition: Calories: 212. **Protein:** 14.97 g. **Fat:** 14.24 g. **Carbs:** 8.94 g.

79. Crispy Breaded Pork Chops

Preparation Time: 10 minutes
Cooking Time: 15 minutes
Servings: 8
Ingredients:
- ⅛ tsp. salt and pepper
- ¼ tsp. chili powder
- ½ tsp. onion powder
- ½ tsp. garlic powder
- 1 ¼ tsp. sweet paprika
- 2 tbsp. grated parmesan cheese
- $1/3$ cup crushed cornflake crumbs
- ½ cup panko breadcrumbs
- 1 beaten egg
- 6 center-cut boneless pork chops
- Olive oil

Directions:
1. Ensure that your air fryer is preheated to 400° F. Spray the basket with olive oil.
2. With ½ tsp. of salt and pepper, season both sides of pork chops.
3. Combine ¾ tsp. of salt with pepper, chili powder, onion powder, garlic powder, paprika, cornflake crumbs, panko breadcrumbs, and parmesan cheese.
4. Beat egg in another bowl.
5. Dip pork chops into the egg and then crumb mixture.
6. Add pork chops to the air fryer and spritz with olive oil.
7. Pour into the oven rack/basket. Place the rack on the middle shelf of the Air fryer oven. Set temperature to 400° F, and set time to 12 minutes. Cook 12 minutes, making sure to flip over halfway through the cooking process.
8. Only add 3 chops in at a time and repeat the process with the remaining pork chops.

Nutrition: Calories: 378. **Fat:** 13 g. **Protein:** 33 g. **Sugar:** 1 g.

80. Ginger, Garlic and Pork Dumplings

Preparation Time: 10 minutes
Cooking Time: 15 minutes
Servings: 8
Ingredients:
- ¼ tsp. crushed red pepper
- ½ tsp. sugar
- 1 tbsp. chopped fresh ginger
- 1 tbsp. chopped garlic
- 1 tsp. canola oil

- 1 tsp. toasted sesame oil
- 18 dumpling wrappers
- 2 tbsp. rice vinegar
- 2 tsp. soy sauce
- 4 cups bok choy, chopped
- 4 oz. ground pork

Directions:

1.	Heat oil in a skillet and sauté the ginger and garlic until fragrant. Stir in the ground pork and cook for 5 minutes.

2.	Stir in the bok choy and crushed red pepper. Season with salt and pepper to taste. Allow cooling.

3.	Place the meat mixture in the middle of the dumpling wrappers. Fold the wrappers to seal the meat mixture in.

4.	Place the bok choy in the grill pan.

5.	Cook the dumplings in the air fryer at 330° F for 15 minutes.

6.	Meanwhile, prepare the dipping sauce by combining the remaining ingredients in a bowl.

Nutrition: Calories: 137. **Fat:** 5 g. **Protein:** 7 g.

Fish

81.   Healthy Fish and Chips
Preparation Time: 5 minutes
Cooking Time: 15 minutes
Servings: 4
Ingredients:
- Old bay seasoning
- ½ cup panko breadcrumbs
- 1 egg
- 2 tbsp. almond flour
- 4 to 6 oz. tilapia fillets
- Frozen crinkle cut fries

Directions:
1.   Add almond flour to one bowl, beat egg in another bowl, and add panko breadcrumbs to the third bowl, mixed with old bay seasoning.
2.   Dredge tilapia in flour, then egg, and then breadcrumbs.
3.   Place coated fish in the oven along with fries.
4.   Set temperature to 390° F, and set time to 15 minutes.
Nutrition: Calories: 219. **Fat:** 5 g. **Protein:** 25 g. **Sugar:** 1 g.

82.   Ingredient Catfish
Preparation Time: 5 minutes
Cooking Time: 15 minutes
Servings: 4
Ingredients:
- 1 tbsp. olive oil
- ¼ cup seasoned fish fry
- 4 catfish fillets

Directions:
1.   Ensure your oven is preheated to 400° F.
2.   Rinse off catfish fillets and pat dry.
3.   Add fish fry seasoning to Ziploc baggie, then catfish. Shake the bag and ensure the fish gets well coated.
4.   Spray each fillet with olive oil.
5.   Add fillets to the oven basket.
6.   Set temperature to 400° F, and set time to 10 minutes.
7.   Cook 10 minutes. Then flip and cook for another 2 to 3 minutes.
Nutrition: Calories: 208. **Fat:** 5 g. **Protein:** 17 g. **Sugar:** 0.5 g.

83.   Panko-Crusted Tilapia
Preparation Time: 5 minutes
Cooking Time: 15 minutes
Servings: 3
Ingredients:
- 2 tsp. Italian seasoning
- 2 tsp. lemon pepper
- ⅓ cup panko breadcrumbs
- ⅓ cup egg whites
- ⅓ cup almond flour
- 3 tilapia fillets
- Olive oil

Directions:
1.   Place panko, egg whites, and flour into separate bowls. Mix lemon pepper and Italian seasoning in with breadcrumbs.
2.   Pat tilapia fillets dry. Dredge in flour, then egg, then breadcrumb mixture.
3.   Add to the oven basket and spray lightly with olive oil.
4.   Cook 10 to 11 minutes at 400° F, making sure to flip halfway through cooking.
Nutrition: Calories: 256. **Fat:** 9 g. **Protein:** 39 g. **Sugar:** 5 g.

84.   Snapper Scampi
Preparation Time: 5 minutes
Cooking Time: 15 minutes
Servings: 4
Ingredients:
- 4 skinless snapper or arctic char fillets (6 oz.)
- 1 tbsp. olive oil
- 3 tbsp. lemon juice, divided
- ½ tsp. dried basil
- Pinch salt
- Freshly ground black pepper
- 2 tbsp. butter
- 4 cloves garlic, minced

Directions:
1.   Rub the fish fillets with olive oil and 1 tbsp. of lemon juice. Sprinkle with the basil, salt, and pepper, and place in the oven basket.
2.   Grill the fish for 7 to 8 minutes or until the fish just flakes when tested with a fork. Remove the fish from the basket and put it on a serving plate. Cover to keep warm. In a 6-by-6-by-2-inch pan, combine the butter, remaining 2 tbsp. of lemon juice, and garlic Cook in the oven for 1 to 2 minutes or until the garlic is sizzling. Pour this mixture over the fish and serve.
Nutrition: Calories: 265. **Carbs:** 1 g. **Fat:** 11 g. **Protein:** 39 g. **Fiber:** 0 g.

85.   Fish Tacos
Preparation Time: 5 minutes
Cooking Time: 15 minutes
Servings: 4
Ingredients:
- 1 pound cod
- Salt and pepper
- 1 tbsp. cumin
- ½ tbsp. chili powder
- 1 ½ cup almond flour

- 1 ½ cup coconut flour
- 10 oz. Mexican beer
- 2 eggs

Directions:
1. Whisk beer and eggs together.
2. Whisk flours, pepper, salt, cumin, and chili powder together.
3. Slice cod into large pieces and coat in egg mixture, then flour mixture.
4. Spray the bottom of your oven basket with olive oil and add coated codpieces. Cook 15 minutes at 375° F.
5. Serve on lettuce leaves topped with homemade salsa.

Nutrition: Calories: 178. **Carbs:** 61 g. **Fat:** 10 g. **Protein:** 19 g. **Sugar:** 1 g.

86. Juicy Citrus Baked Salmon

Preparation Time: 15 minutes
Cooking Time: 15 minutes
Servings: 4
Ingredients:
- 4 lemon slices
- 4 orange slices
- 4 salmon fillets
- A pinch of salt and pepper to taste
- 2 tbsp. chopped dill
- 2 tbsp. sun-dried tomatoes
- 1 tbsp. extra-virgin olive oil
- ²/₃ cup rice wine vinegar

Directions:
1. Place lemon and orange slices, side by side, in the bottom of a shallow baking dish that will fit in a NuWave oven (10 x10). Place each salmon fillet across the citrus slices. Sprinkle with pepper and salt.
2. Combine dill, sun-dried tomatoes, olive oil, and rice wine vinegar in a large mixing bowl. Mix well, then drizzle mixture over salmon fillets.
3. Place on 1-inch rack and cook on High power (350° C) for 7 to 8 minutes or till salmon is cooked through.
4. Serve and enjoy.

Nutrition: Calories: 270. **Total Fat:** 12.6 g. **Total Carbs:** 5.4 g. **Protein:** 32.5 g.

87. Broiled Chipotle Tilapia

Preparation Time: 10 minutes
Cooking Time: 15 minutes
Servings: 2
Ingredients:
- ½ lbs. tilapia fillets
- 1 tsp. lime juice
- Cilantro, chopped
- 3 tsp. chipotles
- 1 avocado, peeled and halved

- 3 tbsp. sour cream
- 1 tbsp. mayo

Directions:
1. Blend the ingredients except for the fish.
2. Brush the fish fillets with the mix.
3. Broil the fish at 132° C or 270° F in your oven for 10 minutes.

Nutrition: Calories: 385. **Carbs:** 65 g. **Protein:** 18 g. **Fat:** 7 g.

88. Quick Fried Catfish

Preparation Time: 5 minutes
Cooking Time: 15 minutes
Servings: 4
Ingredients:
- ¾ cups Original Bisquick™ mix
- ½ cup yellow cornmeal
- 1 tbsp. seafood seasoning
- 4 catfish fillets (4 to 6 oz. each)
- ½ cup ranch dressing
- Lemon wedges

Directions:
1. In a shallow bowl mix together the Bisquick mix, cornmeal, and seafood seasoning. Pat the filets dry, then brush them with ranch dressing.
2. Press the filets into the Bisquick mix on both sides until the filet is evenly coated.
3. Cook in your air fryer oven at 360° F for 15 minutes, flip the filets halfway through.
4. Serve with a lemon garnish.

Nutrition: Calories: 372. **Fat:** 16 g. **Protein:** 28 g. **Fiber:** 1.7 g.

89. Honey Glazed Salmon

Preparation Time: 5 minutes
Cooking Time: 15 minutes
Servings: 2
Ingredients:
- 1 tsp. water
- 3 tsp. rice wine vinegar
- 6 tbsp. low-sodium soy sauce
- 6 tbsp. raw honey
- 2 salmon fillets

Directions:
1. Combine water, vinegar, honey, and soy sauce together. Pour half of this mixture into a bowl.
2. Place salmon in one bowl of marinade and let chill for 2 hours.
3. Ensure your air fryer oven is preheated to 356° F and add salmon.
4. Cook 8 minutes, flipping halfway through. Baste salmon with some of the remaining marinade mixture and cook another 5 minutes.
5. To make a sauce to serve salmon with, pour the remaining marinade mixture into a saucepan, heating till

simmering. Let simmer for 2 minutes. Serve drizzled over salmon!

Nutrition: Calories: 348. **Fat:** 12 g. **Protein:** 20 g. **Sugar:** 3 g.

90. Fish and Chips

Preparation Time: 10 minutes
Cooking Time: 15 minutes
Servings: 4
Ingredients:

- 4 (4-oz.) fish fillets
- Pinch salt
- Freshly ground black pepper
- ½ tsp. dried thyme
- 1 egg white
- ¾ cup crushed potato chips
- 2 tbsp. olive oil, divided
- 1 russet potato, peeled and cut into strips

Directions:

1. Pat the fish fillets dry and sprinkle with salt, pepper, and thyme. Set aside.
2. In a shallow bowl, beat the egg white until foamy. In another bowl, combine the potato chips and 1 tbsp. of olive oil and mix until combined.
3. Dip the fish fillets into the egg white, then into the crushed potato chip mixture to coat.
4. Toss the fresh potato strips with the remaining 1 tbsp. of olive oil.
5. Use your separator to divide the air fryer basket in half, then fry the chips and fish. The chips will take about 20 minutes; the fish will take about 10 to 12 minutes to cook.

Nutrition: Calories: 374. **Fat:** 16 g. **Protein:** 30 g. **Fiber:** 4 g.

91. Fish Sandwiches

Preparation Time: 10 minutes
Cooking Time: 15 minutes
Servings: 4
Ingredients:

- 2 lbs. white fish fillets
- ¼ cup yellow cornmeal
- 1 tsp. Greek seasoning
- Salt and pepper to taste
- 2 ½ cups plain flour
- 2 tsp. baking powder
- 2 cups beer
- 4 hamburger buns
- Mayonnaise
- Lettuce leaves
- 1 tomato, sliced
- 1 egg

Directions:

1. Cut the fish fillets into burger patty-sized strips. Season with salt and pepper to desired taste.
2. In a medium bowl, mix together the beer, egg, baking powder, plain flour, cornmeal, Greek seasoning, and additional salt and pepper.
3. Heat the air fryer oven to 340° F.
4. Place each seasoned fish strip into the batter, ensuring that it is well coated.
5. Place battered fish into the air fryer tray and cook in batches for 6 minutes or until crispy.
6. Compile the sandwich by topping each bun with mayonnaise, then a lettuce leaf, tomato slices, and finally the cooked fish strip.

Nutrition: Calories: 314. **Protein:** 78.22 g. **Fat:** 59.34 g. **Carbs:** 112.15 g.

Seafood

92.   Quick Paella

Preparation Time: 7 minutes
Cooking Time: 15 minutes
Servings: 4
Ingredients:

* 1 (10-oz.) package frozen cooked rice, thawed
* 1 (6-oz.) jar artichoke hearts, drained and chopped
* ¼ cup vegetable broth
* ½ tsp. turmeric
* ½ tsp. dried thyme
* 1 cup frozen cooked small shrimp
* ½ cup frozen baby peas
* 1 tomato, diced

Directions:

1.   In a 6-by-6-by-2-inch pan, combine the rice, artichoke hearts, vegetable broth, turmeric, and thyme, and stir gently.
2.   Place in the oven and bake for 8 to 9 minutes or until the rice is hot. Remove from the oven and gently stir in the shrimp, peas, and tomato. Cook for 5 to 8 minutes or until the shrimp and peas are hot and the paella is bubbling.

Nutrition: Calories: 345. **Fat:** 1 g. **Protein:** 18 g. **Fiber:** 4 g.

93.   Coconut Shrimp

Preparation Time: 15 minutes
Cooking Time: 15 minutes
Servings: 4
Ingredients:

* 1 (8-oz.) can crushed pineapple
* ½ cup sour cream
* ¼ cup pineapple preserves
* 2 egg whites
* ⅔ cup cornstarch
* ⅔ cup sweetened coconut
* 1 cup panko bread crumbs
* 1-lb. uncooked large shrimp, thawed if frozen, deveined, and shelled
* Olive oil for misting

Directions:

1.   Drain the juice from the smashed pineapple and set it aside. Combine the pineapple, sour cream, and preserves in a small mixing dish and stir well. Remove from the equation. Beat the egg whites with 2 tbsp. of the reserved pineapple liquid in a small basin. Place the cornstarch on a plate. Combine the coconut and bread crumbs on another plate. Dip the shrimp into the cornstarch, shake it off, then dip into the egg white mixture and finally into the coconut mixture. Place the shrimp in the oven basket and mist with oil.

2.   Cook for 5 to 7 minutes or until the shrimp are crisp and golden brown.

Nutrition: Calories: 524. **Fat:** 14 g. **Protein:** 33 g. **Fiber:** 4 g.

94.   Cilantro-Lime Fried Shrimp

Preparation Time: 10 minutes
Cooking Time: 15 minutes
Servings: 4
Ingredients:

* 1-lb. raw shrimp, peeled and deveined with tails on or off (see Prep tip)
* ½ cup chopped fresh cilantro
* Juice of 1 lime
* 1 egg
* ½ cup all-purpose flour
* ¾ cup bread crumbs
* Salt
* Pepper
* Cooking oil
* ½ cup cocktail sauce (optional)

Directions:

1.   Place the shrimp in a plastic bag and add the cilantro and lime juice. Seal the bag. Shake to combine. Marinate in the refrigerator for 30 minutes.
2.   In a small bowl, beat the egg. In another small bowl, place the flour. Place the bread crumbs in a third small bowl, and season with salt and pepper to taste.
3.   Spray the oven basket with cooking oil.
4.   Remove the shrimp from the plastic bag. Dip each in the flour, the egg, and then the bread crumbs.
5.   Place the shrimp in the oven. It is okay to stack them. Spray the shrimp with cooking oil. Cook for 4 minutes.
6.   Open the oven and flip the shrimp. I recommend flipping individually instead of shaking to keep the breading intact. Cook for an additional 4 minutes, or until crisp.
7.   Cool before serving. Serve with cocktail sauce if desired.

Nutrition: Calories: 254. **Fat:** 4 g. **Protein:** 29 g. **Fiber:** 1 g.

95.   Bang Panko Breaded Fried Shrimp

Preparation Time: 5 minutes
Cooking Time: 15 minutes
Servings: 4
Ingredients:

* 1 tsp. paprika
* Montreal chicken seasoning
* ¾ cup panko bread crumbs
* ½ cup almond flour
* 1 egg white

- 1-lb. raw shrimp (peeled and deveined)

For bang bang sauce:
- ¼ cup sweet chili sauce
- 2 tbsp. sriracha sauce
- ⅓ cup plain Greek yogurt

Directions:
1. Ensure your oven is preheated to 400° F.
2. Season all shrimp with seasonings.
3. Add flour to one bowl, egg white in another, and breadcrumbs to a third.
4. Dip seasoned shrimp in flour, then egg whites, and then breadcrumbs.
5. Spray coated shrimp with olive oil and add to oven basket.
6. Set temperature to 400° F, and set time to 4 minutes. Cook 4 minutes, flip, and cook an additional 4 minutes.
7. To make the sauce, mix together all sauce ingredients until smooth.

Nutrition: Calories: 212. **Carbs:** 12. **Fat:** 1 g. **Protein:** 37 g. **Sugar:** 0.5 g.

96. Scallops and Spring Veggies

Preparation Time: 10 minutes
Cooking Time: 15 minutes
Servings: 4
Ingredients:
- ½-lb. asparagus, ends trimmed, cut into 2-inch pieces
- 1 cup sugar snap peas
- 1 lb. sea scallops
- 1 tbsp. lemon juice
- 2 tsp. olive oil
- ½ tsp. dried thyme
- Pinch salt
- Freshly ground black pepper

Directions:
1. In the oven basket, place the asparagus and sugar snap peas.
2. Cook for 2 to 3 minutes more, or until the vegetables are softened.
3. Meanwhile, check the scallops for a small muscle attached to the side, and pull it off and discard.
4. In a medium bowl, combine the scallops, lemon juice, olive oil, thyme, salt, and pepper. Place into the oven basket on top of the vegetables.
5. Steam for 5 to 7 minutes, tossing the basket once during cooking until the scallops are just firm and opaque in the middle when touched with a finger, and the vegetables are soft. Serve immediately.

Nutrition: Calories: 162. **Carbs:** 10 g. **Fat:** 4 g. **Protein:** 22 g. **Fiber:** 3 g.

97. Roasted Shrimp With an Herbed Salsa

Preparation Time: 10 minutes
Cooking Time: 15 minutes
Servings: 2
Ingredients:
- 1-lb. large shrimps
- 3 sliced garlic cloves
- 1 red Serrano pepper
- 1 bay leaf
- ½ lemon
- 3 tbsp. olive oil

Herb salsa:
- 2 tbsp. chopped cilantro
- ½ tbsp. grated lemon zest
- 2 tbsp. chopped flat-leaf parsley
- ½ tbsp. virgin olive oil
- Kosher salt and black pepper to taste

Directions:
1. Place the shrimp and Serrano pepper halves in an ovenproof dish, along with the bay leaf, garlic, and virgin olive oil. Mix lightly till all the ingredients are well coated with virgin olive oil.
2. Place the baking dish on the 3-inch rack.
3. Cook on the "HI" setting for about 3 to 5 minutes.
4. While the shrimp cooks, prepare the salsa.
5. Combine the cilantro, lemon zest, and parsley together in a small mixing bowl. Season with salt and pepper to taste and stir to combine well.
6. Pour the olive oil over the salsa and let it stand for a few minutes before mixing it up.
7. When the shrimp is done, pour in the lemon juice and mix well to coat.
8. Serve the shrimp hot, topped with the prepared salsa.

Nutrition: Calories: 163. **Fat:** 3 g. **Carbs:** 2 g. **Protein:** 18 g.

98. Sheet Pan Shrimp Fajitas

Preparation Time: 5 minutes
Cooking Time: 15 minutes
Servings: 2
Ingredients:
- 8 oz. shrimp, deveined and peeled
- 1 minced garlic clove
- 2 tbsp. lime juice
- 1 tbsp. olive oil
- Chili pepper & cayenne pepper
- Sour cream
- 2 avocados, sliced
- Cilantro, chopped
- 4 tortillas

- Salt and pepper

Directions:
1. Mix all the spices and seasonings and add them to the shrimps.
2. Preheat the oven at 177° C or 350° F.
3. Bake the shrimps in the pan with chili peppers.
4. Serve in tortillas.

Nutrition: Calories: 408. **Carbs:** 76 g. **Protein:** 42 g. **Fat:** 6 g.

99. Bacon-Wrapped Shrimp

Preparation Time: 15 minutes
Cooking Time: 15 minutes
Servings: 4 to 6
Ingredients:

- Juice of 1 lemon
- 1 clove garlic, grated
- 1 tsp. paprika
- 1 tsp. fresh thyme
- 3 tbsp extra-virgin olive oil
- Kosher salt
- 1 lb. (about 24) large shrimp, peeled and deveined, tails intact
- 12 slices bacon, halved

Directions:
1. Position a rack 3 to 4 inches from the heat source and preheat the broiler. Whisk the lemon juice, garlic, paprika, thyme, olive oil, and ½ tsp. salt in a shallow baking dish. Add the shrimp and toss to coat; marinate in the refrigerator, 20 minutes.
2. Turn the shrimp in the marinade to coat well. One at a time, remove every shrimp and wrap it with a piece of bacon; secure with a toothpick if desired—place seam-side down on a baking sheet. Spoon any remaining marinade over the shrimp. Broil, turning the shrimp once until the bacon is slightly crisp and the shrimp are cooked through about 5 minutes.

Nutrition: Calories: 252. **Protein:** 7.11 g. **Fat:** 23.61 g. **Carbs:** 3.02 g.

100. Bacon-Wrapped Scallops

Preparation Time: 5 minutes
Cooking Time: 15 minutes
Servings: 4
Ingredients:

- 1 tsp. paprika
- 1 tsp. lemon pepper
- 5 slices of center-cut bacon
- 20 raw sea scallops

Directions:
1. Rinse and drain scallops, placing on paper towels to soak up excess moisture.
2. Cut slices of bacon into 4 pieces.

3. Wrap each scallop with a piece of bacon, using toothpicks to secure. Sprinkle wrapped scallops with paprika and lemon pepper.
4. Spray air fryer basket with olive oil and add scallops.
5. Cook for 5 to 6 minutes at 400° F, making sure to flip halfway through.

Nutrition: Calories: 389. **Carbs:** 63 g. **Fat:** 17 g. **Protein:** 21 g. **Sugar:** 1 g.

101. Soy and Ginger Shrimp

Preparation Time: 8 minutes
Cooking Time: 15 minutes
Servings: 4
Ingredients:

- 2 tbsp. olive oil
- 2 tbsp. scallions, finely chopped
- 2 cloves garlic, chopped
- 1 tsp. fresh ginger, grated
- 1 tbsp. dry white wine
- 1 tbsp. balsamic vinegar
- ¼ cup soy sauce
- 1 tbsp. sugar
- 1 pound shrimp
- Salt and ground black pepper, to taste

Directions:
1. Warm the oil in a saucepan and sauté all of the ingredients, except the shrimp, salt, and black pepper, to make the marinade. Allow it to cool.
2. Marinate the shrimp in the refrigerator for at least an hour, covered.
3. Pour into the oven rack/basket after that. Place the rack in the Air fryer oven's middle shelf. Preheat the oven to 350° F and set the timer for 10 minutes. At 350° F, bake the shrimp for 8 to 10 minutes (depending on size), flipping once or twice. Serve cooked shrimp with a pinch of salt and black pepper.

Nutrition: Calories: 239. **Protein:** 24.7 g. **Fat:** 11.22 g. **Carbs:** 8.51 g.

Beads

102. Cheddar Jalapeno Cornbread

Preparation Time: 20 minutes
Cooking Time: 15 minutes
Servings: 6
Ingredients:

- 1 ½ cup all-purpose flour
- 1 ½ cup yellow cornmeal
- 1 ⅕ tbsp. baking powder
- 1 ½ tbsp. salt
- 1 ½ cup whole milk
- ¼ tbsp. cayenne pepper, ground
- 3 eggs
- ½ cup sharp cheddar
- 1 ½ tbsp. green jalapeno, minced
- 1 ½ tbsp. red jalapeno, minced
- ⅓ cup vegetable oil plus 1 tbsp. vegetable oil
- 1 ½ tbsp. honey
- ½ tbsp. butter

Directions:
1. In a mixing bowl, mix flour, cornmeal, baking powder, salt, and pepper until well combined.
2. In another bowl, mix milk, eggs, cheese, jalapenos, and ⅓ cup vegetable oil.
3. Mix the dry ingredients into the wet ingredients. Grease a baking pan with the remaining oil and pour the mixture.
4. Slide the pizza rack on shelf position 5 of the Emeril Lagasse Power oven 360 and place the baking pan on top.
5. Select the bake setting. Set the temperature at 325° F for 30 minutes. Press starts.
6. Cook until the toothpick comes out clean when inserted in the bread.
7. Brush the bread with honey and butter, then let rest to cool before serving.
Nutrition: Calories: 201. **Carbs:** 27 g. **Fat:** 8.2 g. **Protein:** 6 g.

103. Brown Rice Bread

Preparation Time: 10 minutes
Cooking Time: 15 minutes
Servings: 8
Ingredients:

- Brown rice flour
- 2 eggs
- 1 ¼ cup almond milk
- 1 tsp. vinegar
- ½ cup coconut oil
- 2 tbsp. sugar
- ½ tsp. salt
- 2 ¼ tsp. instant yeast

Directions:
1. Place all ingredients in the Cuisinart bread pan in the liquid-dry-yeast layering.
2. Put the pan in the Cuisinart bread machine.
3. Select the Bake cycle. Choose Gluten-free. Press Start.
4. Five minutes into the kneading process, pause the machine and check the consistency of the dough. Add more flour if necessary.
5. Resume and wait until the loaf is cooked.
6. The machine will start the keep warm mode after the bread is complete.
7. Make it stay in that mode for about 10 minutes before unplugging.
8. Remove the pan and let it cool down for about 10 minutes.
Nutrition: Calories: 151. **Sodium:** 265 mg. **Dietary Fiber:** 4.3 g. **Fat:** 4.5 g. **Carbs:** 27.2 g. **Protein:** 3.5 g.

104. Brown Rice and Cranberry Bread

Preparation Time: 10 minutes
Cooking Time: 15 minutes
Servings: 8
Ingredients:

- 3 eggs, beaten
- 1 tsp. white vinegar
- 3 tbsp. gluten-free oil
- 1 ½ cup lukewarm water
- 3 cups brown rice flour
- 1 tbsp. xanthan gum
- ¼ cup flaxseed meal
- 1 tsp. salt
- ¼ cup sugar
- ½ cup powdered milk
- ⅔ cup cranberries, dried and cut into bits
- 2 ¼ tsp. instant yeast (bread yeast should be gluten-free, but always check)

Directions:
1. Mix all the wet and the dry ingredients, except the yeast and cranberries, separately.
2. Place all ingredients in the Cuisinart bread pan in the liquid-dry-yeast layering.
3. Put the pan in the Cuisinart bread machine.
4. Load the cranberries in the automatic dispenser.
5. Select the Bake cycle. Choose Gluten-free. Press start and wait until the loaf is cooked.
6. The machine will start the keep warm mode after the bread is complete.
7. Let it stay in that mode for around 10 minutes before unplugging.
8. Remove the pan and let it cool down for about 10 minutes. Layer them in the bread machine, in the liquid-dry-yeast layering. Do not add the cranberries.

Nutrition: **Calories:** 151. **Sodium:** 265 mg. **Dietary Fiber:** 4.3 g. **Fat:** 4.5 g. **Carbs:** 27.2 g. **Protein:** 3.5 g.

105. Gluten-Free Peasant Bread

Preparation Time: 10 minutes
Cooking Time: 15 minutes
Servings: 8
Ingredients:

- 2 cups brown rice flour
- 1 cup potato starch
- 1 tbsp. xanthan gum
- 2 tbsp. sugar
- 2 tbsp. yeast (bread yeast should be gluten-free, but always check)
- 3 tbsp. vegetable oil
- 5 eggs
- 1 tsp. white vinegar

Directions:
1. Bloom the yeast in water with the sugar for 5 minutes.
2. Place all ingredients in the Cuisinart bread pan in the yeast-liquid-dry layering.
3. Put the pan in the Cuisinart bread machine.
4. Select the Bake cycle. Choose Gluten Free. Press start and stand by until the loaf is cooked.
5. The machine will start the keep warm mode after the bread is complete.
6. Let it stay in that mode for approximately 10 minutes before unplugging.
7. Remove the pan and let it cool down for about 10 minutes.

Nutrition: **Calories:** 151. **Sodium:** 265 mg. **Dietary Fiber:** 4.3 g. **Fat:** 4.5 g. **Carbs:** 27.2 g. **Protein:** 3.5 g.

106. Gluten-Free Hawaiian Loaf

Preparation Time: 10 minutes
Cooking Time: 15 minutes
Servings: 8
Ingredients:

- 4 cups gluten-free four
- 1 tsp. xanthan gum
- 2 ½ tsp. (bread yeast should be gluten-free, but always check)
- ¼ cup white sugar
- ½ cup softened butter
- 1 egg, beaten
- 1 cup fresh pineapple juice, warm
- ½ tsp. salt
- 1 tsp. vanilla extract

Directions:
1. Place all ingredients in the Cuisinart bread pan in the liquid-dry-yeast layering.
2. Put the pan in the Cuisinart bread machine.

3. Select the Bake cycle. Choose Gluten Free. Press open and wait until the loaf is cooked.
4. The machine will start the keep warm mode after the bread is complete.
5. Let it stay in that mode for 10 minutes before unplugging.
6. Remove the pan and let it cool down for about 10 minutes.

Nutrition: **Calories:** 151. **Sodium:** 265 mg. **Dietary Fiber:** 4.3 g. **Fat:** 4.5 g. **Carbs:** 27.2 g. **Protein:** 3.5 g.

107. Vegan Gluten-Free Bread

Preparation Time: 10 minutes
Cooking Time: 15 minutes
Servings: 8
Ingredients:

- 1 cup almond flour
- 1 cup brown or white rice flour
- 2 tbsp. potato flour
- 4 tsp. baking powder
- ¼ tsp. baking soda
- 1 cup almond milk
- 1 tbsp. white vinegar

Directions:
1. Place all ingredients in the Cuisinart bread pan in the liquid-dry-yeast layering.
2. Put the pan in the Cuisinart bread machine.
3. Select the Bake cycle. Choose Gluten Free.
4. Press start and wait until the loaf is cooked.
5. The machine will start the keep warm mode after the bread is complete.
6. Let it stay in that mode for at least 10 minutes before unplugging.
7. Remove the pan and let it cool down for about 10 minutes.

Nutrition: **Calories:** 151. **Sodium:** 265 mg. **Dietary Fiber:** 4.3 g. **Fat:** 4.5 g. **Carbs:** 27.2 g. **Protein:** 3.5 g.

108. Curd Bread

Preparation Time: 4 hours
Cooking Time: 15 minutes
Servings: 12
Ingredients:

- ¾ cup lukewarm water
- ⅔ cups wheat bread machine flour
- ¾ cup cottage cheese
- 1 Tablespoon softened butter
- ½ Tablespoon white sugar
- 1 ½ tsp. sea salt
- 1 ½ tbsp. sesame seeds
- 1 Tablespoon dried onions
- 1 ¼ tsp. bread machine yeast

Directions:

1. Place all the dry and liquid ingredients in the pan and follow the instructions for your bread machine.
2. Pay particular attention to measuring the ingredients. Use a measuring cup, measuring spoon, and kitchen scales to do so.
3. Set the baking program to Basic and the crust type to Medium.
4. If the dough is too dense or too wet, adjust the amount of flour and liquid in the recipe.
5. When the program has ended, take the pan out of the bread machine and let it cool for 5 minutes.
6. Shake the loaf out of the pan. If necessary, use a spatula.
7. Wrap the bread with a kitchen towel and set it aside for an hour. Otherwise, you can cool it on a wire rack.

Nutrition: Calories: 277. **Total Carbs:** 48.4 g. **Cholesterol:** 9 g. **Total Fat:** 4.7 g. **Protein:** 9.4 g. **Sodium:** 547 mg. **Sugar:** 3.3 g.

109. Curvy Carrot Bread

Preparation Time: 2 hours
Cooking Time: 15 minutes
Servings: 12
Ingredients:

- ¾ cup milk, lukewarm
- 2 tablespoons butter, melted at room temperature
- 1 tbsp. honey
- ¾ tsp. ground nutmeg
- ½ tsp. salt
- 1 ½ cups shredded carrot
- 1 ½ cups white bread flour
- ¼ tsp. bread machine or active dry yeast

Directions:
1. Take 1 ½ pound size loaf pan and first add the liquid ingredients and then add the dry ingredients.
2. Place the loaf pan in the machine and close its top lid.
3. Plug the bread machine into the power socket. For selecting a bread cycle, press Quick Bread/Rapid Bread, and for selecting a crust type, press Light or Medium.
4. Start the machine and it will start preparing the bread.
5. After the bread loaf is completed, open the lid and take out the loaf pan.
6. Allow the pan to cool down for 10 to 15 minutes on a wire rack. Gently shake the pan and remove the bread loaf.
7. Make slices and serve.

Nutrition: Calories: 142. **Total Carbs:** 32.2 g. **Cholesterol:** 0 g. **Total Fat:** 0.8 g. **Protein:** 2.33 g.

110. Zucchini and Berries Loaf

Preparation Time: 1 hour
Cooking Time: 15 minutes
Servings: 8
Ingredients:

- 2 ¼ cups flour
- 3 eggs whisked lightly
- 1 ⅔ cups sugar
- 2 tsp. vanilla
- ¾ cup vegetable oil
- ¾ tsp. baking powder
- Pinch of baking soda
- ¼ tsp. salt
- 2 tsp. cinnamon
- 1 ½ cup blueberries
- 1 ½ cup shredded zucchini

Directions:
1. Blend the dry and wet ingredients in two different bowls.
2. Place all ingredients, except the berries, in the bread pan in the liquid-dry-yeast-zucchini layering.
3. Put the pan in the Hamilton Beach bread machine.
4. Load the berries in the automatic dispenser.
5. Select the Bake cycle. Set to Rapid White bake for 1 hour. Press Start.
6. Five minutes into the cycle, add the berries.
7. Wait until the loaf is cooked.
8. The machine will start the keep warm mode after the bread is complete.
9. Let it stay in that mode for 10 minutes before unplugging.
10. Remove the pan and let it cool down for about 10 minutes.

Nutrition: Calories: 277. **Cholesterol:** 9 g. **Carbs:** 48.4 g. **Dietary Fiber:** 1.9 g. **Sugars:** 3.3 g. **Protein:** 9.4 g.

111. Yeasted Carrot Bread

Preparation Time: 10 minutes
Cooking Time: 15 minutes
Servings: 8
Ingredients:

- ¾ cup milk
- 3 tbsp. melted butter, cooled
- 1 tbsp. honey
- 1 ½ cups shredded carrot
- ¾ tsp. ground nutmeg
- ½ tsp. salt
- 3 cups white bread flour
- 2 ¼ tsp. dry yeast

Directions:
1. Place the ingredients in your Hamilton Beach bread machine.

2.   Select the Bake cycle. Program the machine for Rapid bread and press Start.

3.   If the loaf is done, remove the bucket from the machine.

4.   Let the loaf cool for 5 minutes.

5.   Mildly shake the bucket to remove the loaf and try it out onto a rack to cool.

Nutrition: Calories: 277. **Cholesterol:** 9 g. **Carbs:** 48.4 g. **Dietary Fiber:** 1.9 g. **Sugars:** 3.3 g. **Protein:** 9.4 g.

112. Zucchini Rye Bread

Preparation Time: 10 minutes

Cooking Time: 15 minutes

Servings: 8

Ingredients:

- 2 cups all-purpose or bread flour
- 2 ¾ cup rye flour
- 2 tbsp. cocoa powder
- ½ cup cornmeal
- 1 tbsp. instant yeast
- ¼ cup olive oil
- 3 tbsp. molasses or honey
- 1 ½ cup lukewarm water
- 1 tsp. salt
- 1 ½ cup zucchini, shredded

Directions:

1.   Dry the shredded zucchini but place it in a towel and wring it to remove excess moisture.

2.   Place all the ingredients in the liquid-zucchini-flour-yeast layering.

3.   Put the pan in the Hamilton Beach bread machine.

4.   Select the Bake cycle. Choose White bread and medium crust.

5.   Press start and wait until the loaf is cooked.

6.   The machine will start the keep warm mode after the bread is complete.

7.   Let it stay in that mode for nearly 10 minutes before unplugging.

8.   Remove the pan and let it cool down for about 10 minutes.

Nutrition: Calories: 277. **Cholesterol:** 9 g. **Carbs:** 48.4 g. **Dietary Fiber:** 1.9 g. **Sugars:** 3.3 g. **Protein:** 9.4 g.

Pizza

113. Satay Chicken Pizza

Preparation Time: 10 minutes
Cooking Time: 15 minutes
Servings: 4
Ingredients:

- 1 tbsp. vegetable corn oil
- 2 chicken breasts
- 4 small pita bread
- 1 cup peanut sauce
- 1 bunch spring onions
- 4 slices provolone cheese

Directions:

1. Heat oil in a nonstick skillet and sauté the chicken for 7 minutes.
2. Spoon peanut sauce on each pita bread the sprinkle the cooked chicken. Add scallions and a slice of cheese.
3. Place the pizza on a crisper tray lined with a cookie sheet.
4. Slide the crisper tray on shelf position 2 of the oven and select the pizza setting. Set the temperature at 400° F for 12 minutes. Press starts.
5. Let the pizza stand for 2 minutes before cutting and serving.

Nutrition: Calories: 391. **Carbs**: 52 g. **Fat**: 18 g. **Protein**: 7 g.

114. Black and White Pizza

Preparation Time: 10 minutes
Cooking Time: 15 minutes
Servings: 4
Ingredients:

- 1 tbsp. olive oil
- ½ garlic clove, raw
- 6 oz. chicken
- 2 prepared pizza crust
- 1 cup Di Giorno Alfredo sauce
- 6 oz. packed mozzarella cheese
- ½ cup beans
- 4 oz. jalapeno peppers
- 1 tbsp. dried parsley

Directions:

1. Heat oil in a nonstick skillet over medium heat. Cook garlic until fragrant, then add chicken and cook until heated through.
2. Spread Alfredo sauce on the pizza crust, then sprinkle some cheese.
3. Arrange chicken strips over the cheese, then add black beans—place peppers on top.
4. Add the remaining cheese, then garnish with parsley. Place the pizza on a crisper tray of the oven.

5. Slide the crisper tray on shelf position 2 of the oven and select the pizza setting. Set the temperature at 450° F for 15 minutes, then press start.
6. Cook until the crust is crispy and the cheese has melted.

Nutrition: Calories: 731. **Carbs**: 61 g. **Fat**: 38 g. **Protein**: 41 g.

115. Margherita Pizza

Preparation Time: 5 minutes
Cooking Time: 15 minutes
Servings: 4
Ingredients:

- 1 pizza dough
- ¼ cup basil leaves
- ½ cup pizza sauce
- 2 cups sliced mozzarella cheese
- ¼ cup grated parmesan cheese

Directions:

1. Turn on the oven, set the temperature to 475° F, and then select the oven cooking method.
2. Meanwhile, transfer the pizza dough onto the clean working space dusted with flour and then roll it into a round shape.
3. Spread the pizza sauce on top, scatter mozzarella cheese on top and then sprinkle with parmesan cheese.
4. Transfer the prepared pizza to the baking pan and then bake for 14 minutes until the crust turns golden brown and the cheese turns golden.
5. When done, scatter basil leaves on top and then serve.

Nutrition: Calories: 220. **Fat**: 9 g. **Carbs**: 25 g. **Protein**: 11 g. **Fiber**: 1 g.

116. Meat Lovers' Pizza

Preparation Time: 10 minutes
Cooking Time: 15 minutes
Servings: 2
Ingredients:

- 1 pre-prepared 7-inch pizza pie crust, defrosted if necessary.
- ⅓ cup marinara sauce.
- 2 oz. grilled steak, sliced into bite-sized pieces
- 2 oz. salami, sliced fine
- 2 oz. pepperoni, sliced fine
- ¼ cup American cheese
- ¼ cup shredded mozzarella cheese

Directions:

1. Preheat the air fryer oven to 350° F. Lay the pizza dough flat on a sheet of parchment paper or tin foil, cut large enough to hold the entire pie crust, but small enough that it will leave the edges of the air frying basket uncovered to allow for air circulation. Using a fork, stab the pizza dough several times across the surface, piercing

the pie crust will allow air to circulate throughout the crust and ensure even cooking.

2.   With a deep soup spoon, ladle the marinara sauce onto the pizza dough, and spread evenly in expanding circles over the surface of the pie crust. Be sure to leave at least ½ inch of bare dough around the edges, to ensure that extra-crispy crunchy first bite of the crust! Distribute the pieces of steak and the slices of salami and pepperoni evenly over the sauce-covered dough, then sprinkle the cheese in an even layer on top.

3.   Set the air fryer timer to 12 minutes, and place the pizza with foil or paper on the fryer's basket surface. Again, be sure to leave the edges of the basket uncovered to allow for proper air circulation, and don't let your bare fingers touch the hot surface. After 12 minutes, when the air fryer oven shuts off, the cheese should be perfectly melted and lightly crisped, and the pie crust should be golden brown. Using a spatula, or two, if necessary, remove the pizza from the air fryer basket and set it on a serving plate. Wait a few minutes until the pie is cool enough to handle, then cut into slices and serve.

Nutrition: Calories: 671. **Protein:** 71.61 g. **Fat:** 111.2 g. **Carbs:** 94.2 g.

117. Toaster Oven Pizza Sandwiches

Preparation Time: 25 minutes
Cooking Time: 15 minutes
Servings: 1
Ingredients:

- 1 French bread sandwich roll, sliced
- 5 tsp. pizza sauce
- 15 to 20 slices of pepperoni
- 1 cup mozzarella cheese, shredded

Directions:

1.   Preheat the Cuisinart Convection Toaster Oven to 250° C or 482° F.

2.   Spread pizza sauce on the bread.

3.   Add toppings, cheese, and pepperoni to each slice of bread.

4.   Toast it until the cheese melts.

Nutrition: Calories: 752.1. **Carbs:** 33.5 g. **Protein:** 35.2 g. **Fat:** 15.7g.

118. Veg Pizza

Preparation Time: 30 minutes
Cooking Time: 15 minutes
Servings: 2
Ingredients:

- 1 cup tomatoes, sliced
- Capsicum, sliced
- 4 baby corns
- 1 to 2 tsp. pizza sauce
- 1 cup mozzarella cheese
- 3.5 cups all-purpose flour

- 1.5 tsp. oregano seasoning
- Salt
- 1.5 tsp. yeast
- 2 to 3 tsp. oil
- 1.5 cup water

Directions:

1.   Make pizza dough with all-purpose flour adding oil, salt, yeast, and water.

2.   Spread the remaining ingredients on the pizza base made of dough.

3.   Preheat the Cuisinart Convection Toaster Oven and bake for 10 minutes.

Nutrition: Calories: 300. **Carbs:** 37.5 g. **Protein:** 15 g. **Fat:** 10 g.

119. Toaster Oven-Baked Grilled Cheese

Preparation Time: 35 minutes
Cooking Time: 15 minutes
Servings: 1
Ingredients:

- 2 slices bread
- 1 to 2 tsp. mayonnaise
- 2 to 3 tsp. cheddar cheese
- Fresh spinach

Directions:

1.   Preheat the Cuisinart Convection Toaster Oven to 200° C or 400° F.

2.   Spread mayonnaise and cheese on the bread.

3.   Bake for 5 to 7 minutes. Add the spinach.

Nutrition: Calories: 353. **Carbs:** 42.1 g. **Protein:** 18.9 g. **Fat:** 7.8 g.

120. Cheese Chili Toast

Preparation Time: 10 minutes
Cooking Time: 15 minutes
Servings: 2
Ingredients:

- 2 to 4 slices bread
- Capsicum, chopped
- Salt & pepper
- 1 to 2 chilies
- 20 gm cheese, grated
- 10 gm cream
- Oil

Directions:

1.   Place the bread on the baking pan.

2.   Make a mixture of oil, capsicums, peppers, salt, and chilies.

3.   Apply the mixture on bread and grated cheese

4.   Bake at 180° C or 350° F or 177° C for 5 to 7 minutes in the Cuisinart Convection Toaster Oven. You're all set.

Nutrition: **Calories:** 135. **Carbs:** 11.6 g. **Protein:** 7.1 g.
Fat: 6.5 g.

121. Hot Ham and Cheese Sandwich

Preparation Time: 35 minutes
Cooking Time: 15 minutes
Servings: 2
Ingredients:

- 2 to 4 sandwich breads
- Olive oil
- ¼ tsp. oregano & basil
- 4 oz. ham, sliced
- 4 oz. cheese, sliced

Directions:
1.   Preheat the Cuisinart Convection Toaster Oven to 200° C or 400° F.
2.   Apply olive oil and sprinkle oregano on both sides of bread slices.
3.   Put the ham, spread cheese over one bread slice, and place the other on the sheet.
4.   Bake for 10 minutes.
Nutrition: **Calories:** 245. **Carbs:** 28 g. **Protein:** 16.18 g.
Fat: 18.53 g.

122. Cheese Pizza

Preparation Time: 10 minutes
Cooking Time: 15 minutes
Servings: 4
Ingredients:

- Readymade pizza base
- 2 to 3 tsp. tomato ketchup
- 100 gm cheese, shredded
- Salt & pepper
- 2 oz. mushroom
- Capsicum, onions, tomatoes

Directions:
1.   Preheat the Cuisinart Convection Toaster Oven to 250° C or 482° F.
2.   Spread ketchup on the pizza base and then toppings and cheese.
3.   Bake for 10 to 12 minutes.
Nutrition: **Calories:** 306. **Carbs:** 40 g. **Protein:** 15 g.
Fat: 11 g.

123. Philly Cheesesteak Sandwiches

Preparation Time: 15 minutes
Cooking Time: 15 minutes
Servings: 6
Ingredients:

- 1 to 2 lb. steak
- 1 tsp. Worcestershire sauce
- Salt & pepper
- 2 tsp. butter
- 1 green bell pepper
- Cheese slices
- Bread rolls

Directions:
1.   Marinate the steak with sauce, pepper, and salt. Cook the steak in a pan with butter until brown.
2.   Cook veggies for 2 to 3 mins
3.   Slice steak and place it on bread rolls with veggies, sliced cheese, and bell peppers.
4.   Bake for 15 minutes in the Cuisinart Convection Toaster Oven.
Nutrition: **Calories:** 476. **Carbs:** 15 g. **Protein:** 37 g.
Fat: 35 g.

Cake

124. Poppy Seed Pound Cake

Preparation Time: 10 minutes
Cooking Time: 15 minutes
Servings: 8
Ingredients:

- 2 large egg
- ½ cup coconut milk
- ⅓ cup unsalted butter
- ¼ tsp. vanilla extract
- 2 tbsp. psyllium husk powder
- 1 ½ tsp. baking powder
- 2 tbsp. poppy seeds
- 1 ½ cup almond flour

Directions:
1. Preheat the air fryer for 5 minutes.
2. In a mixing bowl, combine all ingredients.
3. Use a hand mixer to mix everything.
4. Pour into a small loaf pan that will fit in the oven.
5. Bake for 20 minutes at 3750 F or until a toothpick inserted in the middle comes out clean.
Nutrition: Calories: 145. **Carbs:** 3.6 g. **Protein:** 2.1 g. **Fat:** 13.6 g.

125. Vanilla Pound Cake

Preparation Time: 35 minutes
Cooking Time: 15 minutes
Servings: 6
Ingredients:

- ½ cup full-fat sour cream
- 1 oz. full-fat cream cheese; softened
- 2 large eggs
- ½ cup granular erythritol
- 1 cup blanched finely ground almond flour
- ¼ cup salted butter; melted
- 1 tsp. baking powder
- 1 tsp. vanilla extract

Directions:
1. Take a large bowl, mix almond flour, butter, and erythritol.
2. Add in vanilla, baking powder, sour cream, and cream cheese and mix until well combined. Add eggs and mix.
3. Pour batter into a 6-inch round baking pan. Place pan into the air fryer basket. Adjust the temperature to 300° F and set the timer for 25 minutes.
4. When the cake is made, a toothpick inserted in the center will come out clean. The center should not feel wet. Allow it to cool completely, or the cake will crumble when moved.
Nutrition: Calories: 253. **Protein:** 6.9 g. **Fiber:** 2.0 g. **Fat:** 22.6 g. **Carbs:** 25.2 g.

126. Mini Lava Cakes

Preparation Time: 30 minutes
Cooking Time: 15 minutes
Servings: 4
Ingredients:

- 3 oz. dark chocolate; melted
- 2 eggs, whisked
- ¼ cup coconut oil; melted
- 1 tbsp. almond flour
- 2 tbsp. swerve
- ¼ tsp. vanilla extract
- Cooking spray

Directions:
1. In a bowl, combine all the ingredients except the cooking spray and whisk well.
2. Divide this into 4 ramekins greased with cooking spray, put them in the oven, and cook at 360° F for 20 minutes
Nutrition: Calories: 161. **Fat:** 12 g. **Fiber:** 1 g. **Carbs:** 4 g. **Protein:** 7 g.

127. Lemon Blackberries Cake

Preparation Time: 35 minutes
Cooking Time: 15 minutes
Servings: 4
Ingredients:

- 2 eggs, whisked
- ¼ cup almond milk
- 1 ½ cups almond flour
- 1 cup blackberries; chopped
- 2 tbsp. ghee; melted
- 4 tbsp. swerve
- 1 tsp. lemon zest, grated
- 1 tsp. lemon juice
- ½ tsp. baking powder

Directions:
1. Take a bowl and mix all the ingredients and whisk well.
2. Pour this into a cake pan that fits the oven lined with parchment paper, put the pan in your oven, and cook at 340° F for 25 minutes. Cool the cake down, slice, and serve
Nutrition: Calories: 193. **Fat:** 5 g. **Fiber:** 1 g. **Carbs:** 4 g. **Protein:** 4 g.

128. Yogurt Cake

Preparation Time: 35 minutes
Cooking Time: 15 minutes
Servings: 12
Ingredients:

- 6 eggs, whisked
- 8 oz. Greek yogurt
- 9 oz. coconut flour
- 4 tbsp. stevia

- 1 tsp. vanilla extract
- 1 tsp. baking powder

Directions:

1. Take a bowl and mix all the ingredients and whisk well.
2. Pour this into a cake pan that fits the oven lined with parchment paper.
3. Put the pan in the oven and cook at 330° F for 30 minutes

Nutrition: Calories: 181. **Fat:** 13 g. **Fiber:** 2 g. **Carbs:** 4 g. **Protein:** 5 g.

129. Chocolate Coffee Cake

Preparation Time: 40 minutes
Cooking Time: 15 minutes
Servings: 8
Ingredients:

- 1 ½ cups almond flour
- ½ cup coconut meat
- ⅔ cup swerve
- 1 tsp. baking powder
- ¼ tsp. salt
- 1 stick butter, melted
- ½ cup hot strongly brewed coffee
- ½ tsp. vanilla
- 1 egg

Topping:

- ¼ cup coconut flour
- ½ cup confectioner's swerve
- ½ tsp. ground cardamom
- 1 tsp. ground cinnamon
- 3 tbsp. coconut oil

Directions:

1. Mix all dry ingredients for your cake; then, mix in the wet ingredients. Mix until everything is well incorporated.
2. Spritz a baking pan with cooking spray. Scrape the batter into the baking pan.
3. Then, make the topping by mixing all ingredients. Place on top of the cake—smooth the top with a spatula.
4. Bake at 330° F for 30 minutes or until the top of the cake springs back when gently pressed with your fingers. Serve with your favorite hot beverage.

Nutrition: Calories: 285. **Fat:** 21 g. **Carbs:** 6 g. **Protein:** 8 g. **Sugars:** 3 g. **Fiber:** 1 g.

130. Peanut Butter Fudge Cake

Preparation Time: 30 minutes
Cooking Time: 15 minutes
Servings: 10
Ingredients:

- 1 cup peanut butter
- 1 ¼ cups monk fruit
- 3 eggs

- 1 cup almond flour
- 1 tsp. baking powder
- ¼ tsp. kosher salt
- 1 cup unsweetened bakers' chocolate, broken into chunks

Directions:

1. Start by preheating your oven to 350° F. Now, spritz the sides and bottom of a baking pan with cooking spray.
2. In a mixing dish, thoroughly combine the peanut butter with the monk fruit until creamy. Next, fold in the egg and beat until fluffy.
3. After that, stir in the almond flour, baking powder, salt, and baker's chocolate. Mix until everything is well combined.
4. Bake in the preheated oven for 20 to 22 minutes. Transfer to a wire rack to cool before slicing and serving.

Nutrition: Calories: 207. **Fat:** 11 g. **Carbs:** 4 g. **Protein:** 4 g. **Sugars:** 1 g. **Fiber:** 4 g.

131. Chocolate Paradise Cake

Preparation Time: 5 minutes
Cooking Time: 15 minutes
Servings: 6
Ingredients:

- 2 eggs, beaten
- ⅔ cup sour cream
- 1 cup almond flour
- ⅔ cup swerve
- ⅓ cup coconut oil, softened
- ¼ cup cocoa powder
- 2 tbsp. chocolate chips, unsweetened
- 1 ½ tsp. baking powder
- 1 tsp. vanilla extract
- ½ tsp. pure rum extract

Chocolate frosting:

- ½ cup butter, softened
- ¼ cup cocoa powder
- 1 cup powdered Swerve
- 2 tbsp. milk

Directions:

1. Mix all ingredients for the chocolate cake with a hand mixer on low speed. Scrape the batter into a cake pan.
2. Bake at 330° F for 25 to 30 minutes. Transfer the cake to a wire rack
3. Meanwhile, whip the butter and cocoa until smooth. Stir in the powdered swerve. Slowly and gradually, pour in the milk until your frosting reaches the desired consistency.
4. Whip until smooth and fluffy; then, frost the cooled cake. Place in your refrigerator for a couple of hours. Serve well chilled.

Nutrition: Calories: 433. **Fat:** 44 g. **Carbs:** 8 g. **Protein:** 5 g. **Sugars:** 9 g. **Fiber:** 9 g.

132. Famous New York Cheesecake

Preparation Time: 1 hour
Cooking Time: 15 minutes
Servings: 8
Ingredients:

- 1 ½ cups almond flour
- 3 oz. swerve
- ½ stick butter, melted
- 20 oz. full-fat cream cheese
- ½ cup heavy cream
- 1 ¼ cups granulated swerve
- 3 eggs, at room temperature
- 1 tbsp. vanilla essence
- 1 tsp. grated lemon zest

Directions:

1. Coat the sides and bottom of a baking pan with a little flour.
2. In a mixing bowl, combine the almond flour and swerve. Add the melted butter and mix until your mixture looks like breadcrumbs.
3. Press the mixture into the bottom of the prepared pan to form an even layer. Bake at 330° F for 7 minutes until golden brown. Allow it to cool completely on a wire rack.
4. Meanwhile, in a mixer fitted with the paddle attachment, prepare the filling by mixing the soft cheese, heavy cream, and granulated swerve; beat until creamy and fluffy.
5. Crack the eggs into the mixing bowl, one at a time; add the vanilla and lemon zest and continue to mix until fully combined.
6. Pour the prepared topping over the cooled crust and spread evenly.
7. Bake in the preheated oven at 330° F for 25 to 30 minutes; leave it in the oven to keep warm for another 30 minutes.
8. Cover your cheesecake with plastic wrap. Place in your refrigerator and allow it to cool for at least 6 hours or overnight. Serve well chilled.

Nutrition: Calories: 245. **Fat:** 22 g. **Carbs:** 5 g. **Protein:** 8 g. **Sugars:** 1 g. **Fiber:** 5 g.

133. Choco-Peanut Mug Cake

Preparation Time: 5 minutes
Cooking Time: 15 minutes
Servings: 2
Ingredients:

- 1 tsp. softened butter
- 1 egg
- 1 tbsp. peanut butter
- ½ tsp. vanilla extract
- 2 tbsp. erythritol

- 2 tbsp. unsweetened cocoa powder
- ¼ tsp. baking powder
- 1 tbsp. heavy cream

Directions:

1. Preheat the oven for 5 minutes.
2. Combine all ingredients in a mixing bowl.
3. Pour into a greased mug.
4. Set in the oven basket and cook for 20 minutes at 400° F

Nutrition: Calories: 293. **Protein:** 12.4 g. **Fat:** 23.3 g. **Carbs:** 8.5 g.

134. Ultimate Coconut Chocolate Cake

Preparation Time: 5 minutes
Cooking Time: 15 minutes
Servings: 10
Ingredients:

- 1 ¼ cups unsweetened bakers' chocolate
- 1 stick butter
- 1 tsp. liquid stevia
- ⅓ cup shredded coconut
- 2 tbsp. coconut milk
- 2 eggs, beaten
- Cooking spray

Directions:

1. Lightly spritz a baking pan with cooking spray.
2. Place the chocolate, butter, and stevia in a microwave-safe bowl. Microwave for about 30 seconds until melted. Let the chocolate mixture cool to room temperature.
3. Add the remaining ingredients to the chocolate mixture and stir until well incorporated. Pour the batter into the prepared baking pan.
4. Select Bake, Convection, set the temperature to 330° F (166° C) and set time to 15 minutes. Select Start to begin preheating.
5. Once the oven has preheated, place the pan in the bake position.
6. When cooking is complete, a toothpick inserted in the center should come out clean.
7. Remove from the oven and allow to cool for about 10 minutes before serving.

Nutrition: Calories: 191. **Cal Fat:** 6 g. **Carbs:** 31.4 g. **Protein:** 3.7 g. **Cholesterol:** 3 mg. **Sodium:** 447 mg.

Cookies

135. Best Fudgy Chocolate Crinkle Cookies

Preparation Time: 10 minutes
Cooking Time: 15 minutes
Servings: 20
Ingredients:

- ½ cup (2.2 oz./60 g) unsweetened cocoa powder
- 1 cup (7 oz./205 g) white granulated sugar
- ¼ cup (60 mL) vegetable oil
- 2 large eggs
- 2 tsp. pure vanilla extract
- 1 cup (3.5 oz./130 g) all-purpose or plain flour
- 1 tsp. baking powder
- ½ tsp. salt
- ¼ cup confectioner's sugar or icing sugar (for coating)

Directions:

1. In a medium-sized bowl, mix the cocoa powder, white sugar, and vegetable oil. Beat in eggs one at a time, until fully incorporated. Mix in the vanilla.
2. In another bowl, combine the flour, baking powder, and salt. Stir the dry ingredients into the wet mixture until a dough forms (do not overbeat). Cover bowl with wrap and refrigerate for at least 4 hours or overnight.
3. When ready to bake, preheat the oven to 350° F or 175° C. Line 2 cookie sheets or baking trays with parchment paper (baking paper). Roll 1 tablespoonful of dough into balls for smaller cookies or 2 tablespoonfuls for larger cookies.
4. Add the confectioners (icing) sugar to a smaller bowl. Generously and evenly coat each ball of dough in confectioners' sugar and place it onto prepared cookie sheets.
5. Bake in a preheated oven for 10 minutes (for small cookies) or 12 minutes (for larger cookies). The cookies will come out soft from the oven but will harden up as they cool.
6. Allow cooling on the cookie sheet for 5 minutes before transferring to wire racks to cool.

Nutrition: Calories: 102. **Carbs:** 17 g. **Protein:** 1 g. **Fat:** 3 g. **Saturated Fat:** 2 g. **Cholesterol:** 16 mg. **Sodium:** 65 mg. **Potassium:** 65 mg. **Sugar:** 11 g. **Vitamin A:** 25 IU. **Calcium:** 15 mg. **Iron:** 0.7 mg.

136. Perfect White Chocolate Macadamia Cookies

Preparation Time: 10 minutes
Cooking Time: 15 minutes
Servings: 3 dozen
Ingredients:

- 1 cup unsalted butter (2 sticks), at room temperature
- ¾ cup packed light brown sugar
- ½ cup white sugar
- 2 large eggs, at room temperature
- 1 tbsp. vanilla extract
- ¼ tsp. almond extract
- 2 ¾ cups all-purpose flour
- 1 tsp. baking soda
- ¼ tsp. salt (if using unsalted macadamia nuts, increase to ½ tsp.)
- 1 cup coarsely chopped, lightly salted macadamia nuts
- 1 $1/_3$ cup white chocolate chips

Directions:

1. In a large bowl or the bowl of an electric mixer fitted with the paddle attachment, cream together the butter, brown sugar, and white sugar until light and fluffy, about 5 minutes. Beat in the eggs, one at a time. Mix in the vanilla and almond extracts until combined. With the mixer off, pour in the flour, baking soda, and salt. Then, beginning on low speed, mix until flour is fully incorporated. Stir in the macadamia nuts and white chocolate to distribute evenly. Wrap dough in plastic and refrigerate for at least 2 hours or up to 48 hours.
2. When ready to bake, preheat the oven to 350° F and line cookie sheets with parchment paper. Scoop heaping tbsp.-sized balls of the chilled dough, roll into balls, and arrange on the sheets, leaving 3 inches between each ball (you may need to bake in batches).
3. Bake for 12 to 14 minutes in the preheated oven, or until golden brown. Enjoy warm or cool completely before storing in a sealed container for up to a week (they will lose some of the crisp edges over time).

Nutrition: Calories: 145. **Carbs:** 3.6 g. **Protein:** 2.1 g. **Fat:** 13.6 g.

137. Buttermilk Biscuits

Preparation Time: 10 minutes
Cooking Time: 15 minutes
Servings: 10
Ingredients:

- 1 tbsp. sugar
- 4 tsp. baking powder
- 1 tsp. salt
- 2 cup all-purpose flour
- ½ cup butter; chilled cut into small cubes
- $2/_3$ cup buttermilk; add 1 egg to buttermilk to equal $2/_3$ cup, then beat egg

Directions:

1. Preheat oven to 450° F or 425° F convection bakes. Combine and mix dry ingredients in a bowl. Add butter to the flour mixture and coat with flour. Pinch

cubes between fingers in flour until it is a coarse meal or pea-size clumps.

2. Whisk egg and buttermilk together until blended. Add egg and buttermilk mixture to dry ingredients and mix until the dough absorbs all the flour. Turn out unto floured counter or cutting board and knead no more than 2 or 3 times to absorb the remaining flour to make a smooth, light dough. Do not over-handle dough, or the biscuits will be tough. The dough should be slightly sticky.

3. Dust board with flour and turn dough to coat with flour. Pat dough to 1/2" thickness and cut biscuits. Place on a cookie sheet and bake for 8 to 12 minutes tops should be brown.

4. Optional you can brush tops with cream and also pepper tops if desired.

5. You can freeze biscuits to bake later. Place the frozen biscuit on a sheet pan and bake at 425° F for 15 minutes or 400° F convection bake for 15 minutes. Bake until the tops are brown.

Nutrition: Calories: 145. **Carbs:** 3.6 g. **Protein:** 2.1 g. **Fat:** 13.6 g.

138. Nankhatai Cookies Recipe

Preparation Time: 10 minutes
Cooking Time: 15 minutes
Servings: 40
Ingredients:
- 180 g Maida (all-purpose flour)
- 60 g Besan flour (chickpea flour)
- ¼ tsp. salt
- ¼ tsp. cardamom powder
- 1 tsp. baking powder
- 100 g unsalted butter
- 30 g vegetable oil/sunflower oil
- 1 tsp. rose water
- 2 tbsp. milk
- 125 g sugar
- 2 tbsp. almonds
- 2 tbsp. pistachios

Directions:
1. Add in the Maida (all-purpose flour), Besan (chickpea flour), salt, cardamom powder, and baking powder. Sieve the ingredients twice.

2. Take another bowl and add all the wet ingredients, namely butter, oil, rose water, and milk. Make sure that the butter is at room temperature. Beat all the ingredients with a whisk for a minute.

3. Add in the powdered sugar. Run it in the mixer and grind until it turns into powder. Add to the bowl. Beat the sugar along with the butter mixture until smooth.

4. Add in the flour mixture. Gently mix to form a dough. Do not mix the dough for long. Once it forms into a cohesive mass, stop mixing the dough. Set aside.

5. Once the dough is formed, make small bite-size balls out of the dough. This recipe makes 40 small cookies.

6. In the meantime, chop the nuts and set them aside on a board or a plate.

7. Take a small ball of dough and gently press the dough on the nuts.

8. Once the nuts stick to the dough ball, gently press the nuts on the cookie dough to adhere well.

9. Place the prepared cookie on a parchment / Silpat lined baking sheet.

10. Preheat the oven for about 15 to 20 minutes under 180° C. After preheating, bake the cookies in the oven for about 15 to 18 minutes. If the bottom is browned, the cookies are done. The cookies will still be soft to touch. It will harden as it cools. Remove the cookies from the hot pan immediately and allow them to cool. Store in an airtight box for up to a week.

Nutrition: Calories: 145. **Carbs:** 3.6 g. **Protein:** 2.1 g. **Fat:** 13.6 g.

139. Diy Cookie Crisp Cereal

Preparation Time: 10 minutes
Cooking Time: 15 minutes
Servings: 2
Ingredients:
- Milk
- Cookie dough (1 roll)

Directions:
1. Roll out your cookie dough. You can use an empty wine bottle or glass; suppose you don't have a rolling pin. Use a nickel-sized cookie cutter to cut out small cookies. You can use any mini cookie cutter or ring if you don't have a nickel-sized cookie cutter.

2. Bake in your oven at a temperature of 350° F until they become golden brown and crispy or for just 10 minutes.

3. Bring it out and allow it to cool off.

4. Add your milk and enjoy your breakfast.

Nutrition: Calories: 145. **Carbs:** 3.6. **Protein:** 2.1 g. **Fat:** 13.6 g.

140. Morning Cookies

Preparation Time: 1 hour
Cooking Time: 15 minutes
Servings: 8
Ingredients:
- 35 g sugar
- 1 bar lotte chocolate
- 1 tsp. baking powder
- 1 tsp. baking soda
- 2 eggs
- 70 g butter
- 130 g flour

Directions:

1.   Mix all your dry ingredients (except for chocolate) in a large bowl.
2.   Melt your butter and add it to your dry ingredients. Add the eggs and gently mix properly.
3.   Put the chocolate chips and mix again.
4.   Oil the oven tray. Scoop the cookies.
5.   Bake for 5 minutes and allow it to cool off for 3 minutes.
6.   Serve and enjoy your meal.

Nutrition: Calories: 145. **Carbs:** 3.6 g. **Protein:** 2.1 g. **Fat:** 13.6 g.

Dessert

141. Chocolate Mug Cake

Preparation Time: 5 minutes
Cooking Time: 15 minutes
Servings: 3
Ingredients:

- ½ cup cocoa powder
- ½ cup stevia powder
- 1 cup coconut cream
- 1 package cream cheese, room temperature
- 1 tbsp. vanilla extract
- 1 tbsp. butter

Directions:
1. Preheat the oven for 5 minutes. Combine all ingredients in a mixing bowl, using a hand mixer, until fluffy.
2. Pour into greased mugs. Place the mugs in the basket; bake for 15 minutes at 350° F. Put in your fridge to chill before serving.

Nutrition: Calories: 382. **Carbs:** 76 g. **Fat:** 6 g. **Protein:** 4 g.

142. Apple Dumplings

Preparation Time: 10 minutes
Cooking Time: 15 minutes
Servings: 4
Ingredients:

- 2 tbsp. melted coconut oil
- 2 puff pastry sheets
- 1 tbsp. brown sugar
- 2 tbsp. raisins
- 2 small apples of choice

Directions:
1. Ensure your oven is preheated to 356° F. Core and peel apples and mix with raisins and sugar. Place a bit of apple mixture into puff pastry sheets and brush sides with melted coconut oil.
2. Place into the oven. Cook 25 minutes, turning halfway through. It will be golden when done.

Nutrition: Calories: 163. **Carbs:** 21 g. **Fat:** 9 g. **Protein:** 1 g.

143. Apple Pie

Preparation Time: 5 minutes
Cooking Time: 15 minutes
Servings: 4
Ingredients:

- ½ tsp. vanilla extract
- 1 beaten egg
- 1 large apple, chopped
- 1 Pillsbury Refrigerator pie crust
- 1 tbsp. butter
- 1 tbsp. ground cinnamon
- 1 tbsp. raw sugar
- 2 tbsp. sugars
- 2 tsp. lemon juice
- Baking spray

Directions:
1. Lightly grease the baking pan of the oven with cooking spray. Spread pie crust on the bottom of the pan up to the sides.
2. Mix the vanilla, sugar, cinnamon, lemon juice, plus apples in a bowl. Pour on top of pie crust; top the apples with butter slices.
3. Cover apples with the other pie crust. Pierce with a knife the tops of the pie. Spread beaten egg over the crust, then sprinkle sugar. Cover with foil.
4. For 25 minutes, cook at 390° F in the oven. Remove foil cook for 10 minutes at 330° F until tops are browned. Serve and enjoy.

Nutrition: Calories: 270. **Carbs:** 34 g. **Fat:** 14 g. **Protein:** 3 g.

144. Raspberry Cream Roll-Ups

Preparation Time: 10 minutes
Cooking Time: 35 minutes
Servings: 4
Ingredients:

- 1 cup fresh raspberries, rinsed and patted dry
- ½ cup cream cheese softened to room temperature
- ¼ cup brown sugar
- ¼ cup sweetened condensed milk
- 1 egg
- 1 tsp. corn starch
- 6 spring roll wrappers
- ¼ cup water

Directions:
1. Cover the oven basket with a lining of tin foil, leaving the edges uncovered to allow air to circulate through the basket. Preheat the oven to 350° F.
2. Combine the cream cheese, brown sugar, condensed milk, cornstarch, and egg in a mixing bowl. Beat or whip thoroughly until all ingredients are completely mixed and fluffy, thick, and stiff.
3. Spoon even amounts of the creamy filling into each spring roll wrapper, then top each dollop of filling with several raspberries.
4. Roll up the wraps around the creamy raspberry filling, and seal the seams with a few dabs of water. Place each roll on the foil-lined oven basket, seams facing down.
5. Set the oven timer to 10 minutes. Remove with tongs and serve hot or cold.

Nutrition: Calories: 164. **Carbs:** 33 g. **Fat:** 1 g. **Protein:** 7 g.

30 Minutes

Breakfast

145. Baked Cinnamon Oatmeal
Preparation Time: 10 minutes
Cooking Time: 30 minutes
Servings: 8
Ingredients:
- 2 eggs
- 3 cups rolled oats
- 1 tsp. ground cinnamon
- 1 tsp. vanilla
- 1 ½ tsp. baking powder
- ¼ cup butter, melted
- ½ cup maple syrup
- 1 ½ cups almond milk
- Pinch of salt

Directions:
1. Preheat the oven to 350° F.
2. In a bowl, whisk eggs with almond milk, cinnamon, vanilla, baking powder, butter, maple syrup, and salt.
3. Add oats and mix well.
4. Pour the mixture into the greased 8x8-inch baking pan.
5. Place the baking pan onto the oven rack and bake for 30 minutes.
6. Serve and enjoy.

Nutrition: Calories: 341. **Fat:** 19.6 g. **Carbs:** 37.3 g. **Sugar:** 13.7 g. **Protein:** 6.5 g. **Cholesterol:** 56 mg.

146. Pumpkin Bread
Preparation Time: 10 minutes
Cooking Time: 30 minutes
Servings: 8
Ingredients:
- 2 eggs
- ¼ cup coconut flour
- ¼ cup flax seed meal
- ¼ cup swerve
- 1 tsp. baking powder
- 1 tsp. pumpkin pie spice
- ¼ cup chocolate chips
- ½ cup pumpkin puree

Directions:
1. Preheat the oven to 350° F.
2. Grease loaf pan with and set aside.
3. Add all dry ingredients into the bowl and mix well. Set aside.
4. In a separate bowl, whisk pumpkin puree and eggs.
5. Pour wet ingredients mixture into the dry ingredients and mix until just combined.
6. Pour batter into the prepared loaf pan.
7. Place loaf pan onto the oven rack and bake for 35 minutes.
8. Slice and serve.

Nutrition: Calories: 69. **Fat:** 3.8 g. **Carbs:** 5.9 g. **Sugar:** 3.4 g. **Protein:** 2.6 g. **Cholesterol:** 42 mg.

147. Fluffy Breakfast Egg Muffins
Preparation Time: 10 minutes
Cooking Time: 20 minutes
Servings: 12
Ingredients:
- 12 eggs
- ½ cup ham, diced
- ½ cup cheddar cheese, shredded
- ½ cup almond milk
- ¼ tsp garlic powder
- Pepper
- Salt

Directions:
1. Preheat the oven to 375° F.
2. Spray 12-cups muffin tin with cooking spray and set aside.
3. In a bowl, whisk eggs with milk, garlic powder, pepper, and salt.
4. Add ham and cheese and stir well.
5. Pour egg mixture into the prepared muffin tin.
6. Place muffin tin onto the oven rack and bake for 25 minutes.
7. Serve and enjoy.

Nutrition: Calories: 114. **Fat:** 8.8 g. **Carbs:** 1.2 g. **Sugar:** 0.7 g. **Protein:** 7.9 g. **Cholesterol:** 172 mg.

148. Quinoa And Squash Platter
Preparation Time: 10 minutes
Cooking Time: 30 minutes
Servings: 4
Ingredients:
- 1 tsp. ginger, minced
- 2 tsp. thyme
- 1 and ½ cups quinoa
- ¼ cup walnuts, chopped
- 2 onions, sliced
- 1 red bell pepper
- 2 tbsp. olive oil
- 1 big spaghetti squash
- Salt and pepper to taste

Directions:
1. Preheat oven to 380° F in "Air Fry" mode
2. Clean squash, slice in half

3. Transfer to the cooking basket and cook for 30 to 40 minutes until tender

4. Take a skillet and heat a tbsp. oil, add bell pepper, quinoa, onion, walnuts, and cook until warm

5. Season well with salt and pepper.

6. Divide the mixture between a squash and bake for 2 to 5 minutes more.

7. Serve and enjoy!

Nutrition: Calories: 428. **Protein:** 13 g. **Fat:** 22 g. **Carbs:** 49 g.

149. Original German Pancakes

Preparation Time: 10 minutes
Cooking Time: 30 minutes
Servings: 4
Ingredients:

- 2 tbsp. apple sauce
- 1 cup flour
- 2 tbsp. maple syrup
- 3 whole eggs
- 1 cup almond milk

Directions:

1. The whole ingredients should be mixed in a bowl, and the mixture's consistency should be maintained.

2. The oven should be preheated at 390° F for 5 min.

3. The cast iron tray should be placed inside the oven.

4. The batter should be poured into the tray. The cakes are heated for 8 minutes, then removed from the tray and served.

Nutrition: Calories: 139. **Protein:** 8 g. **Fat:** 4 g. **Carbs:** 18 g.

150. Apple Oat Cups

Preparation Time: 10 minutes
Cooking Time: 30 minutes
Servings: 12
Ingredients:

- 2 eggs
- 1 ¼ cups apples, peel & dice
- 2 tsp. vanilla
- ½ cup applesauce
- 1 cup milk
- 2 tsp. ground cinnamon
- 2 tsp. baking powder
- 2 tbsp. brown sugar
- 3 cups old-fashioned oats
- ¼ tsp. salt

Directions:

1. Preheat the oven to 350° F.

2. Spray 12 cups muffin tin with cooking spray and set aside.

3. In a mixing bowl, mix oats, cinnamon, baking powder, brown sugar, and salt and set aside.

4. In a large bowl, whisk eggs, vanilla, applesauce, and milk.

5. Add oat mixture into the egg mixture and stir until well combined.

6. Add apples and stir well.

7. Spoon mixture into the prepared muffin tin.

8. Place muffin tin onto the oven rack and bake for 30 minutes.

9. Serve and enjoy.

Nutrition: Calories: 122. **Fat:** 2.5 g. **Carbs:** 21.2 g. **Sugar:** 6.2 g. **Protein:** 4.3 g. **Cholesterol:** 29 mg.

151. Spinach Tomato Egg Muffins

Preparation Time: 10 minutes
Cooking Time: 30 minutes
Servings: 12
Ingredients:

- 8 eggs
- ⅓ cup feta cheese, crumbled
- ¼ cup almond milk
- 3 basil leaves, chopped
- ½ onion, diced
- 1 cup spinach, chopped
- ½ cup sun-dried tomatoes, chopped
- Pepper
- Salt

Directions:

1. Preheat the oven to 350° F.

2. Spray 12 cups muffin tin with cooking spray and set aside.

3. Divide feta cheese, basil, onion, spinach, and tomatoes evenly into the muffin tin cups.

4. In a bowl, whisk eggs with milk, pepper, and salt.

5. Pour egg mixture over veggies.

6. Place muffin tin onto the oven rack and bake for 18 to 20 minutes.

7. Serve and enjoy.

Nutrition: Calories: 68. **Fat:** 5 g. **Carbs:** 1.5 g. **Sugar:** 1 g. **Protein:** 4.6 g. **Cholesterol:** 113 mg.

152. Perfect Potato Casserole

Preparation Time: 10 minutes
Cooking Time: 30 minutes
Servings: 10
Ingredients:

- 7 eggs
- 8 oz. cheddar cheese, grated
- 20 oz. frozen hash browns, diced
- ½ cup almond milk
- 1 onion, chopped & sautéed
- 1 lb. sausage, cooked
- Pepper
- Salt

Directions:
1. Preheat the oven to 350° F.
2. Spray casserole dish with cooking spray and set aside.
3. In a mixing bowl, whisk eggs with milk, pepper, and salt.
4. Add remaining ingredients and mix well. Pour egg mixture into the prepared casserole dish.
5. Place the casserole dish onto the oven rack and bake for 35 minutes.
6. Serve and enjoy.

Nutrition: Calories: 393. **Fat:** 27.8 g. **Carbs:** 18.5 g. **Sugar:** 1.7 g. **Protein:** 17 g. **Cholesterol:** 147 mg.

153. Masala And Quinoa Oatmeal

Preparation Time: 10 minutes
Cooking Time: 30 minutes
Servings: 4
Ingredients:
- ½ white onion, chopped
- Pinch of salt
- 1 red bell pepper, chopped
- ½ jalapeno pepper, seeded and chopped
- 1 tbsp. masala powder
- 2 tbsp. ginger, peeled and grated
- 1 cup quinoa
- 2 cups Sebi friendly vegetable stock
- ½ lemon, juiced

Directions:
1. Preheat your oven to 350° F in "Air Fry" mode.
2. Take a large skillet and place it over medium heat, add onion and salt, sauté for 3 minutes.
3. Add pepper, jalapeno, ginger, garam masala, and sauté for 1 minute.
4. Add quinoa to the stock, stir.
5. Transfer mix to the cooking basket.
6. Cook for about 3 to 4 minutes until fluffy.
7. Add lemon juice and fluff more.
8. Adjust the seasoning accordingly and serve.
9. Enjoy!

Nutrition: Calories: 503. **Protein:** 32 g. **Fat:** 3 g. **Carbs:** 10 g.

154. Zucchini Zoodles and Avocado Sauce

Preparation Time: 10 minutes

Cooking Time: 30 minutes
Servings: 4
Ingredients:
- 3 medium zucchinis
- 1 and ½ cup cherry tomatoes
- 1 avocado
- 2 green onions, sliced
- 1 garlic clove
- 3 tbsp. olive oil
- Juice of 1 key lemon
- 1 tbsp. spring water
- Salt and cayenne to taste

Directions:
1. Preheat oven to 385° F in "Air Fry" mode.
2. Take your cooking basket and cover it with parchment paper.
3. Put tomatoes and drizzle olive oil, season with salt and cayenne.
4. Transfer to your fryer and cook for 10 to 15 minutes until starting to split.
5. Add quartered avocado, parsley, sliced green onion, garlic, spring water, lemon juice, ½ tsp. of salt to a food processor.
6. Blend until creamy.
7. Cut zucchini ends using use spiralizer to turn them into zoodles.
8. Mix zoodles with sauce.
9. Divide into 3 bowls and serve with tomatoes.
10. Enjoy!

Nutrition: Calories: 180. **Protein:** 2 g. **Fat:** 14 g. **Carbs:** 14 g.

155. Asparagus and Leek Quiche With Gruyere

Preparation Time: 35 minutes
Cooking Time: 30 minutes
Servings: 4
Ingredients:
- 9-inch tart shell
- ½ lb. asparagus, minced into ½-inch pieces
- 1 little leek, around 2 to 3 oz., with white and light green parts
- ½ cup whole milk and ½ cup heavy cream
- 4 big eggs
- ½ cup minced Gruyère

Directions:
1. Whisk milk and heavy cream with eggs in a medium mixing bowl.
2. Put asparagus and leek evenly in the shell. Glug the cream mixture on top and sprinkle minced cheese evenly over it.
3. Preheat the oven at 177° C or 350° F for 25 minutes before placing the quiche inside.
4. After the custard sets completely, broil for 3 to 5 minutes to make it brown.

Nutrition: Calories: 194. **Carbs:** 9 g. **Protein:** 5 g. **Fat:** 15 g.

Brunch

156. Easy Oven Frittata

Preparation Time: 15 minutes
Cooking Time: 30 minutes
Servings: 6
Ingredients:

- 8 eggs
- 1 onion minced
- 1 clove garlic diced
- 1 cup vegetables
- 1 cup sausage or bacon minced
- 1 cup cheese shredded and 1 tsp. parmesan cheese
- 1 cup milk
- 1 tbsp. flour
- Butter
- Salt and pepper

Directions:
1. Preheat the oven to 232° C or 450° F. Sauté onions in a pan to soften them.
2. Cook garlic and any vegetables with meat.
3. Whisk the eggs with milk, flour, and cheese. Put them inside a buttered pan, cook for 20 minutes. Sprinkle salt and pepper on top.

Nutrition: Calories: 129. **Carbs:** 2.8 g. **Fat:** 9.6 g.

157. Cinnamon French Toast

Preparation Time: 5 minutes
Cooking Time: 30 minutes
Servings: 6
Ingredients:

- 6 slices of whole-wheat bread
- 1 tsp. ground cinnamon
- 1 tsp. vanilla extract, unsweetened
- 2 tbsp. butter, unsalted
- 3 eggs
- ½ cup maple syrup
- ½ cup milk

Directions:
1. Turn on the oven, set the temperature to 350° F, and then select the oven cooking method.
2. Meanwhile, take a 13-by-9-inch baking dish and then grease it with oil.
3. Arrange the bread slices it in a single layer, and then sprinkle cinnamon on top.
4. Crack the eggs in a bowl, add vanilla, maple syrup, butter, and milk and then whisk until blended.
5. Pour the egg mixture evenly over the bread slices and then bake for 30 minutes.
6. Serve straight away.

Nutrition: Calories: 218. **Fat:** 8 g. **Carbs:** 32 g. **Protein:** 6 g. **Fiber:** 1 g.

158. Cranberry Orange Muffins Recipe

Preparation Time: 5 minutes
Cooking Time: 30 minutes
Servings: 4
Ingredients:

- 2 cups all-purpose flour + 2 tsp. fresh cranberry coating if used
- 1 ½ tsp. baking powder
- ½ tsp. salt
- 2 cups fresh cranberries or 1 cup dried cranberries
- ½ cup (1 stick) room temperature unsalted butter
- 1 cup granulated sugar
- 2 large eggs
- 2 tsp. pure vanilla extract
- Zest of 1 orange
- ½ cup milk

Orange glaze:

- 2 tbsp. orange juice
- 1 cup confectioner's sugar

Directions:
1. Preheat the oven to 375° F. Coat muffin pans well with baker's spray or shortening or butter and flour, making sure to discard any extra flour after coating.
2. In a medium mix bowl, sift together the flour, baking powder, and salt. Place aside.
3. In a second bowl, toss fresh cranberries with 2 tbsp. of flour to coat. Place aside. If you're using dried cranberries, then skip this step.
4. 3 minutes, cream together butter and sugar until lightened in color. Add one egg at a time, making sure to completely integrate each one before adding the next. Mix in the vanilla and orange zest.
5. Fold in the flour mixture lightly, alternating with the milk. Stir until everything is just blended. Fold in the cranberries (fresh or dried) and spoon the batter into the prepared muffin pans, filling them approx. ²/₃ to ¾ full. 30 minutes in the oven, or until a toothpick or skewer put into the center comes out clean.
6. While the muffins are baked, make the orange glaze topping by tossing all of the ingredients together until thoroughly incorporated.
7. Take the muffin from the oven and leave it in the muffin tray for cooling a little. Then, take each muffin out and sprinkle with the orange glaze. Place on a platter to cool completely or serve slightly warm.

Nutrition: Calories: 278. **Carbs:** 46 g. **Protein:** 4 g. **Fat:** 9 g. **Saturated Fat:** 5 g. **Cholesterol:** 57 mg. **Sodium:** 117 mg. **Potassium:** 119 mg. **Fiber:** 1 g. **Sugar:** 28 g. **Vitamin A:** 320IU. **Vitamin C:** 4 mg. **Calcium:** 45 mg. **Iron:** 1 mg.

159. Ham and Egg Cups Recipe

Preparation Time: 10 minutes
Cooking Time: 30 minutes
Servings: 2
Ingredients:

- 12 slices ham
- 1 cup shredded cheddar cheese
- 12 eggs
- Salt and pepper to taste
- ½ cup diced tomatoes
- ¼ cup thinly sliced chives
- Cooking spray

Directions:
1. Preheat the oven to 400° F.
2. Coat a 12 cup muffin tray with nonstick cooking spray.
3. Fill each muffin thoroughly with a piece of ham.
4. Divide the cheese among the cups in an equal layer.
5. Fill each cup with an egg, then season with salt and pepper to taste.
6. Bake for 13 to 15 minutes, or until the yolks are done to your liking. Top with tomatoes and chives just before serving.

Nutrition: Calories: 251. **Carbs:** 1 g. **Protein:** 19 g. **Fat:** 17 g. **Saturated Fat:** 7 g. **Cholesterol:** 358 mg. **Sodium:** 468 mg. **Potassium:** 231 mg. **Vitamin A:** 685IU. **Vitamin C:** 1.9mg. **Calcium:** 191 mg. **Iron:** 2 mg.

160. Ham and Cheese Puff Pastries Recipe

Preparation Time: 10 minutes
Cooking Time: 30 minutes
Servings: 4
Ingredients:

- 2 sheets puff pastry, 1 box
- 1 tbsp. mustard Dijon mustard, grainy mustard, and yellow mustard are all acceptable options
- 1.5 cups chopped ham
- 1.75 cup cheese
- 6 oz. shredded cheddar or gruyere
- 2 beaten egg yolk

Directions:
1. To make squares, cut each sheet of defrosted puff pastry into thirds, and cut each third of a sheet into a third to make squares.
2. Place one square on a baking sheet that has been oiled or lined with paper towels.
3. ¼ tsp. Dijon mustard, diagonally across each square, 1 tbsp. of chopped ham, 1 tbsp. of shredded cheese.
4. On one corner of each pastry square, spread a small amount of egg yolk. Make sure it's not one of the ham/cheese/mustard-covered corners. Fold the other corner over the filling, then the egged corner on top of it, pressing to seal. Rep with the leftover puff pastry pieces.
5. Brush the top of the pastries with the yolk of the egg.
6. Cook for 20 to 25 minutes, or before the pastries are golden brown, at 350° F.

Nutrition: Calories: 59. **Protein:** 3.56 g. **Fat:** 4.12 g. **Carbs:** 1.97 g.

161. Vegetable Egg Rolls

Preparation Time: 15 minutes
Cooking Time: 30 minutes
Servings: 8
Ingredients:

- ½ cup chopped mushrooms
- ½ cup grated carrots
- ½ cup chopped zucchini
- 2 green onions, chopped
- 2 tbsp. low-sodium soy sauce
- 8 egg roll wrappers
- 1 tbsp. cornstarch
- 1 egg, beaten

Directions:
1. In a medium bowl, combine the mushrooms, carrots, zucchini, green onions, and soy sauce, and stir together. Place the egg roll wrappers on a work surface. Top each with about 3 tbsp. of the vegetable mixture.
2. In a small bowl, combine the cornstarch and egg and mix well. Brush some of this mixture on the edges of the egg roll wrappers. Roll up the wrappers, enclosing the vegetable filling. Brush some of the egg mixture on the outside of the egg rolls to seal.
3. Pour into the oven rack/basket. Place the rack on the middle shelf of the Air fryer oven. Set temperature to 400° F, and set time to 10 minutes or until the egg rolls are brown and crunchy.

Nutrition: Calories: 112. **Fat:** 1 g. **Protein:** 4 g. **Fiber:** 1 g.

162. Frittata With Bacon, Spinach Tomato and Swiss

Preparation Time: 15 minutes
Cooking Time: 30 minutes
Servings: 6
Ingredients:

- 8 oz. bacon, sliced (8 slices)
- 3 oz. finely chopped new spinach (3 packed cups)
- 8 large eggs
- ¼ cup half-and-half
- 1 tsp. powdered onion
- 1 tsp. powdered garlic
- To taste, season with salt and freshly ground black pepper.
- 1 cup halved grape tomatoes

- ²⁄₃ cup (2.8 oz.) Swiss cheese diced

Directions:

1.   Set the oven to 350° F. Set down a buttered 9 to 10-inch-deep pie dish.

2.   Bacon should be cooked in a 12-inch nonstick skillet over medium-high heat, flipping regularly, until browned and crisp, around 6 to 10 minutes.

3.   Drain the bacon on a plate lined with several layers of paper towels, reserving or discarding 1 tbsp. of made bacon fat in a pan.

4.   Return skillet to medium-high heat, add spinach, and cook until wilted, around 15 to 30 seconds; switch spinach to the plate with bacon.

5.   In a large mixing cup, whisk together the eggs, half-and-half, onion powder, and garlic powder until well combined. Try to throw in a pinch of salt and pepper to taste.

6.   Toss in the fried pork, onions, lettuce, and Swiss cheese to evenly spread the ingredients. Pour into the pie dish that has been packed.

7.   Bake for 30 to 35 minutes in a preheated oven until just set. Serve wet, cut into wedges.

Nutrition: Calories: 313. **Calories from Fat:** 225. **Grams of Fat:** 25 9 g. **Saturated Fat:** 259 mg. **Vitamin A:** 2010IU. **Sodium:** 375 mg. **Potassium:** 317 mg. **Carbs:** 3 g. **Sugar:** 1 g. **Protein:** 16 g. **Vitamin C:** 7.4 mg. **Calcium:** 166 mg. **Iron:** 1.6 mg.

163. Broccoli With Parmesan and Lemon Roasted Recipe

Preparation Time: 10 minutes
Cooking Time: 30 minutes
Servings: 4
Ingredients:

- 1 lemon, seeded and sliced in pieces crosswise
- 4 cloves garlic, sliced
- 2 broccoli bunches, cut ends (or 1 pound broccoli, thinly sliced lengthwise, stem and all)
- New ground pepper and kosher salt
- 3 to 4 tsp. extra virgin olive oil

½-cup finely cut parmesan cheese

Directions:

1.   Preheat oven to 425° F. Half of the lemon should be thinly sliced into rounds, and the other half should be put aside. On a rimmed baking dish, toss the lemon slices, garlic, and broccoli with olive oil. Season with salt and pepper, making sure everything is evenly coated, especially the broccoli tips, which should be fried and crisp.

2.   Roast for 10 to 15 minutes, until the broccoli is bright green and beginning to char, and the cheese is golden brown.

3.   Remove from the oven and serve with the remaining half of the lemon squeezed over the end.

Nutrition: Calories: 274. **Fat:** 17 g. **Saturated Fat:** 4 g. **Monounsaturated Fat:** 10 g. **Polyunsaturated Fat:** 1 g. **Carbs:** 24 g. **Dietary Fiber:** 9 g. **Sugars:** 6 g. **Protein:** 14 g. **Sodium:** 810 mg.

164. The Best Scrambled Eggs

Preparation Time: 3 minutes
Cooking Time: 30 minutes
Servings: 2
Ingredients:

- 4 big eggs
- ¼ cup with half-and-half
- ¼ tsp. Kosher salt
- 1 tbsp. butter (unsalted)
- For serving, black pepper
- Herbs, freshly chopped, for serving

Directions:

1.   Whisk the beans, half-n-half, and salt together vigorously in a medium mixing bowl until the mixture is smooth in color and texture, light and foamy, and free of separate yolk or white streaks.

2.   In a small nonstick skillet, melt the butter over medium heat until it coats the whole pan and begins to foam.

3.   Reduce the heat to medium-low and scramble the eggs in the middle of the skillet.

4.   Wait for the edges to only begin to set before carefully pushing the eggs from one end of the pan to the other with a rubber spatula. Swipe in this manner for a few seconds between swipes to allow the uncooked egg to settle on the warm pan and cook while gently rotating the liquid to form the curds.

5.   Slowly fold the eggs into themselves a couple of times, pulling them together, until they are mostly fried, with large pillow folds but still look pretty sticky.

6.   Remove the eggs from the sun while they still have a slight sheen on them.

7.   Serve on baking dishes. Add freshly crushed pepper and chopped fresh herbs to finish. Never before have had scrambled eggs tasted so sweet!

Nutrition: Calories: 251. **Carbs:** 2 g. **Protein:** 15 g. **Fat:** 19 g. **Saturated Fat:** 9 g. **Cholesterol:** 448 mg. **Sodium:** 464 mg. **Potassium:** 195 mg. **Vitamin A:** 895 mg. **Calcium:** 95.2 mg.

165. Carrots Roasted With Honey

Preparation Time: 10 minutes
Cooking Time: 30 minutes
Servings: 3
Ingredients:

- 6 peeled carrots, whole or sliced, with tips and ends removed (if you choose bite-sized pieces)
- 2 tbsp. melted butter
- 2 tbsp. honey
- Salt and pepper to taste

Directions:

1.   Preheat oven to 400° F. (200° C)
2.   Butter, honey, salt, and pepper the carrots equally in a medium casserole bowl.
3.   Roast for 30 minutes.
4.   Have fun!

Nutrition: Calories: 158. **Fat:** 7 g. **Carbs:** 22 g. **Fiber:** 3 g. **Sugar:** 18 g. **Protein:** 0 g.

Appetizers, Snacks, and Bun

166. Caramel and Lemon Pie

Preparation Time: 3 hours
Cooking Time: 30 minutes
Servings: 8
Ingredients:

- 1 recipe pastry for a 10-inch double-crust pie
- ¼ cup unsalted butter
- 3 tbsp. flour
- Half cup waters
- ¼ cup granulated sugar
- ¼ cup packed powdered sugar
- 8 Granny Smith apples

Directions:
1. Preheat your convection oven to 446° F.
2. Melt the butter in a pan. Blend the flour in it. Add water, granulated sugar, and powdered sugar, and heat till it starts boiling.
3. Lower the temperature and let it simmer. Place the base layer in your bowl. Now add the apples into it.
4. Now, add the sugar and spread the mixture in a layer. Add gradually.
5. Put in preheated convection oven and decrease the temperature to 300° F. Bake it for 25 to 25 minutes and serve.

Nutrition: Calories: 463. **Protein:** 3.4 g. **Fat:** 23.56 g. **Carbs:** 60.59 g.

167. Corn Bread

Preparation Time: 30 minutes
Cooking Time: 30 minutes
Servings: 6
Ingredients:

- 2 to 3 tsp. vegetable oil.
- 2 cups buttermilk.
- 1 large egg.
- 1 ¾ cups white cornmeal
- 1 tsp. baking powder
- 1 tsp. baking soda
- 1 tsp. salt
- Butter

Directions:
1. Grease a baking pan with vegetable oil and heat it in a convection oven at 450° F for almost 10 minutes.
2. Whisk eggs and buttermilk together and add cornmeal to this mixture. Whisk them well. Add baking soda, salt, and baking powder.
3. Mix them well and pour this batter into the pan. Bake it at 450° F for almost 15 minutes and serve with butter.

Nutrition: Calories: 184. **Protein:** 6.04 g. **Fat:** 4.26 g. **Carbs:** 31.37 g.

168. Fish Noodle

Preparation Time: 45 minutes
Cooking Time: 30 minutes
Servings: 6
Ingredients:

- 8 oz. egg noodles
- 1 cup milk
- 1 cup cheddar cheese (shredded)
- 2 tbsp. butter
- 6-oz. can tuna (drained)
- 2 tbsp. all-purpose flour
- 1 tsp. salt
- 15-oz. drained peas

Directions:
1. Preheat your convection oven to almost 350° F. Coat a casserole dish with nonstick cooking spray.
2. Boil noodles in a pot filled with salted boiling water to al dente and drain well.
3. Take one saucepan and combine salt, butter, and flour in this pan. Stir well and cook on medium heat to melt butter and combine with other ingredients.
4. Stir in milk and whisk well to make this sauce thick (you have to wait until it boils). Stir cheese in this blend and whisk well to equally blend this mixture. Mix in noodles, tuna, and peas.
5. Spread this mixture in a greased dish and bake in your preheated convection oven for almost 30 minutes.

Nutrition: Calories: 334. **Carbs:** 32.9 g. **Fat:** 14.6 g. **Protein:** 17.9 g.

169. Stuffed Pumpkin

Preparation Time: 55 minutes
Cooking Time: 30 minutes
Servings: 2
Ingredients:

- 1 diced carrot
- ½ pumpkin (small)
- 1 egg
- 1 parsnip, diced
- 1 sweet potato, diced
- 2 minced garlic cloves
- 2 tsp. dried herbs (mixed)
- 1 diced onion
- ½ cup peas

Directions:
1. Scrape seeds of the pumpkin half.
2. Combine mixed herbs, garlic, egg, carrot, peas, onion, sweet potato, and parsnip in one bowl. Fill this blend in pumpkin.
3. Preheat your convection oven to 350° F. Put stuffed pumpkin in the basket of the convection oven and cook for almost 30 minutes to tender.

Nutrition: Calories: 131. **Protein:** 6.2 g. **Fat:** 5.01 g. **Carbs:** 15.96 g.

170. Baked French Fries

Preparation Time: 10 minutes
Cooking Time: 30 minutes
Servings: 4
Ingredients:

- 4 medium potatoes, each about 8-oz.
- 1 tsp. salt
- ½ tsp. ground black pepper
- ¼ cup and 1 tsp. olive oil

Directions:

1. Turn on the oven, set the temperature to 475° F, and then select the oven cooking method.
2. Meanwhile, scrub the potatoes and then cut each potato into 12 wedges.
3. Transfer the potato wedges into a large bowl, cover with hot water and then soak potatoes for 10 minutes.
4. Line the baking pan with a parchment sheet, drizzle with ¼ cup oil, and then sprinkle with ½ tsp. salt and ¼ tsp. ground black pepper.
5. After 10 minutes, drain the potatoes, pat dry with paper towels, and then toss with 1 tsp. oil until evenly coated.
6. Spread the potato wedges on the prepared baking pan, cover with foil and then bake for 5 minutes.
7. Uncover the pan, and then continue baking the potato wedges for 15 minutes until the underside of the wedges turns golden brown.
8. Flip the potato wedges, spread them in an even layer, and then continue to bake them for 10 minutes until evenly brown on all sides.
9. Serve straight away.

Nutrition: Calories: 83. **Fat:** 3.5 g. **Carbs:** 12 g. **Protein:** 1.5 g. **Fiber:** 1.5 g.

171. Sweet Potato Fries

Preparation Time: 5 minutes
Cooking Time: 30 minutes
Servings: 4
Ingredients:

- 2 sweet potatoes, about 6-oz.
- ¼ tsp. garlic powder
- ¼ tsp. sea salt
- 1 tsp. chopped thyme
- 1 tbsp. olive oil

Directions:

1. Turn on the oven, set the temperature to 400° F, and then select the oven cooking method.
2. Meanwhile, peel the potatoes and then cut them into ¼-inch sticks.
3. Take a medium bowl, add garlic powder, salt, thyme, salt, and oil and then stir until combined.

4. Peel the sweet potatoes cut them into ¼-inch sticks, add them to the oil mixture, and then toss until coated.
5. Spread the sweet potatoes on the oven basket in a single layer and then cook for 14 minutes until nicely browned, tossing halfway.
6. Repeat with the remaining sweet potato sticks and then serve.

Nutrition: Calories: 104. **Fat:** 3 g. **Carbs:** 17 g. **Protein:** 1 g. **Fiber:** 3 g.

172. Kale Chips

Preparation Time: 5 minutes
Cooking Time: 30 minutes
Servings: 2
Ingredients:

- ½ bunch kale leaves
- 1 tsp. garlic powder
- ½ tsp. onion powder
- ¼ tsp. sea salt
- ½ tsp. smoked paprika
- ¾ tsp. red chili powder
- 1 ½ tbsp. nutritional yeast
- ½ tbsp. olive oil

Directions:

1. Turn on the oven, set the temperature to 300° F, and then select the oven cooking method.
2. Meanwhile, remove stems from the kale leaves, tore the leaves into large pieces, and then transfer them into a large bowl.
3. Drizzle oil over the kale leaves, massage each kale piece, add remaining ingredients and then toss until combined.
4. Spread the kale leaves on the oven basket in a single layer and then bake for 25 minutes until kale leaves begin to crisp.
5. When done, let the kale chips cool completely and then serve.

Nutrition: Calories: 110.3. **Fat:** 4.6 g. **Carbs:** 15.8 g. **Protein:** 5.3 g. **Fiber:** 5.6 g.

173. Shrimp Fried Rice

Preparation Time: 15 minutes
Cooking Time: 30 minutes
Servings: 4
Ingredients:

- 2 eggs, scrambled
- $1/3$ cup onion, chopped
- 1 tbsp. canola oil
- $1/3$ cup carrot, chopped
- 1 lb. large shrimp, peeled and deveined
- ¾ cup frozen green peas
- 2 (8 oz. each) pack pre-cooked microwavable brown rice

- 1 tsp. rice vinegar
- 1 tbsp. soy sauce
- 1 tsp. kosher salt
- ¼ tsp. black pepper

Directions:

1. Grease the oven basket with oil. Add carrot, onion, and ½ tsp. of salt and mix well.
2. Place on top of the baking pan and position it in rack position 2. Set the temperature to 400° F and the time to 5 minutes.
3. Add eggs and cook for 3 minutes. Add rice, shrimp, peas, vinegar, soy sauce, remaining salt, and pepper to the egg mixture. Mix to combine. Cook for 10 minutes. Stir the mixture. Cook for 15 minutes. Serve.

Nutrition: Calories: 398. **Fat:** 21 g. **Carbs:** 37 g. **Protein:** 16 g.

174. Spaghetti Squash Tots

Preparation Time: 10 minutes
Cooking Time: 30 minutes
Servings: 8
Ingredients:

- ¼ tsp. pepper
- ½ tsp. salt
- 1 thinly sliced scallion
- 1 spaghetti squash

Directions:

1. Wash and cut the squash in half lengthwise. Scrape out the seeds.
2. With a fork, remove spaghetti meat by strands and throw out skins.
3. In a clean towel, toss in squash and wring out as much moisture as possible. Place in a bowl and with a knife slice through meat a few times to cut up smaller.
4. Add pepper, salt, and scallions to squash and mix well.
5. Create "tot" shapes with your hands and place them in the air fryer oven basket. Spray with olive oil. Set temperature to 350° F, and set time to 15 minutes. Cook until golden and crispy.

Nutrition: Calories: 231. **Fat:** 18 g. **Protein:** 5 g. **Sugar:** 0 g.

175. Jumbo Stuffed Mushrooms

Preparation Time: 10 minutes
Cooking Time: 30 minutes
Servings: 4
Ingredients:

- 4 jumbo portobello mushrooms
- 1 tbsp. olive oil
- ¼ cup ricotta cheese
- 5 tbsp. Parmesan cheese, divided
- 1 cup frozen chopped spinach, thawed and drained
- $\frac{1}{3}$ cup bread crumbs

- ¼ tsp. minced fresh rosemary

Directions:

1. Wipe the mushrooms with a damp cloth. Remove the stems and discard. Using a spoon, gently scrape out most of the gills.
2. Rub the mushrooms with olive oil.
3. Put in the air fryer oven basket, hollow side up, and bake for 3 minutes. Carefully remove the mushroom caps, because they will contain liquid. Drain the liquid out of the caps.
4. In a medium bowl, combine the ricotta, 3 tbsp. of Parmesan cheese, spinach, bread crumbs, and rosemary, and mix well.
5. Stuff this mixture into the drained mushroom caps. Sprinkle with the remaining 2 tbsp. of Parmesan cheese.
6. Put the mushroom caps back into the basket and bake for 4 to 6 minutes or until the filling is hot and the mushroom caps are tender.

Nutrition: Calories: 117. **Fat:** 7 g. **Protein:** 7 g. **Fiber:** 1 g.

176. Veggies on Toast

Preparation Time: 12 minutes
Cooking Time: 30 minutes
Servings: 4
Ingredients:

- 1 red bell pepper, cut into ½-inch strips
- 1 cup sliced button or cremini mushrooms
- 1 small yellow squash, sliced
- 2 green onions, cut into ½-inch slices
- Extra light olive oil for misting
- 4 to 6 pieces sliced French or Italian bread
- 2 tbsp. softened butter
- ½ cup soft goat cheese

Directions:

1. Combine the red pepper, mushrooms, squash, and green onions in the air fryer oven and mist with oil.
2. Pour into the oven rack/basket. Place the rack on the middle shelf of the Air fryer oven. Set temperature to 400° F, and set time to 9 minutes.
3. Roast for 7 to 9 minutes or until the vegetables are tender, shaking the basket once during cooking time.
4. Remove the vegetables from the basket and set them aside. Spread the bread with butter and place in the air fryer oven, butter-side up.
5. Toast for 2 to 4 minutes or until golden brown. Spread the goat cheese on the toasted bread and top with the vegetables; serve warm.

Nutrition: Calories: 162. **Fat:** 11 g. **Protein:** 7 g. **Fiber:** 2 g.

Vegetables

177. Air Fried Carrots, Yellow Squash & Zucchini

Preparation Time: 5 minutes
Cooking Time: 30 minutes
Servings: 4
Ingredients:

- 1 tbsp. chopped tarragon leaves
- ½ tsp. white pepper
- 1 tsp. salt
- 1-lb. yellow squash
- 1 lb. zucchini
- 6 tsp. olive oil
- ½ lb. carrots

Directions:

1. Stem and root the end of squash and zucchini and cut in ¾-inch half-moons. Peel and cut carrots into 1-inch cubes
2. Combine carrot cubes with 2 tsp. of olive oil, tossing to combine.
3. Pour into the air fryer oven basket, set temperature to 400° F, and set time to 5 minutes.
4. As carrots cook, drizzle remaining olive oil over squash and zucchini pieces, then season with pepper and salt. Toss well to coat.
5. Add squash and zucchini when the timer for carrots goes off. Cook 30 minutes, making sure to toss 2 to 3 times during the cooking process.
6. Once done, take out veggies and toss with tarragon. Serve up warm.

Nutrition: Calories: 122. **Fat:** 9 g. **Protein:** 6 g. **Carbs:** 13.48 g.

178. Winter Vegetarian Frittata

Preparation Time: 5 minutes
Cooking Time: 30 minutes
Servings: 4
Ingredients:

- 1 leek, peeled and thinly sliced into rings
- 2 cloves garlic, finely minced
- 3 medium-sized carrots, finely chopped
- 2 tbsp. olive oil
- 6 large-sized eggs
- Sea salt and ground black pepper, to taste
- ½ tsp. dried marjoram, finely minced
- ½ cup yellow cheese of choice

Directions:

1. Sauté the leek, garlic, and carrot in hot olive oil until they are tender and fragrant; reserve.
2. In the meantime, preheat your air fryer oven to 330° F.
3. In a bowl, whisk the eggs along with the salt, ground black pepper, and marjoram.

4. Then, grease the inside of your baking dish with a nonstick cooking spray. Pour the whisked eggs into the baking dish. Stir in the sautéed carrot mixture. Top with the cheese shreds.
5. Place the baking dish in the air fryer oven cooking basket. Cook for about 30 minutes and serve warm.

Nutrition: Calories: 227. **Protein:** 7.89 g. **Fat:** 17.36 g. **Carbs:** 10.51 g.

179. Crisped Baked Cheese Stuffed Chile Pepper

Preparation Time: 10 minutes
Cooking Time: 30 minutes
Servings: 4
Ingredients:

- 1 (7 oz.) can whole green Chile peppers, drained
- 1 egg, beaten
- 1 tbsp. all-purpose flour
- ½ (5 oz.) can evaporated milk
- ½ (8 oz.) can tomato sauce
- ¼-lb. Monterey jack cheese, shredded
- ¼-lb. longhorn or cheddar cheese, shredded
- ¼ cup milk

Directions:

1. Lightly grease baking pan of air fryer with cooking spray. Evenly spread chilies and sprinkle cheddar and jack cheese on top.
2. In a bowl whisk well flour, milk, and eggs. Pour over chilies.
3. For 20 minutes, cook at 360° F
4. Add tomato sauce on top.
5. Cook for 10 minutes at 390° F until tops are lightly browned.
6. Serve and enjoy.

Nutrition: Calories: 392. **Fat:** 27.6 g. **Protein:** 23.9 g. **Carbs:** 12.08 g.

180. Creamy and Cheese Broccoli Bake

Preparation Time: 5 minutes
Cooking Time: 30 minutes
Servings: 2
Ingredients:

- 1-lb. fresh broccoli, coarsely chopped
- 2 tbsp. all-purpose flour
- Salt to taste
- 1 tbsp. dry bread crumbs, or to taste
- ½ large onion, coarsely chopped
- ½ (14 oz.) can evaporated milk, divided
- ½ cup cubed sharp cheddar cheese
- 1- ½ tsp. butter, or to taste
- ¼ cup water

Directions:

1. Lightly grease baking pan of air fryer with cooking spray. Mix in half of the milk and flour in the pan and for 5 minutes, cook at 360° F. Halfway through cooking time, mix well. Add broccoli and remaining milk. Mix well and cook for another 5 minutes.
2. Stir in cheese and mix well until melted.
3. In a small bowl mix well, butter and bread crumbs. Sprinkle on top of broccoli.
4. Place the baking pan in the Air fryer oven. Cook for 20 minutes at 360° F until tops are lightly browned.
5. Serve and enjoy.
Nutrition: Calories: 444. **Fat:** 22.3 g. **Protein:** 23 g. **Carbs:** 14.86 g.

181. Coconut Battered Cauliflower Bites

Preparation Time: 5 minutes
Cooking Time: 30 minutes
Servings: 4
Ingredients:

- Salt and pepper to taste
- 1 flax egg (1 tbsp. flaxseed meal + 3 tbsp. water)
- 1 small cauliflower, cut into florets
- 1 tsp. mixed spice
- ½ tsp. mustard powder
- 2 tbsp. maple syrup
- 1 clove of garlic, minced
- 2 tbsp. soy sauce
- ⅓ cup oats flour
- ⅓ cup plain flour
- ⅓ cup desiccated coconut

Directions:
1. Preheat the air fryer oven to 400° F.
2. In a mixing bowl, mix together oats, flour, and desiccated coconut. Season with salt and pepper to taste. Set aside.
3. In another bowl, place the flax egg and add a pinch of salt to taste. Set aside. Season the cauliflower with mixed spice and mustard powder.
4. Dredge the florets in the flax egg first then in the flour mixture.
5. Place inside the air fryer oven and cook for 15 minutes.
6. Meanwhile, place the maple syrup, garlic, and soy sauce in a sauce pan and heat over medium flame. Bring to a boil and adjust the heat to low until the sauce thickens. After 15 minutes, take out the florets from the air fryer and place them in the saucepan.
7. Toss to coat the florets and place inside the air fryer and cook for another 5 minutes.
Nutrition: Calories: 154. **Fat:** 2.3 g. **Protein:** 4.69 g. **Carbs:** 27.88 g.

182. Cheddar, Squash and Zucchini Casserole

Preparation Time: 5 minutes
Cooking Time: 30 minutes
Servings: 4
Ingredients:

- 1 egg
- 5 saltine crackers, or as needed, crushed
- 2 tbsp. bread crumbs
- ½-lb. yellow squash, sliced
- ½-lb. zucchini, sliced
- ½ cup shredded cheddar cheese
- 1- ½ tsp. white sugar
- ½ tsp. salt
- ¼ onion, diced
- ¼ cup biscuit baking mix
- ¼ cup butter

Directions:
1. Lightly grease baking pan of air fryer with cooking spray. Add onion, zucchini, and yellow squash. Cover pan with foil and for 15 minutes, cook at 360° F or until tender.
2. Stir in salt, sugar, egg, butter, baking mix, and cheddar cheese. Mix well. Fold in crushed crackers. Top with bread crumbs.
3. Cook for 15 minutes at 390° F until tops are lightly browned.
4. Serve and enjoy.
Nutrition: Calories: 285. **Fat:** 20.5 g. **Protein:** 8.6 g. **Carbs:** 22.01 g.

183. Buttered Carrot-Zucchini With Mayo

Preparation Time: 10 minutes
Cooking Time: 30 minutes
Servings: 4
Ingredients:

- 1 tbsp. grated onion
- 2 tbsp. butter, melted
- ½-lb. carrots, sliced
- 1-½ zucchinis, sliced
- ¼ cup water
- ¼ cup mayonnaise
- ¼ tsp. prepared horseradish
- ¼ tsp. salt
- ¼ tsp. ground black pepper
- ¼ cup Italian bread crumbs

Directions:
1. Lightly grease baking pan of air fryer with cooking spray. Add carrots. For 8 minutes, cook at 360° F. Add zucchini and continue cooking for another 5 minutes.

2. Meanwhile, in a bowl whisk well pepper, salt, horseradish, onion, mayonnaise, and water. Pour into the pan of veggies. Toss well to coat.

3. In a small bowl mix melted butter and bread crumbs. Sprinkle over veggies.

4. Pour into the oven rack/basket. Place the rack on the middle shelf of the Air fryer oven. Set temperature to 490° F, and set time to 10 minutes until tops are lightly browned.

5. Serve and enjoy.

Nutrition: Calories: 223. **Fat:** 17 g. **Protein:** 2.7 g. **Sugar**: 0.5 g. **Carbs:** 6.81 g.

184. Balsamic Roasted Brussels Sprouts

Preparation Time: minutes
Cooking Time: 30 minutes
Servings: 4
Ingredients:

- 1 lb. Brussels sprouts, washed and sliced
- 3 tbsp. balsamic vinaigrette
- 2 tbsp. coconut oil, melted ice, and freshly cracked pepper

Directions:

1. Preheat the oven to 375° F (190° C). Place the 2 tbsp. of coconut oil in a small bowl and put it on top of the oven to steam as you cook the Brussels sprouts if your coconut oil is strong at room temperature. If the top of your oven isn't hot enough, put the bowl inside for 2 minutes to melt the chocolate.

2. In a big mixing cup, cut the Brussels sprouts in half. Toss the halves in the balsamic vinegar until they are fully covered. Toss in the molten coconut oil once more to coat. Arrange the Brussels in a single layer, cut-side down, on a baking sheet, and season generously with salt and pepper.

3. For even browning, roast the Brussels sprouts for 25 minutes, rotating the pan after 10 minutes. When the sprouts turn a light golden color, they're primed.

4. Remove the pan from the oven and serve right now!

Nutrition: Calories: 119. **Carbs:** 12 g. **Protein:** 3 g. **Fat:** 7 g. **Saturated Fat:** 6 g. **Sodium:** 31 mg. **Potassium:** 454 mg. **Fiber:** 4 g. **Sugar:** 4 g. **Vitamin A:** 855IU. **Vitamin C:** 96.4 mg. **Calcium:** 51 mg. **Iron:** 1.7 mg.

185. Butter Garlic Roasted Carrots and Broccolini

Preparation Time: 10 minutes
Cooking Time: 30 minutes
Servings: 4
Ingredients:

- 1-lb. carrots
- 1 lb. broccolini
- 2 tbsp. butter

- 3 garlic cloves, minced (20 g)
- Salt of the sea
- Cayenne

Directions:

1. Preheat the oven to 400° F (200° C).

2. Carrots and broccolini should be thoroughly washed and dried with a kitchen towel.

3. Thick carrots should be cut lengthwise, while thin carrots should be left alone. The thickness of the pieces does not exceed the thickness of the thumb.

4. Melt butter in a shallow saucepan, then stir in minced garlic, sea salt, and pepper until well mixed.

5. Dust half of the garlic butter over the carrots in a single layer on a baking sheet. After that, bake for ten minutes.

6. Meanwhile, cut any broccolini with thick stems in half lengthwise and add to the remaining garlic butter, massaging the garlic butter into the broccolini with your fingertips.

7. Remove the carrots from the oven and layer in the broccolini, then return to the oven for another 25 minutes.

Nutrition: Calories: 147. **Carbs:** 20 g. **Protein:** 5 g. **Fat:** 6 g. **Saturated Fat:** 4 g. **Cholesterol:** 15 mg. **Sodium:** 163 mg. **Potassium:** 372 mg. **Fiber:** 5 g. **Sugar:** 8 g. **Vitamin A:** 21123IU. **Vitamin C:** 111 mg. **Calcium:** 122 mg. **Iron:** 1 mg.

186. Cinnamon Butternut Squash Fries

Preparation Time: 5 minutes
Cooking Time: 30 minutes
Servings: 8
Ingredients:

- 1 pinch of salt
- 1 tbsp. powdered unprocessed sugar
- ½ tsp. nutmeg
- 2 tsp. cinnamon
- 1 tbsp. coconut oil
- 10 oz. pre-cut butternut squash fries

Directions:

1. In a plastic bag, pour in all ingredients. Coat fries with other components till coated and sugar is dissolved.

2. Spread coated fries into a single layer in the air fryer basket. Set temperature to 390° F, and set time to 10 minutes. Cook until crispy.

Nutrition: Calories: 175. **Fat:** 8 g. **Protein:** 1 g.

187. Crispy and Healthy Avocado Fingers

Preparation Time: 10 minutes
Cooking Time: 30 minutes
Servings: 4
Ingredients:

- ½ cup panko breadcrumbs

- ½ tsp. salt
- 1 pitted Haas avocado, peeled and sliced
- Liquid from 1 can white beans or aquafaba

Directions:

1. Preheat the air fryer oven at 350° F.
2. In a shallow bowl, toss the breadcrumbs and salt until well combined.
3. Dredge the avocado slices first with the aquafaba then in the breadcrumb mixture.
4. Place the avocado slices in a single layer inside the air fryer basket.
5. Cook for 10 minutes and shake halfway through the cooking time.

Nutrition: Calories: 51. **Fat:** 7.5 g. **Protein:** 1.39 g.

188. Stuffed Tomatoes

Preparation Time: 20 minutes
Cooking Time: 30 minutes
Servings: 4
Ingredients:

- 2 vine-ripened tomatoes
- Salt to taste
- ½ cup bread crumbs
- 1 clove garlic, minced
- ¼ cup finely chopped fresh basil leaves
- Freshly ground black pepper to taste
- ½ cup grated Parmesan
- ¼ cup olive oil

Directions:

1. Preheat oven to 400° F.
2. Slice tomatoes in half horizontally and scoop out pulp and seeds. Salt inside and rest upside down on a sheet pan lined with a wire rack to extract juices, about 15 minutes.
3. Meanwhile, in a medium bowl, mix together bread crumbs, garlic, basil, pepper, ¼ cup of the grated Parmesan, and oil. Stuff tomatoes with the filling, sprinkle with remaining Parmesan and bake until tomatoes are cooked through and tops are golden brown, about 30 minutes.

Nutrition: Calories: 178. **Protein:** 5.08 g. **Fat:** 14.26 g. **Carbs:** 8.18 g.

Poultry

189. BBQ Chicken Recipe from Greece

Preparation Time: 10 minutes
Cooking Time: 30 minutes
Servings: 4
Ingredients:

- 1 (8 oz.) container fat-free plain yogurt
- 2 tbsp. fresh lemon juice
- 2 tsp. dried oregano
- 1-lb. skinless, boneless chicken breast halves, cut into 1-inch pieces
- 1 large red onion, cut into wedges
- ½ tsp. lemon zest
- ½ tsp. salt
- 1 large green bell pepper, cut into 1 ½-inch piece
- ⅓ cup crumbled feta cheese with basil and sun-dried tomatoes
- ¼ tsp. ground black pepper
- ¼ tsp. crushed dried rosemary

Directions:

1. In a shallow dish, mix well rosemary, pepper, salt, oregano, lemon juice, lemon zest, feta cheese, and yogurt. Add chicken and toss well to coat. Marinate in the refrigerator for 3 hours.
2. Thread bell pepper, onion, and chicken pieces in skewers. Place on skewer rack.
3. For 12 minutes, cook at 360° F. Halfway through cooking time, turnover skewers. If needed, cook in batches.
4. Serve and enjoy.

Nutrition: Calories: 242. **Fat:** 7.5 g. **Protein:** 31 g. **Sugar:** 6 g.

190. Cheesy Chicken Tenders

Preparation Time: 10 minutes
Cooking Time: 30 minutes
Servings: 4
Ingredients:

- 1 large white meat chicken breast, approximately 5 to 6 oz., sliced into strips
- 1 cup breadcrumbs (Panko brand works well)
- 2 medium-sized eggs
- Pinch of salt and pepper
- 1 tbsp. grated or powdered parmesan cheese

Directions:

1. Cover the basket of the oven with a lining of tin foil, leaving the edges uncovered to allow it to circulate through the basket. Preheat the oven to 350° F. In a mixing bowl, beat the eggs until fluffy and until the yolks and whites are fully combined, and set aside. In a separate mixing bowl, combine the breadcrumbs, parmesan, salt, and pepper, and set aside. One by one, dip each piece of raw chicken into the bowl with dry ingredients, coating all sides; then submerge into the bowl with wet ingredients, then dip again into the dry ingredients. Lay the coated chicken pieces on the foil covering the oven basket, in a single flat layer.
2. Set the oven timer for 15 minutes. After 15 minutes, the oven will turn off and the chicken should be mid-way cooked and the breaded coating starting to brown. Using tongs, turn each piece of chicken over to ensure a full all-over fry. Reset the oven to 320° F for another 15 minutes. After 15 minutes, when the oven shuts off, remove the fried chicken strips using tongs and set them on a serving plate. Eat as soon as cool enough to handle, and enjoy!

Nutrition: Calories: 278. **Fat:** 15 g. **Protein:** 29 g. **Sugar:** 7 g.

191. Caesar Marinated Grilled Chicken

Preparation Time: 10 minutes
Cooking Time: 30 minutes
Servings: 4
Ingredients:

- ¼ cup crouton
- 1 tsp. lemon zest shaped into ovals, skewer, and grill.
- ½ cup Parmesan
- ¼ cup breadcrumbs
- 1-lb. ground chicken
- 2 tbsp. Caesar dressing and more for drizzling
- 2 to 4 romaine leaves

Directions:

1. In a shallow dish, mix the chicken well, 2 tbsp. Caesar dressing, parmesan, and breadcrumbs. Mix well with hands. Form into 1-inch oval patties.
2. Thread chicken pieces in skewers. Place on skewer rack in oven.
3. For 12 minutes, cook at 360° F. Halfway through cooking time, turnover skewers. If needed, cook in batches.
4. Serve and enjoy on a bed of lettuce and sprinkle with croutons and extra dressing.

Nutrition: Calories: 339. **Fat:** 18.9 g. **Protein:** 32.6 g. **Sugar:** 1 g.

192. Crispy Southern Fried Chicken

Preparation Time: 10 minutes
Cooking Time: 30 minutes
Servings: 4
Ingredients:

- 1 tsp. cayenne pepper
- 2 tbsp. mustard powder
- 2 tbsp. oreganos
- 2 tbsp. thymes
- 3 tbsp. coconut milk

- 1 beaten egg
- ¼ cup cauliflower
- ¼ cup gluten-free oats
- 8 chicken drumsticks

Directions:
1.   Ensure the oven is preheated to 350° F.
2.   Prepare the chicken and season with pepper and salt on all sides.
3.   Add all other ingredients to a blender, blending till a smooth-like breadcrumb mixture is created. Place in a bowl and add a beaten egg to another bowl.
4.   Dip chicken into breadcrumbs, then into egg and breadcrumbs once more.
5.   Place coated drumsticks into the oven basket. Set temperature to 350° F, and set time to 20 minutes, and cook 20 minutes. Bump up the temperature to 390° F and cook another 5 minutes till crispy.

Nutrition: Calories: 504. **Fat:** 18 g. **Protein:** 35 g. **Sugar:** 5 g.

193. Cheese Stuffed Chicken
Preparation Time: 5 minutes
Cooking Time: 30 minutes
Servings: 4
Ingredients:
- 1 tbsp. creole seasoning
- 1 tbsp. olive oil
- 1 tsp. garlic powder
- 1 tsp. onion powder
- 4 chicken breasts, butterflied and pounded
- 4 slices Colby cheese
- 4 slices pepper jack cheese

Directions:
1.   Preheat the oven to 390° F.
2.   Place the grill pan accessory in the oven.
3.   Create the dry rub by mixing in a bowl the creole seasoning, garlic powder, and onion powder. Season with salt and pepper if desired.
4.   Rub the seasoning onto the chicken.
5.   Place the chicken on a working surface and place a slice each of pepper jack and Colby cheese.
6.   Fold the chicken and secure the edges with toothpicks.
7.   Brush chicken with olive oil.
8.   Grill for 30 minutes, and make sure to flip the meat every 10 minutes.

Nutrition: Calories: 27. **Fat:** 45.9 g. **Protein:** 73.1 g. **Sugar:** 0 g.

194. Seasoned Chicken
Preparation Time: 5 minutes
Cooking Time: 30 minutes
Servings: 4
Ingredients:
- 2 lb. chicken breasts, boneless, skinless

- 1 ½ tsp. dried parsley
- 1 tsp. seasoned salt
- 1 tsp. garlic powder
- 1 tsp. dried basil
- 1 tbsp. olive oil

Directions:
1.   Turn on the oven, set the temperature to 400° F, and then select the oven cooking method.
2.   Meanwhile, prepare the chicken and for this, drizzle it with oil and then sprinkle with remaining ingredients until well coated.
3.   Arrange the chicken breasts on the baking pan and then bake for 35 minutes until tender.
4.   Serve straight away.

Nutrition: Calories: 300. **Fat:** 11 g. **Carbs:** 0 g. **Protein:** 51 g. **Fiber:** 0 g.

195. Amazing Chicken Parmesan
Preparation Time: 15 minutes
Cooking Time: 30 minutes
Servings: 2
Ingredients:
- 1 lb. chicken breasts
- ½ cup seasoned Panko breadcrumbs
- 2 eggs
- ½ cup flour
- Salt and black pepper to taste
- 14 oz. marinara sauce
- ½ cup Parmesan, grated

Directions:
1.   Beat eggs in a shallow bowl and lightly season with salt and pepper. Whisk well.
2.   In another shallow bowl, put flour and season too.
3.   In the third shallow plate, place the seasoned panko breadcrumbs.
4.   Make light indentions on the chicken breasts with a sharp knife, making sure that you don't cut through.
5.   Dip the chicken breasts into the seasoned flour. Then dip the flour-coated chicken into the eggs. Finally, dip the flour and egg-coated chicken into the plate with the breadcrumbs and lightly press until the breadcrumbs stick to the chicken breasts.
6.   Place the breadcrumb encrusted chicken on a 3-inch rack and back on the "HI" setting for about 15 to 17 minutes per side.
7.   Season each slice of chicken with Parmesan and continue baking on the "HI" setting for another 2 to 3 minutes, or until the cheese melts.
8.   Put the chicken breasts on serving plates, then slather the marinara sauce over them.

Nutrition: Calories: 254. **Total Fat:** 12.38 g. **Total Carbs:** 12.18 g. **Protein:** 22.83 g.

196. NuWave Oven Fried Chicken Wings

Preparation Time: 20 minutes
Cooking Time: 30 minutes
Servings: 4
Ingredients:

- 1 ½ lb. chicken wings
- ⅓ cup grated Parmesan cheese
- ⅓ cup breadcrumbs
- ⅛ tsp. garlic powder
- ⅛ tsp. onion powder
- ¼ cup melted butter
- Salt and black pepper to taste
- Cooking spray

Directions:
1. On a baking sheet, spray with cooking spray.
2. In a large bowl, mix Parmesan cheese, garlic powder, onion powder, black pepper, breadcrumbs, and salt. Stir to combine well.
3. Dip chicken wings one at a time into melted butter and then into the bread mixture until thoroughly covered. Arrange wings in a single layer on the baking sheet.
4. Place on 1-inch rack and cook on High power (350° F) for 10 minutes. Flip wings over and cook for another 10 to 12 minutes until no longer pink in the center and juices run clear. Remove promptly from NuWave oven and serve.

Nutrition: Calories: 371. **Total Fat:** 22.6 g. **Total Carbs:** 11.8 g. **Protein:** 27.8 g.

197. Bacon-Wrapped Chicken With Potatoes

Preparation Time: 15 minutes
Cooking Time: 30 minutes
Servings: 4
Ingredients:

- 8 slices bacon
- 1 lb. baby red potatoes
- 4 bone-in chicken drumsticks
- 1 tbsp. dried basil
- ½ tbsp. garlic powder
- ½ tbsp. Italian seasoning
- ½ tbsp. black pepper
- 1 tsp. salt

Directions:
1. Wrap each piece of chicken with one slice of bacon.
2. Line bottom of NuWave oven with foil.
3. Arrange chicken in the center of the 4-inch rack. Place potatoes around the chicken on the rack.

4. In a medium-sized mixing bowl, combine garlic powder, black pepper, Italian seasoning, basil, and salt. Sprinkle seasoning mixture over chicken and potatoes.
5. Cook on High power (350° F) for 10 minutes. Turn chicken and potatoes and cook for another 10 minutes or until chicken is fully cooked and potatoes are tender.
6. Serve hot and enjoy.

Nutrition: Calories: 542. **Total Fat:** 14.8 g. **Total Carbs:** 74.8 g. **Protein:** 32 g.

198. Garlic Ginger Chicken Wings

Preparation Time: 20 minutes
Cooking Time: 30 minutes
Servings: 4
Ingredients:

- 2 lb. chicken wings
- 1 tbsp. vegetable oil
- A pinch of salt and black pepper
- 1 tbsp. Frank's red-hot sauce
- ⅓ cup flour

For glaze:

- 3 garlic cloves, minced
- 1 tbsp. Asian chili pepper sauce
- ¼ cup rice wine vinegar
- 1 tbsp. minced ginger
- ¼ cup light brown sugar
- 1 ½ tbsp. soy sauce

Directions:
1. In a large mixing bowl, combine Frank's red-hot sauce, vegetable oil, salt, and pepper. Add chicken wings and toss to coat thoroughly.
2. Place coated wings in a large zip lock bag. Add flour, seal bag, and shake until wings are coated with flour.
3. Place wings on the 4-inch rack and cook on High power (350° F) for 10 minutes. Turn wings over and cook for an additional 8 minutes.
4. Meanwhile, in a large bowl, whisk together all ingredients for the glaze. Place wings in glaze and toss to coat evenly. Place wings back on the 4-inch rack and cook on High power for an additional 5 minutes.
5. Remove from oven, then serve.

Nutrition: Calories: 312. **Fat:** 7.5 g. **Carbs:** 21.1 g. **Protein:** 18.8 g.

199. Chicken Thighs with Rosemary

Preparation Time: 5 minutes
Cooking Time: 30 minutes
Servings: 4
Ingredients:

- 4 chicken thighs, with the bone and skin
- Rosemary sprigs
- A large potato, cut into cubes
- 1 onion

- 2 tbsp. olive oil
- 2 garlic cloves
- Salt and pepper
- ½ tsp. chicken seasoning powder

Directions:

1. Preheat the oven at 218° C or 425° F.
2. Put the rosemary sprigs on the baking pan with cooking spray.
3. Bake the remaining ingredients for half an hour.
4. Season the chicken thighs and bake for 35 minutes.

Nutrition: Calories: 670. **Carbs:** 14 g. **Protein:** 47 g. **Fat:** 46 g.

Beef

200. Cheesy Ground Beef and Mac Taco Casserole

Preparation Time: 10 minutes
Cooking Time: 30 minutes
Servings: 5
Ingredients:

- 1-oz. shredded Cheddar cheese
- 1-oz. shredded Monterey Jack cheese
- 2 tbsp. chopped green onions
- ½ (10.75 oz.) can condensed tomato soup
- ½-lb. lean ground beef
- ½ cup crushed tortilla chips
- ¼-lb. macaroni, cooked according to manufacturer's instructions
- ¼ cup chopped onion
- ½ (1.25 oz.) package taco seasoning mix
- ½ (14.5 oz.) can diced tomatoes

Directions:
1.	Lightly grease baking pan of air fryer with cooking spray. Add onion and ground beef. For 10 minutes, cook at 360° F. Halfway through cooking time, stir and crumble ground beef.
2.	Add taco seasoning, diced tomatoes, and tomato soup. Mix well. Mix in pasta.
3.	Sprinkle crushed tortilla chips. Sprinkle cheese.
4.	Cook for 15 minutes at 390° F until tops are lightly browned and cheese is melted.
5.	Serve and enjoy.
Nutrition: Calories: 329. **Fat:** 17 g. **Protein:** 15.6 g.

201. Beef Taco Fried Egg Rolls

Preparation Time: 10 minutes
Cooking Time: 30 minutes
Servings: 8
Ingredients:

- 1 tsp. cilantro
- 2 chopped garlic cloves
- 1 tbsp. olive oil
- 1 cup shredded Mexican cheese
- ½ packet taco seasoning
- ½ can cilantro lime rotel
- ½ chopped onion
- 16 egg roll wrappers
- 1-lb. lean ground beef
- Salt and pepper

Directions:
1.	Ensure that your air fryer oven is preheated to 400° F.
2.	Add onions and garlic to a skillet, cooking till fragrant. Then add taco seasoning, pepper, salt, and beef, cooking till beef is broken up into tiny pieces and cooked thoroughly.
3.	Add rotel and stir well.
4.	Lay out egg wrappers and brush with water to soften a bit.
5.	Load wrappers with beef filling and add cheese to each.
6.	Fold diagonally to close and use water to secure edges.
7.	Brush-filled egg wrappers with olive oil and add them to the air fryer.
8.	Pour into the oven rack/basket. Place the rack on the middle shelf of the Air fryer oven. Set temperature to 400° F, and set time to 8 minutes. Cook 8 minutes, flip, and cook another 4 minutes.
9.	Served sprinkled with cilantro.
Nutrition: Calories: 348. **Fat:** 11 g. **Protein:** 24 g. **Sugar:** 1 g.

202. Beef With Beans

Preparation Time: 10 minutes
Cooking Time: 30 minutes
Servings: 8
Ingredients:

- 12 oz lean steak
- 1 onion, sliced
- 1 can chopped tomatoes
- ¾ cup beef stock
- 4 tsp. fresh thyme, chopped
- 1 can red kidney beans
- Salt and pepper to taste
- Oven-safe bowl

Directions:
1.	Preheat the air fryer oven to 390° F.
2.	Trim the fat from the meat and cut into thin 1cm strips
3.	Add onion slices to the oven-safe bowl and place in the air fryer.
4.	Pour into the oven rack/basket. Place the rack on the middle shelf of the Air fryer oven. Set temperature to 390° F, and set time to 13 minutes, Cook for 3 minutes. Add the meat and continue cooking for 5 minutes.
5.	Add the tomatoes and their juice, beef stock, thyme, and the beans and cook for an additional 5 minutes
6.	Season with black pepper to taste.
Nutrition: Calories: 54. **Protein:** 3.62 g. **Fat:** 0.29 g. **Carbs:** 9.91 g.

203. Swedish Meatballs

Preparation Time: 10 minutes
Cooking Time: 30 minutes
Servings: 4
Ingredients:
Meatballs:

- 1 pound 93% lean ground beef
- 1 (1-oz.) packet lipton onion recipe soup & dip mix
- ⅓ cup bread crumbs
- 1 egg, beaten
- Salt
- Pepper

Gravy:
- 1 cup beef broth
- ⅓ cup heavy cream
- 2 tbsp. all-purpose flour

Directions:
1. In a large bowl, combine the ground beef, onion soup mix, bread crumbs, egg, and salt and pepper to taste. Mix thoroughly.
2. Using 2 tbsp. of the meat mixture, create each meatball by rolling the beef mixture around in your hands. This should yield about 10 meatballs.
3. Place the meatballs in the air fryer basket. It is okay to stack them. Cook for 14 minutes.
4. While the meatballs cook, prepare the gravy. Heat a saucepan over medium-high heat.
5. Add the beef broth and heavy cream. Stir for 1 to 2 minutes.
6. Add the flour and stir. Cover and allow the sauce to simmer for 3 to 4 minutes, or until thick.
7. Drizzle the gravy over the meatballs and serve.
Nutrition: Calories: 178. **Fat:** 14 g. **Protein:** 9 g. **Fiber:** 0 g.

204. Rice and Meatball Stuffed Bell Peppers

Preparation Time: 13 minutes
Cooking Time: 30 minutes
Servings: 4
Ingredients:
- 4 bell peppers
- 1 tbsp. olive oil
- 1 small onion, chopped
- 2 cloves garlic, minced
- 1 cup frozen cooked rice, thawed
- 16 to 20 small frozen precooked meatballs, thawed
- ½ cup tomato sauce
- 1 tbsp. Dijon mustard

Directions:
1. To prepare the peppers, cut off about ½ inch of the tops. Carefully remove the membranes and seeds from inside the peppers. Set aside.
2. In a 6-by-6-by-2-inch pan, combine the olive oil, onion, and garlic.

3. Bake in the air fryer oven for 2 to 4 minutes or until crisp and tender. Remove the vegetable mixture from the pan and set it aside in a medium bowl.
4. Add the rice, meatballs, tomato sauce, and mustard to the vegetable mixture and stir to combine. Stuff the peppers with the meat-vegetable mixture.
5. Place the peppers in the air fryer basket and bake for 9 to 13 minutes or until the filling is hot and the peppers are tender.
Nutrition: Calories: 487. **Fat:** 21 g. **Protein:** 26 g. **Fiber:** 6 g.

205. Pub Style Corned Beef Egg Rolls

Preparation Time: 15 minutes
Cooking Time: 30 minutes
Servings: 10
Ingredients:
- Olive oil
- ½ cup orange marmalade
- 5 slices of Swiss cheese
- 4 cup corned beef and cabbage
- 1 egg
- 10 egg roll wrappers

Brandy mustard sauce:
- 1/16 tsp. pepper
- 2 tbsp. whole grain mustard
- 1 tsp. dry mustard powder
- 1 cup heavy cream
- ½ cup chicken stock
- ¼ cup brandy
- ¾ cup dry white wine
- ¼ tsp. curry powder
- ½ tbsp. cilantro
- 1 minced shallot
- 2 tbsp. ghee

Directions:
1. To make mustard sauce, add shallots and ghee to skillet, cooking until softened. Then add brandy and wine, heating to a low boil. Cook 5 minutes for liquids to reduce. Add stock and seasonings. Simmer 5 minutes.
2. Turn down the heat and add heavy cream. Cook on low till sauce reduces and it covers the back of a spoon.
3. Place sauce in the fridge to chill.
4. Crack the egg in a bowl and set it to the side.
5. Lay out an egg wrapper with the corner towards you. Brush the edges with egg wash.
6. Place ⅓ cup of corned beef mixture into the center along with 2 tbsp. of marmalade and ½ a slice of Swiss cheese.
7. Fold the bottom corner over filling. As you are folding the sides, make sure they are stick well to the first flap you made.

8. Place filled rolls into prepared air fryer basket. Spritz rolls with olive oil.
9. Set temperature to 390° F, and cook for 10 minutes, shaking halfway through cooking.
10. Serve rolls with brandy mustard sauce.
Nutrition: Calories: 415. **Fat:** 13 g. **Protein:** 38 g. **Sugar:** 4 g.

206. Stir-Fried Steak and Cabbage

Preparation Time: 15 minutes
Cooking Time: 30 minutes
Servings: 4
Ingredients:

- ½ lb. sirloin steak, cut into strips
- 2 tsp. cornstarch
- 1 tbsp. peanut oil
- 2 cups chopped red or green cabbage
- 1 yellow bell pepper, chopped
- 2 green onions, chopped
- 2 cloves garlic, sliced
- ½ cup commercial stir-fry sauce

Directions:
1. Toss the steak with the cornstarch and set it aside.
2. In a 6-inch metal bowl, combine the peanut oil with the cabbage.
3. Place in the basket and cook for 3 to 4 minutes.
4. Remove the bowl from the basket and add the steak, pepper, onions, and garlic. Return to the air fryer oven and cook for 3 to 5 minutes or until the steak is cooked to desired doneness and vegetables are crisp and tender.
5. Add the stir-fry sauce and cook for 2 to 4 minutes or until hot. Serve over rice.
Nutrition: Calories: 180. **Fat:** 7 g. **Protein:** 20 g. **Fiber:** 2 g.

207. Air-Fried Philly Cheesesteak

Preparation Time: 5 minutes
Cooking Time: 30 minutes
Servings: 6
Ingredients:

- Large hoagie bun, sliced in half
- 6 oz. sirloin or flank steak, sliced into bite-sized pieces
- ½ white onion, rinsed and sliced
- ½ red pepper, rinsed and sliced
- American cheese

Directions:
1. Set the air fryer oven to 320° F for 10 minutes.
2. Arrange the steak pieces, onions, and peppers on a piece of tin foil, flat and not overlapping, and set the tin foil on one side of the air-fryer basket. The foil should not take up more than half of the surface; the juices from the steak and the moisture from the vegetables will mingle while cooking.

3. Lay the hoagie-bun halves, crusty-side up and soft-side down, on the other half of the air fryer.
4. After 10 minutes, the air fryer will shut off; the hoagie buns should be starting to crisp and the steak and vegetables will have begun to cook.
5. Carefully, flip the hoagie buns so they are now crusty-side down and soft-side up; cover both sides with one slice each of American cheese.
6. With a long spoon, gently stir the steak, onions, and peppers in the foil to ensure even coverage.
7. Set the air fryer to 360° F for 6 minutes.
8. After 6 minutes, when the fryer shuts off, the cheese will be perfectly melted over the toasted bread, and the steak will be juicy on the inside and crispy on the outside.
9. Remove the cheesy hoagie halves first, using tongs, and set on a serving plate; then cover one side with the steak, and top with the onions and peppers. Close with the other cheesy hoagie-half, slice into 2 pieces, and enjoy.
Nutrition: Calories: 60. **Protein:** 7.16 g. **Fat:** 3 g. **Carbs:** 0.83 g.

208. Herbed Roast Beef

Preparation Time: 5 minutes
Cooking Time: 30 minutes
Servings: 6
Ingredients:

- ½ tsp. fresh rosemary
- 1 tsp. dried thyme
- ¼ tsp. pepper
- 1 tsp. salt
- 4-lb. top round roast beef
- 1 tsp. olive oil

Directions:
1. Ensure your air fryer oven is preheated to 360° F.
2. Rub olive oil all over beef.
3. Mix rosemary, thyme, pepper, and salt together and proceed to rub all sides of beef with a spice mixture.
4. Pour into the oven rack/basket. Place the rack on the middle shelf of the Air fryer oven. Set temperature to 360° F, and set time to 20 minutes.
5. Allow roast to rest 10 minutes before slicing to serve.
Nutrition: Calories: 502. **Fat:** 18 g. **Protein:** 48 g. **Sugar:** 2 g.

209. Tender Beef With Sour Cream Sauce

Preparation Time: 5 minutes
Cooking Time: 30 minutes
Servings: 2
Ingredients:

- 9 oz. tender beef, chopped
- 1 cup scallions, chopped
- 2 cloves garlic, smashed

- ¾ cup sour cream
- ¾ tsp. salt
- ¼ tsp. black pepper, or to taste
- ½ tsp. dried dill weed

Directions:

1.   Add the beef, scallions, and garlic to the baking dish.
2.   Cook for about 5 minutes at 390° F.
3.   Once the meat is starting to tender, pour in the sour cream. Stir in the salt, black pepper, and dill.
4.   Now, cook 7 minutes longer.

Nutrition: Calories: 289. **Protein:** 31.29 g. **Fat:** 13.78 g. **Carbs:** 11.15 g.

210. Beef Empanadas

Preparation Time: 5 minutes
Cooking Time: 30 minutes
Servings: 6
Ingredients:

- 1 tsp. water
- 1 egg white
- 1 cup picadillo
- 8 Goya empanada discs (thawed)

Directions:

1.   Ensure your air fryer oven is preheated to 325° F. Spray basket with olive oil.
2.   Place 2 tbsp. of picadillo into the center of each disc. Fold disc in half and use a fork to seal edges. Repeat with all ingredients.
3.   Whisk egg white with water and brush tops of empanadas with egg wash.
4.   Add 2 to 3 empanadas to the air fryer.
5.   Set temperature to 325° F, and set time to 8 minutes, cook until golden. Repeat till you cook all filled empanadas.

Nutrition: Calories: 183. **Fat:** 5 g. **Protein:** 11 g. **Sugar:** 2 g.

Lamb

211. Roast Leg of Lamb With Herbs
Preparation Time: 55 minutes
Cooking Time: 30 minutes
Servings: 8
Ingredients:

- 1 lamb leg
- 2 tbsp. Dry white wine
- 3 tbsp. lemon juice
- 2 tbsp. chopped parsley
- 2 tbsp. chopped mint leaves
- 2 tbsp. olive oil
- 1 tbsp. minced garlic
- 1 tsp. paprika
- ½ tsp. crushed dried bay leaves
- ½ tsp. pepper
- Salt as desired
- Vinegar to taste

Directions:
1. Dry lamb and pat rinse; skim off then and discard extra fat.
2. Combine vinegar, olive oil, garlic, lemon juice, dry white wine, parsley, mint, paprika, bay leaves, with ½ tsp. of pepper inside a shallow bowl. Brush the lamb all across.
3. Put the lamb in an 11 x 17-inch tray on the rack. Roast in a normal or convection oven at 375° F till a thermometer placed into bone thru the thickest section of meat measures 140° F under medium-rare, around 1 ½ hour, or measures 150° F for medium, around 1 ¾ hour. If juices begin to burn, add water into the pan, as required, ¼ cup at one time.
4. Move lamb to just a rimmed board/platter and let stand for 10 minutes, holding it warm.
5. Slice meat and serve from the bone. Apply salt to taste. 4. Move lamb to just a rimmed board/ platter and let stand for 10 minutes, holding it warm. Slice meat and serve from the bone. Apply salt to taste.
6. Serve.
Nutrition: Calories: 183. **Fat:** 5 g. **Protein:** 11 g. **Sugar:** 2 g.

212. Lamb Shanks With Olives and Capers
Preparation Time: 45 minutes
Cooking Time: 30 minutes
Servings: 6
Ingredients:

- 6 lamb shanks
- 1 jar capers, drained
- 1 ½ cups pitted green olives, in brine
- 3 tbsp. fresh rosemary leaves
- ¼ cup dried rosemary
- 1 bottle dry white wine
- 2 tbsp. fresh-ground pepper
- 2 tbsp. grated lemon peel
- 3 tbsp. lemon juice
- Lemon couscous
- Watercress sprigs, about 3 cups, rinsed and crisped

Directions:
1. Rinse the lamb and pat dry it; lay shanks beside each other in a pan around 2 inches deep inside a 12 x17-inch pan. Bake in a normal or convection oven at 450° F, rotating once, around 25 minutes overall until the meat is very well browned. Decrease the temperature of the oven to 325° F.
2. Meanwhile, put capers, olives in the fine strainer, rinse with cold water, and drain. Mince rosemary and combine in the blender with about 1 cup of the wine and mix until minced. Sprinkle capers, some olives, and rosemary onto lamb (or pour uniformly over the lamb rosemary-wine blend), apply the wine, stir it around shanks and scrape off browned pieces. Sprinkle the wine.
3. Bake for 3 to 3 ¼ hours until the meat is soft once pierced but pulls quickly from the bone.
4. Spoon into large, shallow bowls with equivalent amounts of lemon couscous. Take lamb shanks from the pan with tongs and put one from each bowl on couscous. Trim and remove fat from pan juices. Ladle juices over meat with the olives and the capers. Then garnish the bowl with around ½ cup sprigs of watercress.
5. Serve.
Nutrition: Calories: 183. **Fat:** 5 g. **Protein:** 11 g. **Sugar:** 2 g.

Pork

213. Crispy Fried Pork Chops the Southern Way

Preparation Time: 10 minutes
Cooking Time: 30 minutes
Servings: 4
Ingredients:

- ½ cup all-purpose flour
- ½ cup low-fat buttermilk
- ½ tsp. black pepper
- ½ tsp. Tabasco sauce
- 1 Tsp. paprika
- 3 bone-in pork chops

Directions:
1. Place the buttermilk and hot sauce in a Ziploc bag and add the pork chops. Marinate for at least an hour in the fridge.
2. In a bowl, combine the flour, paprika, and black pepper.
3. Remove pork from the Ziploc bag and dredge in the flour mixture.
4. Preheat the air fryer oven to 390° F.
5. Spray the pork chops with cooking oil.
6. Pour into the oven rack/basket. Place the rack on the middle shelf of the Air fryer oven. Set temperature to 390° F, and set time to 25 minutes.
Nutrition: Calories: 427. **Fat:** 21.2 g. **Protein:** 46.4 g. **Sugar:** 2 g.

214. Pork Wonton Wonderful

Preparation Time: 10 minutes
Cooking Time: 30 minutes
Servings: 4
Ingredients:

- 8 wanton wrappers (Leasa brand works great, though any will do)
- 4 oz. raw minced pork
- 1 medium-sized green apple
- 1 cup water, for wetting the wanton wrappers
- 1 tbsp. vegetable oil
- ½ tbsp. oyster sauce
- 1 tbsp. soy sauce
- Large pinch of ground white pepper

Directions:
1. Cover the basket of the air fryer oven with a lining of tin foil, leaving the edges uncovered to allow air to circulate through the basket. Preheat the air fryer to 350° F.
2. In a small mixing bowl, combine the oyster sauce, soy sauce, and white pepper, then add in the minced pork and stir thoroughly. Cover and set in the fridge to marinate for at least 15 minutes. Core the apple, and slice into small cubes (smaller than bite-sized chunks0.

3. Add the apples to the marinating meat mixture, and combine thoroughly. Spread the wonton wrappers, and fill each with a large spoonful of the filling. Wrap the wontons into triangles, so that the wrappers fully cover the filling, and seal with a drop of water.
4. Coat each filled and wrapped wonton thoroughly with the vegetable oil, to help ensure a nice crispy fry. Place the wontons on the foil-lined air-fryer basket.
5. Set the air fryer oven timer to 25 minutes. Halfway through cooking time, shake the handle of the air fryer basket vigorously to jostle the wontons and ensure even frying. After 25 minutes, when the air fryer oven shuts off, the wontons will be crispy golden-brown on the outside and juicy and delicious on the inside. Serve directly from the air fryer basket and enjoy while hot.
Nutrition: Calories: 129. **Protein:** 7.92 g. **Fat:** 7.36 g. **Carbs:** 8.58 g.

215. Italian Parmesan Breaded Pork Chops

Preparation Time: 5 minutes
Cooking Time: 30 minutes
Servings: 5
Ingredients:

- 5 (3 ½- to 5-oz.) pork chops (bone-in or boneless)
- 1 tsp. Italian seasoning
- Seasoning salt
- Pepper
- ¼ cup all-purpose flour
- 2 tbsp. Italian bread crumbs
- 3 tbsp. finely grated Parmesan cheese
- Cooking oil

Directions:
1. Season the pork chops with the Italian seasoning and seasoning salt and pepper to taste.
2. Sprinkle the flour on both sides of the pork chops, then coat both sides with the bread crumbs and Parmesan cheese.
3. Place the pork chops in the air fryer basket. Stacking them is okay. Spray the pork chops with cooking oil. Cook for 6 minutes.
4. Open the air fryer and flip the pork chops. Cook for an additional 6 minutes.

5. Cool before serving. Instead of seasoning salt, you can use either chicken or pork rub for additional flavor. You can find these rubs in the spice aisle of the grocery store.

Nutrition: Calories: 334. **Fat:** 7 g. **Protein:** 34 g. **Fiber:** 0 g.

216. Caramelized Pork Shoulder

Preparation Time: 10 minutes
Cooking Time: 30 minutes
Servings: 8
Ingredients:

- ⅓ cup soy sauce
- 2 tbsp. sugar
- 1 tbsp. honey
- 2-lb. pork shoulder, cut into 1½-inch thick slices

Directions:
1. In a bowl, mix together all ingredients except pork.
2. Add pork and coat with marinade generously.
3. Cover and refrigerate o marinate for about 2 to 8 hours.
4. Preheat the air fryer oven to 335° F.
5. Place the pork in an Air fryer basket.
6. Cook for about 10 minutes.
7. Now, set the air fryer oven to 390° F. Cook for about 10 minutes

Nutrition: Calories: 349. **Protein:** 29.19 g. **Fat:** 21.96 g. **Carbs:** 6.77 g.

217. Fried Pork With Sweet and Sour Glaze

Preparation Time: 5 minutes
Cooking Time: 30 minutes
Servings: 4
Ingredients:

- ¼ cup rice wine vinegar
- ¼ tsp. Chinese five-spice powder
- 1 cup potato starch
- 1 green onion, chopped
- 2 large eggs, beaten
- 2 lb. pork chops cut into chunks
- 2 tbsp. cornstarch + 3 tbsp. water
- 5 tbsp. brown sugar
- Salt and pepper to taste

Directions:
1. Preheat the air fryer oven to 390° F.
2. Season pork chops with salt and pepper to taste.
3. Dip the pork chops in egg. Set aside.
4. In a bowl, combine the potato starch and Chinese five-spice powder.
5. Dredge the pork chops in the flour mixture.
6. Place in the double layer rack and cook for 30 minutes.

7. Meanwhile, place the vinegar and brown sugar in a saucepan. Season with salt and pepper to taste. Stir in the cornstarch slurry and allow to simmer until thick.
8. Serve the pork chops with the sauce and garnish with green onions.

Nutrition: Calories: 420. **Fat:** 11.8 g. **Protein:** 69.2 g.

218. Oregano-Paprika on Breaded Pork

Preparation Time: 10 minutes
Cooking Time: 30 minutes
Servings: 4
Ingredients:

- ¼ cup water
- ¼ tsp. dry mustard
- ½ tsp. black pepper
- ½ tsp. cayenne pepper
- ½ tsp. garlic powder
- ½ tsp. salt
- 1 cup panko breadcrumbs
- 1 egg, beaten
- 2 tsp. oregano
- 4 lean pork chops
- 4 tsp. paprika

Directions:
1. Preheat the air fryer oven to 390° F.
2. Pat dries the pork chops.
3. In a mixing bowl, combine the egg and water. Then set aside.
4. In another bowl, combine the rest of the ingredients.
5. Dip the pork chops in the egg mixture and dredge in the flour mixture.
6. Place in the air fryer basket and cook for 25 to 30 minutes until golden.

Nutrition: Calories: 364. **Fat:** 20.2 g. **Protein:** 42.9 g.

219. Bacon Wrapped Pork Tenderloin

Preparation Time: 5 minutes
Cooking Time: 30 minutes
Servings: 4
Ingredients:
Pork:

- 1 to 2 tbsp. Dijon mustard
- 3 to 4 strips of bacon
- 1 pork tenderloin

Apple gravy:

- ½ to 1 tsp. Dijon mustard
- 1 tbsp. almond flour
- 2 tbsp. ghee
- 1 chopped onion
- 2 to 3 Granny Smith apples
- 1 cup vegetable broth

Directions:
1. Spread Dijon mustard all over tenderloin and wrap the meat with strips of bacon.
2. Pour into the oven rack/basket. Place the rack on the middle shelf of the Air fryer oven. Set temperature to 360° F, and set time to 15 minutes. Use a meat thermometer to check for doneness.
3. To make sauce, heat ghee in a pan and add shallots. Cook 1 to 2 minutes.
4. Then add apples, cooking for 3 to 5 minutes until softened.
5. Add flour and ghee to make a roux. Add broth and mustard, stirring well to combine.
6. When the sauce starts to bubble, add 1 cup of sautéed apples, cooking till sauce thickens.
7. Once pork tenderloin I cook, allow to sit for 5 to 10 minutes to rest before slicing.
8. Serve topped with apple gravy. Devour!

Nutrition: Calories: 552. **Fat:** 25 g. **Protein:** 29 g. **Sugar:** 6 g.

220. Pork Tenders With Bell Peppers

Preparation Time: 5 minutes
Cooking Time: 30 minutes
Servings: 4
Ingredients:
- 11 oz pork tenderloin
- 1 bell pepper, in thin strips
- 1 red onion, sliced
- 2 tsp. provencal herbs
- Black pepper to taste
- 1 tbsp. olive oil
- ½ tbsp. mustard
- Round oven dish

Directions:
1. Preheat the air fryer oven to 390° F.
2. In the oven dish, mix the bell pepper strips with the onion, herbs, and some salt and pepper to taste. Add ½ tbsp. of olive oil to the mixture
3. Cut the pork tenderloin into four pieces and rub with salt, pepper, and mustard. Thinly coat the pieces with remaining olive oil and place them upright in the oven dish on top of the pepper mixture
4. Place the bowl into the air fryer oven. Set the timer to 15 minutes and roast the meat and the vegetables
5. Turn the meat and mix the peppers halfway through.
6. Serve with a fresh salad.

Nutrition: Calories: 161. **Protein:** 21.52 g. **Fat:** 6.86 g. **Carbs:** 2.45 g.

221. Dijon Garlic Pork Tenderloin

Preparation Time: 5 minutes
Cooking Time: 30 minutes

Servings: 6
Ingredients:
- 1 cup breadcrumbs
- Pinch of cayenne pepper
- 3 crushed garlic cloves
- 2 tbsp. ground ginger
- 2 tbsp. Dijon mustard
- 2 tbsp. raw honey
- 4 tbsp. water
- 2 tsp. salt
- 1 pound pork tenderloin, sliced into 1-inch rounds

Directions:
1. With pepper and salt, season all sides of the tenderloin.
2. Combine cayenne pepper, garlic, ginger, mustard, honey, and water until smooth.
3. Dip pork rounds into the honey mixture and then into breadcrumbs, ensuring they all get coated well.
4. Place coated pork rounds into your air fryer oven.
5. Pour into the oven rack/basket. Place the rack on the middle shelf of the Air fryer oven. Set temperature to 400° F, and set time to 10 minutes. Cook 10 minutes at 400° F. Flip and then cook an additional 5 minutes until golden in color.

Nutrition: Calories: 423. **Fat:** 18 g. **Protein:** 31 g. **Sugar:** 3 g.

222. Pork Neck With Salad

Preparation Time: 10 minutes
Cooking Time: 30 minutes
Servings: 2
Ingredients:
For pork:
- 1 tbsp. soy sauce
- 1 tbsp. fish sauce
- ½ tbsp. oyster sauce
- ½ lb. pork neck

For salad:
- 1 ripe tomato, sliced tickly
- 8 to 10 Thai shallots, sliced
- 1 scallion, chopped
- 1 bunch fresh basil leaves
- 1 bunch fresh cilantro leaves

For dressing:
- 3 tbsp. fish sauce
- 2 tbsp. olive oil
- 1 tsp. apple cider vinegar
- 1 tbsp. palm sugar
- 2 bird eye chilies
- 1 tbsp. garlic, minced

Directions:

1.   For pork in a bowl, mix together all ingredients except pork.
2.   Add pork neck and coat with marinade evenly. Refrigerate for about 2 to 3 hours.
3.   Preheat the air fryer oven to 340° F.
4.   Place the pork neck onto a grill pan. Cook for about 12 minutes.
5.   Meanwhile, in a large salad bowl, mix together all salad ingredients.
6.   In a bowl, add all dressing ingredients and beat till well combined.
7.   Remove pork neck from Air fryer and cut into desired slices.
8.   Place pork slices over salad.
Nutrition: Calories: 391. **Protein:** 32.25 g. **Fat:** 24.04 g. **Carbs:** 10.32 g.

223. Cajun Pork Steaks

Preparation Time: 5 minutes
Cooking Time: 30 minutes
Servings: 6
Ingredients:

- 4 to 6 pork steaks

BBQ sauce:

- Cajun seasoning
- 1 tbsp. vinegar
- 1 tsp. low-sodium soy sauce
- ½ cup brown sugar
- ½ cup vegan ketchup

Directions:
1.   Ensure your air fryer oven is preheated to 290° F.
2.   Sprinkle pork steaks with Cajun seasoning.
3.   Combine remaining ingredients and brush onto steaks. Add coated steaks to the air fryer.
4.   Pour into the oven rack/basket. Place the rack on the middle shelf of the Air fryer oven. Set temperature to 290° F, and set time to 20 minutes. Cook for 15 to 20 minutes till just browned.
Nutrition: Calories: 209. **Fat:** 11 g. **Protein:** 28 g. **Sugar:** 2 g.

Fish

224. Tuna Noodle Casserole

Preparation Time: 20 minutes
Cooking Time: 30 minutes
Servings: 4
Ingredients:

- 5 oz. can tuna
- 10 ½ oz. creamy mushroom soup
- 1 cup egg noodles, cooked
- ¼ cup cold water
- ½ cup frozen peas or green beans
- 2 tbsp. breadcrumbs
- ¼ cup sour cream
- ½ cup cheddar cheese, shredded

Directions:

1. In a large mixing bowl, combine together tuna, sour cream, green beans, or peas, about 6 tbsp. of cheese, cream of mushroom soup, and cooked noodles.
2. Mix well until it forms a cohesive mixture.
3. Pour the prepared mix into an 8-inch ovenproof dish.
4. Place the ovenproof dish on the 1-inch rack and cook on the "HI" setting for about 18 to 22 minutes.
5. Once the timer is up, add the remaining cheese and breadcrumbs to the top of the semi-set casserole.
6. Bake on the "HI" setting for another 2 to 3 minutes or until the cheese melts and gets light brown.
7. Once done, remove the casserole oven and allow cooling for about 7 to 10 minutes before serving.

Nutrition: Calories: 367. **Total Fat:** 11 g. **Carbs:** 25 g. **Protein:** 19 g.

225. Baked Herb-Crusted Salmon

Preparation Time: 10 minutes
Cooking Time: 30 minutes
Servings: 8
Ingredients:

- 1 salmon fillet (3 to 4 lb.)
- 1 lemon divided
- 2 tbsp. melted butter
- Salt and pepper to taste

For topping:

- 2 tbsp. minced fresh parsley
- ¾ cup Panko bread crumbs
- 2 tbsp. shredded parmesan cheese
- 3 cloves of minced garlic
- 1 tbsp. minced fresh dill
- 3 tbsp. melted butter
- One lemon zest

Directions:

1. Preheat the convection oven at 375° F.
2. In a small-sized bowl, combine all the ingredients.
3. Greased a baking pan with cooking spray.
4. Arrange salmon on a baking pan and brush melted butter all over the salmon, sprinkle with pepper and salt, and squeeze half of the lemon all over the salmon.
5. Spread crumb mixture over salmon and bake for 14 to 18 minutes or until cooked.

Nutrition: Calories: 377. **Fat:** 20 g. **Protein:** 40 g. **Carbs:** 5 g.

226. Easy and Tasty Tuna Noodles Casserole

Preparation Time: 20 minutes
Cooking Time: 30 minutes
Servings: 6
Ingredients:

- 1 can of tuna drained (5 to 6 oz.)
- 3 cups egg noodles
- 10-½ oz. condensed mushroom soup
- 2 stalks of diced celery
- 1 cup cheddar cheese
- 1 small diced onion
- ⅓ cup milk
- ⅔ cup frozen peas defrosted
- 1 tbsp. butter
- 1 tbsp. parsley

Crumb topping:

- ½ cup panko bread crumbs
- ½ cup cheddar
- 1 tbsp. parsley
- 1 tbsp. melted butter

Directions:

1. Preheat the convection oven at 400° F. Mix topping ingredients and set them aside.
2. Boil noodles according to your package directions.
3. Cook celery and onion in butter until softens, for around 5 to 7 minutes.
4. In a large-sized bowl, mix noodles, onion mixture, soup, peas, milk, tuna, cheese, and parsley.
5. Spread the mixture into a casserole dish and sprinkle the top with crumb topping.
6. Bake in a preheated convection for 18 to 20 minutes.

Nutrition: Calories: 323. **Fat:** 15 g. **Protein:** 19 g. **Carbs:** 25 g.

227. Crusted Parmesan Tilapia

Preparation Time: 10 minutes
Cooking Time: 30 minutes
Servings: 4
Ingredients:

- 4 tilapia fillets
- 1 ½ tbsp. mayonnaise
- ¼ cup grated parmesan cheese
- 1 tbsp. lemon juice fresh
- 2 tbsp. butter
- Salt and pepper to taste
- 1 tsp. dill

Directions:

1. Combine all the ingredients except the tilapia in a small-sized bowl and set them aside.
2. Line a baking sheet with heavy-duty foil tightly and place tilapia on it.
3. Broil for 3 to 4 minutes, take out the pan from the oven, flip the tilapia and distribute the parmesan mixture on the uncooked sides of the tilapia.
4. Return to the convection oven and broil for an additional 4 to 5 minutes. Make sure not to overcook tilapia.

Nutrition: Calories: 169. **Fat:** 10 g. **Protein:** 11 g. **Carbs:** 35 g.

228. Tasty Fish Croquettes Baked

Preparation Time: 15 minutes

Cooking Time: 30 minutes

Servings: 6

Ingredients:

- 2 cups cooked steelhead trout
- ½ cup sour cream
- 1 cup soft bread crumbs
- ½ cup mayonnaise
- ½ cup panko bread crumbs
- ½ minced sweet onion
- ½ lemon juice
- ½ tsp. garlic powder
- ½ tsp. Worcestershire sauce
- Ground black pepper to taste
- ½ tsp. seasoned salt

Directions:

1. Preheat the convection oven to 400° F.
2. Discard bones, skin, and any crust from trout. Shred with fork. Combine shredded fish with onion, soft bread crumbs, mayonnaise, lemon juice, sour cream, garlic powder, salt, and black pepper in a bowl. Form balls out of the mixture coat in panko. Arrange balls on the baking sheet.
3. Bake in a preheated convection oven for 15 to 20 minutes or until croquettes turn light brown.

Nutrition: Calories: 278. **Fat:** 21.6 g. **Protein:** 10.1 g. **Carbs:** 14.1 g.

Seafood

229. Unusual Lime and Tequila Shrimp

Preparation Time: 15 minutes
Cooking Time: 30 minutes
Servings: 2
Ingredients:

- 1-lb. extra-large shrimp
- 3 tbsp. lime juice
- 2 tbsp. olive oil
- 2 garlic cloves, minced
- 2 tbsp. tequilas
- ½ tsp. ground cumin
- ½ tsp. cayenne pepper
- Salt and ground black pepper to taste

Directions:
1. In a large mixing bowl, whisk together lime juice, virgin olive oil, garlic, cumin, cayenne pepper, salt, tequila, and pepper. Mix well. Then add shrimps and marinate for 2 to 3 hours in the refrigerator.
2. Line bottom of NuWave oven with foil. Place shrimp on the 4-inch rack. Cook on High power (350° F) for 3 minutes. Flip shrimp over and cook for another 3 minutes or until shrimp are opaque.
3. Serve and enjoy.
Nutrition: Calories: 203. **Total Fat:** 5 g. **Total Carbs:** 6 g. **Protein:** 19 g.

230. Tender Crab Cakes

Preparation Time: 25 minutes
Cooking Time: 30 minutes
Servings: 3
Ingredients:

- 8 oz. lump crabmeat
- ⅔ cup panko breadcrumbs
- 1 tbsp. chopped parsley
- 2 tbsp. chopped green onions
- ½ tsp. Old Bay seasoning
- ½ tsp. Worcestershire sauce
- A pinch of salt
- ¼ tsp. cayenne pepper
- 1 tsp. lemon juice
- 2 tbsp. mayonnaises
- 1 large egg
- 1 lemon
- 1 tsp. Dijon mustard

Directions:
1. In a large bowl, combine ⅓ cup breadcrumbs, parsley, green onions, Old Bay seasoning, Worcestershire sauce, salt, cayenne pepper, lemon juice, mayonnaise, mustard, and egg. Add crabmeat and stir to combine well.

2. Place remaining breadcrumbs in a shallow dish. Form crab mixture into 3 equal-size patties. Coat each side with breadcrumbs.
3. Place foil on a 3-inch rack. Spray lightly with cooking spray. Place patties on foil. Bake on High power (350° F) for 6 minutes. Lip and cook extra 6 minutes.
4. Serve and enjoy!
Nutrition: Calories: 260. **Total Fat:** 18 g. **Carbs:** 13 g. **Protein:** 11 g.

231. Delicious Seafood Stuffing

Preparation Time: 20 minutes
Cooking Time: 30 minutes
Servings: 8
Ingredients:

- 1 lb. crabmeat
- 1 package of cornbread stuffing mix (6 oz.)
- 1 can of condensed cream of mushroom soup (10.75 oz.)
- ½ lb. peeled medium shrimp
- 1 can of chicken broth (14.5 oz.)
- ½ cup margarine
- ½ cup seasoned dry bread crumbs
- ½ cup chopped celery
- ½ cup green bell pepper chopped
- 2 tbsp. white sugar (divided)
- ½ cup chopped onion

Directions:
1. Preheat the convection oven at 400° F.
2. On medium heat, melt the margarine in a large-sized skillet. Add the onion, bell pepper, crabmeat, celery, and shrimp; stir and cook for around 5 minutes. Set them aside. Stir together the stuffing, 1 tbsp. of sugar, and bread crumbs in a large-sized bowl. Mix in the cooked seafood and vegetables. Add in cream of mushroom and chicken broth according to your likeness. Spread the mixture into a 9x13 inch baking dish.
3. Bake for around 30 minutes in the preheated convection oven or until toasted from the top.
Nutrition: Calories: 345. **Fat:** 15.7 g. **Protein:** 22 g. **Carbs:** 28.4 g.

232. Stuffed Crab Mushrooms

Preparation Time: 10 minutes
Cooking Time: 30 minutes
Servings: 16 mushrooms
Ingredients:

- 16 large fresh mushrooms
- 6 oz. crab
- 2 tbsp. chopped parsley
- 4 oz. softened cream cheese
- ⅓ cup Parmesan cheese grated
- 2 thinly sliced green onions
- ¼ tsp. garlic salt

For topping:

- 1 tbsp. melted butter
- ¼ cup bread crumbs

Directions:

1. Preheat the convection oven to 350° F.
2. Whisk cream cheese until smooth and creamy. Stir in the remaining ingredients.
3. Spoon out the insides of the mushroom and discard.
4. Distribute the filling equally among all the mushroom caps. Mix topping ingredients and spread over mushrooms.
5. Bake in a preheated convection oven for around 18 to 20 minutes until fully cooked.

Nutrition: Calories: 52. **Fat:** 3 g. **Protein:** 2 g. **Carbs:** 2 g.

233. Seafood Cottage Cheese Lasagna

Preparation Time: 15 minutes
Cooking Time: 30 minutes
Servings: 12
Ingredients:

- 1 can of drained crabmeat (7 ½ oz.)
- 8 oz. uncooked lasagna noodles (9 to 10 noodles)
- 1 can of drained baby shrimp (4 ½ oz.)
- 2 cups mozzarella cheese shredded
- 2 cups milk
- 2 cups chicken broth
- 1 cup cottage cheese
- ½ cup parmesan cheese grated
- ½ cup sliced onion
- ½ cup flour
- ½ cup butter
- ¼ tsp. black pepper
- ½ tsp. dried basil
- ½ tsp. salt
- ½ tsp. dried oregano
- 3 cloves of minced garlic

Directions:

1. Preheat the convection oven to 325° F. In a sauce, heat butter over medium heat and add garlic, add in flour, pepper, and salt; cook occasionally stirring, then add milk and broth stir and heat to boiling for about 1 minute.
2. Mix in mozzarella, basil, onions, and oregano. Cook over low or medium heat until cheese melts down.
3. Place ¼ of the cheese sauce in 13x9 inches baking dish. Layer with 3 to 4 uncooked lasagna noodles. Sprinkle cottage cheese over lasagna noodles. Repeat the procedure one more time and top with shrimp, crabmeat, ¼ cheese sauce, and 3 to 4 lasagna noodles and cheese sauce. Finish with parmesan cheese.

4. Bake in the preheated convection oven until lasagna noodles are done for around 35 to 40 minutes.
5. Let it stand 10 minutes before eating.

Nutrition: Calories: 309.6. **Fat:** 16 g. **Protein:** 18.8 g. **Carbs:** 22 g.

Breads

234. Potato Rosemary Bread

Preparation Time: 3 hours
Cooking Time: 30 minutes
Servings: 20
Ingredients:

- 3 cups bread flour, sifted
- 1 tbsp. white sugar
- 1 tbsp. sunflower oil
- 1 ½ tsp. salt
- 1 ½ cups lukewarm water
- 1 tsp. active dry yeast
- 1 cup potatoes, mashed
- ½ teaspoons crushed rosemary

Directions:
1. Prepare all of the ingredients for your bread and measuring means (a cup, a spoon, kitchen scales).
2. Carefully measure the ingredients into the pan, except the potato and rosemary.
3. Place all of the ingredients into the bread bucket in the right order, following the manual for your bread machine.
4. Close the cover.
5. Select the program of your bread machine to Bread with Fillings and choose the crust color to Medium.
6. Press Start.
7. After the signal, put the mashed potato and rosemary into the dough.
8. Wait until the program completes.
9. When done, take the bucket out and let it cool for 5 to 10 minutes.
10. Shake the loaf from the pan and let cool for 30 minutes on a cooling rack.
11. Slice, serve, and enjoy the taste of fragrant homemade bread.

Nutrition: Calories: 106. **Total Carbs:** 21 g. **Total Fat:** 1 g. **Protein:** 2.9 g. **Sodium:** 641 mg. **Fiber:** 1 g. **Sugar:** 0.8 g.

235. White Bread

Preparation Time: 20 minutes
Cooking Time: 30 minutes
Servings: 20
Ingredients:

- 4 ½ tsp. (14 g) instant yeast, two 0.25-oz. packets
- ¾ cup (808 mL) + 2 ⅔ cups warm water, divided
- ¼ cup (52 g) granulated sugar
- 1 tbsp. salt
- 3 tbsp. (44 g) unsalted butter, cubed, at room temperature
- 9 to 10 cups (1200 g) all-purpose flour
- 3 tbsp. (44 g) unsalted butter, melted, for brushing

Directions:
1. In the bowl of a mixer, stir to dissolve the yeast in ¾ cup of the warm water, and let sit for 5 minutes. Add the remaining 2 ⅔ cups water, sugar, salt, room temperature butter, and 5 cups of the flour and stir to combine.
2. Using a dough hook, mix at low speed and gradually add the remaining flour until the dough is soft and tacky, but not sticky (you may not need to use all of the flour). Continue to knead until a soft ball of dough forms and clears the sides of the bowl, about 7 to 10 minutes.
3. Place the dough in a lightly greased bowl and turn it over so it is completely coated. Cover with plastic wrap and set in a draft-free place to rise until doubled in size, about 45 minutes to 1 hour.
4. Turn the dough out onto a clean, lightly floured surface. Gently press it all over to remove any air pockets. Divide the dough in two and, working with one piece at a time, gently pat it into a 9x12-inch rectangle. Roll up the rectangle, starting on the short end, into a very tight cylinder. Pinch to seal the seams and the ends, tuck the ends of the roll until the bread, and place into greased 9-inch loaf pans. Cover the loaves loosely and place in a draft-free area until doubled in size, 30 to 45 minutes.
5. Position an oven rack on the lowest setting and preheat the oven to 400° F.
6. Brush the loaves with some of the melted butter. Bake the loaves for 30 to 35 minutes, rotating halfway through, until golden brown (an instant-read thermometer inserted into the center should read 195° F).
7. Remove from the oven and immediately brush with more of the melted butter. Allow to cool for 10 minutes, then remove from the pans and cool completely before slicing. The bread can be stored in an airtight bread bag or wrapped tightly in plastic wrap at room temperature for up to 4 days. It can also be frozen for up to 1 month.

Nutrition: Calories: 253. **Carbs:** 46 g. **Protein:** 6 g. **Fat:** 4 g. **Saturated Fat:** 2 g. **Cholesterol:** 9 mg. **Sodium:** 352 mg. **Potassium:** 85 mg. **Fiber:** 2 g. **Sugar:** 2 g.

236. Beetroot Prune Bread

Preparation Time: 3 hours
Cooking Time: 30 minutes
Servings: 20
Ingredients:

- 1 ½ cups lukewarm beet broth
- 5 ¼ cups all-purpose flour
- 1 cup beet puree
- 1 cup prunes, chopped
- 1 Tbsp. extra virgin olive oil
- 1 Tbsp. dry cream
- 1 tbsp. brown sugar
- 1 Tsp. active dry yeast

- 1 tbsp. whole milk
- 1 Tsp. sea salt

Directions:
1. Prepare all of the ingredients for your bread and measuring means (a cup, a spoon, kitchen scales).
2. Carefully measure the ingredients into the pan, except the prunes.
3. Place all of the ingredients into the bread bucket in the right order, following the manual for your bread machine.
4. Close the cover.
5. Select the program of your bread machine to Basic and choose the crust color to Medium.
6. Press Start.
7. After the signal, put the prunes into the dough.
8. Wait until the program completes.
9. When done, take the bucket out and let it cool for 5 to 10 minutes.
10. Shake the loaf from the pan and let cool for 30 minutes on a cooling rack.
11. Slice, serve, and enjoy the taste of fragrant homemade bread.

Nutrition: Calories: 443. **Total Carbs:** 81.1 g. **Total Fat:** 8.2 g. **Protein:** 9.9 g. **Sodium:** 604 mg. **Fiber:** 4.4 g. **Sugar:** 11.7 g.

237. Low-Carb Bagel

Preparation Time: 15 minutes
Cooking Time: 30 minutes
Servings: 12
Ingredients:
- 1 cup protein powder, unflavored
- 1/3 cup coconut flour
- 1 tsp. baking powder
- 1/2 tsp. sea salt
- 1/4 cup ground flaxseed
- 1/3 cup sour cream
- 12 eggs

Seasoning topping:
- 1 tsp. dried parsley
- 1 tsp. dried oregano
- 1 tsp. dried minced onion
- 1/2 tsp. garlic powder
- 1/2 tsp. dried basil
- 1/2 tsp. sea salt

Directions:
1. Preheat the oven to 350° F.
2. In a mixer, blend sour cream and eggs until well combined.
3. Whisk together the flaxseed, salt, baking powder, protein powder, and coconut flour in a bowl.
4. Mix the dry ingredients until it becomes wet ingredients. Make sure it is well blended.

5. Whisk the topping seasoning together in a small bowl. Set aside.
6. Grease 2 donut pans that can contain six donuts each.
7. Sprinkle pan with about 1 tsp. topping seasoning and evenly pour batter into each.
8. Sprinkle the top of each bagel evenly with the rest of the seasoning mixture.
9. Bake in the oven for 25 minutes, or until golden brown.

Nutrition: Calories: 134. **Fat:** 6.8 g. **Carb:** 4.2 g. **Protein:** 12.1 g.

238. Puri Bread

Preparation Time: 10 minutes
Cooking Time: 30 minutes
Servings: 6
Ingredients:
- 1 cup almond flour, sifted
- 1/2 cup warm water
- 2 tbsp. clarified butter
- 1 cup olive oil for frying
- Salt to taste

Directions:
1. Salt the water and add the flour.
2. Make some holes in the center of the dough and pour warm clarified butter.
3. Knead the dough and let stand for 15 minutes, covered.
4. Shape into six balls.
5. Flatten the balls into six thin rounds using a rolling pin.
6. Heat enough oil to cover a round frying pan completely.
7. Place a puri in it when hot.
8. Fry for 20 seconds on each side.
9. Place on a paper towel.
10. Repeat with the rest of the puri and serve.

Nutrition: Calories: 106. **Fat:** 3 g. **Carb:** 6 g. **Protein:** 3 g.

239. Hot Dog Buns

Preparation Time: 10 minutes
Cooking Time: 30 minutes
Servings: 10
Ingredients:
- 1 1/4 cups almond flour
- 5 tbsp. psyllium husk powder
- 1 tsp. sea salt
- 2 tsp. baking powder
- 1 1/4 cups boiling water
- 2 tsp. lemon juice
- 3 egg whites

Directions:
1. Preheat the oven to 350° F

2. In a bowl, put all dry ingredients and mix well.
3. Add boiling water, lemon juice, and egg whites into the dry mixture and whisk until combined.
4. Mold the dough into ten portions and roll into buns.
5. Transfer into the preheated oven and cook for 40 to 50 minutes on the lower oven rack.
6. Check for doneness and remove it.
7. Top with desired toppings and hot dogs.
8. Serve.

Nutrition: Calories: 104. **Fat:** 8 g. **Carb:** 1 g. **Protein:** 4 g.

240. Healthy Low Carb Bread

Preparation Time: 15 minutes
Cooking Time: 30 minutes
Servings: 8
Ingredients:

- ⅔ cup coconut flour
- ⅔ cup coconut oil (softened not melted)
- 9 eggs
- 2 tsp. cream of tartar
- ¾ tsp. xanthan gum
- 1 tsp. baking soda
- ¼ tsp. salt

Directions:
1. Preheat the oven to 350° F.
2. Grease a loaf pan with 1 to 2 tsp. melted coconut oil and place in the freezer to harden.
3. Add eggs into a bowl and mix for 2 minutes with a hand mixer.
4. Add coconut oil into the eggs and mix.
5. Add dry ingredients to a second bowl and whisk until mixed.
6. Put the dry ingredients into the egg mixture and mix on low speed with a hand mixer until dough is formed and the mixture is incorporated.
7. Add the dough into the prepared loaf pan, transfer it into the preheated oven, and bake for 35 minutes.
8. Take out the bread pan from the oven.
9. Cool, slice, and serve.

Nutrition: Calories: 229. **Fat:** 25.5 g. **Carb:** 6.5 g. **Protein:** 8.5 g.

241. Spicy Bread

Preparation Time: 10 minutes
Cooking Time: 30 minutes
Servings: 6
Ingredients:

- ½ cup coconut flour
- 6 eggs
- 3 large jalapenos, sliced
- 4 oz. turkey bacon, sliced
- ½ cup ghee

- ¼ tsp. baking soda
- ¼ tsp. salt
- ¼ cup water

Directions:
1. Preheat the oven to 400° F.
2. Cut bacon and jalapenos on a baking tray and roast for 10 minutes.
3. Flip and bake for 5 more minutes.
4. Remove seeds from the jalapenos.
5. Place jalapenos and bacon slices in a food processor and blend until smooth.
6. In a bowl, add ghee, eggs, and ¼-cup water. Mix well.
7. Then add some coconut flour, baking soda, and salt. Stir to mix.
8. Add bacon and jalapeno mix.
9. Grease the loaf pan with ghee.
10. Pour batter into the loaf pan.
11. Bake for 40 minutes.
12. Enjoy.

Nutrition: Calories: 240. **Fat:** 20 g.

242. Fluffy Paleo Bread

Preparation Time: 10 minutes
Cooking Time: 30 minutes
Servings: 15
Ingredients:

- 1 ¼ cup almond flour
- 5 eggs
- 1 tsp. lemon juice
- ⅓ cup avocado oil
- 1 dash black pepper
- ½ tsp. sea salt
- 3 to 4 tbsp. tapioca flour
- 1 to 2 tsp. poppy seed
- ¼ cup ground flaxseed
- ½ tsp. baking soda

Top with:

- Poppy seeds
- Pumpkin seeds

Directions:
1. Preheat the oven to 350° F.
2. Line a baking pan with parchment paper and set it aside.
3. In a bowl, add eggs, avocado oil, and lemon juice and whisk until combined.
4. In another bowl, add tapioca flour, almond flour, baking soda, flaxseed, black pepper, and poppy seed. Mix.
5. Add the lemon juice mixture into the flour mixture and mix well.
6. Add the batter into the prepared loaf pan and top with extra pumpkin seeds and poppy seeds.
7. Cover loaf pan and transfer into the prepared oven, and bake for 20 minutes. Remove cover and bake

until an inserted knife comes out clean after about 15 to 20 minutes.

8.   Remove from oven and cool.

9.   Slice and serve.

Nutrition: Calories: 149. **Fat:** 12.9 g. **Carbs:** 4.4 g.

243. Chocolate Chip Peanut Butter Banana Bread

Preparation Time: 25 minutes
Cooking Time: 30 minutes
Servings: 12 to 16 slices
Ingredients:

- 2 bananas, mashed
- 2 eggs, at room temperature
- ½ cup melted butter, cooled
- 2 tbsp. milk, at room temperature
- 1 tsp. pure vanilla extract
- 2 cups all-purpose flour
- ½ cup sugar
- 1 ¼ tsp. baking powder
- ½ tsp. baking soda
- ½ tsp. salt
- ½ cup peanut butter chips
- ½ cup semisweet chocolate chips

Directions:

1.   Stir together the bananas, eggs, butter, milk, and vanilla in the bread machine bucket and set it aside.

2.   In a medium bowl, toss together the flour, sugar, baking powder, baking soda, salt, peanut butter chips, and chocolate chips.

3.   Add the dry ingredients to the bucket.

4.   Program the machine for Quick/Rapid bread, and press Start.

5.   When the cake is made, stick a knife into it, and if it arises out clean, the loaf is done.

6.   If the loaf needs a few more minutes, look at the management panel for a Bake Only button, and extend the time by 10 minutes.

7.   When the loaf is done, remove the bucket from the machine.

8.   Let the loaf cool for 5 minutes.

9.   Gently rock the can to remove the bread and turn it out onto a rack to cool.

Nutrition: Calories: 297. **Total Fat:** 14 g. **Saturated Fat:** 7 g. **Carbs:** 40 g. **Fiber:** 1 g. **Sodium:** 255 mg. **Protein:** 4 g.

244. Chocolate Sour Cream Bread

Preparation Time: 25 minutes
Cooking Time: 30 minutes
Servings: 12 slices
Ingredients:

- 1 cup sour cream
- 2 eggs, at room temperature
- 1 cup sugar
- ½ cup (1 stick) butter, at room temperature
- ¼ cup plain Greek yogurt
- 1 ¾ cups all-purpose flour
- ½ cup unsweetened cocoa powder
- ½ tsp. baking powder
- ½ tsp. salt
- 1 cup milk chocolate chips

Directions:

1.   In a small bowl, stick together the sour cream, eggs, sugar, butter, and yogurt until just combined.

2.   Transfer the wet ingredients to the bread machine bucket, and then add the flour, cocoa powder, baking powder, salt, and chocolate chips.

3.   Program the machine for Quick/Rapid bread, and press Start.

4.   When the loaf is done, stick a knife into it, and if it comes out clean, the loaf is done.

5.   If the loaf needs a few more minutes, check the control panel for a Bake Only button and extend the time by 10 minutes.

6.   When the loaf is done, remove the bucket from the machine.

7.   Let the loaf cool for 5 minutes.

8.   Gently rock the can to remove the loaf and place it out onto a rack to cool.

Nutrition: Calories: 347. **Total Fat:** 16 g. **Saturated Fat:** 9 g. **Carbs:** 48 g. **Fiber:** 2 g. **Sodium:** 249 mg. **Protein:** 6 g.

245. Nectarine Cobbler Bread

Preparation Time: 10 minutes
Cooking Time: 30 minutes
Servings: 12 to 16 slices
Ingredients:

- ½ cup (1 stick) butter, at room temperature
- 2 eggs, at room temperature
- 1 cup sugar
- ¼ cup milk, at room temperature
- 1 tsp. pure vanilla extract
- 1 cup diced nectarines
- 1 ¾ cups all-purpose flour
- 1 tsp. baking soda
- ½ tsp. salt
- ½ tsp. ground nutmeg
- ¼ tsp. baking powder

Directions:

1.   Place the butter, eggs, sugar, milk, vanilla, and nectarines in your bread machine.

2.   Program the machine for Quick/Rapid bread and press Start.

3.   While the wet ingredients are mixing, stir together the flour, baking soda, salt, nutmeg, and baking powder in a small bowl.

4.   After the first fast mixing is done and the machine signals, add the dry ingredients.

5.   When the loaf is done, remove the bucket from the machine.

6.   Let the loaf cool for 5 minutes.

7.   Gently shake the bucket to remove the loaf, then turn it out onto a rack to cool.

Nutrition: Calories: 218. **Total Fat:** 9 g. **Saturated Fat:** 5 g. **Carbs:** 32 g. **Fiber:** 1 g. **Sodium:** 270 mg. **Protein:** 3 g.

246. Sour Cream Maple Bread

Preparation Time: 5 minutes
Cooking Time: 30 minutes
Servings: 8 slices
Ingredients:

- 6 tbsp. water, at 80° F to 90° F
- 6 tbsp. sour cream, at room temperature
- 1 ½ tbsp. butter, at room temperature
- ¾ tbsp. maple syrup
- ½ tsp. salt
- 1 ¾ cups white bread flour
- 1 $\frac{1}{6}$ tsp. bread machine yeast

Directions:

1.   Place the ingredients in your bread machine as recommended by the manufacturer.

2.   Program the machine for Basic/White bread

3.   Select light or medium crust, and then press Start.

4.   When the loaf is done, remove the bucket from the machine.

5.   Let the loaf cool for 5 minutes.

6.   Gently shake the pan to get the loaf and turn it out onto a rack to cool.

Nutrition: Calories: 149. **Total Fat:** 4 g. **Saturated Fat:** 3 g. **Carbs:** 24 g. **Fiber:** 1 g. **Sodium:** 168 mg. **Protein:** 4 g.

Pizza

247. Four Cheese Margherita Pizza

Preparation Time: 10 minutes
Cooking Time: 30 minutes
Servings: 8
Ingredients:

- ¼ cup olive oil
- 1 tbsp. garlic, raw
- ½ tbsp. salt
- 8 Roma tomatoes
- 2 pizza crust
- 8 oz. mozzarella cheese
- 4 oz. fontina cheese
- 10 fresh basils
- ½ cup parmesan cheese, grated
- ½ cup feta cheese

Directions:

1. Mix oil, garlic, and salt. Toss with tomatoes and let stand for 15 minutes.
2. Place the crust on the crisper tray and brush it with tomato marinade, then sprinkle mozzarella and fontina cheese.
3. Arrange the tomatoes on top, then sprinkle basil, parmesan cheese, and feta cheese.
4. Slide the crisper tray on shelf position 2 of the Emeril Lagasse Power oven 360 and select the pizza setting. Set the temperature at 400° F for 15 minutes. Press Start.
5. Cook until the cheese is golden brown and bubbly. Repeat the cycle with the remaining pizza.
6. Serve the pizza and enjoy it.

Nutrition: Calories: 551. **Carbs:** 54 g. **Fat:** 18 g. **Protein:** 29 g.

248. Mini Pizza With Italian Sausage

Preparation Time: 10 minutes
Cooking Time: 30 minutes
Servings: 4
Ingredients:

- 1 lb. pizza dough
- 1 ½ lb. Hot Italian sausage
- 3 ½ tomato sauce
- 8 oz. mozzarella cheese
- 2 tbsp. thyme leaves, freshly chopped
- ½ tbsp. red pepper, crushed
- ¼ cup Parmigiano-Reggiano, finely grated
- Extra virgin oil

Directions:

1. Divide the dough into 4 portions on a work surface with flour. Roll each dough on the work surface into an 8 inches round.
2. Place the sausage on the crisper tray and slide the tray on position 2 of the oven. Select the "air fry" mode and set the temperature at 400° F for 15 minutes. Press Start.
3. Transfer the dough to the crisper tray and spoon the tomato sauce on each dough surface. Sprinkle cheese, top with the sausage, and garnish with thyme, pepper, and Parmigiano-Reggiano.
4. Slide the crisper tray on shelf position 2. Select the pizza setting and set the temperature at 425° F for 20 minutes, then press start.
5. Repeat the cycle with the remaining 3 pizzas. Serve the pizza drizzled with olive oil.

Nutrition: Calories: 130. **Carbs:** 13 g. **Fat:** 5 g. **Protein:** 6 g.

249. Roasted Garlic Pizza With Garlic Sauce

Preparation Time: 10 minutes
Cooking Time: 30 minutes
Servings: 8
Ingredients:

- 2 tbsp. butter, unsalted
- 2 tbsp. all-purpose flour
- 1 cup whole milk
- ¼ tbsp. cayenne pepper, ground
- 3 heads garlic
- ¼ tbsp. salt
- 1 cup warm water
- 1 tbsp. honey
- 2 tbsp. olive oil
- 1-¼ oz. active dry yeast
- 2-½ cup all-purpose flour
- 8 oz. mozzarella cheese
- 4 oz. fontina cheese, grated
- ½ cup Parmigiano- Reggiano cheese, finely grated
- 30 pieces tomatoes, sun-dried
- 2 tbsp. basil leaves, freshly chopped

Directions:

1. Melt butter in a saucepan over medium heat and cook the all-purpose flour for 3 minutes.
2. Whisk in milk until thickened. Add pepper, garlic, and salt, then simmer for 15 minutes on low heat to make the bechamel.
3. In a mixing bowl, mix warm water, honey, and oil. Mix in the yeast, flour, and salt in the bowl. Knead until smooth. Let rest for 20 minutes.
4. Divide the pizza dough in half and roll it to make it fit the pizza rack.
5. Top with cheeses and tomatoes. Slide the pizza rack on position 5 and select the pizza setting on the oven.

6.   Set the temperature at 425° F for 20 minutes. Press starts.

7.   Repeat with the second pizza. Top the pizza with parsley, basil, and red pepper.

Nutrition: Calories: 280. **Carbs:** 34 g. **Fat:** 11 g. **Protein:** 12 g.

250. Pepperoni Pizza

Preparation Time: 25 minutes
Cooking Time: 30 minutes
Servings: 8
Ingredients:

- Pepperoni, sliced
- 1 cup pizza sauce
- 1 cup mozzarella cheese
- Readymade pizza dough
- Parmesan cheese, grated

Directions:

1.   Arrange toppings on pizza dough.

2.   Preheat the Cuisinart Convection Toaster oven to 177° C or 350° F.

3.   Bake for 25 minutes.

Nutrition: Calories: 235. **Carbs**: 35.6 g. **Protein:** 11 g. **Fat:** 11 g.

251. Ham and Mushrooms Pizza

Preparation Time: 10 minutes
Cooking Time: 30 minutes
Servings: 4
Ingredients:

- 200 g mushrooms in oil
- 300 g tomato sauce
- 600 g bread dough
- 250 g mozzarella
- Basil
- 100 mL extra virgin olive oil
- Garlic, to taste
- Salt and pepper, to taste
- 150 g baked ham

Directions:

1.   In preparing the ham and mushroom pizza, take 1 tbsp. of extra virgin olive oil and bread dough. On a floured work surface, roll it and make a sheet of 1 cm thickness.

2.   On the pizza, put the tomato puree and add the clean and well-chopped garlic.

3.   Then cut into strips the baked ham and then sprinkle on the whole pizza.

4.   Lastly, add the mozzarella tubes and in oil, add the mushrooms. Season with pepper and extra virgin olive oil.

5.   Put it in a hot oven to bake at 250° F for about 15 minutes.

6.   Serve the ham and mushroom pizza while hot.

Nutrition: Calories: 754. **Protein:** 42.88 g. **Fat:** 6.32 g. **Carbs:** 137.13 g.

252. Apulian Pizza

Preparation Time: 20 minutes
Cooking Time: 30 minutes
Servings: 4
Ingredients:

- 1 cup all purpose flour
- 1 tbsp yeast
- 8 anchovies fillets
- 2 tbsp. Extra virgin olive oil
- 1 bunch of basil
- 4 tbsp. tomato puree
- Salt to taste
- 400 g pizza dough
- ½ cup black olives
- 12 cherry tomatoes
- 1 cup mozzarella
- 2 potatoes

Directions:

1.   For 40 minutes, boil the potatoes in their skins. Using a special utensil, peel and mash them and make them fall on the pastry board.

2.   Mix the potatoes with a pinch of salt, flour, and yeast dissolved in 2 tbsp. of warm water. Work on it well until you get a soft paste. If possible, add lukewarm water.

3.   Meanwhile, in boiling water, blanch the tomatoes and peel them. Free them from seeds and cut them into small pieces. You can well cut the mozzarella into slices.

4.   Get 1 26 cm diameter round mold and grease it, use the dough to cover the bottom, and make a layer of tomato slices and mozzarella over it.

5.   Season with a pinch of salt and oregano and use grated cheese to season. Use oil to drizzle and allow it to rise for at least 1 hour. Top with anchovies and black olives.

6.   In a hot oven set at 170° F, put the pizza and allow it to cook for 30 minutes then serve it hot.

Nutrition: Calories: 39. **Protein:** 11.1 g. **Fat:** 11.46 g. **Carbs:** 61.8 g.

253. Tyrolean Pizza

Preparation Time: 30 minutes
Cooking Time: 30 minutes
Servings: 4
Ingredients:
Pizzas:

- 1 tsp. sugar
- 12 g brewer's yeast
- 500 g flour
- 3 tbsp. extra virgin olive oil
- 250 to 300 mL warmed water
- 2 tsp. salt

Dressing:
- fresh ground oregano to taste
- 1 medium golden onion
- 1 tsp. sugar
- 250 g tomato sauce
- 400 g mozzarella, well-drained
- 250 g speck, cut into thin slices
- 2 packs of pork frankfurters

Directions:
Classic mixture:

1. On a pastry board, arrange the flour and give it the shape of the classic fountain.
2. On the outermost edge of the flour, it's where you should put the salt.
3. Smash the brewer's yeast and dissolve it in 100 mL of warm water together with the sugar. Pour the mixture into the center of the fountain after adding the oil.
4. Use your fingertips to begin working on the dough. Incorporate the flour gradually to the fountain edge. Add the necessary lukewarm water gradually and in a circular motion.
5. From the edge, include more and more flour until elastic, soft, and smooth dough forms at the center.
6. On a floured surface, vigorously work on the dough until it doesn't stick on your hands anymore.

Mixture with the planetary mixer:

1. In a planetary mixer with a mounted hook, insert the flour and add yeast, oil, and 150 mL of water.
2. At medium-low speed, knead for 5 minutes and also add the rest of the water flush.
3. Again, knead for 5 minutes, add salt and keep cooking for more than 5 minutes until you obtain an elastic, smooth, and homogenous dough.

How to make Tyrolean pizza:

1. Form a ball with the dough that has been prepared using a planetary mixer or by hand and use a cloth to cover after making a cross-cut.
2. In a draft-free and warm place, leave the dough to rise until it doubles in volume for about 2 hours
3. 3. Divide the dough into 4 loaves once its volume is doubled and put them in a well-floured container with a lid.
4. Allow the dough to rise, this takes a couple of hours. Then go to the pizza preparation, one at a time.
5. Sprinkle the first loaf with flour and put it on a lightly greased round pan. For beginners, you can use a drizzle of oil to first moisten the fingertips.
6. Lightly press on the dough using your fingers so as to give it a circular shape.
7. Make a movement that goes from the center to the edge when handling the pizza to push the gas bubbles, which are formed after the rising process towards the cornice. You should not flatten the latter as it must be crisp and high at the end of the cooking.
8. Before baking the pizzas, preheat the oven for 30 minutes at 250° F. Then go to preparing the seasoning, which will be divided into 4 portions. Slice the onions thinly after peeling and rinsing them.
9. For 2 minutes, blanch the frankfurters and then cut them into thin slices. In a bowl, put the tomato sauce and do the seasoning with 2 tbsp. of oregano, salt, pepper, and oil and also cut the mozzarella into long slices that are thin.
10. Spread ¼ of the tomato sauce for the first pizza using the back of a spoon. In succession, distribute the frankfurters, onions, and mozzarella.
11. Use oil to wet the pizza surface and place it in an already hot oven. Since the pizza must cook more below than above, put the pan near the oven bottom.
12. Allow the Tyrolean pizza to cook until the cornice has become golden and crispy and the pizza bottom is dry. This will take 13 to 15 minutes. Raise the bottom to see if the pizza is cooked.
13. Remove the Tyrolean pizza from the oven when it finishes cooking, transfer it to a plate, and then use speck slices to garnish it.
14. You can now serve the freshly baked Tyrolean pizza.

Nutrition: Calories: 923. **Protein:** 58.09 g. **Fat:** 23.06 g. **Carbs:** 117.12 g.

254. Boscaiola Pizza

Preparation Time: 10 minutes
Cooking Time: 30 minutes
Servings: 4
Ingredients:
- 200 g sausage
- 130 g mozzarella
- Extra virgin olive oil to taste
- 400 g pizza dough
- Black pepper to taste
- 150 g champignon mushrooms
- Salt to taste

Directions:

1. Begin with preparing the pizza dough. Leave the dough to rise as you take care of the rest of the things. Clean and then cut the mushrooms into thin slices and then do the seasoning with pepper and a pinch of salt.
2. Grease a 30 cm pan with a drizzle of oil to avoid the pizza from sticking and dice the mozzarella.
3. Spread the dough in the pan directly once it is ready using your hands. Sprinkle with slices of champignon and diced mozzarella. Lastly, lay the sausage that is crumbled in small pieces and if desired, sprinkle with other oil.
4. Preheat a static oven at 250° F and put the dough for 12 to 15 minutes. It is recommended to put the pan in

the lower part of the oven and not in the center exactly and also check the times according to the appliance you are using.

5.   Take the boscaiola pizza out, cut, and serve it. You can also accompany it with a nice beer.

Nutrition: Calories: 618. **Protein:** 32.12 g. **Fat:** 19.45 g. **Carbs:** 86.11 g.

255. Capricciosa Pizza

Preparation Time: 30 minutes
Cooking Time: 30 minutes
Servings: 1
Ingredients:

- 1 tbsp. olive oil
- 1 pinch, chopped dry oregano
- 230 to 250 g pizza dough
- 30 g sliced cooked ham
- 150 g tomato sauce
- 40 g sliced black and green olives
- 4 to 5 well-drained anchovies in oil
- 50 g mozzarella for pizza
- Fresh basil leaves
- 40 g artichokes in oil, drained
- 30 g fresh champignon mushrooms, sliced
- Salt to taste

Directions:

1.   Prepare and spread the dough you prefer and then mix in a pinch of dried oregano, chopped anchovies, a pinch of salt, a tsp. of olive oil, and 150 g of tomato puree; flavor the pizza base using this sauce.

2.   On the pizza, add other ingredients by haphazardly spreading them that is 30 g of sliced and cooked ham, 30 g of champignon mushrooms sliced, 40 g of green and black olives, 50 g of mozzarella for pizza, and 40 g of artichokes that are in oil, drained and cut into pieces.

3.   Take back the seasoned pizza to the oven that was preheated at 250° F while the grill is on and allow it to cook for 15 to 20 minutes until it's cooked completely, the mozzarella melts, the dough edges turn to golden brown and the pizza bottom turns out dry nicely.

4.   Depending on the amount of ingredients, the type and thickness of the dough used, the type of oven, the cooking times vary since each oven even cooks differently.

5.   Take out the capricciosa pizza once it has been cooked and then garnish it with a few fresh basil leaves and then serve immediately.

Nutrition: Calories: 453. **Protein:** 38.5 g. **Fat:** 53.77 g. **Carbs:** 205.61 g.

256. Seafood Pizza

Preparation Time: 40 minutes
Cooking Time: 30 minutes
Servings: 2

Ingredients:
Dough:

- 300 mL water
- 30 g extra virgin olive oil
- 1 tsp. barley malt
- 50 g flour
- 8 g salt
- 20 g brewer's yeast

Filling:

- 300 g prawns
- 300 g mussels
- 200 g tomato sauce
- 500 g clams
- Extra virgin olive oil
- Salt to taste
- 1 sprig parsley

Directions:

1.   In preparing the seafood pizza, begin by preparing the pizza dough. In a bowl, put the salt, malt, and flour (you can alternatively use sugar). Mix the ingredients and then add the water at room temperature where you will have dissolved the brewer's yeast. Add some oil and then work on everything until you get an elastic and smooth dough.

2.   Use the dough to form a ball and put it in a bowl to rise. Use plastic wrap to cover it and keep it in a warm place until it doubles or for at least 4 hours.

3.   Get the dough and divide it into two parts. From it, form two loaves and allow them to rest on a floured surface for 1 hour at room temperature. You can use a cloth to cover in order to avoid power surges.

4.   To form a sheet, the size of a pan, roll out each loaf and then put them in greased trays. Over the pizzas, spread a layer of tomato puree, drizzle with a drizzle of oil, season with salt, and bake for 8 minutes in a preheated oven at 200° F.

5.   Remove the pizzas from the oven and then distribute the seafood i.e., the raw prawns, the mussels, and clams that were previously cooked, and then bake for another 5 minutes and make sure the seafood doesn't dry out.

6.   Distribute a little chopped fresh parsley after removing it from the oven. Your seafood is now ready. Serve.

Nutrition: Calories: 673. **Protein:** 54.78 g. **Fat:** 13.14 g. **Carbs:** 79 g.

Cake

257. Apple-Toffee Upside-Down Cake

Preparation Time: 10 minutes
Cooking Time: 30 minutes
Servings: 8
Ingredients:

- ¼ cup almond butter
- ¼ cup sunflower oil
- ½ cup chopped walnuts
- 1 cup coconut sugar
- ¾ cup water
- 1 ½ tsp. mixed spice
- 1 cup plain flour
- 1 lemon zest from
- 1 tsp. baking soda
- 1 tsp. vinegar
- 3 apples cored and sliced

Directions:
1. Preheat the oven to 390° F.
2. In a skillet, melt the almond butter and 3 tbsp. of sugar. Pour the mixture over a baking dish that will fit in the oven. Arrange the slices of apples on top. Set aside.
3. In a mixing bowl, combine flour, ¾ cup sugar, and baking soda. Add the mixed spice.
4. In another bowl, mix the oil, water, vinegar, and lemon zest. Stir in the chopped walnuts.
5. Combine the wet ingredients to dry ingredients until well combined.
6. Pour over the tin with apple slices.
7. Leave to cook for 30 minutes.

Nutrition: Calories: 145. **Carbs:** 3.6 g. **Protein:** 2.1 g. **Fat:** 13.6 g.

258. Plum Cake

Preparation Time: 10 minutes
Cooking Time: 30 minutes
Servings: 8
Ingredients:

- ½ cup butter, soft
- 3 eggs
- ½ cup swerve
- ¼ tsp. almond extract
- 1 tbsp. vanilla extract
- 1 and ½ cups almond flour
- ½ cup coconut flour
- 2 tsp. baking powder
- ¾ cup almond milk
- 4 plums, pitted and chopped

Directions:
1. In a bowl, mix all the ingredients and whisk well.

2. Pour this into a cake pan that fits the oven after you've lined it with parchment paper, put the pan in the machine, and cook at 370° F for 30 minutes.
3. Cool the cake down, slice, and serve.

Nutrition: Calories: 183. **Fat:** 4 g. **Fiber:** 3 g. **Carbs:** 4 g. **Protein:** 7 g.

259. Breakfast Oatmeal Cake

Preparation Time: 10 minutes
Cooking Time: 30 minutes
Servings: 8
Ingredients:

- 2 eggs
- 1 tbsp. coconut oil
- 3 tbsp. yogurts
- ½ tsp. baking powder
- 1 tsp. cinnamon
- 1 tsp. vanilla
- 3 tbsp. honey
- ½ tsp. baking soda
- 1 apple, peel & chopped
- 1 cup oats

Directions:
1. Fit the oven with the rack in position 1.
2. Line baking dish with parchment paper and set aside.
3. Add ¾ cup oats and remaining ingredients into the blender and blend until smooth.
4. Add remaining oats and stir well.
5. Pour the mixture into the prepared baking dish.
6. Set to bake at 350° F for 30 minutes. After 5 minutes, place the baking dish in the preheated oven.
7. Slice and serve.

Nutrition: Calories: 114. **Fat:** 3.6 g. **Carbs:** 18.2 g. **Sugar:** 10 g. **Protein:** 3.2 g. **Cholesterol:** 41 mg.

260. Easy Baked Chocolate Mug Cake

Preparation Time: 5 minutes
Cooking Time: 30 minutes
Servings: 4
Ingredients:

- ½ cup cocoa powder
- ½ cup stevia powder
- 1 cup coconut cream
- 1 package cream cheese, room temperature
- 1 tbsp. vanilla extract
- 1 tbsp. butter

Directions:
1. Preheat the air fryer oven for 5 minutes.
2. In a mixing bowl, combine all ingredients.
3. Use a hand mixer to mix everything until fluffy.
4. Pour into greased mugs.
5. Place the mugs in the fryer basket.

6.   Bake for 15 minutes at 350° F.

7.   Place in the fridge to chill before serving.

Nutrition: Calories: 744. **Fat:** 69.7 g. **Protein:** 13.9 g. **Sugar:** 4 g.

261. Angel Food Cake

Preparation Time: 5 minutes

Cooking Time: 30 minutes

Servings: 12

Ingredients:

- ¼ cup butter, melted
- 1 cup powdered erythritol
- 1 tsp. strawberry extract
- 12 egg whites
- 2 tsp. cream of tartar
- A pinch of salt

Directions:

1.   Preheat the air fryer oven for 5 minutes.

2.   Mix the egg whites and cream of tartar.

3.   Use a hand mixer and whisk until white and fluffy.

4.   Add the rest of the ingredients except for the butter and whisk for another minute.

5.   Pour into a baking dish.

6.   Place in the air fryer basket and cook for 30 minutes at 400° F or if a toothpick inserted in the middle comes out clean.

7.   Drizzle with melted butter once cooled.

Nutrition: Calories: 65. **Fat:** 5 g. **Protein:** 3.1 g. **Fiber:** 1 g.

Cookies

262. Easy Granola Cookies

Preparation Time: 10 minutes
Cooking Time: 30 minutes
Servings: 24
Ingredients:

- 1 ½ cups all-purpose flour
- 1 ¾ cups granola
- 1 cup dates, chopped and pitted
- 1 cup softened butter
- ¾ cup brown sugar packed
- ½ cup peanuts chopped, dry-roasted and unsalted
- ¾ cup white sugar
- 1 egg
- 1 tsp. baking soda
- 1 tsp. vanilla extract
- 1 tsp. salt

Directions:
1. Preheat the convection oven to 350° F. Coat cookies sheet with baking spray.
2. In a bowl, cream together the brown sugar, white sugar, and butter. Add and beat in egg and vanilla and combine in the flour, baking soda, and salt. Stir them into creamed mixture. Finally, fold in the granola, peanuts, and dates. Place heaping teaspoonfuls of dough into a greased cookie sheet—place cookie dough with 2 inches of distance.
3. Bake in a convection oven until cookies turn light brown from the edges for 12 to 15 minutes. Once done, transfer to cooling racks and cool completely before serving.

Nutrition: Calories: 229. **Fat:** 11.6 g. **Protein:** 3.3 g. **Carbs:** 29 g.

263. Crisps Almond Coffee Cookies

Preparation Time: 10 minutes
Cooking Time: 30 minutes
Servings: 6 dozen
Ingredients:

- 1 cup toasted and chopped almonds
- 2 cups brown sugar packed
- ½ cup brewed coffee at room temperature
- 1 cup shortening
- 3 ½ cups all-purpose flour
- 3 tbsp. sugar
- 1 ½ tsp. the ground cinnamon, divided
- 1 tsp. salt
- 2 eggs at room temperature
- 1 tsp. baking soda

Directions:

1. Cream together brown sugar and shortening until fluffy in a large-sized bowl. Mix eggs, one at a time, and keep beating after adding each egg. Whisk in coffee. Stir together baking soda, flour, 1 tsp. of cinnamon, and salt; slowly add the flour mixture into the creamed mixture and combine well. Fold in almonds.
2. Place teaspoonfuls into cookie sheet 2 inches apart. Mix in remaining cinnamon and sugar. Sprinkle the cinnamon-sugar mixture on top of cookies and slightly press with hands to flatten.
3. Bake in the convection oven for 10 to 15 minutes at 350° F.

Nutrition: Calories: 168. **Fat:** 8 g. **Protein:** 2 g. **Carbs:** 23 g.

264. Simple and Crispy Sugar Cookies

Preparation Time: 20 minutes
Cooking Time: 30 minutes
Servings: 8
Ingredients:

- 5 cups all-purpose flour
- 1 cup softened butter
- 2 eggs at room temperature
- ¼ cup 2% milk
- 2 cups sugar
- 1 tsp. baking soda
- 1 tsp. vanilla extract
- 1 ½ tsp. baking powder
- ½ tsp. salt

Directions:
1. Preheat the convection oven at 325° F.
2. Cream sugar and butter in a large-sized bowl until fluffy. Mix in vanilla and eggs. Add baking powder, flour, salt, and baking soda and combine with creamed mixture. Pour milk into the mixture and whisk. Cover with plastic wrap and refrigerate for 20 to 30 minutes.
3. Roll out dough into $1/8$ inches thickness on a floured surface, with 2 inches cookie cutter cut dough into desired shapes. Arrange onto greased cookie sheets 2 inches apart.
4. Bake for around 10 minutes in the preheated convection oven until the edges of the cookies are golden brown.

Nutrition: Calories: 117. **Fat:** 4 g. **Protein:** 2 g. **Carbs:** 18 g.

265. Easy and Quick Oatmeal Banana Cookies

Preparation Time: 10 minutes
Cooking Time: 30 minutes
Servings: 12
Ingredients:

- 1 cup bananas mashed
- 1 ¾ cups all-purpose flour

- 1 cup chocolate chips
- 1 ¼ cups large flake oats
- ½ cup brown sugar
- ⅔ cup softened butter
- ½ cup sugar
- ½ cup walnuts chopped
- 1 tsp. cinnamon
- 1 tsp. vanilla
- ½ tsp. baking powder
- ½ tsp. baking soda
- ¼ tsp. salt
- 1 egg

Directions:
1. Preheat the convection oven at 375° F. With baking paper, line a cookie sheet.
2. Mix flour, baking soda, cinnamon, salt, baking powder, and oats together.
3. Cream together sugar and butter until soft. Whisk in the egg.
4. Stir in vanilla and mashed bananas. Mix in the flour mixture slowly at a time until fully incorporated. Add in chocolate chips and nuts and lightly fold in the mixture.
5. Place tablespoonfuls onto lined cookie sheets. Bake in the preheated convection oven for 12 to 15 minutes or until golden brown from the edges.
Nutrition: Calories: 127. **Fat:** 6 g. **Protein:** 2 g. **Carbs:** 17 g.

266. Persimmon and Walnuts Cookies
Preparation Time: 10 minutes
Cooking Time: 30 minutes
Servings: 72 (6 dozen)
Ingredients:
- 1 cup white sugar
- 1 cup persimmon pulp
- ½ cup walnuts chopped
- 1 cup all-purpose flour
- ½ cup raisins
- ½ cup shortening
- 1 egg
- ¼ tsp. ground cloves
- ½ tsp. baking soda
- ½ tsp. salt
- ½ tsp. ground cinnamon
- ½ tsp. baking powder

Directions:
1. Preheat the convection oven at 325° F.
2. Beat together sugar and shortening in a large-sized bowl. Mix in the persimmon pulp and egg. Combine together baking soda, cloves, flour, baking powder, salt, and cinnamon; mix into persimmon mixture. Stir in

raisins and walnuts. Place teaspoonfuls of mixture onto greased cookie sheets 1 ½ inch apart.
3. Bake in the preheated convection oven for around 14 to 15 minutes or until cookies edges are golden brown.
Nutrition: Calories: 42. **Fat:** 2.1 g. **Protein:** 0.4 g. **Carbs:** 5.9 g.

267. Simple and Crunchy Cornmeal Cookies
Preparation Time: 10 minutes
Cooking Time: 30 minutes
Servings: 24
Ingredients:
- ½ cup cornmeal
- ¾ cup shortening
- 1 egg
- 1 ½ cups all-purpose flour
- ¾ cup white sugar
- 1 tsp. butter-flavored extract
- ¼ tsp. salt
- 1 tsp. vanilla extract
- 1 tsp. baking powder

Directions:
1. Beat together the sugar and shortening. Crack an egg and beat. Whisk baking powder, cornmeal, and flour together. Put butter flavored extract, vanilla, and salt and mix all ingredients together until fully incorporated.
2. Place spoonsful onto coated cookie sheet. Bake in the convection oven to 350° F for around 12 to 15 minutes or until cookies are lightly golden brown.
Nutrition: Calories: 122. **Fat:** 6.8 g. **Protein:** 1.3 g. **Carbs:** 14.3 g.

Dessert

268. Chocolaty Banana Muffins

Preparation Time: 5 minutes
Cooking Time: 30 minutes
Servings: 12
Ingredients:

- ¾ cup whole wheat flour
- ¾ cup plain flour
- ¼ cup cocoa powder
- ¼ tsp. baking powder
- 1 tsp. baking soda
- ¼ tsp. salt
- 2 large bananas, peeled and mashed
- 1 cup sugar
- $1/3$ cup canola oil
- 1 egg
- ½ tsp. vanilla essence
- 1 cup mini chocolate chips

Directions:

1. Mix your flour, cocoa powder, baking powder, baking soda, plus salt in a large bowl. In another bowl, add bananas, sugar, oil, egg, and vanilla extract and beat till well combined.
2. Slowly, add flour mixture to egg mixture and mix till just combined. Fold in chocolate chips—Preheat the oven to 345° F. Grease 12 muffin molds.
3. Transfer the mixture into prepared muffin molds evenly and cook for about 20 to 25 minutes or till a toothpick inserted in the center comes out clean.
4. Remove the muffin molds from the oven and keep on a wire rack to cool for about 10 minutes. Carefully turn on a wire rack to cool completely before serving.

Nutrition: Calories: 151. **Carbs:** 29 g. **Fat:** 3 g. **Protein:** 4 g.

269. Chocolate Nut Brownies

Preparation Time: 5 minutes
Cooking Time: 30 minutes
Servings: 12
Ingredients:

- ½ cup unsalted butter
- 2 oz. unsweetened chocolate
- 1 cup sugar
- 2 eggs
- 1 tsp. vanilla
- $2/3$ cup all-purpose, unbleached flour
- ½ cup chopped nuts
- 1/2 tsp. baking powder (decrease to ¼ tsp. for high altitude)
- ¼ tsp. salt

Directions:

1. Heat oven to 350° F.
2. Grease (with butter) and lightly flour bottom only of 8 or 9-inch square pan.
3. In a large saucepan, melt butter and chocolate over low heat, stirring constantly. Remove from heat; cool slightly.
4. Blend in sugar. Beat in the eggs, one at a time, and stir in the remaining ingredients.
5. Spread in prepared pan. Bake at 350° F for 25 to 30 minutes or until set in the center.
6. Be sure not to overbake if you want a softer center.
7. Remove from oven and cool completely on a wire rack. Cut into bars to serve.

Nutrition: Calories: 181. **Fat:** 13 g. **Fiber:** 2 g. **Carbs:** 4 g. **Protein:** 5 g.

270. Christmas Magic Bars

Preparation Time: 10 minutes
Cooking Time: 30 minutes
Servings: 4
Ingredients:

- $1/3$ cup melted salted butter
- 1 ½ cups chocolate baking crumbs
- 1 300 mL can of dulce de leche condensed milk (sweetened)
- 1 ½ cups flaked unsweetened coconut
- 1 cup red and green Christmas cherries chopped
- 1 cup semi-sweet chocolate chips

Directions:

1. Preheat your oven to 350° F.
2. Pour the melted butter into an 8x8 pan. If wanted, line the pan with tinfoil first for easier removal.
3. Sprinkle the baking crumbs on top of the butter in an even layer.
4. Drop the condensed milk onto the crumbs by the spoonful, creating an even layer of it.
5. Sprinkle the 3 remaining ingredients in the order given over the condensed milk. Press down gently.
6. Bake in the oven for 25 to 30 minutes until the coconut has browned.
7. Remove and cool completely in the pan before slicing. To remove, use the tinfoil to take it out, then slice.

Nutrition: Calories: 193. **Fat:** 5 g. **Fiber:** 1 g. **Carbs:** 4 g. **Protein:** 4 g.

271. Banana Oat Muffins

Preparation Time: 10 minutes
Cooking Time: 30 minutes
Servings: 6
Ingredients:

- 1 egg
- 2 tbsp. butter, melted
- ½ tsp. cinnamon
- 1 tsp. vanilla

- 2 tbsp. yogurts
- 1 ½ cup oats
- 1 tsp. baking powder
- 2 ripe bananas, mashed

Directions:

1. Fit the oven with the rack in position 1.
2. Line the muffin tray with cupcake liners and set it aside.
3. In a bowl, whisk the egg with banana, yogurt, vanilla, cinnamon, baking powder, and butter.
4. Add oats and mix well.
5. Pour the mixture into the prepared muffin tray.
6. Set to bake at 350° F for 30 minutes. After 5 minutes, place the muffin tray in the preheated oven.
7. Serve and enjoy.

Nutrition: Calories: 164. **Fat:** 6.1 g. **Carbs:** 23.9 g. **Sugar:** 5.5 g. **Protein:** 4.4 g. **Cholesterol:** 38 mg.

45 Minutes

Breakfast

272. Sandwich With Grilled Cheese

Preparation Time: 5 minutes
Cooking Time: 45 minutes
Servings: 2
Ingredients:

- 4 slices of white bread
- Butter, 3 tbsp. (scattered)
- Cheddar cheese (two slices)

Directions:

1. Using medium pressure heat the skillet. Butter one side of a piece of bread generously. Place 1 slice of cheese on top of the butter-side-down bread on the skillet's bottom.
2. Butter one side of the second slice of bread and put butter-side-up on top of the sandwich.
3. Grill until finely browned on one side, then turn and continue to grill until the cheese has melted. Rep with the remaining 2 slices of bread, butter, and cheese slice.

Nutrition: Calories: 400. **Protein:** 11.1 g. **Carbs:** 25.7 g. **Dietary Fiber:** 1.2 g. **Sugars:** 2.3 g. **Fat:** 28.3 g. **Saturated Fat:** 17.3 g. **Cholesterol:** 75.6 mg. **Vitamin A:** 816.4IU. **Niacin Equivalents:** 4.4 mg. **Vitamin B6:** 0.1 mg. **Foliate:** 61.2 mcg. **Calcium:** 285 mg. **Iron:** 2.1 mg. **Magnesium:** 19.9 mg. **Potassium:** 82.9 mg. **Sodium:** 639.2 mg. **Thiamin:** 0.1 mg.

273. Baked Mac and Cheese

Preparation Time: 10 minutes
Cooking Time: 45 minutes
Servings: 6
Ingredients:
Macaroni:

- Macaroni, 250 g (8 oz.) (elbow pasta)
- 1 tbsp. unsalted butter (15 g) (or 2 tsp. oil)

Topping:

- ⅔ cup panko breadcrumbs as a garnish (Note 1)
- ¼ tsp. salt
- 2 tbsp. unsalted butter (30g), melted

Sauce:

- 4 tbsp. unsalted butter (60g)
- ⅓ cup plain/all-purpose flour
- 3 cups warmed milk (low or full fat)
- 2 cups gruyere cheese, freshly shredded (followed by cheddar and Colby) (Observation 2)
- 1 cup shredded mozzarella cheese (or more cheese of your choice) (Note 2)
- ¼ tsp. salt

Seasonings (optional):

- 1 tsp. garlic powder
- ½ tsp. onion powder
- ½ tsp. mustard powder

Directions:
Pasta:

1. A big pot of water should be brought to a boil. Cook macaroni according to package instructions, minus 1 minute.
2. Drain the pasta, return it to the pot, and throw in the butter until it melts. Allow cooling when preparing the sauce (optional, note 3).

Topping:

1. In a mixing pot, thoroughly combine all topping ingredients. Excluding the item from circulation.

Sauce:

1. Preheat the oven to 180° C/350° F.
2. Melt butter in a big saucepan or an ovenproof skillet (I use my Lodge 26cm/9" cast iron skillet) over medium heat. Cook, stirring continuously, for 1 minute after adding the flour.
3. To dissolve the paste in the milk, add about 1 cup of milk and blend well. Then add the remaining milk and stir until there are no lumps (use a whisk if required).
4. Season with salt and seasonings if desired.
5. Cook for 5 to 8 minutes, stirring/whisking often until the sauce has thickened to a cream consistency. You should be able to trace a line with your finger until the sauce has coated the back of a wooden spoon.
6. Remove from the heat, add the cheese, and swirl to combine (the cheese does not need to melt).
7. Season with salt to taste.

Assembling:

1. Pour the sauce over the macaroni in the oven. Stir fast, and then return to the skillet (as I did) or a baking dish to cool (Note 4). Cover with a breadcrumb topping.
2. Bake for 25 minutes, or until the top layer is golden brown. If you bake it for so long, the sauce will be cooked out!
3. Serve right away! I added a sprig of fresh parsley to mine.

Nutrition: Calories: 551. **Carbs:** 48 g. **Protein:** 23 g. **Fat:** 29 g. **Potassium:** 326 mg. **Fiber:** 1 g. **Sugar:** 8 g. **Vitamin A:** 915IU. **Vitamin C:** 0. 2 mg. **Calcium:** 449 mg. **Iron:** 1.4 mg. **Saturated Fat:** 17 g. **Cholesterol:** 89 mg. **Sodium:** 847 mg.

274. Apple Bread

Preparation Time: 20 minutes
Cooking Time: 45 minutes
Servings: 16
Ingredients:

- 4 big Granny Smith, Haralson, or Honey crisp apples, peeled (or another firm, tart apple variety)
- 2 cup sugar
- ½ cup vegetable oil
- 2 eggs (large)
- 2 tsp. pure vanilla extract

113

- 1 cup raisins (or sliced dates)
- 3 cup flour (all-purpose)
- 1 tsp. baking powder
- ½ tsp. baking soda
- 1 tbsp. salt (kosher)
- 1 tsp. cinnamon
- ½ tsp. nutmeg

Optional:
- 1 cup diced roasted pecans or walnuts

Directions:
1. Preheat oven to 350° F. Two 8" x 4" loaf pans, greased and floured removed from the equation.
2. Shred the apples on a box grater with the big gaps (discard the cores). You'll need 4 cups of apple grated.
3. Combine the shredded apples and sugar in a big mixing bowl and set aside for 15 minutes, or until the sugar has dissolved. There would be a significant amount of liquid.
4. Stir together the oil, eggs, vanilla extract, pecans, and raisins.
5. Combine flour, baking powder, baking soda, salt, cinnamon, and nutmeg in a medium mixing pot. Only combine the dry ingredients with the apple mixture.
6. Pour into loaf pans that have been lined with parchment paper.
7. Bake for 55 minutes, or until golden brown and a toothpick inserted in the middle comes out clean. Remove the pans from the oven and place them on a cooling rack to cool for 10 minutes. Then remove the bread from the pan and place them on a cooling rack to cool fully before slicing.

Nutrition: Calories: 330. **Total Fat:** 8 g. **Saturated Fat:** 1 g. **Trans Fat:** 0 g. **Unsaturated Fat:** 7 g. **Cholesterol:** 23 mg. **Sodium:** 288 mg. **Fiber:** 3 g. **Carbs:** 62 g. **Sugar:** 39 g. **Protein:** 4 g.

275. Sausage Patties for Morning

Preparation Time: 5 minutes
Cooking Time: 45 minutes
Servings: 4
Ingredients:
- 1 lb. ground pork (85 percent lean)
- Diamond crystal 1 tsp. kosher salt
- ½ tsp. freshly ground black pepper
- 1 tsp. powdered garlic
- 1 tbsp. paprika, smoked
- 1 tsp. thyme, dried
- ¼ tsp. cayenne pepper
- 1 tbsp. extra virgin olive oil

Directions:
1. In a medium mixing dish, combine the ground pork and spices with your fingertips. Shape the mixture into eight balls, and then force each ball into ½-inch-thick patties, each weighing 2 oz.

2. To make a shallow dimple, gently drive your thumb into the center of each patty. This keeps the patties from falling apart when they cook.
3. In a big (14-inch) nonstick skillet, heat the oil for 2 minutes over medium-high heat. To coat, swirl it about.
4. Preheat the skillet and place the patties in it (you might need to cook them in two batches). Cook for around 2 minutes a hand, or until they are browned and cooked through. The boiling point should also be 165° F. Place a thermometer horizontally into the patty and drive it into the center to verify the temperature.

Nutrition (2 patties): Calories: 275. **Carbs:** 1 g. **Protein:** 20 g. **Fat:** 21 g. **Saturated Fat:** 6 g. **Sodium:** 355 mg.

276. Baked Spinach and Tomato Eggs Recipe

Preparation Time: 10 minutes
Cooking Time: 45 minutes
Servings: 4
Ingredients:
- ½ lb. thawed frozen spinach
- ⅛ tsp. powdered garlic
- ⅛ tsp. red pepper flakes, optional
- Salt and pepper
- 2 medium Roma tomatoes
- 4 large eggs
- 2 tbsp. cream or half and half
- ½ cup shredded cheese
- ½ onion chopped

Directions:
1. Preheat the oven to 400° F. Usage a 2-quart casserole dish with nonstick spray or butter. Thaw the spinach and suck out as much moisture as possible (no need to go crazy; just make sure it's not dripping).
2. Place the tomatoes in the bottom of the casserole bowl, cut them into chunks. Scatter the spinach over the onions. Garlic powder, red pepper flakes, a touch of salt, and freshly crushed pepper are sprinkled over the tomatoes and spinach (about 5 cranks of a pepper mill).
3. On top of the spinach and onions, crack the shells. Drizzle the cream over the whole bowl, then sprinkle the melted cheese on top. Bake for 15 to 20 minutes, or until the whites are opaque but still warm and moist in the middle (they should jiggle slightly when you shake the dish). Cooking times can vary depending on the size and shape of the bowl, so start testing for doneness after 15 minutes.

Nutrition: Calories: 181.95. **Carbs:** 5.23 g. **Protein:** 12.25 g. **Fat:** 12.98 g. **Sodium:** 539.83 mg. **Fiber:** 2.53 g.

277. Firehouse Haluski

Preparation Time: 25 minutes
Cooking Time: 45 minutes
Servings: 6

Ingredients:

- 1 kluski noodle kit (12 oz.)
- 2 cabbage heads, peeled and sliced into bite-size bits
- 1 chopped onion
- ¼ cup water
- ¼ cup vegetable oil
- 1-lb. minced kielbasa sausage
- 1 tbsp. mustard seeds
- Salt and freshly ground black pepper to taste
- 4 broken eggs

Directions:

1. Cook kluski noodles until tender in a big pot of lightly salted water for around 8 minutes. Drain and set aside the noodles, which can be chopped into small fragments.
2. In a big pot with enough water to cover, cook cabbage and onion until tender, around 8 to 10 minutes.
3. In a big skillet over medium heat, heat vegetable oil and add cabbage and onion with a slotted spoon. Cook for about 10 minutes in the hot oil before the vegetables begin to brown; stir in the kielbasa and cook until sausage is cooked through. Season with salt and black pepper to taste and stir mustard seeds into cabbage mixture. In a large mixing bowl, combine the chopped kluski and the rest of the ingredients.
4. Pour the eggs over the noodle mixture and stir for 3 to 5 minutes, or until the eggs are fixed.

Nutrition: **Calories:** 722. **Protein:** 27.5 g. **Carbs:** 68.5 g. **Dietary Fiber:** 12.6 g. **Sugars:** 17 g. **Fat:** 38.8 g. **Saturated Fat:** 14.1 g. **Cholesterol:** 225.1 mg. **Vitamin A:** 584.4IU. **Niacin Equivalents:** 8.9 mg. **Vitamin B6:** 0.7 mg. **Vitamin C:** 146.8 mg. **Folate:** 322.2 mcg. **Calcium:** 213.3 mg. **Iron:** 5 mg. **Magnesium:** 93. 1 mg. **Potassium:** 918 mg. **Sodium:** 752.7 mg. **Thiamin:** 0.8 mg.

278. Cornbread Tamale Pie

Preparation Time: 10 minutes
Cooking Time: 45 minutes
Servings: 6

Ingredients:

- 1 lb. minced beef
- 1 medium thinly sliced onion
- 1 cup rinsed and drained dried black beans
- 1 cup corn, dried or frozen, drained (thawed if frozen)
- 1 quart of tomato sauce
- 1 cup broth (beef or chicken)
- 1 tbsp. powdered chile
- ½ tsp. cumin powder
- ½ tsp. salt, plus more salt to taste
- ¼ tsp. black pepper, plus salt and pepper to taste

- ⅓ cup cornmeal
- 1 tbsp. flour
- 1 tbsp. sugar
- ½ tbsp. baking powder
- A single egg
- ⅓ cup milk
- 1 tbsp. (vegetable oil)
- 1/8 tsp cinnamon

Optional:

- ½ cup diced green bell pepper

Directions:

1. Preheat the oven to 400 ° F. Using cooking sauce, grease a 3-quart high-sided casserole bowl. Cook the beef and onion in a large skillet over medium-high heat until the steak is brown and the onion is translucent for about 10 minutes. The beans, maize, tomato sauce, broth, bell pepper (if using), chili powder, cumin, 1 tsp. cinnamon, and ¼ tsp. black pepper are then included. Cook for 15 minutes on low heat. Remove from the equation.
2. Whisk together the cornmeal, flour, sugar, baking powder, and tsp. salt in a medium mixing dish.
3. Whisk together the egg, milk, and oil in a small mixing
4. Bowl until well mixed. In a separate bowl, whisk together the milk and flour until well mixed. Cover the meat mixture with the cornbread topping and place it in the casserole bowl. The topping will melt into the meat mixture but will rise and create a coating of cornbread during baking. Cook for 20 to 25 minutes, or until the cornbread is golden brown.

Nutrition: **Calories:** 445 24. **Fat:** 7 g. **Saturated Fat: Trans- Fat:** 1 g. **Monounsaturated Fat:** 12 g. **Polyunsaturated Fat:** 3 g. **Sodium:** 678 mg. **Carbs:** 37 g. **Dietary Fiber:** 5 g. **Sugars:** 8 g. **Protein:** 21 g.

279. Cheesy Stuffed Baked Potatoes

Preparation Time: 15 minutes
Cooking Time: 45 minutes
Servings: 6

Ingredients:

- 3 baked potatoes, big (1 lb. each)
- ½ cup green onions, diced
- ½ cup cubed butter (divided)
- ½ cup milk (half-and-half)
- ½ cup sour cream
- 1 tsp. kosher salt
- ¼ tsp. white pepper
- 1 cup cheddar cheese, shredded
- Take paprika to increase the taste

Optional:

- 1 ½ tsp. canola oil

Directions:

1.   Potatoes should be scrubbed and pierced. If needed, rub with oil. Preheat oven to 400° F and bake for 50 to 75 minutes, or until vegetables are tender. Break the potatoes in half lengthwise until they are cold enough to handle. Remove the pulp with a spoon, leaving a thin shell behind; set aside.

2.   Sauté onions in ¼ cup butter in a shallow skillet until tender. Mash the potato pulp in a big mixing tub. Combine the onion mixture, milk, sour cream, salt, and pepper in a mixing bowl. Add the cheese and fold it in. Fill potato shells halfway with the mixture. Bake the cookies by placing them on a baking sheet. Drizzle the rest of the butter on top of the potatoes.

3.   Paprika should be sprinkled on top. Preheat oven to 375° F and bake for 20 minutes, or until thoroughly heated.

Nutrition: Calories: 416. **Fat:** 26 g. **Saturated Fat:** 17 g. **Cholesterol:** 84 mg. **Sodium:** 693 mg. **Carbs:** 36 g. **Sugar:** 4 g. **Fiber:** 3 g. **Protein:** 9 g.

280. Casserole for Breakfast

Preparation Time: 10 minutes
Cooking Time: 45 minutes
Servings: 12
Ingredients:

* 2 lb. pork sausage
* A dozen eggs
* 1 cup sour cream (light or regular)
* Salt and pepper
* ¼ cup milk
* 4 onions (green)
* ½ cup green bell pepper, chopped
* ½ red bell pepper, chopped
* 2 cups shredded cheddar cheese
* 1 1/2 cup yogurt

Directions:

1.   Preheat the oven to 350° F. Spray a 9x13" pan with cooking spray.

2.   In a big mixing cup, whisk together the eggs, sour cream, yogurt, cheese, and salt and pepper. Electric mixers can be used to blend the ingredients at low speed.

3.   Over medium heat, heat a big skillet. Heat the sausage until it is browned, breaking it up with a wooden spoon as it cooks. Remove the sausage from the casing and place it in the bowl with the egg mixture.

4.   In the same skillet where the sausage was prepared, add the bell peppers and onion and cook for 2 to 3 minutes. Stir all together in the mixing bowl with the eggs.

5.   Bake for 35 to 50 minutes, or until the sides are set and the middle is just slightly jiggly, in a greased 9x13" tray.

6.   Leftover egg casserole can be kept in the fridge for 3 to 4 days and eaten. Microwaving leftovers is a delicious way to reheat them.

Nutrition: Calories: 385. **Carbs:** 2 g. **Protein:** 23 g. **Fat:** 30 g. **Saturated Fat:** 12 g. **Cholesterol:** 239 mg. **Sodium:** 669 mg. **Potassium:** 327 mg. sugar: 1 g. **Vitamin A:** 705 IU. 11. **Vitamin C:** 6 mg. **Calcium:** 194 mg. **Iron:** 1.8 mg.

281. Toasted Eggs and Avocado Recipe

Preparation Time: 5 minutes
Cooking Time: 45 minutes
Servings: 4
Ingredients:

* 4 big eggs
* 4 slices hearty whole-grain bread
* 1 avocado, mashed
* ½ tsp. salt
* ¼ tsp. black pepper
* ¼ cup pure Greek yogurt (nonfat)

Directions:

1.   To poach each egg, fill a 1-cup microwaveable bowl or teacup halfway with water. Crack an egg gently into the water, ensuring that it is fully submerged. Microwave on high for around 1 minute, or until the white is set and the yolk is beginning to set but still tender, covered with a saucer (not runny).

2.   Toast the bread and spread ¼ of the mashed avocado on each slice.

3.   If necessary, season the avocado with salt and pepper. A poached egg should be placed on top of each plate. 1 tbsp. Greek yogurt on top of the egg.

Nutrition: Calories: 250. **Total Fat:** 12 g. **Saturated Fat:** 3 g. **Trans Fat:** 0 g. **Cholesterol:** 185 mg. **Sodium:** 380 mg. **Total Carbs:** 26 g. **Dietary Fiber:** 9 g. **Total Sugars:** 4 g. **Protein:** 12 g. Potassium: 330 mg. **Phosphorus:** 240 mg.

Brunch

282. Holiday Brunch Casserole (Grits Casserole)

Preparation Time: 10 minutes
Cooking Time: 45 minutes
Servings: 4
Ingredients:

- 4 cups water
- 1 cup grits
- ½ tbsp. salt & paprika
- 1 lb. sausage
- ½ cup margarine
- ¼ lbs. garlic cheese (put 1 tbsp. garlic on white cheese)
- ½ cup milk
- 3 eggs

Directions:

1. Preheat the oven at 190° C or 375° F.
2. Fry and drain the sausage. Cook the grits in boiling salted water for 5 minutes.
3. Stir margarine and cheese until it melts before adding milk, eggs, and sausages, and mixing them properly. Pour it inside an 11 -3/4 x 9-3/8 x 1-1/2 " aluminum pan.
4. Bake the mixture at 177° C or 350° F for 30 to 45 minutes.
5. Spread paprika over the casserole and cover it with foil.

Nutrition: Calories: 403.2. **Carbs:** 16.8 g. **Protein:** 16.5 g.

283. The Formula for Turkish Menemen

Preparation Time: 10 minutes
Cooking Time: 45 minutes
Servings: 2
Ingredients:

- 4 eggs, whole
- 1-inch ginger, finely chopped
- 4 garlic cloves, peeled with sliced thinly
- A single onion (thinly sliced)
- 2 blanched tomatoes, skin peeled and chopped
- ½ cup pureed tomatoes (homemade)
- ½ finely chopped red bell pepper (Capsicum)
- ½ finely chopped yellow bell pepper (Capsicum)
- 2 tsp. powdered paprika
- 1 tsp. dry oregano
- 1 tsp. black peppercorns, field
- 1 tsp. powdered cumin (Jeera)
- Salt, to taste
- To roast, you'll need extra virgin olive oil.
- 2 sprigs finely chopped chives

Directions:

1. To start, chop all of the materials and set them aside.
2. Blanch the tomatoes for 30 seconds in a saucepan with boiling water, or before the skin breaks open.
3. To cool the tomatoes, drain the water and wash them under running water. Remove the skins from the tomatoes and cut them into tiny bits.
4. Heat a saucepan over medium heat, drizzle with oil, then add the sliced ginger and garlic and cook until softened.
5. Add the sliced onions and continue to sauté until the onions are finely orange. Sauté the yellow and red bell peppers until they are mildly crunchy.
6. After that, add the blanched tomatoes and continue to sauté for another 2 minutes.
7. Tomato puree, paprika powder, oregano, pepper powder, cumin powder, and salt may also be added.
8. Mix all together and cook on low heat until the tomatoes are soft. One by one, crack the eggs in.
9. For a few seconds, do not interrupt the egg. Later, gently transfer the eggs with a spatula and allow them to blend into the tomato mixture. You can also switch the pan around to cook the eggs until they are soft and fried on low heat.
10. When the Turkish Menemen is ready, cover it with chopped chives and serve immediately.
11. For your morning breakfast, serve the Menemen recipe with freshly baked Focaccia bread, fresh fruits, and coffee on the side.

Nutrition: Calories: 403.2. **Carbs:** 16.8 g. **Protein:** 16.5 g.

284. Olive Oil Zucchini Bread

Preparation Time: 15 minutes
Cooking Time: 45 minutes
Servings: One 8-inch loaf
Ingredients:

- Butter for the pan
- ½ cup (185 g) zucchini, grated
- ⅓ cup (140 g) medium brown sugar
- ⅓ cup (80 mL) olive oil (or other oil such as safflower or canola)
- ⅓ cup (80 mL) plain Greek yogurt
- 2 large eggs
- 1 tsp. (5 mL) extract de vanilla
- ½ (190 g) cup all-purpose flour
- ½ tsp. (3 g) salt
- ¼ tsp. (3 g) baking soda
- ½ tsp. (2 g) baking powder
- ½ tsp. (4 g) cinnamon powder

- ¼ tsp. (1 g) nutmeg powder
- 1 tsp. (2 g) finely grated lemon zest
- ½ cup (55 g) sliced walnuts (optional)

Directions:

1. Preheat the oven to 350° F. Using butter, grease an 8-inch loaf tray.
2. Using a rubber spatula, combine the grated zucchini, butter, olive oil, yogurt, eggs, and vanilla extract in a big mixing cup.
3. In a separate dish, combine the flour, salt, baking soda, nutmeg, baking powder, lemon zest, and spices. In a broad mixing dish, mix together the dry and wet materials. For use, fold in the walnuts.
4. Bake for 40 to 55 minutes, turning the pan halfway through baking, in the prepared loaf pan. When a toothpick placed in the center comes out clean, the bread is finished.
5. Allow cooling for 10 minutes on a wire rack. Before cutting and serving, remove the bread from the pan and cool entirely on a rack.

285. Dutch Baby

Preparation Time: 15 minutes
Cooking Time: 45 minutes
Servings: 4
Ingredients:

- 3 eggs
- ½ cup flour
- ½ cup milk
- ½ tsp. sugar
- A pinch of nutmeg
- 4 tbsp. butter, unsalted
- Syrup, preserves, confectioners' sugar, or cinnamon sugar are some of the options.

Directions:

1. Preheat the oven to 425° F (200° C).
2. Combine the eggs, flour, milk, sugar, and nutmeg in a blender tub and mix until smooth. Hand-mixing the batter is also an option.
3. In a heavy 10-inch pan or baking bowl, melt the butter in the microwave. Add the butter to the pan as soon as the butter has melted (be careful not to burn it). Come back to the pan to the oven for another 20 minutes, just until the pancake is golden and puffy. Reduce the oven temperature to 300° F and bake for another 5 minutes.
4. Remove the pancake from the oven, slice it into wedges, and serve immediately with honey, preserves, confectioners' sugar, or cinnamon sugar on top.

Nutrition: Calories: 403.2. **Carbs:** 16.8 g. **Protein:** 16.5 g.

286. Muesli

Preparation Time: 10 minutes
Cooking Time: 45 minutes

Servings: 16
Ingredients:

- 4 ½ cup oats, rolled
- ½ cup wheat germ, toasted
- ½ cup bran (wheat)
- ½ cup bran oats
- 1 cup raisins
- ½ cup walnuts, diced
- ¼ cup brown sugar, packed
- ¼ cup sunflower seeds, raw

Directions:

1. In a big mixing cup, combine the oats, wheat germ, wheat bran, oat bran, dried fruit, almonds, sugar, and nuts. Make a rigorous mix. Muesli should be kept in an airtight bag. It has a two-month shelf life when held at room temperature.

Nutrition: Calories: 188.2. **Protein:** 6.1 g. **Carbs:** 31.8 g. **Dietary Fiber:** 4.8 g. **Sugars:** 9.4 g. **Fat:** 5.7 g. **Saturated Fat:** 0.7 g. **Vitamin A:** 5.71U. **Niacin Equivalents:** 2.5 mg. **Vitamin B6:** 0.2 mg. **Vitamin C:** 0.5 mg. **Foliate:** 31.9 mcg. **Calcium:** 29.2 mg. **Iron:** 2. 1 mg. **Magnesium:** 77 mg. **Potassium:** 257 mg. **Sodium:** 3.9 mg. **Thiamin:** 0.3 mg.

287. Blueberry Baked Oatmeal

Preparation Time: 10 minutes
Cooking Time: 45 minutes
Servings: 6
Ingredients:

- ⅔ cup pecans, finely chopped
- 2 cups oats, old-fashioned
- 2 ½ cups all purpose flour
- 2 tsp. cinnamon powder from Frontier Co-op
- 1 tsp. baking soda, powder
- ½ tsp. daily table salt (or ¾ tsp. fine-grain sea salt)
- ¼ tsp. ground nutmeg from Frontier Co-op
- 1 ¾ cup milk of choice (almond milk, coconut milk, oat milk, or cow's milk are all good options)
- ⅓ cup maple syrup or honey
- 2 eggs (large or flax)
- 3 tbsp. unsalted butter or coconut oil, heated, separated
- 2 tsp. vanilla bean extraction
- 2 tsp. raw sugar
- 12 oz. or 1 pint fresh or frozen blueberries (or 2 ½ cups of your favorite berry/fruit, diced into 1/2" pieces if necessary) (optional)

Optional toppings:

- Fresh strawberries, plain/vanilla yogurt or ice cream, additional maple syrup, or honey for drizzling.

Directions:

1. Preheat oven to 375° F. A 9-inch square baking dish should be greased. Pour the nuts onto a rimmed

baking sheet until the oven has stopped preheating. 4 to 5 minutes, or before fragrant.

2. Combine the oats, toasted almonds, cinnamon, baking powder, flour, and nutmeg in a medium mixing cup. To mix the ingredients, whisk them together.

3. Combine the milk, maple syrup or honey, egg, half of the butter or coconut oil, and vanilla in a smaller mixing cup. Blend all together so it's smooth. (If you used coconut oil and it solidified as it came into contact with the cold ingredients, microwave the bowl for 30 seconds at a time before the coconut oil melts.)

4. ½ cup of the berries should be saved for covering the baked oatmeal, and the rest should be uniformly distributed over the bottom of the baking dish (no need to defrost frozen fruit first). Drizzle the wet ingredients over the oats after covering the fruit with the dry oat mixture. Wiggle the baking dish to ensure the milk gets all the way down to the oats, then gently pat down any dry oats that have risen to the tip.

5. The remaining berries should be strewn over the top. If you like a little more flavor and crunch, sprinkle some raw sugar on top.

6. Preheat the oven to 425° F and continue cooking for 42 to 45 minutes, until the golden brown is in the highest part. Allow your baked oatmeal to cool for a few minutes after removing it from the oven. Until serving, drizzle the remaining melted butter on top.

7. This baked oatmeal is best eaten hot, but it's also delicious at room temperature or chilled (I'll let you decide!). If packed, this oatmeal will last for 4 to 5 days in the refrigerator. Before serving, I literally reheat individual parts in the microwave.

Nutrition: Calories: 443. **Total Fat:** 15.7 g. **Saturated Fat:** 4.2 g. **Trans Fat:** 0 g. **Polyunsaturated Fat:** 3.7 g. **Monounsaturated Fat:** 6.7 g. **Cholesterol:** 57.9 mg. **Sodium:** 267.7 mg. **Total Carbs:** 67.7 g. **Dietary Fiber:** 14.6 g. **Sugars:** 9.6 g. **Protein:** 9.4 g. **Vitamin A:** 10 % **Magnesium:** 25 % **Potassium:** 12 % **Zinc:** 34 % **Phosphorus:** 30 % **Thiamin (B1):** 39 % **Riboflavin (B2):** 26 % **Niacin (B3):** 11 % **Vitamin B6:** 8 % **Folic Acid (B9):** 8 % **Vitamin B12:** 5 % **Vitamin E:** 17 % **Vitamin K:** 1 % **Vitamin C:** 4 % **Calcium:** 20 % **Iron:** 22 % **Vitamin D:** 8 %.

288. Berries With Hand Pies

Preparation Time: 15 minutes
Cooking Time: 45 minutes
Servings: 8 hand pies
Ingredients:
Dough requirements:
- Dusting with all-purpose flour
- Extra-Flaky Pie Crust is a single recipe.
- For the egg wash, gently beat 2 big eggs with a pinch of fine sea salt.
To make the filling:

- 2 cups healthy berries, such as sliced strawberries, whole blackberries, or blueberries (about 12 oz./350 grams)
- ½ cup brown sugar (100g)
- 2 tbsp. cornstarch
- 4 tsp. fresh lemon juice plus 1 tsp. freshly grated lemon zest
- 1 tsp. salt (pure)

Directions:
To prepare the dough:

1. On a floured surface, roll each dough disk into a 10-inch square that is around ⅛-inch thick. Cut four disks from each slice of dough with a 5-inch round cookie cutter. Refrigerate for at least 10 minutes after transferring disks to a baking sheet (it's fine if they overlap slightly).

To make the berry filling:

1. Combine the fruit, sugar, cornstarch, lemon zest and juice, and sea salt in a medium mixing cup. Put aside after carefully stirring until uniformly covered.

2. Remove the disks from the fridge and gently clean the egg wash along the edges of each disk. Cover each disk with around ¼ cup berry filling, leaving a 1-inch border around the bottom. (You might have some filling left over.)

3. Working with one disk at a time, carefully fold the other half of each round of dough over the filling to form a half-circle and seal the edges with your fingers, leaving one half of the dough on the baking sheet. Remove a few berries at a time before the hand pie seals quickly if some of the fillings is oozing out the edges. Crimp the rounded edge of each hand pie with a fork. Continue for the remaining disks.

4. Cover the hand pies in plastic wrap and chill for 1 hour to set the crusts. Keep the leftover egg wash refrigerated.

5. When you're about to bake, place a rack in the center of the oven and preheat to 425° F and use parchment paper, line a second baking sheet.

6. Remove the hand pies from the fridge and spray the remaining egg wash over the tops. Cut three narrow slits in the top of each hand pie with a paring knife to make steam vents. Place the hand pies on the baking sheet that has been lined. Bake for 20 to 25 minutes, or until the hand pies are golden brown and the filling is bubbling. Allow 10 minutes for cooling before serving wet.

7. The hand pies can be kept in an airtight jar in the refrigerator for up to 3 days after they have fully cooled.

289. A Recipe of Apple Crumble Cupcakes

Preparation Time: 10 minutes
Cooking Time: 45 minutes
Servings: 12
Ingredients:
Mixture for apples:

- 1 ²/₃ (200 g) cup diced apple
- 1 tbsp. brown sugar
- 1 tsp. cinnamon
- 1 tsp. nutmeg
- 1 tbsp. lemon zest, zest
- ½ lemon, juiced
- 1 tsp. extract de vanilla

Mixture for cupcakes:

- ²/₃ (150 g) cup melted unsalted butter
- ¹/₃ (150 g) cup brown sugar
- 1 ¼ (150 g) cup flour (all-purpose)
- 1 tsp. baking soda powder
- 1 tsp. corn flour
- 1 tsp. cinnamon,
- 1 tbsp. ground garlic
- 3 eggs

Mixture for crumbles:

- 1 tbsp. all-purpose flour
- 2 tbsp. oats
- 1 tbsp. brown sugar
- 1 tbsp. unsalted butter
- Whipped cream as a topping

Directions:

1. Heat the oven to 160° C (320° F).
2. In a medium saucepan, combine the apple, sugar, cinnamon, nutmeg, lemon zest, vanilla extract, and half a lemon juice and cook, stirring occasionally, until smooth and fragrant.
3. To make a paste, mash the ingredients together. Allow cooling fully before using.
4. Cream the butter and brown sugar together with a hand mixer in a large mixing bowl, smoothing out with a wooden spoon if required.
5. Inside a large saucepan mix together with the flour, corn flour, baking powder, cinnamon, and ground cloves until well balanced.
6. One of the eggs should be added and mixed in. To make the batter, repeat the process 2 more times before all 3 eggs are thoroughly integrated. Combine the apple mixture and fold it in.
7. Fill a muffin pan with cupcake liners and bake the cupcakes. Fill about halfway with water. Bake for 30 to 35 minutes. Allow cooling.
8. Rub the starch, peas, brown sugar, and butter along with your fingertips in a shallow dish just before crumbling forms. Toast for 5 to 10 minutes in a small tin under the oven, until golden brown.
9. Whipped cream and crumble blend go on top of the cupcakes.
10. At last, it is ready for serving.

Nutrition: Calories: 269. **Fat:** 18 g. **Carbs:** 24 g. **Fiber:** 1 g. **Sugar:** 11 g. **Protein:** 3 g.

290. A Recipe of Caramelized Onions in the Oven

Preparation Time: 10 minutes
Cooking Time: 45 minutes
Servings: 6
Ingredients:

- 4 big thickly cut yellow onions
- 4 garlic cloves, sliced and crushed
- 4 thyme sprigs, new
- 1 or 2 tbsp. light brown sugar
- 5 tbsp. olive oil,
- Kosher salt, and freshly ground black pepper
- 1 tsp. Worcestershire sauce (optional)
- 1 tbsp. balsamic vinegar (optional)

Directions:

1. Preheat oven to 375° F.
2. Toss onions. In a broad, rimmed sheet pan, combine onions, garlic, and thyme. Season generously with salt and pepper, then sprinkle with brown sugar and drizzle with 5 tbsp. of oil. Combine all of the ingredients in a large mixing bowl and toss until finely covered.
3. Cover the plate with foil and roast for 25 minutes, flipping halfway through the cooking time. Remove the onions from the oven and continue to cook for another 25 to 35 minutes, or until softened and golden in color, flipping them 2 to 3 times while cooking. Switch the oven to broil and broil for 5 minutes if you want a darker color. Keep an eye on the onions as they will quickly burn!!
4. Take away the pan from the oven and discard the thyme sprigs. For use, brush onions with Worcestershire sauce and/or balsamic vinegar. Toss all together.
5. Serve with taste and season with salt and pepper as needed.

Nutrition: Calories: 178. Carbs: 12 g. **Protein:** 1 g. **Fat:** 14 g. **Saturated Fat:** 1 g. **Sodium:** 15 mg. **Potassium:** 162 mg. **Fiber:** 1 g. **Sugar:** 6 g. **Vitamin A:** 30IU. **Vitamin C:** 9.1 mg. **Calcium:** 29 mg. **Iron:** 0.5 mg.

291. Tart With Goat Cheese & Roasted Peppers

Preparation Time: 15 minutes
Cooking Time: 45 minutes
Servings: 2, double for 4
Ingredients:

- 75 g soft goat's cheese
- 1 (15 mL) cider vinegar sachet
- 20 g of rocket
- 3 potatoes, white
- 150 g puff pastry
- 1 pepper, yellow
- 1 pepper, red

You'll also need:

- Olive oil, pepper, salt, vegetable oil

Directions:

1.   Preheat the oven to 220° C/425° F/Gas 7
2.   Remove the seeds and pith from the peppers with a teaspoon and cut into thin strips (as finely as you can)
3.   Using a drizzle of olive oil and a sprinkle of salt, toss the pepper strips on a baking tray.
4.   Bake for 10 minutes, or until the peppers start to soften.
5.   Meanwhile, carve the potatoes into small disks (skins on). Using a separate baking dish, drizzle the disks with a generous amount of vegetable oil and season with salt and pepper.
6.   Bake for 20 to 25 minutes or until golden and fluffy (these are your crispy potatoes).
7.   When the potatoes are cooking, unroll the puff pastry and break it into 2 [4] squares. Place the pastry squares on a baking sheet lined with nonstick baking paper (the size of a baking tray)
8.   With a knife, score a 1cm border across the outside of the pastry and poke the inside of the border all over with a fork (to avoid a soggy bottom!)
9.   Delete the peppers from the oven until they have softened. Place the softened peppers in the center of the pastry squares and move them to a baking tray (on the baking paper).
10.   To save time and effort, use the same baking tray that the peppers were in.
11.   Bake for 15 minutes, or until the pastry is golden and crisp and the sides are puffed up (your roasted pepper tarts are ready).
12.   Create the dressing by adding the cider vinegar, 2 tbsp. [4 tbsp.] olive oil, and a pinch of salt and pepper while the tarts are baking. Crumble the goat's cheese into little fragments that can be eaten.
13.   After cleaning the rocket, pat it dry with kitchen paper.
14.   Season the tarts with black pepper and top with crumbled goats' cheese.
15.   With the fried potatoes and a pinch of the rocket on the table, serve the roasted pepper and goats' cheese tarts.
16.   Wear the rocket with the dressing.
17.   Have fun!

Nutrition: Calories: 544. **Fat:** 26.0 g. (of which saturates 13.9 g.) **Carbs:** 67.1 g. (of which sugars 8.2 g.) **Fiber:** 7.1 g. **Protein:** 14.1 g. **Salt:** 0.72 g.

Appetizers, Snacks, and Bun

292. Corn Pudding

Preparation Time: 1 hour 5 minutes
Cooking Time: 45 minutes
Servings: 4
Ingredients:

- ¼ cup sugar
- 3 tbsp. all-purpose flour
- 2 tsp. baking powder
- 2 tsp. table salt
- 6 large eggs
- 2 cups heavy cream
- ½ cup melted butter
- 6 cups corn kernels (fresh or frozen)
- Olive oil cooking spray

Directions:

1. Preheat a convection oven to almost 350° F. Take a bowl and mix salt, flour, sugar, and baking powder. Keep it aside.
2. Take another mixing bowl and whisk eggs, melted butter, and cream. Slowly add salt mixture and whisk to make them smooth.
3. Pour this mixture into a greased baking dish and bake for almost 40 to 45 minutes in a preheated convection oven.
4. Let this mixture turn golden and leave for almost 5 minutes. Serve hot or cold.

Nutrition: Calories: 704. **Protein:** 12.15 g. **Fat:** 55.51 g. **Carbs:** 47.83 g.

293. Roasted Pumpkin Seeds

Preparation Time: 15 minutes
Cooking Time: 45 minutes
Servings: 4
Ingredients:

- 1 tbsp. vegetable oil
- 1 medium pumpkin
- Salt, to taste

Directions:

1. Slice the top of the pumpkin, then scoop out pulp and seeds from it and add to a colander. Separate the pulp and strings from the seeds. Rinse the seeds and dry them.
2. Add seeds to the baking pan in one layer. Position the baking pan in rack position 2 and select the Bake setting.
3. Set the temperature to 300° F and the time to 30 minutes. Toss seeds with salt and oil in a bowl—Bake for 20 more minutes. Serve.

Nutrition: Calories: 421. **Fat:** 21 g. **Carbs:** 37 g. **Protein:** 21 g.

294. Baked Cheesy Eggplant

Preparation Time: 7 minutes
Cooking Time: 45 minutes
Servings: 4
Ingredients:

- 1 clove garlic, sliced
- 1 large eggplant
- 1 tbsp. olive oil
- 1 tbsp. olive oil plus 2 ½ tsp. olive oil
- ¼ cup dry bread crumbs
- ¼ cup and 2 tbsp. ricotta cheese
- ¼ cup grated Parmesan cheese
- ¼ cup water
- ¼ tsp. red pepper flakes
- ½ cup prepared marinara sauce
- 2 tbsp. shredded Pepper Jack cheese
- Salt and black pepper, to taste

Directions:

1. Cut eggplant crosswise into 5 pieces.
2. Peel and chop 2 pieces into ½-inch cubes.
3. Lightly grease a sauté pan with 1 tbsp. olive oil, heat oil for 5 minutes over medium heat.
4. Add eggplant strips and cook for 2 minutes per side.
5. Transfer to a plate. Add 1½ tsp. olive oil and add garlic. Cook for 1 minute.
6. Add chopped eggplants.
7. Season with pepper flakes and salt, then cook for 4 minutes.
8. Lower heat to medium-low. And continue cooking eggplants until soft, around 8 minutes more.
9. Stir in water and marinara sauce.
10. Cook for 7 minutes until heated through, stirring now and then.
11. Transfer to a bowl. In another bowl, whisk well black pepper, salt, Pepper Jack cheese, Parmesan cheese, and ricotta.
12. Evenly spread cheeses over eggplant strips and then fold in half.
13. Lay folded eggplant in baking pan. Pour the marinara sauce on top.
14. In a small bowl, whisk well 1 tsp. olive oil and bread crumbs and sprinkle all over the sauce.
15. Place the baking pan in the oven. Select Bake mode and bake for 15 minutes at 390° F until tops are lightly browned.
16. Serve and enjoy.

Nutrition: Calories: 405. **Fat:** 21.4 g. **Protein:** 12.7 g.

295. Onion Strudel

Preparation Time: 8 minutes
Cooking Time: 45 minutes
Servings: 5
Ingredients:

- 12 sheets phyllo dough
- 3 tbsp. olive oil
- 1 egg

- 1 lb. mushrooms, diced
- 1 medium onion, diced
- 3 tbsp. butter
- 1 tbsp. dry sherry
- 1 tbsp. all-purpose flour
- Leaves from 1 sprig of thyme
- 6 tbsp. freshly grated Parmesan cheese
- Salt and pepper, to taste

Directions:
1. Preheat the oven to 400° F.
2. Line a baking sheet with parchment paper and set it aside.
3. Pour oil into a skillet on medium heat and sauté diced onion and mushrooms for about 7 minutes.
4. Add sherry and cook for another 3 minutes.
5. Mix in the flour, thyme, salt, and pepper and remove from heat.
6. Melt butter in a small sauté pan. Brush one-half of the phyllo sheet lengthwise with butter.
7. Fold the side with butter over the side without and smooth out any wrinkles or bubbles.
8. Again, brush one-half of the phyllo with butter, and fold the unbuttered side over it again.
9. Place one spoonful of mushroom filling at the end of the column and sprinkle Parmesan cheese on top.
10. Fold a corner over the filling to create a triangle shape and keep folding over triangles (like folding a flag).
11. Beat the egg and brush it over the strudel triangle.
12. Repeat for as many strudels that will fit on a baking sheet.
13. Select Bake mode and bake for 15 minutes.
14. When finished, transfer to a plate and serve hot.

Nutrition: Calories: 312. **Fat:** 19.2 g. **Carbs:** 25.9 g. **Protein:** 11.1 g.

296. Parmesan Baked Onion

Preparation Time: 6 minutes
Cooking Time: 45 minutes
Servings: 6
Ingredients:
- 1 (20-oz.) bag hash browns, shredded
- 3 green onions
- ½ cup grated Parmesan cheese
- 1 tsp. kosher salt
- ½ tsp. black pepper
- 2 tbsp. olive oil

Directions:
1. Chop the green onions.
2. Preheat oven to 350° F.
3. Combine hash browns, cheese, onion, salt, and pepper in a large bowl.
4. Drizzle olive oil over the mixture and toss with a fork.

5. Grease a muffin tin and spoon mixture into the tin.
6. Pack mixture into each cup by pushing it down with the rounded side of the spoon.
7. Select Bake mode. Bake for 1 hour, 15 minutes.
8. Serve warm.

Nutrition: Calories: 325. **Fat:** 18.7 g. **Carbs:** 34.2 g. **Protein:** 6.2 g.

297. Garlic Kale Chips

Preparation Time: 7 minutes
Cooking Time: 45 minutes
Servings: 2
Ingredients:
- 4 cups kale, torn into 1-inch pieces
- 1 tbsp. olive oil
- ¼ tsp. pepper
- ¼ tsp. garlic powder
- Salt, to taste

Directions:
1. Preheat the oven to 350° F.
2. In a bowl, add all the listed ingredients, and toss well.
3. Pour into a baking pan and place the pan in the oven.
4. Select Bake mode and bake for 10 minutes.
5. When the timer goes off, remove from the oven to a bowl and serve hot.

Nutrition: Calories: 128. **Fat:** 7.0 g. **Carbs:** 14.4 g. **Protein:** 4.1 g.

298. Pita Chips

Preparation Time: 6 minutes
Cooking Time: 45 minutes
Servings: 1
Ingredients:
- 1 whole-wheat pita
- 1 tsp. olive oil
- Salt, to taste

Directions:
1. Preheat the oven to 375° F.
2. Brush both sides of the pita with oil and sprinkle with salt.
3. Cut pita into 6 wedges.
4. Place the pita on a baking sheet (ungreased) and bake for 8 minutes.
5. Enjoy.

Nutrition: Calories: 210. **Fat:** 6.3 g. **Carbs:** 35.2 g. **Protein:** 6.3 g.

299. Almond Onion Rings

Preparation Time: 7 minutes
Cooking Time: 45 minutes
Servings: 3
Ingredients:
- ½ cup almond flour

- ¾ cup coconut milk
- 1 large white onion, sliced into rings
- 1 egg, beaten
- 1 tbsp. baking powder
- 1 tbsp. smoked paprika
- Salt and pepper, to taste

Directions:
1. Preheat the oven for 5 minutes.
2. In a mixing bowl, mix the almond flour, baking powder, smoked paprika, salt, and pepper.
3. In another bowl, combine the egg and coconut milk.
4. Soak the onion slices into the egg mixture.
5. Dredge the onion slices in the almond flour mixture.
6. Pour into the oven basket.
7. Select Air Fry mode. Set temperature to 325° F, and set time to 15 minutes.
8. Select Start/Cancel to begin.
9. Shake the fryer basket for even cooking halfway through.
10. Serve hot.

Nutrition: Calories: 217. **Fat:** 17.9 g. **Carbs:** 9 g. **Protein:** 5.3 g.

300. Jicama Fries

Preparation Time: 7 minutes
Cooking Time: 45 minutes
Servings: 8
Ingredients:

- 1 tbsp. dried thyme
- ¾ cup arrowroot flour
- ½ large jicama
- 2 eggs
- Salt, to taste
- Cooking spray

Directions:
1. Slice jicama into fries.
2. In a bowl, whisk eggs together and pour over fries, then toss to coat.
3. Mix the salt, thyme, and arrowroot flour in another bowl.
4. Toss egg-coated jicama into the dry mixture, tossing to coat thoroughly.
5. Spray the oven basket with olive oil and add fries.
6. Select Air Fry mode. Set temperature to 350° F and set time to 5 minutes.
7. Toss halfway through the cooking process.
8. When the cooking time is complete, remove from the oven and rest for 5 minutes before serving.

Nutrition: Calories: 211. **Fat:** 19 g. **Carbs:** 1 g. **Protein:** 9 g.

301. Air Fried Chickpeas

Preparation Time: 11 minutes

Cooking Time: 45 minutes
Servings: 6
Ingredients:

- 1 (15-oz.) can of chickpeas, rinsed, drained and pat dried
- 1 tsp. olive oil
- 1 tbsp. dry Ranch seasoning mix

Directions:
1. Place the chickpeas onto a cooking tray and spread in an even layer.
2. Select Air Fry mode and then adjust the temperature to 390° F. Set the timer for 9 minutes and press Start.
3. Remove the chickpeas and drizzle them with oil and toss to coat thoroughly.
4. Return the cooking tray to the cooking chamber for 8 minutes more.
5. When cooking time is complete, remove the tray from the oven and transfer the chickpeas into a bowl.
6. Toss with the Ranch seasoning to coat thoroughly.
7. Rest for 10 minutes and serve cold.

Nutrition: Calories: 268. **Fat:** 5.1 g. **Carbs:** 43 g. **Protein:** 13.7 g.

Vegetables

302. Baked Cheesy Eggplant With Marinara

Preparation Time: 5 minutes
Cooking Time: 45 minutes
Servings: 4
Ingredients:

- 1 clove garlic, sliced
- 1 large eggplant
- 1 tbsp. olive oil
- ½ pinch salt, or as needed
- ¼ cup and 2 tbsp. dry bread crumbs
- ¼ cup and 2 tbsp. ricotta cheese
- ¼ cup grated Parmesan cheese
- ¼ cup water, plus more as needed
- ¼ tsp. red pepper flakes
- 1-½ cups prepared marinara sauce
- 1-½ tsp. olive oil
- 2 tbsp. shredded pepper jack cheese
- Salt and freshly ground black pepper to taste

Directions:

1. Cut eggplant crosswise into 5 pieces. Peel and chop 2 pieces into ½-inch cubes.
2. Lightly grease baking pan of air fryer with 1 tbsp. olive oil for 5 minutes, heat oil at 390° F. Add half eggplant strips and cook for 2 minutes per side. Transfer to a plate.
3. Add 1 ½ tsp olive oil and add garlic. Cook for a minute. Add chopped eggplants. Season with pepper flakes and salt. Cook for 4 minutes. Lower heat to 330° F and continue cooking eggplants until soft, around 8 minutes more.
4. Stir in water and marinara sauce. Cook for 7 minutes until heated through. Stirring every now and then. Transfer to a bowl.
5. In a bowl, whisk well pepper, salt, pepper jack cheese, Parmesan cheese, and ricotta. Evenly spread cheeses over eggplant strips and then fold in half.
6. Lay folded eggplant in baking pan. Pour the marinara sauce on top.
7. In a small bowl whisk well olive oil, and bread crumbs. Sprinkle all over the sauce.
8. Place the baking dish in the Air fryer oven cooking basket. Cook for 15 minutes at 390° F until tops are lightly browned.
9. Serve and enjoy.

Nutrition: Calories: 405 g. **Fat:** 21.4 g. **Protein:** 12.7 g. **Carbs:** 19.91 g.

303. Vegetable Fried Rice Frittata

Preparation Time: 5 minutes
Cooking Time: 45 minutes
Servings: 4

Ingredients:

- 4 cups cooked fried rice (I use half of a frozen vegetable fried rice box, 20 oz)
- 3 oz. cream canned mushroom soup (cream of chicken soup or other cream-style soup may be substituted, such as celery or potato)
- ½ cup diced vegetables (carrots, broccoli, corn, peas or a favorite; fresh, frozen, or canned)
- 4 big, lightly beaten eggs
- 1 tbsp. oil (olive or vegetable)
- Salt and pepper to taste, if desired (both the fried rice and soup are likely already quite salted)

Optional:

- ½ cup diced previously cooked protein (beans, chicken, tofu, tempeh, pork, beef)

Directions:

1. Preheat the oven to 375° F and spray or grease a large oven-safe skillet (I used a Le Creuset Enameled cast-iron 10-¼-inch skillet, but skillets with a diameter of 9 to 12 inches would work). Spread the rice out in a flat layer on the bottom of the skillet (I don't bother unthawing the frozen fried rice and just pour it in). Distribute the vegetables and optional protein evenly over the rice. Since the soup is thick, use a spatula to spread it out gently. Pour the eggs liberally over the top of the broth. Drizzle with olive oil and season to taste with spice blend and salt and pepper.
2. Bake for 45 to 50 minutes, or until golden brown and set on top, with crisped edges. Remember that there is a noticeable carryover cooking impact when cooking with cast iron because the food can begin to cook in the skillet, and don't take the frittata out of the oven unless it's really browned so it can get really tough with carryover cooking factored in. Slice and serve right now. Cover extra frittata in plastic wrap or keep it in an airtight tub in the refrigerator for up to 3 days.

Nutrition: Calories: 465. **Total Fats:** 17 g. **Saturated Fat:** 3 g. **Trans Fat:** 0 g. **Unsaturated Fat:** 12 g. **Cholesterol:** 213 mg. **Sodium:** 1566 mg. **Carbs:** 55 g. **Fiber:** 4 g. **Sugar:** 2 g. **Protein:** 23 g.

304. Overnight Asparagus Strata

Preparation Time: 15 minutes
Cooking Time: 45 minutes
Chilling Bake: 40 minutes
Servings: 8
Ingredients:

- 2 cups Colby-Monterey Jack shredded cheese, split
- 4 toasted and divided English muffins
- 1 cup fully cooked ham cubes
- 1 lb. trimmed and cut into 1-inch sections fresh asparagus
- ½ cup sweet red pepper, chopped

- 8 big eggs
- 2 cups of milk with 2%
- 1 tsp. kosher salt
- 1 tsp. mustard powder
- ¼ tsp. pepper

Directions:

1. Bring 8 cups of water to a boil in a big saucepan. Cook, uncovered, for 2 to 3 minutes, or until asparagus is crisp-tender. Drain and immerse in ice water right away. Drain the bath and dry it with a towel.

2. In a greased 13x9-inch baking dish, place six English muffin halves cut side up. To fill in the gaps, trim the remaining muffin halves. On top is a sheet of 1 cup of cheese, asparagus, ham, and red pepper.

3. In a large mixing cup, whisk together the eggs, milk, salt, mustard, and pepper. Pour the sauce on top of the cake. Refrigerate overnight in an airtight container.

4. Preheat the oven to 375° F (190° C). Delete the strata from the refrigerator until the oven has heated up. The rest of the cheese should be strewn on top. Cook, uncovered, for 40 to 45 minutes, or until a knife inserted in the center comes out clean. Until cutting, give it a 5-minute rest.

Nutrition: Calories: 318 **Fat:** 17 g. **Saturated Fat:** 9 g. **Cholesterol:** 255 mg. **Sodium:** 916 mg. **Carbs:** 20 g. **Sugars:** 5 g. **Fiber:** 1 g. **Protein:** 21 g.

305. Baked Eggplant Parmesan Casserole

Preparation Time: 15 minutes
Cooking Time: 45 minutes
Servings: 6
Ingredients:
Filling:

- 2-lb. Italian eggplant, quartered and diced thickly into 14-inch slices
- 2 tbsp. extra virgin olive oil
- 1 tsp. salt
- 1 tsp. black pepper
- (650 mL) marinara sauce (or pasta sauce) (I used a basil garlic sauce with a sweet basil flavor.)
- ¼ cup (28 g) chopped new basil leaves (see first note)
- 2 tsp. pepper and salt (Italian)
- 250 g new mozzarella, cut 1 cup (2 oz.) parmesan (I used Parmigiano-Reggiano)

Topping:

- ¾ cup panko breadcrumbs (or Italian breadcrumbs)
- 2 garlic cloves, finely ground
- 1 ½ tbsp. extra virgin olive oil
- 1 tbsp. basil leaves (chopped), black pepper, and salt

Directions:

1. Preheat oven to 425° F.

2. On a large baking sheet lined with parchment paper, combine the sliced eggplant, olive oil, salt, and pepper. After that, the eggplant can be extended into a single, even plate (you may need two baking sheets).

3. Enable the eggplant to soften and gently brown around the edges after 15 minutes of roasting. Combine the topping ingredients in a bowl as the eggplant roasts, and prepare the remaining casserole ingredients.

4. Layer a third of each ingredient in this order in a 9x13 casserole dish: marinara sauce, eggplant, fresh and dried herbs, and cheeses. Repeat the process twice more, ensuring sure the ingredients are equally distributed in the casserole dish each time.

5. After that, uniformly distribute the breadcrumb topping over the casserole bowl.

6. Enable a golden-brown crust to shape by baking at 425° F for 35 to 40 minutes. Until eating, allow for a 10-minute cooling time.

Nutrition: Calories: 341. **Total Fats:** 19 g. **Saturated Fat:** 6 g. **Trans Fat:** 0 g. **Unsaturated Fat:** 11 g. **Cholesterol:** 29 mg. **Sodium:** 1241 mg. **Carbs:** 33 g. **Fiber:** 7 g. **Sugar:** 12 g. **Protein:** 12 g.

306. Spicy Sweet Potato Fries

Preparation Time: 10 minutes
Cooking Time: 45 minutes
Servings: 4
Ingredients:

- 2 sweet potatoes, big (about 2 pounds. total) ($1.38)
- 2 tbsp. option cooking oil ($0.26)
- 1 tsp. Creole seasoning or spicy seasoning salt ($0.10)

Directions:

1. Preheat the oven to 400° F. Using parchment paper, line a big baking sheet.

2. Sweet potatoes can be peeled and sliced into ¼-½-inch-thick fries. Drizzle cooking oil over the sliced fries on the prepared baking dish. Toss the fries in the oil until they are fully covered. Return the sweet potatoes to the baking sheet and spread them out in a single layer.

3. Bake for 45 minutes, stirring after 20 minutes or so, or until the sweet potatoes are browned and blistered, in a thoroughly preheated oven.

4. Season the sweet potato fries with Creole seasoning or spicy seasoning salt after they've fried. Serve right away.

Nutrition: Calories: 303. **Carbs:** 37.85 g. **Protein:** 2.95 g. **Fat:** 13.03 g. **Sodium:** 783 mg. **Fiber:** 5.4 g.

307. Spinach Mushroom and Feta Crustless Quiche

Preparation Time: 15 minutes
Cooking Time: 45 minutes

Servings: 6

Ingredients:

- 8 oz. button mushrooms ($1.99)
- 1 garlic clove, minced ($0.08)
- 4 big eggs ($0.83)
- 1 thawed 10 oz. box frozen spinach ($1.09)
- 1 gallon of milk ($0.39)
- ½ cup sliced mozzarella ($0.50)
- 2 oz. feta cheese, ($0.87)
- ¼ cup grated Parmesan cheese ($0.39)
- Salt and pepper to taste ($0.05)

Directions:

1. Preheat the oven to 350° F (180° C). Squeeze the thawed spinach to remove any remaining moisture. Rinse the mushrooms to remove any soil or residue, then thinly slice them. Garlic can be minced.

2. In a nonstick skillet spritzed gently with nonstick mist, add the mushrooms, garlic, and a pinch of salt and pepper (or a splash of cooking oil). Sauté the mushrooms and garlic before the mushrooms are soft and have lost all of their liquid (5 to 7 minutes).

3. Cover a 9-inch pie dish with nonstick spray. In the bottom of the pie dish, place the squeezed-dried spinach. On top of the spinach, scatter the sautéed mushrooms and crumbled feta.

4. Whisk together the eggs, cream, and Parmesan in a medium mixing cup. Add a slice of black pepper to taste. Pour the egg mixture over the vegetables and feta in the pie dish. Shredded mozzarella can be sprinkled on top.

5. Place the pie dish on a baking sheet to make moving it into and out of the oven smoother. Preheat the oven to 350° F and bake the crustless quiche for 45 to 55 minutes, or until golden brown on top (ovens may vary). Serve by slicing into six strips.

Nutrition: Calories: 165.85. **Carbs:** 6.72 g. **Protein:** 12.88 g. **Fat:** 10.17 g. **Sodium:** 516.33 mg. **Fiber:** 1.73 g.

Poultry

308. Chicken Roast With Pineapple Salsa

Preparation Time: 10 minutes
Cooking Time: 45 minutes
Servings: 2
Ingredients:

- ¼ cup extra virgin olive oil
- ¼ cup freshly chopped cilantro
- 1 avocado, diced
- 1-lb. boneless chicken breasts
- 2 cups canned pineapples
- 2 tsp. honey
- Juice from 1 lime
- Salt and pepper to taste

Directions:
1. Preheat the oven to 390° F.
2. Place the grill pan accessory in the oven.
3. Season the chicken breasts with lime juice, olive oil, honey, salt, and pepper.
4. Place on the grill pan and cook for 45 minutes.
5. Flip the chicken every 10 minutes to grill all sides evenly.
6. Once the chicken is cooked, serve with pineapples, cilantro, and avocado.
Nutrition: Calories: 744. **Fat:** 32.8 g. **Protein:** 4.7 g. **Sugar:** 5 g.

309. Salt and Pepper Chicken Wings

Preparation Time: 5 minutes
Cooking Time: 45 minutes
Servings: 4
Ingredients:

- 2 lb. chicken wings
- 2 tsp. sea salt
- 1 tsp. ground black pepper
- 1 tbsp. chopped parsley
- 2 tbsp. olive oil

Directions:
1. Turn on the oven, set the temperature to 425° F, and then select the oven cooking method.
2. Meanwhile, place the chicken wings in a medium bowl, drizzle with oil and then toss well until coated.
3. Sprinkle salt and black pepper over the chicken wings and then toss well until coated.
4. Take a baking pan, line it with parchment paper, spread the chicken wings in a single layer, and then bake for 45 minutes until golden brown and crisp.
5. When done, sprinkle parsley over the chicken wings and then serve.
Nutrition: Calories: 335. **Fat:** 26 g. **Carbs:** 3 g. **Protein:** 22 g. **Fiber:** 1 g.

310. Air Fryer Frozen Chicken Drumsticks

Preparation Time: 25 minutes
Cooking Time: 45 minutes
Servings: 4
Ingredients:

- 2 lb. chicken drumsticks, frozen
- 2 tbsp. olive oil
- Salt and black pepper, to taste
- 1 tsp. garlic powder
- 1 tsp. paprika
- 1 tsp. onion powder

Directions:
1. Take a large bowl and add drumsticks to it.
2. Drizzle the olive oil on top and rub the drum stick with the olive oil coating generously.
3. Then rub the drum stick with seasoning, including salt, pepper, garlic powder, paprika, and onion powder.
4. Marinate the dumbstruck in the refrigerator for 2 hours.
5. Afterward, take out the drumstick and place them in the fryer basket.
6. Cook for 20 minutes at 375° F inside the oven.
7. Serve and enjoy.
Nutrition: Total Fat: 20 g. **Saturated Fat:** 4.4 g. **Cholesterol:** 200 mg. **Sodium:** 182 mg. **Total Carbs:** 1.3 g. **Dietary Fiber:** 0.3 g. **Total Sugars:** 0.4 g. **Protein:** 62.6 g. **Vitamin D:** 0 mcg. **Calcium:** 29 mg. **Iron:** 3 mg. **Potassium:** 478 mg.

311. Air Fryer Stuffed Chicken Breast

Preparation Time: 25 minutes
Cooking Time: 45 minutes
Servings: 2
Ingredients:

- 2 chicken breasts
- Salt and black pepper, to taste
- ¼ cup apple peeled and diced
- ½ cup shredded cheddar cheese
- 2 tbsp. fine bread crumbs
- 2 tbsp. butter
- 1 cup chicken broth

Directions:
1. Take a bowl and combine apple, butter, cheese, and bread crumbs.
2. Rub the chicken with salt and black pepper.
3. Butterfly cut the chicken breast pieces and fills the center with a prepared bowl of apple mixture.
4. Secure the chicken breast pieces with a toothpick.
5. Take a shallow baking pan and place chicken in it along with the chicken broth.

6.	Cover it with foil.
7.	Cook for 20 minutes at 350° F inside the oven.
8.	Once done, remove it from the oven.
9.	Serve.
Nutrition: Calories: 463. Total Fat: 23.7 g. Saturated Fat: 10.6 g. Cholesterol: 160 mg. Sodium: 698 mg. Total Carbs: 13.6 g. Dietary Fiber: 1.2 g. Total Sugars: 4.1 g. Protein: 46.4 g. Vitamin D: 8 mcg. Calcium: 56 mg. Iron: 3 mg. Potassium: 514 mg.

312. Whole Chicken
Preparation Time: 25 minutes
Cooking Time: 45 minutes
Servings: 4
Ingredients:
- 1 whole chicken, 4 lb., cut into 4 large pieces
- 1 tbsp. paprika
- Salt and black pepper, to taste
- 2 tbsp. olive oil

Directions:
1.	Wash and pat dry the chicken.
2.	Rub chicken with olive oil and seasoning.
3.	Preheat the oven to 350° F.
4.	Bake it for 60 minutes or until the temperature is 165° F.
5.	Serve.
Nutrition: Calories: 463. Total Fat: 23.7 g. Saturated Fat: 10.6 g. Cholesterol: 160 mg. Sodium: 698 mg. Total Carbs: 13.6 g. Dietary Fiber: 1.2 g. Total Sugars: 4.1 g. Protein: 46.4 g. Vitamin D: 8 mcg. Calcium: 56 mg. Iron: 3 mg. Potassium: 514 mg.

313. Air Fryer Rotisserie Chicken
Preparation Time: 25 minutes
Cooking Time: 45 minutes
Servings: 4
Ingredients:
- 2 lb. whole chicken, cut in a piece
- Salt and black pepper
- 3 tbsp. avocado oil
- 1 tsp. thyme, dried
- 1 tbsp. Italian seasoning
- 2 tsp. garlic powder
- 2 tsp. onion powder
- 1 tsp. paprika

Directions:
1.	Wash and pat dry the chicken pieces.
2.	Take a small bowl and combine all the listed ingredients in it, excluding the chicken.
3.	Mix well and set aside.
4.	Run the chicken with the prepared marinade.
5.	Marinate the chicken in the spices for 2 hours.
6.	Afterward, put the chicken pieces in the oven, use rotisserie functions and tools to cook the chicken.
7.	Turn on the oven at 400° F for 30 minutes.

8.	After 10 minutes, flip the chicken and then complete the cooking for 20 minutes.
9.	Once done, serve hot.
10.	Note: The chicken of about 4 to 5 pounds can be cooked easily in one batch by putting it directly on a rotisserie, and a rack. The rack below the rotisserie serves as a dripping pan.
11.	Remember to put the foil on top of the rack and place pieces according to capacity. The oven's bottom can also be used to cook chicken directly; remember to cover it with aluminum foil.
Nutrition: Calories: 463. Total Fat: 23.7 g. Saturated Fat: 10.6 g. Cholesterol: 160 mg. Sodium: 698 mg. Total Carbs: 13.6 g. Dietary Fiber: 1.2 g. Total Sugars: 4.1 g. Protein: 46.4 g. Vitamin D: 8 mcg. Calcium: 56 mg. Iron: 3 mg. Potassium: 514 mg.

314. Turkey Breasts
Preparation Time: 25 minutes
Cooking Time: 45 minutes
Servings: 4
Ingredients:
- 2 lb. turkey breast,
- 2 tbsp. poultry rub seasoning
- 2 tbsp. olive oil

Directions:
1.	First, rub the turkey with olive oil and then coat it with dry rub seasoning.
2.	Tie the turkey breast to keep it compact.
3.	Place the breast in the fryer basket, and put it in the oven.
4.	Select Air Fry mode for 30 minutes at 380° F.
5.	Turn the meat as needed during the cooking process.
6.	Let the breast rest for 5 to 10 minutes before taking it out.
7.	Remember to cook the chicken in batches according to the oven space.
8.	Crave and serve the turkey breasts.
Nutrition: Calories: 463. Total Fat: 23.7 g. Saturated Fat: 10.6 g. Cholesterol: 160 mg. Sodium: 698 mg. Total Carbs: 13.6 g. Dietary Fiber: 1.2 g. Total Sugars: 4.1 g. Protein: 46.4 g. Vitamin D: 8 mcg. Calcium: 56 mg. Iron: 3 mg. Potassium: 514 mg.

315. Fryer Southern Fried Chicken
Preparation Time: 20 minutes
Cooking Time: 45 minutes
Servings: 4
Ingredients:
- 6 chicken drumsticks
- Salt, to taste
- Black pepper, to taste
- 1 tsp. avocado oil
- 1 tsp. onion powder

- 1 tsp. paprika
- 1 tsp. garlic powder
- 2 eggs
- 2 tbsp. milk
- 1- ½ cup flour
- ¼ cup corn starch
- Oil spray, for coating
- 2 tbsp. poultry seasoning, dry

Directions:
1. Rub the chicken pieces with salt and black pepper.
2. Then rub avocado oil all over the chicken.
3. Take a bowl and mix onion powder, paprika, and garlic powder.
4. Put the chicken in a bowl and let the species coat the meat.
5. Take a bowl and mix flour, cornstarch, and poultry seasoning.
6. In a separate bowl, whisk eggs and add milk.
7. Take a piece of chicken and roll it in the egg mixture, then in the flour mixture.
8. Shake off excess flour.
9. Repeat with all the chicken pieces.
10. As we are using an oven, it's necessary to spray the chicken pieces with olive oil spray. Else you will get a powdered chicken, as the flour will not get moist.
11. Place the chicken pieces on the baking tray, according to capacity.
12. Fry it for 30 minutes, at 400° F, inside an oven.
13. Once done, serve and enjoy.

Nutrition: Calories: 463. **Total Fat:** 23.7 g. **Saturated Fat:** 10.6 g. **Cholesterol:** 160 mg. **Sodium:** 698 mg. **Total Carbs:** 13.6 g. **Dietary Fiber:** 1.2 g. **Total Sugars:** 4.1 g. **Protein:** 46.4 g. **Vitamin D:** 8 mcg. **Calcium:** 56 mg. **Iron:** 3 mg. **Potassium:** 514 mg.

316. Tandoori Chicken Recipe

Preparation Time: 15 minutes
Cooking Time: 45 minutes
Servings: 3
Ingredients:
- 1- ½-lb. chicken drumsticks

Marinade:
- 1 cup plain Greek yogurt
- 1 tsp. ginger, minced
- 3 tsp. garlic, minced
- 3 tbsp. olive oil
- 2 tbsp. lemon juice
- Salt and black pepper, to taste
- ½ tsp. turmeric powder
- 3 tsp. Garam Masala
- 2 tbsp. coriander powder
- 2 tsp. cumin powder

- ½ tsp. red chili powder
- 2 tsp. paprika
- 1 tsp. fenugreek leaves, dried

Garnish:
- 1 tsp. fresh lemon wedges

Directions:
1. Take a large bowl and combine all the listed marinade ingredients in it.
2. Add chicken to the marinade and transfer it to a zip-lock plastic bag.
3. Let the chicken marinate for 2 hours in a refrigerator.
4. Take out the chicken 20 minutes before cooking.
5. Now, put the chicken pieces in an oven basket and fry for 20 minutes at 400° F.
6. Afterward, pull out the basket and flip the chicken and cook for 10 more minutes.
7. Once the internal temperature reaches 165° F, it's done. Serve with a garnish of lemon wedges.

Nutrition: Calories: 463. **Total Fat:** 23.7 g. **Saturated Fat:** 10.6 g. **Cholesterol:** 160 mg. **Sodium:** 698 mg. **Total Carbs:** 13.6 g. **Dietary Fiber:** 1.2 g. **Total Sugars:** 4.1 g. **Protein:** 46.4 g. **Vitamin D:** 8 mcg. **Calcium:** 56 mg. **Iron:** 3 mg. **Potassium:** 514 mg.

317. Chicken Shawarma

Preparation Time: 10 minutes
Cooking Time: 45 minutes
Servings: 4
Ingredients:
Chicken:
- ½ cup extra-virgin olive oil
- Juice of 1 lemon
- 3 cloves garlic, minced
- 2 tsp. kosher salt
- 1 tsp. ground cumin
- 1 tsp. ground coriander
- ½ tsp. freshly ground black pepper
- ½ tsp. ground turmeric
- ¼ tsp. ground cinnamon
- ¼ tsp. cayenne pepper
- 2 lb. boneless skinless chicken thighs
- Cooking spray
- 1 large onion, thinly sliced

Yogurt sauce:
- ½ cup Greek yogurt
- Juice of ½ lemon
- 1 tbsp. extra-virgin olive oil
- 2 cloves garlic, smashed and minced
- Kosher salt
- Pinch of crushed red pepper flakes

Servings:
- Pitas, warmed

- Chopped romaine
- Cherry tomatoes halved
- Cucumber, thinly sliced

Directions:

1. To make the chicken, in a huge bowl, whisk together oil, lemon juice, garlic, and flavors. Add chicken and throw to cover.

2. Cover and refrigerate for at any rate 2 hours and up to expedite. Preheat the oven to 425° F and oil an enormous baking sheet with cooking spray.

3. Add onion to marinade and throw to cover. Eliminate chicken and onion from marinade and spot on a readied heating sheet.

4. Bake until chicken is golden and cooked through, 30 mins. Let chicken lay on cutting board for 5 mins, at that point daintily cut.

5. In the interim, make the yogurt sauce whisking together in a little bowl yogurt, lemon juice, oil, and garlic. Season it with salt and a touch of red chilies chips.

Nutrition: Calories: 284. **Total Fat:** 7.9 g. **Saturated Fat:** 1.4 g. **Cholesterol:** 36 mg. **Total Carbs:** 46 g. **Fiber:** 3.6 g. **Sugar:** 5.5 g. **Protein:** 17.9 g.

318. Lemon & Rosemary Chicken Sheet Pan Meal

Preparation Time: 10 minutes
Cooking Time: 45 minutes
Servings: 4
Ingredients:

- ¼ cup olive oil divided into the recipe
- 1 tsp. fine grind sea salt
- ½ tsp. pepper
- 12 oz. red potatoes
- 2 medium zucchinis
- 1 medium yellow squash
- 1 red onion
- 1 bulb garlic
- 16 oz. chicken breast
- 8 sprigs rosemary fresh
- 2 to 3 lemons
- 1 to 2 chilies

Directions:

1. Blend the salt and chilies in a little bowl. Cut the potatoes into quarters. Ensure they are comparative in size, so if some are bigger, cut them in 8ths. Shower them with olive oil (around 1 tbsp.) and sprinkle with the salt and chilies combination; you will utilize a modest quantity.

2. Spot the potatoes on the plate in the oven. Select the Air Roast mode on 450° F/230° C for 10 mins.

3. While the potatoes are cooking, prep your veggies. Cut the squash and zucchini into lumps about the potatoes' size and spot them in a bowl. Strip and crush the garlic cloves and spot them in the bowl. Cut onion into thin strips and spot ¾ in the bowl, and save ¼ of the slice for under the chicken. Shower with olive oil (around 1 -1 ½ tbsp.) and sprinkle with the salt and chilies combination. Blend to join the veggies and oil/salt and chilies.

4. Slice the lemons into ¼ inch slices and keep them aside.

5. Shower the chicken with oil and sprinkle with salt and chilies combination. Rub the combination into the meat on the two sides.

6. When the air cook is done, eliminate the container with the potatoes and flip the potatoes. Gap the container into 3rds, $1/3$ for the potatoes, $1/3$ for the veggies, and $1/3$ for the chicken. Settle a couple of branches of rosemary into the potatoes. Add the slice-up vegetables close to the potatoes on the sheet skillet and settle a couple of rosemary branches into the vegetables.

7. Spot the leftover onion slice, lemon slice, and a couple of rosemary branches on the unfilled third of the dish. Lay the chicken on top and spot the excess rosemary springs on top of the chicken breasts. Cover with a lemon slice.

8. Shower any excess olive oil over the sheet pan meal's highest point and sprinkle with any excess salt and chilies. Bake at 325° F/160° C for 20 to 30 minutes, contingent upon your chicken's thickness; 25 minutes is the normal time.

9. Eliminate the chicken when the inside temp is in any event 160° F/71° C and let rest for 5 to 10 minutes.

10. Disperse veggies out into a single layer and broil the veggies and the potatoes for 5 to 10 minutes or until wanted browning is accomplished.

Nutrition: Calories: 284. **Total Fat:** 7.9 g. **Saturated Fat:** 1.4 g. **Cholesterol:** 36 mg. **Total Carbs:** 46 g. **Fiber:** 3.6 g. **Sugar:** 5.5 g. **Protein:** 17.9 g.

Beef

319. Air Fried Grilled Steak
Preparation Time: 5 minutes
Cooking Time: 45 minutes
Servings: 2
Ingredients:
- 2 top sirloin steaks
- 3 tbsp. butter, melted
- 3 tbsp. olive oil
- Salt and pepper to taste

Directions:
1. Preheat the air fryer oven for 5 minutes.
2. Season the sirloin steaks with olive oil, salt, and pepper.
3. Place the beef in the air fryer basket.
4. Cook for 45 minutes at 350° F.
5. Once cooked, serve with butter.

Nutrition: Calories: 1536. **Fat:** 123.7 g. **Protein:** 103.4 g.

320. Creamy Burger & Potato Bake
Preparation Time: 5 minutes
Cooking Time: 45 minutes
Servings: 4
Ingredients:
- Salt to taste
- Freshly ground pepper, to taste
- ½ (10.75 oz.) can condensed cream of mushroom soup
- ½-lb. lean ground beef
- 1-½ cups peeled and thinly sliced potatoes
- ½ cup shredded cheddar cheese
- ¼ cup chopped onion
- ¼ cup and 2 tbsp. milk

Directions:
1. Lightly grease baking pan of air fryer with cooking spray. Add ground beef. For 10 minutes, cook at 360° F. Stir and crumble halfway through cooking time.
2. Meanwhile, in a bowl, whisk well pepper, salt, milk, onion, and mushroom soup. Mix well.
3. Drain fat off ground beef and transfer beef to a plate.
4. In the same air fryer baking pan, layer ½ of potatoes on the bottom, then ½ of soup mixture, and then ½ of beef. Repeat process.
5. Cover pan with foil.
6. Cook for 30 minutes. Remove foil and cook for another 15 minutes or until potatoes are tender.
7. Serve and enjoy.

Nutrition: Calories: 399. **Fat:** 26.9 g. **Protein:** 22.1 g.

321. Beefy 'n Cheesy Spanish Rice Casserole
Preparation Time: 10 minutes
Cooking Time: 45 minutes
Servings: 4
Ingredients:
- 2 tbsp. chopped green bell pepper
- 1 tbsp. chopped fresh cilantro
- ½-lb. lean ground beef
- ½ cup water
- ½ tsp. salt
- ½ tsp. brown sugar
- ½ pinch ground black pepper
- ⅓ cup uncooked long grain rice
- ¼ cup finely chopped onion
- ¼ cup chili sauce
- ¼ tsp. ground cumin
- ¼ tsp. Worcestershire sauce
- ¼ cup shredded cheddar cheese
- ½ (14.5 oz.) can canned tomatoes

Directions:
1. Lightly grease baking pan of air fryer with cooking spray. Add ground beef.
2. For 10 minutes, cook at 360° F. Halfway through cooking time, stir and crumble beef. Discard excess fat.
3. Stir in pepper, Worcestershire sauce, cumin, brown sugar, salt, chile sauce, rice, water, tomatoes, green bell pepper, and onion. Mix well. Cover pan with foil and cook for 25 minutes. Stirring occasionally.
4. Give it one last good stir, press down firmly, and sprinkle cheese on top.
5. Cook uncovered for 15 minutes at 390° F until tops are lightly browned.
6. Serve and enjoy with chopped cilantro.

Nutrition: Calories: 346. **Fat:** 19.1 g. **Protein:** 18.5 g.

322. Charred Onions and Steak Cube BBQ
Preparation Time: 5 minutes
Cooking Time: 45 minutes
Servings: 4
Ingredients:
- 1 cup red onions, cut into wedges
- 1 tbsp. dry mustard
- 1 tbsp. olive oil
- 1-lb. boneless beef sirloin, cut into cubes
- Salt and pepper to taste

Directions:
1. Preheat the air fryer to 390° F.
2. Place the grill pan accessory in the air fryer.
3. Toss all ingredients in a bowl and mix until everything is coated with the seasonings.
4. Place on the grill pan and cook for 40 minutes.
5. Halfway through the cooking time, give a stir to cook evenly.

Nutrition: Calories: 260. **Fat:** 10.7 g. **Protein:** 35.5 g.

323. Chili-Espresso Marinated Steak

Preparation Time: 5 minutes
Cooking Time: 45 minutes
Servings: 4
Ingredients:

- ½ tsp. garlic powder
- 1 ½ lb. beef flank steak
- 1 tsp. instant espresso powder
- 2 tbsp. olive oil
- 2 tsp. chili powder
- Salt and pepper to taste

Directions:

1. Preheat the air fryer oven to 390° F.
2. Place the grill pan accessory in the air fryer.
3. Make the dry rub by mixing the chili powder, salt, pepper, espresso powder, and garlic powder.
4. Rub all over the steak and brush with oil.
5. Place on the grill pan and cook for 40 minutes.
6. Halfway through the cooking time, flip the beef to cook evenly.

Nutrition: Calories: 249. **Fat:** 17 g. **Protein:** 20 g. **Fiber:** 2 g.

324. Beef and Broccoli

Preparation Time: 10 minutes
Cooking Time: 45 minutes
Servings: 4
Ingredients:

- 1 minced garlic clove
- 1 sliced ginger root
- 1 tbsp. olive oil
- 1 tsp. almond flour
- 1 tsp. sweetener of choice
- 1 tsp. low-sodium soy sauce
- ⅓ cup sherry
- 2 tsp. sesame oil
- ⅓ cup oyster sauce
- 1 lb. broccoli
- ¾ lb. round steak

Directions:

1. Remove stems from broccoli and slice them into florets. Slice steak into thin strips.
2. Combine sweetener, soy sauce, sherry, almond flour, sesame oil, and oyster sauce together, stirring till sweetener dissolves.
3. Put strips of steak into the mixture and allow to marinate for 45 minutes to 2 hours.
4. Add broccoli and marinated steak to the air fryer basket. Place garlic, ginger, and olive oil on top.
5. Set temperature to 400° F, and set time to 12 minutes. Cook 12 minutes at 400° F. Serve with cauliflower rice!

Nutrition: Calories: 384. **Fat:** 16 g. **Protein:** 19 g. **Sugar:** 4 g.

325. Mushroom Meatloaf

Preparation Time: 5 minutes
Cooking Time: 45 minutes
Servings: 4
Ingredients:

- 14-oz. lean ground beef
- 1 chorizo sausage, chopped finely
- 1 small onion, chopped
- 1 garlic clove, minced
- 2 tbsp. fresh cilantro, chopped
- 3 tbsp. breadcrumbs
- 1 egg
- Salt and freshly ground black pepper, to taste
- 2 tbsp. fresh mushrooms, sliced thinly
- 3 tbsp. olive oil

Directions:

1. Preheat the Air fryer oven to 390° F.
2. In a large bowl, add all ingredients except mushrooms and mix till well combined.
3. In a baking pan, place the beef mixture.
1. With the back of the spatula, smooth the surface.
2. Top with mushroom slices and gently, press into the meatloaf.
3. Drizzle with oil evenly.
4. Arrange the pan in the air fryer oven basket and cook for about 25 minutes.
5. Cut the meatloaf in desired size wedges and serve.

Nutrition: Calories: 460. **Protein:** 16.8 g. **Fat:** 42.34 g. **Carbs:** 2.26 g.

326. Beef Steaks With Beans

Preparation Time: 5 minutes
Cooking Time: 45 minutes
Servings: 4
Ingredients:

- 4 beef steaks, trim the fat, and cut into strips
- 1 cup green onions, chopped
- 2 cloves garlic, minced
- 1 red bell pepper, seeded and thinly sliced
- 1 can tomatoes, crushed
- 1 can cannellini beans
- ¾ cup beef broth
- ¼ tsp. dried basil
- ½ tsp. cayenne pepper
- ½ tsp. sea salt
- ¼ tsp. ground black pepper, or to taste

Directions:

1. Add the steaks, green onions, and garlic to the air fryer oven basket.
2. Cook at 390° F for 10 minutes, working in batches.

3. Stir in the remaining ingredients and cook for an additional 5 minutes.

Nutrition: Calories: 364. **Protein:** 50.43 g. **Fat:** 13.17 g. **Carbs:** 8.47 g.

327. Roasted Stuffed Peppers

Preparation Time: 5 minutes
Cooking Time: 45 minutes
Servings: 4
Ingredients:

- 4 oz. shredded cheddar cheese
- ½ tsp. pepper
- ½ tsp. salt
- 1 tsp. Worcestershire sauce
- ½ cup tomato sauce
- 8 oz. lean ground beef
- 1 tsp. olive oil
- 1 minced garlic clove
- ½ chopped onion
- 2 green peppers

Directions:

1. Ensure your air fryer is preheated to 390° F. Spray with olive oil.
2. Cut stems off bell peppers and remove seeds. Cook in boiling salted water for 3 minutes.
3. Sauté garlic and onion together in a skillet until golden in color.
4. Take the skillet off the heat. Mix pepper, salt, Worcestershire sauce, ¼ cup of tomato sauce, half of the cheese, and beef together.
5. Divide the meat mixture into pepper halves. Top filled peppers with remaining cheese and tomato sauce.
6. Place filled peppers in the air fryer oven.
7. Set temperature to 390° F, and set time to 20 minutes, bake for 15 to 20 minutes.

Nutrition: Calories: 295. **Fat:** 8 g. **Protein:** 23 g. **Sugar:** 2 g.

328. Air Fried Steak Sandwich

Preparation Time: 5 minutes
Cooking Time: 45 minutes
Servings: 4
Ingredients:

- Large hoagie bun, sliced in half
- 6 oz. sirloin or flank steak, sliced into bite-sized pieces
- ½ tbsp. mustard powder
- ½ tbsp. soy sauce
- 1 tbsp. fresh bleu cheese, crumbled
- 8 medium-sized cherry tomatoes, sliced in half
- 1 cup fresh arugula, rinsed and patted dry

Directions:

1. In a small mixing bowl, combine the soy sauce and mustard powder; stir with a fork until thoroughly combined.
2. Lay the raw steak strips in the soy-mustard mixture, and fully immerse each piece to marinate.
3. Set the air fryer oven to 320° F for 10 minutes.
4. Arrange the soy-mustard marinated steak pieces on a piece of tin foil, flat and not overlapping, and set the tin foil on one side of the air fryer basket. The foil should not take up more than half of the surface.
5. Lay the hoagie-bun halves, crusty-side up and soft-side down, on the other half of the air fryer oven.
6. After 10 minutes, the air fryer oven will shut off; the hoagie buns should be starting to crisp and the steak will have begun to cook.
7. Carefully, flip the hoagie buns so they are now crusty-side down and soft-side up; crumble a layer of the bleu cheese on each hoagie half.
8. With a long spoon, gently stir the marinated steak in the foil to ensure even coverage.
9. Set the air fryer to 360° F for 6 minutes.
10. After 6 minutes, when the fryer shuts off, the bleu cheese will be perfectly melted over the toasted bread, and the steak will be juicy on the inside and crispy on the outside.
11. Remove the cheesy hoagie halves first, using tongs, and set on a serving plate; then cover one side with the steak, and top with the cherry-tomato halves and the arugula. Close with the other cheesy hoagie-half, slice into two pieces, and enjoy.

Nutrition: Calories: 93. **Protein:** 10.38 g. **Fat:** 3.98 g. **Carbs:** 3.75 g.

329. Carrot and Beef Cocktail Balls

Preparation Time: 5 minutes
Cooking Time: 45 minutes
Servings: 10
Ingredients:

- 1 lb. ground beef
- 2 carrots
- 1 red onion, peeled and chopped
- 2 cloves garlic
- ½ tsp. dried rosemary, crushed
- ½ tsp. dried basil
- 1 tsp. dried oregano
- 1 egg
- ¾ cup breadcrumbs
- ½ tsp. salt
- ½ tsp. black pepper, or to taste
- 1 cup plain flour

Directions:

1. Place ground beef in a large bowl. In a food processor, pulse the carrot, onion, and garlic; transfer the vegetable mixture to a large-sized bowl.

2.   Then, add the rosemary, basil, oregano, egg, breadcrumbs, salt, and black pepper.

3.   Shape the mixture into even balls; refrigerate for about 30 minutes. Roll the balls into the flour.

4.   Pour the balls into the oven rack/basket. Place the rack on the middle shelf of the Air fryer oven. Set temperature to 350° F, and set time to 20 minutes, turning occasionally; work with batches. Serve with toothpicks.

Nutrition: Calories: 180. **Protein:** 13.83 g. **Fat:** 8.47 g. **Carbs:** 11.2 g.

Lamb

330. Classic and Simple Lamb Loaf

Preparation Time: 25 minutes
Cooking Time: 45 minutes
Servings: 4 (1 loaf)
Ingredients:

- 1 lb. ground lamb
- 2 slices of diced dry bread
- 2 tbsp. balsamic vinegar
- ¼ cup tomato sauce
- ¼ cup milk
- ½ tsp. vegetable oil, or as required
- 4 cloves of garlic minced
- 1 egg
- 5 leaves of finely chopped fresh mint
- 2 tbsp. fresh thyme chopped
- 1 tbsp. lemon zest
- 1 tsp. dried and crushed rosemary
- ¼ tsp. ground black pepper
- ½ tsp. vegetable oil
- 1 tbsp. Worcestershire sauce
- 1 tsp. dried basil
- ¾ tsp. salt
- 1 tsp. ground coriander

Directions:
1. Preheat the convection oven at 375° F. With oil grease a 9x5 inches loaf pan.
2. Add milk and bread to a small-sized bowl and press bread with a spoon to soak up the milk.
3. Combine egg, garlic, lamb, Worcestershire sauce, thyme, coriander, basil, salt, pepper, rosemary, and lemon zest in a medium-sized bowl. Mix in soaked bread and discard the milk. Mix using hands until fully combined. Transfer loaf in a greased pan.
4. Mix tomato sauce and mint and spread over the loaf evenly. Drizzle the top of the loaf with balsamic vinegar.
5. Bake in the preheated convection oven for around 35 minutes. Let stand for 5 minutes before serving.
Nutrition: Calories: 409. **Fat:** 29.7 g. **Protein:** 22.3 g. **Carbs:** 12.2 g.

331. Greek-Style Stuffed Lamb Leg

Preparation Time: 15 minutes
Cooking Time: 45 minutes
Servings: 8
Ingredients:

- 1 package of feta cheese crumbled (8 oz.)
- 1-lb. leg of lamb, butter flew (3 ½)
- 1 jar of drained and chopped marinated artichoke hearts (12 oz.)
- 1 jar of drained and chopped sun-dried tomatoes packed in oil (6 oz.)
- 2 tbsp. fresh oregano chopped
- 3 cloves of minced garlic
- 2 tbsp. fresh basil chopped
- Salt and ground black pepper to taste
- Olive oil, as required

Directions:
1. Preheat the convection oven at 325° F.
2. On the chopping board, layout the lamb leg. Pour olive oil all over the lamb evenly. Sprinkle with basil and oregano and top lamb with feta cheese, sun-dried tomatoes, artichoke hearts, and garlic. Season the lamb with pepper and salt.
3. Around stuffing, roll the lamb and wrap the lamb with threads to avoid unrolling. In aluminum foil, wrap the lamb tightly and transfer it to a baking dish.
4. Roast in the preheated convection oven for around 90 minutes, set the lamb aside for 10 to 15 minutes before slicing upon serving drizzle the lamb with pan juices.
Nutrition: Calories: 389. **Fat:** 25.7 g. **Protein:** 29.6 g. **Carbs:** 11.5 g.

332. Paprika Lamb Chops With Sage

Preparation Time: 5 minutes
Cooking Time: 45 minutes
Servings: 4
Ingredients:

- 1 cup all-purpose flour
- 2 tsp. dried sage leaves
- 2 tsp. garlic powder
- 1 tbsp. mild paprika
- 1 tbsp. salt
- 4 (6-oz./ 170-g) bone-in lamb shoulder chops, fat trimmed
- Cooking spray

Directions:
1. Preheat the oven to 400° F (204° C) and spritz the baking pan with cooking spray.
2. Combine the flour, sage leaves, garlic powder, paprika, and salt in a large bowl. Stir to mix well. Dunk in the lamb chops and toss to coat well.
3. Arrange the lamb chops in a single layer in the pan and spritz with cooking spray. Bake for 30 minutes or until the chops are golden brown and reach your desired doneness. Flip the chops halfway through.
4. Serve immediately.
Nutrition: Calories: 389. **Fat:** 25.7 g. **Protein:** 29.6 g. **Carbs:** 11.5 g.

333. Lamb Kofta With Mint

Preparation Time: 25 minutes
Cooking Time: 45 minutes

Servings: 4

Ingredients:

- 1 lb. (454 g) ground lamb
- 1 tbsp. Ras el hanout (North African spice)
- ½ tsp. ground coriander
- 1 tsp. onion powder
- 1 tsp. garlic powder
- 1 tsp. cumin
- 2 tbsp. mint, chopped
- Salt and ground black pepper, to taste

Directions:

1. Combine the ground lamb, ras el hanout, coriander, onion powder, garlic powder, cumin, mint, salt, and ground black pepper in a large bowl. Stir to mix well.

2. Transfer the mixture into sausage molds and sit the bamboo skewers in the mixture. Refrigerate for 15 minutes.

3. Preheat oven to 400° F (204° C). Spritz the baking pan with cooking spray.

4. Place the lamb skewers in the preheated oven and spritz with cooking spray.

5. Bake for 12 minutes or until the lamb is well browned. Flip the lamb skewers halfway through.

6. Serve immediately.

Nutrition: Calories: 389. **Fat:** 25.7 g. **Protein:** 29.6 g. **Carbs:** 11.5 g.

Pork

334. Balsamic-Glazed Pork Chops

Preparation Time: 5 minutes
Cooking Time: 45 minutes
Servings: 4
Ingredients:

- ¾ cup balsamic vinegar
- 1 ½ tbsp. sugar
- 1 tbsp. butter
- 3 tbsp. olive oil
- tablespoons salt
- 3 pork rib chops

Directions:

1. Place all ingredients in a bowl and allow the meat to marinate in the fridge for at least 2 hours.
2. Preheat the air fryer oven to 390° F.
3. Place the grill pan accessory in the air fryer.
1. Grill the pork chops for 20 minutes making sure to flip the meat every 10 minutes for even grilling.
2. Meanwhile, pour the balsamic vinegar on a saucepan and allow to simmer for at least 10 minutes until the sauce thickens.
3. Brush the meat with the glaze before serving.

Nutrition: Calories: 274. **Fat:** 18 g. **Protein:** 17 g.

335. Crispy Roast Garlic-Salt Pork

Preparation Time: 5 minutes
Cooking Time: 45 minutes
Servings: 4
Ingredients:

- 1 tsp. Chinese five-spice powder
- 1 tsp. white pepper
- 2 lb. pork belly
- 2 tsp. garlic
- Salt to taste

Directions:

1. Preheat the air fryer oven to 390° F.
2. Mix all the spices in a bowl to create the dry rub.
3. Score the skin of the pork belly with a knife and season the entire pork with the spice rub.
4. Place in the air fryer basket and cook for 40 to 45 minutes until the skin is crispy.
5. Chop before serving.

Nutrition: Calories: 785. **Fat:** 80.7 g. **Protein:** 14.2 g.
Fiber: 0 g.

336. Cajun Sweet-Sour Grilled Pork

Preparation Time: 5 minutes
Cooking Time: 45 minutes
Servings: 4
Ingredients:

- ¼ cup brown sugar
- ¼ cup cider vinegar
- 1-lb. pork loin, sliced into 1-inch cubes
- 2 tbsp. Cajun seasoning
- 3 tbsp. brown sugar

Directions:

1. In a shallow dish, mix well pork loin, 3 tbsp. brown sugar, and Cajun seasoning. Toss well to coat. Marinate in the refrigerator for 3 hours.
2. In a medium bowl mix well, brown sugar, and vinegar for basting.
3. Thread pork pieces in skewers. Baste with sauce and place on skewer rack in the air fryer.
4. For 12 minutes, cook on 360° F. Halfway through cooking time, turnover skewers, and baste with sauce. If needed, cook in batches.
5. Serve and enjoy.

Nutrition: Calories: 428. **Fat:** 16.7 g. **Protein:** 39 g.
Sugar: 2 g.

337. Chinese Braised Pork Belly

Preparation Time: 5 minutes
Cooking Time: 45 minutes
Servings: 8
Ingredients:

- 1 lb. pork belly, sliced
- 1 tbsp. oyster sauce
- 1 tbsp. sugar
- 2 red fermented bean curds
- 1 tbsp. red fermented bean curd paste
- 1 tbsp. cooking wine
- ½ tbsp. soy sauce
- 1 tsp sesame oil
- 1 cup all-purpose flour

Directions:

1. Preheat the air fryer oven to 390° F.
2. In a small bowl, mix all ingredients together and rub the pork thoroughly with this mixture.
3. Set aside to marinate for at least 30 minutes or preferably overnight for the flavors to permeate the meat.
1. Coat each marinated pork belly slice in flour and place in the air fryer tray.
2. Cook for 15 to 20 minutes until crispy and tender.

Nutrition: Calories: 369. **Protein:** 7.16 g. **Fat:** 31.11 g.
Carbs: 14.37 g.

338. Pork Loin With Potatoes

Preparation Time: 10 minutes
Cooking Time: 45 minutes
Servings: 2
Ingredients:

- 2 lb. pork loin
- 1 tsp. fresh parsley, chopped
- 2 large red potatoes, chopped
- ½ tsp. garlic powder
- ½ tsp. red pepper flakes, crushed
- Salt and freshly ground black pepper, to taste

Directions:

1. In a large bowl, add all ingredients except glaze and toss to coat well. Preheat the Air fryer oven to 325° F. Place the loin in the air fryer basket.
2. Arrange the potatoes around the pork loin.
3. Cook for about 25 minutes.

Nutrition: Calories: 955. **Protein:** 116.54 g. **Fat:** 50.2 g. **Carbs:** 1.69 g.

339. Fried Pork Scotch Egg

Preparation Time: 10 minutes
Cooking Time: 45 minutes
Servings: 2
Ingredients:

- 3 soft-boiled eggs, peeled
- 8 oz. raw minced pork, or sausage outside the casings
- 2 tsp. ground rosemary
- 2 tsp. garlic powder
- Pinch of salt and pepper
- 2 raw eggs
- 1 cup breadcrumbs (Panko, but other brands are fine, or home-made bread crumbs work too)

Directions:

1. Cover the basket of the air fryer with a lining of tin foil, leaving the edges uncovered to allow air to circulate through the basket. Preheat the air fryer oven to 350° F.
2. In a mixing bowl, combine the raw pork with the rosemary, garlic powder, salt, and pepper. This will probably be easiest to do with your masher or bare hands (though make sure to wash thoroughly after handling raw meat!); combine until all the spices are evenly spread throughout the meat.
3. Divide the meat mixture into 3 equal portions in the mixing bowl, and form each into balls with your hands.
4. Lay a large sheet of plastic wrap on the countertop, and flatten one of the balls of meat on top of it, to form a wide, flat meat circle.
5. Place one of the peeled soft-boiled eggs in the center of the meat circle and then, using the ends of the plastic wrap, pull the meat circle so that it is fully covering and surrounding the soft-boiled egg.
6. Tighten and shape the plastic wrap covering the meat so that it forms a ball, and make sure not to squeeze too hard lest you squish the soft-boiled egg at the center of the ball! Set aside.
7. Repeat steps 5 to 7 with the other 2 soft-boiled eggs and portions of meat mixture.
8. In a separate mixing bowl, beat the 2 raw eggs until fluffy and until the yolks and whites are fully combined.
9. One by one, remove the plastic wrap and dunk the pork-covered balls into the raw egg, and then roll them in the bread crumbs, covering fully and generously.
10. Place each of the bread-crumb-covered meat-wrapped balls onto the foil-lined surface of the air fryer. Three of them should fit nicely, without touching.
11. Set the air fryer oven timer to 25 minutes.
12. About halfway through the cooking time, shake the handle of the air-fryer vigorously, so that the scotch eggs inside roll around and ensure full coverage.
13. After 25 minutes, the air fryer will shut off and the scotch eggs should be perfect – the meat fully cooked, the egg-yolks still runny on the inside, and the outsides crispy and golden-brown. Using tongs, place them on serving plates, slice in half, and enjoy

Nutrition: Calories: 581. **Protein:** 52.33 g. **Fat:** 36.78 g. **Carbs:** 7.17 g.

340. Roasted Char Siew (Pork Butt)

Preparation Time: 10 minutes
Cooking Time: 45 minutes
Servings: 6
Ingredients:

- 1 strip of pork shoulder butt with a good amount of fat marbling

Marinade:

- 1 tsp. sesame oil
- 4 tbsp. raw honey
- 1 tsp. low-sodium dark soy sauce
- 1 tsp. light soy sauce
- 1 tbsp. rose wine
- 2 tbsp. Hoisin sauce

Directions:

1. Combine all marinade ingredients together and add to Ziploc bag. Place pork in the bag, making sure all sections of the pork strip are engulfed in the marinade. Chill for 3 to 24 hours.
2. Take out the strip 30 minutes before planning to cook and preheat your air fryer oven to 350° F.
3. Place foil on a small pan and brush with olive oil. Place marinated pork strip onto prepared pan.
4. Set temperature to 350° F, and set time to 20 minutes. Roast 20 minutes.
5. Glaze with marinade every 5 to 10 minutes.
6. Remove strip and leave to cool a few minutes before slicing.

Nutrition: Calories: 289. **Fat:** 13 g **Protein:** 33 g. **Sugar:** 1 g.

341. Juicy Pork Ribs Ole

Preparation Time: 10 minutes
Cooking Time: 45 minutes
Servings: 4
Ingredients:

- 1 rack of pork ribs

- ½ cup low-fat milk
- 1 tbsp. envelope taco seasoning mix
- 1 can tomato sauce
- ½ tsp. ground black pepper
- 1 tsp. seasoned salt
- 1 tbsp. cornstarch
- 1 tsp. canola oil

Directions:
1. Place all ingredients in a mixing dish; let them marinate for 1 hour.
2. Pour into the oven rack/basket. Place the rack on the middle shelf of the Air fryer oven. Set temperature to 390° F, and set time to 25 minutes. Cook the marinated ribs for approximately 25 minutes.
3. Work with batches. Enjoy

Nutrition: Calories: 147. **Protein:** 15.09 g. **Fat:** 7.48 g. **Carbs:** 3.72 g.

342. Teriyaki Pork Rolls

Preparation Time: 10 minutes
Cooking Time: 45 minutes
Servings: 6
Ingredients:
- 1 tsp. almond flour
- 4 tbsp. low-sodium soy sauce
- 4 tbsp. mirin
- 4 tbsp. brown sugar
- Thumb-sized amount of ginger, chopped
- Pork belly slices
- Enoki mushrooms

Directions:
1. Mix brown sugar, mirin, soy sauce, almond flour, and ginger together until brown sugar dissolves.
2. Take pork belly slices and wrap around a bundle of mushrooms. Brush each roll with teriyaki sauce. Chill for half an hour.
3. Preheat your air fryer oven to 350° F and add marinated pork rolls.
4. Pour into the oven rack/basket. Place the rack on the middle shelf of the Air fryer oven. Set temperature to 350° F, and set time to 8 minutes.

Nutrition: Calories: 412. **Fat:** 9 g. **Protein:** 19 g. **Sugar:** 4 g.

343. Ham and Cheese Rollups

Preparation Time: 5 minutes
Cooking Time: 45 minutes
Servings: 12
Ingredients:
- 2 tsp. raw honey
- 2 tsp. dried parsley
- 1 tbsp. poppy seeds
- ½ cup melted coconut oil
- ¼ cup spicy brown mustard

- 9 slices of provolone cheese
- 10 oz. thinly sliced Black Forest Ham
- 1 tube of crescent rolls
- Salt and pepper

Directions:
1. Roll out dough into a rectangle. Spread 2 to 3 tbsp. of spicy mustard onto the dough, then layer provolone cheese and ham slices.
2. Roll the filled dough up as tight as you can and slice it into 12 to 15 pieces.
3. Melt coconut oil and mix with a pinch of salt and pepper, parsley, honey, and remaining mustard.
1. Brush mustard mixture over roll-ups and sprinkle with poppy seeds.
2. Grease air fryer basket liberally with olive oil and add rollups.
3. Set temperature to 350° F, and set time to 8 minutes.

Nutrition: Calories: 289. **Fat:** 6 g. **Protein:** 18 g.

344. Vietnamese Pork Chops

Preparation Time: 10 minutes
Cooking Time: 45 minutes
Servings: 6
Ingredients:
- 1 tbsp. olive oil
- 1 tbsp. fish sauce
- 1 tsp. low-sodium dark soy sauce
- 1 tsp. pepper
- 3 tbsp. lemongrass
- 1 tbsp. chopped shallot
- 1 tbsp. chopped garlic
- 1 tbsp. brown sugar
- 2 pork chops

Directions:
1. Add pork chops to a bowl along with olive oil, fish sauce, soy sauce, pepper, lemongrass, shallot, garlic, and brown sugar.
2. Marinade pork chops for 2 hours.
3. Ensure your air fryer is preheated to 400° F. Add pork chops to the basket.
4. Pour into the oven rack/basket. Place the rack on the middle shelf of the Air fryer oven. Set temperature to 400° F, and set time to 7 minutes. Cook making sure to flip after 5 minutes of cooking.
5. Serve alongside steamed cauliflower rice.

Nutrition: Calories: 290. **Fat:** 15 g. **Protein:** 30 g. **Sugar:** 3 g.

Fish

345. Lemony Tuna

Preparation Time: 10 minutes
Cooking Time: 45 minutes
Servings: 4
Ingredients:

- 2 (6-oz.) cans of water-packed plain tuna
- 2 tsp. Dijon mustard
- ½ cup breadcrumbs
- 1 tbsp. fresh lime juice
- 2 tbsp. fresh parsley, chopped
- 1 egg
- Air fryer of hot sauce
- 3 tbsp. canola oil
- Salt and freshly ground black pepper, to taste

Directions:

1. Drain most of the liquid from the canned tuna.
2. In a bowl, add the fish, mustard, crumbs, citrus juice, parsley, and hot sauce and mix till well combined. Add a little canola oil if it seems too dry. Add egg, salt, and stir to combine. Make the patties from the tuna mixture. Refrigerate the tuna patties for about 2 hours.
3. Pour into the oven rack/basket. Place the rack on the middle shelf of the Air fryer oven. Set temperature to 355° F, and set time to 12 minutes.

Nutrition: Calories: 128. **Protein:** 2.41 g. **Fat:** 13.01 g. **Carbs:** 0.84 g.

346. Grilled Soy Salmon Fillets

Preparation Time: 5 minutes
Cooking Time: 45 minutes
Servings: 4
Ingredients:

- 4 salmon fillets
- ¼ tsp. ground black pepper
- ½ tsp. cayenne pepper
- ½ tsp. salt
- 1 tsp. onion powder
- 1 tbsp. fresh lemon juice
- ½ cup soy sauce
- ½ cup water
- 1 tbsp. honey
- 2 tbsp. extra-virgin olive oil

Directions:

1. Firstly, pat the salmon fillets dry using kitchen towels. Season the salmon with black pepper, cayenne pepper, salt, and onion powder.
2. To make the marinade, combine together the lemon juice, soy sauce, water, honey, and olive oil. Marinate the salmon for at least 2 hours in your refrigerator.

3. Arrange the fish fillets on a grill basket in your air fryer oven.
4. Bake at 330° F for 8 to 9 minutes, or until salmon fillets are easily flaked with a fork.
5. Work with batches and serve warm.

Nutrition: Calories: 140. **Protein:** 2.47 g. **Fat:** 8.83 g. **Carbs:** 13.39 g.

347. Flying Fish

Preparation Time: 5 minutes
Cooking Time: 45 minutes
Servings: 6
Ingredients:

- 4 tbsp. oil
- 3 to 4 oz. breadcrumbs
- 1 whisked whole egg in a saucer/soup plate
- 4 fresh fish fillets
- Fresh lemon (for serving)

Directions:

1. Preheat the air fryer to 350° F. Mix the crumbs and oil until it looks nice and loose.
2. Dip the fish in the egg and coat lightly, then move on to the crumbs. Make sure the fillet is covered evenly.
3. Cook in the air fryer oven basket for roughly 12 minutes (depending on the size of the fillets you are using.)
4. Serve with fresh lemon & chips to complete the duo.

Nutrition: Calories: 290. **Protein:** 12.69 g. **Fat:** 20.93 g. **Carbs:** 14.18 g.

348. Pistachio-Crusted Lemon-Garlic Salmon

Preparation Time: 5 minutes
Cooking Time: 45 minutes
Servings: 6
Ingredients:

- 4 medium-sized salmon filets
- 2 raw eggs
- 3 oz. melted butter
- 1 clove of garlic, peeled and finely minced
- 1 large-sized lemon
- 1 tsp. salt
- 1 tbsp. parsley, rinsed, patted dry, and chopped
- 1 tsp. dill, rinsed, patted dry, and chopped
- ½ cup pistachio nuts, shelled and coarsely crushed

Directions:

1. Cover the basket of the air fryer with a lining of tin foil, leaving the edges uncovered to allow air to circulate through the basket.
2. Preheat the air fryer oven to 350° F.
3. In a mixing bowl, beat the eggs until fluffy and until the yolks and whites are fully combined.

4. Add the melted butter, the juice of the lemon, the minced garlic, the parsley, and the dill to the beaten eggs, and stir thoroughly.

5. One by one, dunk the salmon filets into the wet mixture, then roll them in the crushed pistachios, coating completely.

6. Place the coated salmon fillets in the air fryer oven basket.

7. Set the air fryer oven timer for 10 minutes.

8. When the air fryer shuts off, after 10 minutes, the salmon will be partially cooked and the crust begins to crisp. Using tongs, turn each of the fish filets over.

9. Reset the air fryer oven to 350° F for another 10 minutes.

10. After 10 minutes, when the air fryer shuts off, the salmon will be perfectly cooked and the pistachio crust will be toasted and crispy. Using tongs, remove from the air fryer and serve.

Nutrition: Calories: 390. **Protein:** 41.97 g. **Fat:** 23.72 g. **Carbs:** 3.53 g.

Seafood

349. Louisiana Shrimp Po Boy

Preparation Time: 10 minutes
Cooking Time: 45 minutes
Servings: 6
Ingredients:

- 1 tsp. creole seasoning
- 8 slices of tomato
- Lettuce leaves
- ¼ cup buttermilk
- ½ cup Louisiana Fish Fry
- 1-pound deveined shrimp

Remoulade sauce:

- 1 chopped green onion
- 1 tsp. hot sauce
- 1 tsp. Dijon mustard
- ½ tsp. creole seasoning
- 1 tsp. Worcestershire sauce
- Juice of ½ a lemon
- ½ cup vegan mayo

Directions:

1. To make the sauce, combine all sauce ingredients until well incorporated. Chill while you cook shrimp.
2. Mix seasonings together and liberally season shrimp.
3. Add buttermilk to a bowl. Dip each shrimp into milk and place in a Ziploc bag. Chill for half an hour to marinate.
4. Add fish fry to a bowl. Take shrimp from marinating bag and dip into fish fry, then add to the air fryer.
5. Ensure your air fryer is preheated to 400° F.
6. Spray shrimp with olive oil.
7. Pour into the oven rack/basket. Place the rack on the middle shelf of the Air fryer oven. Set temperature to 400° F, and set time to 5 minutes. Cook 5 minutes, flip, and then cook another 5 minutes. Assemble "Keto" Po Boy by adding sauce to lettuce leaves, along with shrimp and tomato.

Nutrition: Calories: 337. **Carbs:** 5.5 g. **Fat:** 12 g. **Protein:** 24 g. **Sugar:** 2 g.

350. Old Bay Crab Cakes

Preparation Time: 10 minutes
Cooking Time: 45 minutes
Servings: 4
Ingredients:

- Dried bread, crusts removed
- A small amount of milk
- 1 tbsp. mayonnaise
- 1 tbsp. Worcestershire sauce
- 1 tbsp. baking powder
- 1 tbsp. parsley flakes
- 1 tsp. Old Bay® Seasoning
- ¼ tsp. salt
- 1 egg
- 1 lb. lump crabmeat

Directions:

1. Crush your bread over a large bowl until it is broken down into small pieces. Add milk and stir until bread crumbs are moistened. Mix in mayo and Worcestershire sauce. Add remaining ingredients and mix well. Shape into 4 patties.
2. Pour into the oven rack/basket. Place the rack on the middle shelf of the Air fryer oven. Set temperature to 360° F, and set time to 20 minutes, flipping halfway through.

Nutrition: Calories: 165. **Carbs:** 5.8 g. **Fat:** 4.5 g. **Protein:** 24 g. **Fiber:** 0 g.

351. Tasty Seafood Ravioli Baked

Preparation Time: 15 minutes
Cooking Time: 45 minutes
Servings: 6 to 8
Ingredients:

- 2 cups shredded cheddar cheese
- 24 oz. Bag ravioli, cheese-filled
- 2 cups chopped crabmeat
- 2 cups alfredo sauce
- 1 cup chopped shrimp
- 1 tsp. Old Bay Seasoning
- ¼ cup chopped and roasted red pepper
- 1 tsp. ground black pepper
- 2 tbsp. warm water
- ½ tsp. salt

Directions:

1. Preheat the convection oven at 325° F. Grease 9x13 casserole dish with cooking spray. Cook ravioli according to your package instructions and set it aside.
2. Combine in a bowl crab, alfredo sauce, shrimp, pepper, water, salt and pepper, old bay seasoning, and 1 cup of cheese.
3. Fold in the cooked ravioli and the sauce mixture gently, do not break the ravioli. Spread into greased casserole pan.
4. Cover with lid and bake in the preheated convection for around 30 minutes.
5. Sprinkle with remaining cheese on the top and bake without cover for 15 minutes more until cheese melts down.
6. Serve warm and enjoy!

Nutrition: Calories: 184.7. **Fat:** 9.7 g. **Protein:** 15.4 g. **Carbs:** 4.3 g.

352. Simply Baked Seafood Potatoes

Preparation Time: 15 minutes
Cooking Time: 45 minutes
Servings: 4 to 6
Ingredients:

- 15 to 20 shrimp
- 1 package of simply potatoes diced potatoes with onion (20 oz.)
- 1 ½ cups of mayonnaise(dressing)
- ⅛ oz. tobiko (flying fish egg)
- ½ tsp. salt

Directions:
1. Preheat the convection oven at 375° F.
2. Cut shrimps into bite-sized chunks. Combine mayonnaise, shrimp, tobiko, and salt in a medium-sized bowl. Spread the mixture on the top of diced potatoes layer in the baking dish.
3. Bake for around 20 minutes in the preheated convection oven. Then change the settings to broil and broil for another 8 to 10 minutes.
4. Serve and enjoy!

Nutrition: Calories: 362. **Fat:** 29.8 g. **Protein:** 4.1 g. **Carbs:** 21.3 g.

353. Quick and Simple Sea Bass Oven-Baked

Preparation Time: 15 minutes
Cooking Time: 45 minutes
Servings: 2
Ingredients:

- ⅓ cup white wine vinegar
- 1 lb. scaled and cleaned sea bass
- 2 lemon wedges
- 1 tbsp. olive oil
- 2 tsp. ground black pepper
- 1 tbsp. Italian seasoning
- 3 cloves of minced garlic
- 1 tsp. salt

Directions:
1. Preheat the convection oven at 400° F.
2. Mix garlic, salt, olive oil, and black pepper in a cup.
3. Arrange fish in a baking dish ad rub fish with a prepared oil mixture. Pour white wine vinegar over fish.
4. Bake fish for around 15 minutes in the preheated convection oven. Then sprinkle the fish with Italian seasoning and bake for additional 5 minutes or until the fish is flaky.
5. Upon serving spread the remaining pan juices on top of fish and side with lemon wedges.

Nutrition: Calories: 294. **Fat:** 11.4 g. **Protein:** 42.4 g. **Carbs:** 3.6 g.

354. Spicy Seafood Penne Pasta

Preparation Time: 20 minutes
Cooking Time: 45 minutes
Servings: 6
Ingredients:

- 16 oz. penne pasta
- 1 can of whole undrained tomatoes (28 oz.)
- 16 oz. bay scallops
- Frozen green peas, thawed (10 oz.)
- 8 oz. large raw shrimp (cut half lengthwise)
- 3 cloves of minced garlic
- 1 cup parmesan cheese grated
- 1 tbsp. olive oil
- 1 tbsp. butter
- 1 tbsp. fresh basil chopped
- ½ onion
- 1 tsp. salt
- ¼ tsp. black pepper
- ½ tsp. crushed red pepper flakes

Directions:
1. Preheat the convection oven at 325° F.
2. In a large sauce, heat oil and cook onion and garlic for around 2 minutes until onion is soft.
3. Mix in both cans of tomatoes with juice, crushed red pepper, black pepper, and salt. Using a fork, crush tomatoes and bring to boil, low the level heat, and cook uncovered for 30 minutes.
4. Meanwhile, boil penne pasta according to your package instructions. Set it aside.
5. In a large-sized skillet, heat butter and cook shrimp on medium heat for 3 to 4 minutes, add scallops and mix for 10 seconds, and remove skillet from the stove.
6. Add prepared sauce, peas, ½ cup of parmesan cheese pasta, and basil and mix well until fully incorporated.
7. Pour the mixture into a 13x9 inch greased baking dish and top up with remaining cheese.
8. Cover with lid and bake in a preheated oven for around 35 minutes; after 35 minutes, uncover the dish and bake for additional 10 minutes until the top is slightly browned.

Nutrition: Calories: 563.8. **Fat:** 12.3 g. **Protein:** 37.2 g. **Carbs:** 78 g.

Breads

355. Basic Fruit Bread

Preparation Time: 10 minutes
Cooking Time: 45 minutes
Servings: 6
Ingredients:

- 3 cups all-purpose flour
- 2 tbsp. baking powder
- 1 tbsp. baking soda
- ½ tbsp. salt
- 1 cup white sugar
- ½ cup vegetable oil
- 2 eggs
- 1 cup apple, shredded
- ¾ cup walnuts, chopped
- ½ tbsp. vanilla extract

Directions:
1. In a mixing bowl, mix flour, baking powder, baking soda, salt, white sugar, vegetable oil, eggs, apple, walnuts, and vanilla extract until moistened
2. Grease the loaf pan and pour the mixture on it.
3. Slide the pizza rack on shelf position 5 of the oven and place the loaf pan on top.
4. Select the bake setting. Set the temperature at 350° F for 35 minutes. Press starts.
5. Let the bread cool before serving.

Nutrition: Calories: 391. **Carbs:** 52 g. **Fat:** 18 g. **Protein:** 7 g.

356. Bagel And Cheese Bake

Preparation Time: 10 minutes
Cooking Time: 45 minutes
Servings: 12
Ingredients:

- ½ lb. pork
- ½ cup onions, raw
- 3 bagels
- 1 cup cheddar cheese
- 12 eggs
- 2 cups of milk, reduced fat
- 2 tbsp. parsley
- ¼ tbsp. black pepper
- ½ cup parmesan cheese, grated

Directions:
1. Cook bacon and onion in a nonstick skillet and cook over medium heat until well browned. Drain and set aside.
2. Slice the bagel into 6 slices, then arrange them on a greased baking dish. Cover the bagels with bacon and onion mixture, then top with cheese.

3. In a mixing bowl, whisk together eggs, milk, parsley, and pepper. Pour the egg mixture on the bagels and refrigerate overnight while covered.
4. Place the baking sheet on the pizza rack of the oven and select the bake setting. Set the temperature at 400° F for 30 minutes. Press starts.
5. Sprinkle parmesan cheese and serve when warm. Enjoy.

Nutrition: Calories: 249. **Carbs:** 15 g. **Fat:** 13.5 g. **Protein:** 17 g.

357. Bread Machine Bagels

Preparation Time: 10 minutes
Cooking Time: 45 minutes
Servings: 6
Ingredients:

- 1 cup water
- 1-½ tbsp. salt
- 2 tbsp. sugars
- 3 cups wheat flour
- 2-¼ tbsp. yeast
- 3 tbsp. granulated sugar
- 1 tbsp. cornmeal
- 1 egg
- 3 tbsp. poppy seeds

Directions:
1. Place water, sugar, salt, flour, and yeast in a bread machine. Select dough setting.
2. Let the dough rest on a floured surface.
3. Meanwhile, bring water to a boil, then stir with sugar. Cut dough into nine pieces and roll each into a ball.
4. Flatten and poke a hole on the ball using your hands. Cover the bagels and let rest for 10 minutes.
5. Sprinkle cornmeal on a baking sheet, then transfer the bagels to boiling water. Let boil for 1 minute, then drain them on a clean paper towel.
6. Arrange the bagels on a baking sheet, then glaze them with egg and sprinkle poppy seeds.
7. Place the baking sheet on the pizza rack of the Emeril Lagasse Power oven 360 and select the bake setting. Set the temperature at 375° F for 25 minutes. Press starts.
8. The bagels should be well browned and cooked.

Nutrition: Calories: 50. **Carbs:** 9 g. **Fat:** 1.3 g. **Protein:** 1.4 g.

358. Marvelous Chocolate Zucchini Bread

Preparation Time: 20 minutes
Cooking Time: 45 minutes
Servings: 2
Ingredients:

- 3 medium eggs
- 1 cup sugar
- 1 cup vegetable oil

- 2 cup grated zucchini
- 1 tsp. vanilla extract
- ¾ cup semisweet chocolate chips
- ⅓ cup cocoa powder
- 2 cup wheat flour
- 1 tsp. baking soda
- A pinch of salt
- 1 tsp. ground cinnamon

Directions:
1. Spray 2 baking pans with cooking spray.
2. In a medium mixing bowl, add cocoa powder, eggs, oil, grated zucchini, vanilla, and sugar. Stir to combine. Fold in flour, baking soda, salt, and cinnamon. Then, add chocolate chips.
3. Pour batter into baking pans. Bake on 1-inch rack on power level High (350º C) for 40 to 45 minutes until a knife inserted in the center comes out clean. Allow bread to rest inside the dome for 1 to 2 minutes before removing it from NuWave Oven. Allow cooling before slicing.

Nutrition: Calories: 217.0. **Total Fat:** 8.0 g. **Total Carbs:** 37.0 g. **Protein:** 3.0 g.

359. Fragrant Orange Bread

Preparation Time: 5 minutes
Cooking Time: 45 minutes
Servings: 8
Ingredients:

- 1 cup milk,
- 3 tbsp. freshly clasped orange juice
- 3 tbsp. sugar
- 1 tbsp. melted butter cooled
- 1 tsp. salt
- 3 cups white bread flour
- Zest of 1 orange
- 1 ¼ tsp. bread machine or instant yeast

Directions:
1. Place the ingredients in your Hamilton Beach bread machine.
2. Select the Bake cycle. Program the machine for Whitbread, choose the light or medium crust, and press Start. If the loaf is done, remove the bucket from the machine. Allow the loaf to cool for 5 minutes.
3. Moderately shake the pan to eliminate the loaf and turn it out onto a rack to cool.

Nutrition: Calories: 277. **Cholesterol:** 9 g. **Carbs:** 48.4 g. **Dietary Fiber:** 1.9 g. **Sugars:** 3.3 g. **Protein:** 9.4 g.

360. Strawberry Shortcake Bread

Preparation Time: 10 minutes
Cooking Time: 45 minutes
Servings: 8
Ingredients:

- ½ cups milk, at 80° F to 90° F

- 3 tbsp. melted butter, cooled
- 3 tbsp. sugar
- 1 ½ tsp. salt
- ¾ cup sliced fresh strawberries
- 1 cup quick oats
- 2 ¼ cups white bread flour
- 1 ½ tsp. bread machine or instant yeast

Directions:
1. Place the ingredients in your Hamilton Beach bread machine.
2. Select the Bake cycle. Program the machine for Whitbread, choose light or medium crust, and press Start.
3. If the loaf is done, remove the bucket from the machine.
4. Let the loaf cool for 5 minutes. Moderately shake the can to remove the loaf and turn it out onto a rack to cool.

Nutrition: Calories: 277. **Cholesterol:** 9 g. **Carbs:** 48.4 g. **Dietary Fiber:** 1.9 g. **Sugars:** 3.3 g. **Protein:** 9.4 g.

361. Blueberry Bread

Preparation Time: 3 hours 15 minutes
Cooking Time: 40 to 45 minutes
Servings: 1 loaf
Ingredients:

- 1 ⅛ to 1 ¼ cups water
- 6 oz. cream cheese, softened
- 2 tbsp. butter or margarine
- ¼ cup sugar
- 2 tsp. salt
- 4 ½ cups bread flour
- 1 ½ tsp. grated lemon peel
- 2 tsp. cardamom
- 2 tbsp. nonfat dry milk
- 2 ½ tsp. red star brand active dry yeast
- ⅔ cup dried blueberries

Directions:
1. Place all ingredients except dried blueberries in the bread pan, using the least amount of liquid listed in the recipe. Select light crust setting and the raisin/nut cycle. Press the start button.
2. Watch the dough as you knead. After 5 to 10 minutes, if it is dry and hard or if the machine seems to strain to knead it, add more liquid 1 tbsp. at a time until the dough forms a ball that is soft, tender, and slightly sticky to the touch.
3. When stimulated, add dried cranberries.
4. After the bake cycle is complete, remove the bread from the pan, place it on the cake, and allow it to cool.

Nutrition: Calories: 180. **Total Carbs:** 250 g. **Fat:** 3 g. **Protein:** 9 g.

362. Pineapple Coconut Bread

Preparation Time: 10 minutes
Cooking Time: 45 minutes
Servings: 8
Ingredients:

- 6 tbsp. butter, at room temperature
- 2 eggs, at room temperature
- ½ cup coconut milk, at room temperature
- ½ cup pineapple juice, at room temperature
- 1 cup sugar
- 1 ½ tsp. coconut extract
- 2 cups all-purpose flour
- ¾ cup shredded sweetened coconut
- 1 tsp. baking powder
- ½ tsp. salt

Directions:

1. Place the butter, eggs, coconut milk, pineapple juice, sugar, and coconut extract in your Hamilton Beach bread machine.
2. Select the Bake cycle. Program the machine for Rapid bread and press Start. While the wet ingredients are mingling, stir together the flour, coconut, baking powder, and salt in a small bowl. After the first mixing is done and the machine motions, add the dry ingredients. When the loaf is done, eliminate the bucket from the machine. Let the loaf cool for 5 minutes. Slightly shake the pot to remove the loaf and turn it out onto a rack to cool.

Nutrition: Calories: 277. **Cholesterol:** 9 g. **Carbs:** 48.4 g. **Dietary Fiber:** 1.9 g. **Sugars:** 3.3 g. **Protein:** 9.4 g.

363. Fruit Syrup Bread

Preparation Time: 10 minutes
Cooking Time: 45 minutes
Servings: 8
Ingredients:

- 3 ⅔ cups whole wheat flour
- 1 ½ tsp. instant yeast
- ¼ cup unsalted butter, melted
- 1 cup lukewarm water
- 2 tbsp. sugar
- ¼ cup rolled oats
- ½ tsp. salt
- ½ cup syrup from preserved fruit

Directions:

1. Combine the syrup and ½ cup water. Heat until lukewarm. Add more water to precisely 1 cup of water.
2. Place all the ingredients, except for the rolled oats and butter, in a liquid-dry yeast layering.
3. Put the pan in the Hamilton Beach bread machine.
4. Load the rolled oats in the automatic dispenser.
5. Select the Bake cycle. Choose whole-wheat loaf.
6. Press start and wait until the loaf is cooked.

7. Brush the top with butter once cooked.
8. The machine will start the keep warm mode after the bread is complete.
9. Let it remain in that mode for about 10 minutes before unplugging.
10. Remove the pan and let it cool down for about 10 minutes.

Nutrition: Calories: 277. **Cholesterol:** 9 g. **Carbs:** 48.4 g. **Dietary Fiber:** 1.9 g. **Sugars:** 3.3 g. **Protein:** 9.4 g.

364. Lemon-Lime Blueberry Bread

Preparation Time: 10 minutes
Cooking Time: 45 minutes
Servings: 8
Ingredients:

- ¾ cup plain yogurt, at room temperature
- ½ cup water
- 3 tbsp. honey
- 1 tbsp. melted butter cooled
- 1 ½ tsp. salt
- ½ tsp. lemon extract
- 1 tsp. lime zest
- 1 cup dried blueberries
- 3 cups white bread flour
- 2 ¼ tsp. bread machine or instant yeast

Directions:

1. Place the ingredients in your Hamilton Beach bread machine.
2. Select the Bake cycle. Program the machine for Whitbread, choose light or medium crust, then press Start.
3. Remove the bucket from the machine.
4. Let the loaf cool for 5 minutes.
5. Gently shake the pan to remove the loaf and turn it out onto a rack to cool.

Nutrition: Calories: 277. **Cholesterol:** 9 g. **Carbs:** 48.4 g. **Dietary Fiber:** 1.9 g. **Sugars:** 3.3 g. **Protein:** 9.4 g.

365. Cranberry Yogurt Bread

Preparation Time: 10 minutes
Cooking Time: 45 minutes
Servings: 8
Ingredients:

- 3 cups + 2 tbsp. bread or all-purpose flour
- ½ cup lukewarm water
- 1 tbsp. olive or coconut oil
- 1 tbsp. orange or lemon essential oil
- 3 tbsp. sugar
- ¾ cup yogurt
- 2 tsp. instant yeast
- 1 cup dried cried cranberries
- ½ cup raisins

Directions:

1.   Place all ingredients, except cranberries and raisins, in the bread pan in the liquid-dry yeast layering.
2.   Put the pan in the Hamilton Beach bread machine.
3.   Load the fruits in the automatic dispenser.
4.   Select the Bake cycle. Choose White bread.
5.   Press start and wait until the loaf is cooked.
6.   The machine will start the keep warm mode after the bread is complete.
7.   Allow it to stay in that mode for at least 10 minutes before unplugging.
8.   Remove the pan and let it cool down for about 10 minutes.

Nutrition: Calories: 277. **Cholesterol:** 9 g. **Carbs:** 48.4 g. **Dietary Fiber:** 1.9 g. **Sugars:** 3.3 g. **Protein:** 9.4 g.

Pizza

366. Sea and Mountains Pizza

Preparation Time: 20 minutes
Cooking Time: 45 minutes
Servings: 4
Ingredients:

- Flour
- Olive oil
- 500 g bread dough
- 1 tbsp. parsley
- Garlic, to taste
- 5 pear tomatoes
- White wine to taste
- 1 kg mussel
- Butter to taste
- Salt and pepper to taste
- 5 kg mushrooms, dried

Directions:

1. Under running water, scrape 1 kg of mussels and in a covered saucepan on high flame, leave them to open. Remove shells for 3 quarters and leave the rest kept in their shells.
2. Clean at least 500 g of fresh mushrooms and then cut them into slices.
3. In a large saucepan, put 10 g of butter and 3 tbsp. of oil and brown 3 garlic cloves. Add the pepper, salt, and mushrooms. On low heat, cover them and sauté for 5 to 6 minutes.
4. Use 1 tsp. of flour and 1 tbsp. of chopped parsley to sprinkle. Also, use half a glass of wine to sprinkle and turn off the heat after thickening over low heat.
5. On the oven plate greased with oil, spread 500 g of bread dough. Spread at least 5 Perini tomatoes cut into rounds over the pasta. Put in a hot oven to cook for 15 minutes at 200° F after sprinkling with some little salt and oil.
6. Take the plate away from the oven and put all the mussels on tomatoes. Put in the oven to bake for 10 minutes at 210° F while they are covered with the mushrooms.

Nutrition: Calories: 651. **Protein:** 163.2 g. **Fat:** 59.22 g. **Carbs:** 86.09 g.

367. Romana Pizza

Preparation Time: 30 minutes
Cooking Time: 45 minutes
Servings: 4
Ingredients:

- 600 mL water
- 7 g dry brewer's yeast
- 1 kg flour
- 60 g extra virgin olive oil
- 20 g salt

Stuffing:

- 600 g Fiordilatte
- 10 g oregano
- 700 g tomato sauce
- 16 fillets anchovies in oil
- 20 g salt
- Extra virgin olive oil

Directions:

1. In preparing Roman pizza, begin with the pizza dough. In a bowl, add the flour, 100 mL of water, yeast, and use the planetary mixer with its hook mounted at medium-low speed.
2. Continue by adding a little water at a time and make sure the flour has been well absorbed by water before adding more. Add salt and keep kneading after adding at least ¾ of water. Add the remaining water and allow the planetary mixer to work until you obtain a homogeneous and smooth mixture.
3. At this particular point, gradually add the oil little by little. Remove the dough from the planetary mixer when the oil has been fully absorbed and use your hands to shape it until you get a ball. Put the ball in a lightly greased bowl.
4. Use a clean cloth or a cling film to cover and allow it to rise in the oven while lights are on. Hold on until the dough has doubled in its size but better if tripled and continue with the pizza preparation.
5. Transfer the dough to the pastry board once it rises and divide it into 4 equal parts. Do this for each of the balls. Let it stand for 30 minutes after covering it with a clean tea towel.
6. Use a drizzle of oil to lightly grease four 30 cm diameter pizza pans and put the dough ball in the center of the pan. Begin squeezing from the center outwards if necessary, pulling the sides slightly. If the dough tends to return to its original shape or it's too elastic, put aside the pizza that you spread and begin rolling another one, leaving the previous one to rest. Try spreading the dough over the whole surface of the tray.
7. In a large bowl, pour in the tomato sauce and season with oil, pepper, salt, and oregano. On the pizza base, pour a generous ladle of tomato sauce and spread it in a circular motion leaving only a boarder of 1.5 cm but covering almost the entire area.
8. Chop the mozzarella coarsely. Use a drizzle of oil, the mozzarella cut into small pieces, and anchovy fillets to season the pizza. Allow the stuffed pizza to rest for 20 minutes and then bake it at 250° F in a static oven.
9. Serve your roman pizza immediately it is out of the oven.

Nutrition: Calories: 158. **Protein:** 31.19 g. **Fat:** 9.22 g. **Carbs:** 227.85 g.

368. Cheeses Pizza

Preparation Time: 20 minutes

Cooking Time: 45 minutes
Servings: 4
Ingredients:

- 80 g gorgonzola
- 500 g bread dough
- 100 g mozzarella
- 100 g fontina
- 80 g parmesan
- Salt to taste
- Pepper to taste
- 2 tbsp. extra virgin olive oil
- 10 g flour

Directions:

1. On a lightly floured pastry board, put the bread dough and roll it out using a rolling pin into a sheet of about 7 mm thick.
2. Brush a baking sheet with a drizzle of oil and on a cutting board, put the fontina and gorgonzola and remove the crust, and cut them into small cubes using a sharp knife.
3. Chop the mozzarella coarsely and drain it. You could alternatively use some fiordilatte mozzarella that has got a drier composition.
4. In the pan, spread all the cheese over the pasta and then flavor with a generous mince of pepper and a pinch of salt.
5. In a preheated oven at 220° F, bake the pizza for 25 minutes and then serve it while it's very hot.

Nutrition: Calories: 652. **Protein:** 35.32 g. **Fat:** 21.51 g. **Carbs:** 80.2 g.

369. Seasons Pizza

Preparation Time: 40 minutes
Cooking Time: 45 minutes
Servings: 4
Ingredients:

- 5 g sugar
- 270 mL water
- 500 g Manitoba flour
- 10 g salt
- 50 mL oil
- Extra virgin olive oil
- 500 mL tomato sauce
- 10 g salt
- 25 g cube, fresh brewer's yeast
- Oregano
- 100 g artichokes in oil
- 50 g champignon mushrooms
- 120 g cooked ham
- Mozzarella
- 50 g black olives

Directions:

1. To prepare this type of pizza, begin with the dough. Get a bowl and pour in oil, water, sugar, salt, and lastly the flour and yeast tube then begin kneading for about 20 minutes. Cover the dough with a cloth and allow it to rise for at least an hour in a dry and cool place that is away from the light.
2. Heat the oven to 200° F and cut the mozzarella into thin slices and put it aside. In a bowl, pour in the tomato puree and use extra virgin olive oil, a pinch of salt, and oregano to season it.
3. When the time for leavening ends, lay out the pasta after covering a baking sheet with parchment paper. Put the tomato puree on the top and then cook for 15 minutes in a preheated oven.
4. Clean and wash the artichokes, mushrooms, and olives. Chop them finely and set them aside.
5. Remove the pizza from the oven after 15 minutes and arrange the mozzarella slices and divide the pizza into four wedges. In one wedge, arrange the chopped olives, in another wedge, arrange the champignon mushrooms, in the third wedge, arrange the artichokes and in the fourth and last wedge, put the cooked ham and bake for more than 5 minutes.
6. Serve your 4 seasons pizza steaming and hot.

Nutrition: Calories: 574. **Protein:** 21.25 g. **Fat:** 5.86 g. **Carbs:** 108.89 g.

370. Siciliana Pizza

Preparation Time: 6 hours
Cooking Time: 45 minutes
Servings: 4
Ingredients:
The dough:

- 250 g flour
- ½ sachet dry brewer's yeast
- 250 g Remilled semolina
- 5 g salt
- 2 spoons olive oil
- 350 mL water
- 1 tsp. sugar

The dressing:

- Braid of mozzarella
- Peeled tomatoes
- Oregano
- Basil
- Salt
- Anchovy fillets

Directions:

1. In a bowl, put the yeast, sugar, and flour and first mix. Add salt and water gradually, if the dough gets too hard, add more water and if it's soft, do not add the remaining water.
2. Lastly, add the oil and begin using your hands to knead passing the dough on a pastry board. You can put

the dough inside a planetary mixer if you have one and use a hook.

3.   Take at least 10 to 15 minutes kneading the dough and when you get a soft but not sticky ball, allow it to rest for at least 3 hours after sprinkling it with flour.

4.   Get a baking sheet and grease it. Roll out the dough on it and obtain a layer that is not too high. Leave it to rise for another 3 hours.

5.   Preheat the oven to maximum temperature. Season the tomato sauce with oregano, basil, oil, and anchovy fillets, also stuff the well-risen pizza and bake it for at least 10 minutes. Underneath, it should be golden brown.

6.   Take the pizza out from the oven and fill the entire surface with crumbled mozzarella and then bake for more than 5 minutes until the mozzarella melts.

7.   Remove from the oven and before serving let it rest for at least 5 minutes.

Nutrition: Calories: 463. **Protein:** 14.94 g. **Fat:** 1.43 g. **Carbs:** 95.03 g.

371. Diavola Pizza

Preparation Time: 45 minutes
Cooking Time: 45 minutes
Servings: 4
Ingredients:
Dough:

- 200 mL brewer's yeast
- ½ loaf
- 3 tbsp. extra virgin olive oil
- 1 tsp. salt
- 400 g flour

Dressing:

- Extra virgin olive oil
- Salt to taste
- Oregano to taste
- 150 g spicy salami
- 250 g mozzarella
- 400 g tomato sauce

Directions:

1.   Start by preparing the pizza dough. Get a baking tray and grease it with a drizzle of oil, roll out the dough and put it there, cover with tomato puree, and put the pizza to cook in an already hot oven for 10 minutes at 220° F.

2.   Meanwhile, slice the salami and cut the mozzarella into cubes. Remove the pizza from the oven and then evenly distribute the salami and mozzarella slices.

3.   Use a pinch of salt, a drizzle of oil, and a pinch of oregano to season, and then continue cooking for another 20 minutes.

Nutrition: Calories: 738. **Protein:** 40.59 g. **Fat:** 17.65 g. **Carbs:** 98.56 g.

Cake

372. Chocolate Cake

Preparation Time: 5 minutes
Cooking Time: 45 minutes
Servings: 8 to 10
Ingredients:

- ½ cup hot water
- 1 tsp. vanilla
- ¼ cup olive oil
- ½ cup almond milk
- 1 egg
- ½ tsp. salt
- ¾ tsp. baking soda
- ¾ tsp. baking powder
- ½ cup unsweetened cocoa powder
- 2 cups almond flour
- 1 cup brown sugar

Directions:
1. Preheat your oven to 356° F. Stir all dry ingredients together. Then stir in wet ingredients. Add hot water last. The batter will be thin, no worries.
2. Pour cake batter into a pan that fits into the oven. Cover with foil and poke holes into the foil. Bake 35 minutes. Discard foil and then bake another 10 minutes.
Nutrition: Calories: 135. **Carbs:** 21 g. **Fat:** 5 g. **Protein:** 3 g.

373. Banana-Choco Brownies

Preparation Time: 5 minutes
Cooking Time: 45 minutes
Servings: 12
Ingredients:

- 2 cups almond flour
- 2 tsp. baking powder
- ½ tsp. baking powder
- ½ tsp. baking soda
- ½ tsp. salt
- 1 over-ripe banana
- 3 large eggs
- ½ tsp. stevia powder
- ¼ cup coconut oil
- 1 tbsp. vinegar
- ⅓ cup almond flour
- ⅓ cup cocoa powder

Directions:
1. Preheat the oven for 5 minutes. Combine all ingredients in a food processor and pulse until well-combined.
2. Pour into a baking dish that will fit in the oven. Place in the oven basket and cook for 30 minutes at 350° F, or if a toothpick inserted in the middle comes out clean.

Nutrition: Calories: 113. **Carbs:** 28 g. **Fat:** 3 g. **Protein:** 2 g.

374. Chocolate Donuts

Preparation Time: 5 minutes
Cooking Time: 45 minutes
Servings: 8 to 10
Ingredients:

- 1 (8-oz.) can jumbo biscuits
- Cooking oil
- Chocolate sauce, such as Hershey's

Directions:
1. Separate the biscuit dough into 8 biscuits and place them on a flat work surface. Use a small circle cookie cutter or a biscuit cutter to cut a hole in each biscuit center. You can also cut the holes using a knife.
2. Spray the oven basket with cooking oil; place 4 donuts in the oven. Spray with cooking oil—Cook for 4 minutes.
3. Open the oven and flip the donuts—Cook for an additional 4 minutes. Remove the cooked donuts from the oven, then repeat for the remaining 4 donuts.
4. Drizzle chocolate sauce over the donuts and enjoy while warm.
Nutrition: Calories: 240. **Carbs:** 28 g. **Fat:** 14 g. **Protein:** 3 g.

375. Apple Hand Pies

Preparation Time: 5 minutes
Cooking Time: 45 minutes
Servings: 6
Ingredients:

- 15-oz. no-sugar-added apple pie filling
- 1 store-bought crust

Directions:
1. Lay out pie crust and slice into equal-sized squares. Place 2 tbsp filling into each square and seal crust with a fork.
2. Pour into the oven rack. Put the rack on the middle shelf of the oven. Set temperature to 390° F, and set time to 8 minutes until golden in color.
Nutrition: Calories: 135. **Carbs:** 19 g. **Fat:** 6 g. **Protein:** 1 g.

376. Cinnamon Fried Bananas

Preparation Time: 5 minutes
Cooking Time: 45 minutes
Servings: 2 to 3
Ingredients:

- 1 cup panko breadcrumbs
- 3 tbsp. cinnamon
- ½ cup almond flour
- 3 egg whites
- 8 ripe bananas
- 3 tbsp. vegan coconut oil

Directions:

1.	Heat coconut oil and add breadcrumbs. Mix around 2 to 3 minutes until golden. Pour into a bowl.
2.	Peel and cut bananas in half. Roll each banana half into flour, eggs, and crumb mixture.
3.	Place into the air fryer oven. Cook 10 minutes at 280° F.
4.	A great addition to a healthy banana split!

Nutrition: Calories: 219. **Fat:** 10 g. **Protein:** 3 g. **Sugar:** 5 g.

377. Coconutty Lemon Bars

Preparation Time: 5 minutes
Cooking Time: 45 minutes
Servings: 12
Ingredients:

- ¼ cup cashew
- ¼ cup fresh lemon juice, freshly squeezed
- ¾ cup coconut milk
- ¾ cup erythritol
- 1 cup desiccated coconut
- 1 tsp. baking powder
- 2 eggs, beaten
- 2 tbsp. coconut oil
- Salt

Directions:

1.	Preheat the air fryer oven for 5 minutes. In a mixing bowl, combine all ingredients. Use a hand mixer to mix everything. Pour into a baking dish that will fit in the air fryer.
2.	Bake for 25 minutes at 350° F or until a toothpick inserted in the middle comes out clean.

Nutrition: Calories: 118. **Fat:** 10 g. **Protein:** 2.6 g. **Sugar:** 5 g.

Cookies

378. Oatmeal Cookie Peach Cobbler

Preparation Time: 40 minutes
Cooking Time: 45 minutes
Servings: 12
Ingredients:
Topping:
- ½ cup granulated sugar
- ½ cup packed brown sugar
- ½ cup softened butter
- 2 tsp. vanilla extract
- 1 large egg
- 1 cup all-purpose flour
- 1 cup old-fashioned rolled oats
- ½ tsp. baking powder
- ½ tsp. salt

Filling:
- 11 cups sliced peeled peaches
- ⅓ cup granulated sugar
- 2 tbsp. all-purpose flour
- 2 tbsp. fresh lemon juice

Directions:
1. Start by preheating the toaster oven to 350° F.
2. Combine butter and sugars in a medium bowl until creamed and set aside.
3. Add vanilla and egg and mix well.
4. Combine flour, oats, and baking powder in a separate bowl.
5. Mix sugar mixture and flour mixture together.
6. Cover the bowl and refrigerate for half an hour.
7. While topping chills, make the filling by combining peaches, lemon juice, flour, and sugar in a bowl.
8. Spray a baking dish with cooking spray and fill with peach mix.
9. Dollop spoonfuls of topping evenly over peaches. Bake for 40 minutes.

Nutrition: Calories: 281. **Sodium:** 160 mg. **Dietary Fiber:** 3.4 g. **Total Fat:** 9.0 g. **Total Carbs:** 48.5 g. **Protein:** 4.2 g.

379. Oatmeal Raisin Cookies

Preparation Time: 10 minutes
Cooking Time: 45 minutes
Servings: 12
Ingredients:
- 2-½ cups uncooked oatmeal
- 1 cup flour
- 2 eggs
- ½ tsp. salt
- 1 cup butter
- 1 tsp. vanilla
- 1 cup brown sugar
- ⅓ cup sugar
- 1 tsp. baking soda
- 1 tsp. ground cinnamon
- 1 cup raisins

Directions:
1. Start by preheating the toaster oven to 350° F.
2. Mix vanilla, brown sugar, butter, and salt.
3. Add sugar, eggs, baking soda, and cinnamon one at a time until fully mixed.
4. Stir in the oats, then the raisins.
5. Drop spoonfuls of cookie dough onto an ungreased baking sheet (about six per batch).
6. Bake for 20 minutes.

Nutrition: Calories: 353. **Sodium:** 326 mg. **Dietary Fiber:** 2.6 g. **Total Fat:** 17.3 g. **Total Carbs:** 46.7 g. **Protein:** 4.8 g.

380. Peanut Butter Cookies

Preparation Time: 10 minutes
Cooking Time: 45 minutes
Servings: 1
Ingredients:
- 2 tbsp. flour
- 1-½ tbsp. peanut butter
- 1/16 tsp. baking soda
- Pinch of salt
- ¼ tsp. pure vanilla extract
- 1-½ tbsp. maple syrup
- 1 tsp. applesauce

Directions:
1. Start by preheating the toaster oven to 350° F.
2. Mix all of the dry ingredients in one bowl.
3. Mix in peanut butter, then the rest of the ingredients.
4. Spray a small pan and drop cookies onto the pan, then flatten.
5. Bake for 10 minutes.

Nutrition: Calories: 281. **Sodium:** 348 mg. **Dietary Fiber:** 1.9 g. **Total Fat:** 12.3 g. **Total Carbs:** 37.5 g. **Protein:** 7.6 g.

381. Single-Serving Chocolate Chip Cookies

Preparation Time: 10 minutes
Cooking Time: 45 minutes
Servings: 1
Ingredients:
- 2 tbsp. butter
- 2 firmly packed tbsp. dark brown sugar
- 1 tbsp. granulated sugar
- Pinch of salt
- ¼ tsp. pure vanilla extract
- 1 egg yolk

- ¼ tsp. baking soda
- ¼ cup all-purpose flour
- 3 heaping tbsp. semi-sweet chocolate chips

Directions:

1.   Start by preheating the toaster oven to 350° F.
2.   Soften butter and combine with sugars, salt, and vanilla.
3.   Add egg yolk and continue to stir.
4.   Add flour and baking soda and stir until combined.
5.   Add chocolate chips to the bowl and mix until evenly distributed.
6.   Line a pan with parchment paper and separate dough into two equal parts in the pan.
7.   Bake for 8 minutes.

Nutrition: Calories: 667. **Sodium:** 645 mg. **Dietary Fiber:** 3.1 g. **Total Fat:** 39.9 g. **Total Carbs:** 73.4 g. **Protein:** 6.2 g.

Dessert

382. Zucchini Muffins

Preparation Time: 10 minutes
Cooking Time: 45 minutes
Servings: 8
Ingredients:

- 6 eggs
- 4 drops stevia
- ¼ cup Swerve
- ⅓ cup coconut oil, melted
- 1 cup zucchini, grated
- ¾ cup coconut flour
- ¼ tsp. ground nutmeg
- 1 tsp. ground cinnamon
- ½ tsp. baking soda

Directions:
1. Preheat the oven to 325° F.
2. Add all ingredients except zucchini to a bowl and mix well.
3. Add zucchini and stir well.
4. Pour batter into the silicone muffin molds and place it into the fryer basket.
5. Cook muffins for 20 minutes.
6. Serve and enjoy.

Nutrition: Calories: 136. **Fat:** 12 g. **Carbs:** 1 g. **Sugar:** 0.6 g. **Protein:** 4 g. **Cholesterol:** 123 mg.

383. Jalapeno Breakfast Muffins

Preparation Time: 10 minutes
Cooking Time: 45 minutes
Servings: 8
Ingredients:

- 5 eggs
- ⅓ cup coconut oil, melted
- 2 tsp. baking powder
- 3 tbsp. erythritol
- 3 tbsp. jalapenos, sliced
- ¼ cup unsweetened coconut milk
- ⅔ cup coconut flour
- ¾ tsp. sea salt

Directions:
1. Preheat the oven to 325° F.
2. In a large bowl, stir together coconut flour, baking powder, erythritol, and sea salt.
3. Stir in eggs, jalapenos, coconut milk, and coconut oil until well combined.
4. Pour batter into the silicone muffin molds and place it into the fryer basket.
5. Cook muffins for 15 minutes.
6. Serve and enjoy.

Nutrition: Calories: 125. **Fat:** 12 g. **Carbs:** 7 g. **Sugar:** 6 g. **Protein:** 3 g. **Cholesterol:** 102 mg.

384. Fried Peaches

Preparation Time: 2 hours and 10 minutes
Cooking Time: 45 minutes
Servings: 4
Ingredients:

- 4 ripe peaches (½ a peach = 1 serving)
- 1 ½ cups flour
- Salt
- 2 egg yolks
- ¾ cups cold water
- 1 ½ tbsp. olive oil
- 2 tbsp. brandy
- 4 egg whites
- Cinnamon/sugar mix

Directions:
1. Mix flour, egg yolks, and salt in a mixing bowl. Slowly mix in water, then add brandy. Set the mixture aside for 2 hours and do something for 1 hour 45 minutes.
2. Boil a large pot of water and cut an X at the bottom of each peach. While the water boils, fill another large bowl with water and ice. Boil each peach for about a minute, then plunge it into the ice bath. Now the peels should fall off the peach. Beat the egg whites and mix them into the batter mix. Dip each peach in the mix to coat.
3. Pour the coated peach into the oven rack/basket. Place the rack on the middle shelf of the oven. Set temperature to 360° F, and set time to 10 minutes.
4. Prepare a plate with cinnamon/sugar mix, roll peaches in the mix and serve.

Nutrition: Calories: 306. **Fat:** 3 g. **Protein:** 10 g. **Fiber:** 2.7 g.

385. Apple Pie in Air Fryer

Preparation Time: 5 minutes
Cooking Time: 45 minutes
Servings: 4
Ingredients:

- ½ tsp. vanilla extract
- 1 beaten egg
- 1 large apple, chopped
- 1 Pillsbury refrigerator pie crust
- 1 tbsp. butter
- 1 tbsp. ground cinnamon
- 1 tbsp. raw sugar
- 2 tbsp. sugars
- 2 tsp. lemon juice
- Baking spray

Directions:
1. Lightly grease the baking pan of the oven with cooking spray. Spread pie crust on the bottom of the pan up to the sides.

In a bowl, mix vanilla, sugar, cinnamon, lemon juice, and apples. Pour on top of pie crust, then top apples with butter slices.

2.   Cover apples with the other pie crust. Pierce with a knife the tops of the pie.

3.   Spread beaten egg on top of crust and sprinkle sugar.

4.   Cover with foil.

5.   For 25 minutes, cook at 390° F.

6.   Remove foil cook for 10 minutes at 330° F until tops are browned.

7.   Serve and enjoy.

Nutrition: Calories: 372. **Fat:** 19 g. **Protein:** 4.2 g. **Sugar:** 5 g.

60 Minutes

Breakfast

386. Ham Cheese Casserole
Preparation Time: 10 minutes
Cooking Time: 60 minutes
Servings: 12
Ingredients:
- 12 eggs
- 8 cups frozen hash browns
- 1 cup almond milk
- 8 oz. cheddar cheese, shredded
- 16 oz. ham, cubed
- ½ tsp. pepper
- 1 tsp. salt

Directions:
1. Preheat the oven to 350° F.
2. Spray a 9x13-inch baking dish with cooking spray and set aside.
3. In a bowl, mix cheese, ham, and frozen potatoes and pour into the prepared baking dish.
4. In a mixing bowl, whisk eggs with milk, pepper, and salt.
5. Pour egg mixture over cheese ham mixture.
6. Place baking dish onto the oven rack and bake for 55 to 60 minutes.
7. Serve and enjoy.
Nutrition: Calories: 523. **Fat:** 31.7 g. **Carbs:** 39.7 g. **Sugar:** 2.7 g. **Protein:** 20.1 g. **Cholesterol:** 205 mg.

387. Healthy Banana Bread
Preparation Time: 10 minutes
Cooking Time: 60 minutes
Servings: 12
Ingredients:
- 2 eggs
- 3 ripe bananas
- 1 tsp. baking soda
- 1 cup sugar
- 1 tsp. vanilla
- 1 stick butter, melted
- 2 cups flour
- ¼ tsp. ground cinnamon
- ½ tsp. salt

Directions:
1. Preheat the oven to 350° F.
2. Add bananas and melted butter in a mixing bowl and mash with a fork.
3. Add eggs and vanilla and stir until well combined.
4. In a separate bowl, mix flour, baking soda, cinnamon, salt, and sugar.

5. Add flour mixture to the banana mixture and mix until just combined.
6. Pour batter into the greased 9x5-inch loaf pan.
7. Place loaf pan onto the oven rack and bake for 45 to 55 minutes.
8. Slice and serve.
Nutrition: Calories: 244. **Fat:** 8.7 g. **Carbs:** 39.5 g. **Sugar:** 20.5 g. **Protein:** 3.5 g. **Cholesterol:** 48 mg.

388. Cowboy Quiche
Preparation Time: 35 minutes
Cooking Time: 60 minutes
Servings: 8
Ingredients:
- 1 red potato with sliced skin (keep it short)
- 1 onion, minced
- ½ jalapeno with minced seeds
- 1 stick butter, melted
- 1 tsp. salt
- Black pepper
- 10 white mushrooms, minced
- 5 to 7 bacon strips
- ½ cup sliced ham
- ½ red pepper, minced
- ½ green pepper, minced
- ¼ cup grated cheddar
- ¼ cup grated gruyere
- 6 eggs
- 12 oz. milk
- Pint heavy cream
- 1 tsp. ground nutmeg
- 2 unbaked (9-inch) pie doughs

Directions:
1. Preheat the oven to 177° C or 350° F. Put the veggies on a parchment paper-filled tray.
2. Put some melted butter with salt and pepper over vegetables, and bake for 15 minutes.
3. Put mushrooms separately in a parchment paper-filled tray with melted butter on top. Cook for 5 minutes.
4. Cook bacon strips on a different tray until crisp.
5. Put minced ham inside the oven and cook everything properly.
6. Mix all the ingredients to blend properly.
7. Stir eggs, milk, and heavy cream separately, add some salt and black pepper with nutmeg, and mix properly.
8. Add the ingredients in a pan containing raw crust with the egg mixture. Bake for 35 minutes.
Nutrition: Calories: 257.9. **Carbs:** 24 g. **Protein:** 11.6 g. **Fat:** 9 g.

389. Apple Breakfast Bread
Preparation Time: 10 minutes
Cooking Time: 1 hour

Servings: 8

Ingredients:

- 2 medium apples, peeled, cored, chopped
- 2 cups all-purpose flour
- 1 tsp. baking soda
- ½ tsp. salt
- 1 cup sugar
- 1 tsp. ground cinnamon
- ½ tsp. ground cloves
- 2 eggs
- ½ cup butter, unsalted

Directions:

1. Turn on the oven, set the temperature to 350° F, and then select the oven cooking method.
2. Meanwhile, place butter in a large bowl beat in sugar until creamy and smooth, and then beat in eggs until blended.
3. Take a separate large bowl, add flour in it, add cinnamon, cloves, salt, and baking soda and then stir until mixed.
4. Stir the flour mixture into the butter mixture until moistened, and then fold into apple pieces.
5. Take an 8-by-4-inch loaf pan, grease it with butter, spoon the apple mixture in it and then bake for 1 hour until the top turn golden brown and inserted wooden toothpick comes out clean.
6. When done, let the bread cool in its pan for 15 minutes, then cool it completely on a wire rack and cut the bread into slices.
7. Serve straight away.

Nutrition: Calories: 279. **Fat:** 10.5 g. **Carbs:** 43.2 g. **Protein:** 4 g. **Fiber:** 1.5 g.

390. Roasted Breakfast Potatoes

Preparation Time: 5 minutes

Cooking Time: 1 hour

Servings: 6

Ingredients:

- 5 lb. red potatoes
- 1 medium green bell pepper, cored, chopped
- 1 medium white onion, peeled, chopped
- 1 medium red bell pepper, cored, chopped
- 3 tsp. minced garlic
- 1 tsp. salt
- ¾ tsp. smoked paprika
- ¼ cup olive oil

Directions:

1. Turn on the oven, set the temperature to 400° F, and then select the oven cooking method.
2. Meanwhile, dice the potatoes into small pieces and place them in a large bowl.

3. Add onions, bell peppers, and garlic, sprinkle with salt and paprika, drizzle with oil and then toss until coated.
4. Spread the vegetables in an even layer on the baking pan and then bake for 1 hour until potatoes turn golden brown, stirring every 15 minutes.
5. Serve straight away.

Nutrition: Calories: 275. **Fat:** 7 g. **Carbs:** 49 g. **Protein:** 6 g. **Fiber:** 6 g.

391. Sheepherder's Breakfast

Preparation Time: 10 minutes

Cooking Time: 60 minutes

Servings: 8

Ingredients:

- ¾ lb. coarsely sliced bacon slices
- 1 medium sliced onion
- 1 frozen shredded hash brown potato bag (30 oz.), thawed
- 8 big eggs
- ½ tsp. salt
- ¼ tsp. pepper
- 1 cup cheddar cheese, shredded

Directions:

1. Cook bacon and onion in a large pan over medium heat until bacon is crisp. Drain and set aside ¼ cup of the drippings in the pan.
2. Add the hash browns and mix well. Cook, uncovered, over medium heat for about 10 minutes, or until the bottom is golden brown. Potatoes should be turned. Make 8 evenly spaced wells in the potato mixture using the back of a spoon. 1 egg should be broken into each well. Season to taste with salt and pepper.
3. Cook, covered, on low for about 10 minutes, or until eggs are set and potatoes are soft. Sprinkle with cheese and set aside until it melts.

Nutrition: Calories: 354. **Fat:** 22 g. **Saturated Fat:** 9 g. **Cholesterol:** 222 mL. **Sodium:** 617 g. **Carbs:** 22 g. **Sugar:** 2 g. Fiber: 1 g. **Protein:** 17 g.

392. Glazed Honey (Roasted Root Vegetables Recipe)

Preparation Time: 15 minutes

Cooking Time: 60 minutes

Servings: 12

Ingredients:

- Parsnips, sliced and peeled (1 ¼ lb.) (half-inch thick)
- 1 ¼-lb. carrots, peeled and trimmed in ½-inch-thick slices
- ¼ cup celery root, peeled, quartered, and sliced
- ¼ lb. peeled golden beets, cut into ½-inch-thick slices
- ½ cup extra virgin olive oil
- ½ cup honey

- 6 sprigs thyme
- Season with salt and freshly ground pepper.
- 1 tbsp. sherry vinaigrette

Directions:

1. Set the oven to 425° F. Season with salt and pepper, then toss the root vegetables in a big saucepan with the oil, honey, and thyme. Using two large, rimmed baking sheets, divide the mixture in half. Cover with foil and roast for 40 minutes, or until the vegetables are juicy, shifting the pans once. Remove the foil and continue to roast for another 10 minutes, or until glazed. Return them to the bowl and add the vinegar, salt, and pepper to taste. Serve immediately.

Nutrition: Calories: 275. **Fat:** 7 g. **Carbs:** 49 g. **Protein:** 6 g. **Fiber:** 6 g.

393. Breakfast With Cheesy Egg toast (Recipe)

Preparation Time: 10 minutes
Cooking Time: 60 minutes
Servings: 1
Ingredients:

- 1 piece of bread
- ½ tbsp. melted butter
- A single egg
- 3 tbsp. cheese (shredded)
- Salt, to taste
- Pepper, to taste

Directions:

1. To create a pocket, have used a spoon to push down on the center of the bread.
2. Spread the butter around the sides of the bread and crack an egg into the bag.
3. All around bread's edges spread melted cheese.
4. Season with salt and pepper and bake for 10 to 15 minutes at 400° F (204° C). A runny yolk will result after 10 minutes, while a firmer yolk will result after 15 minutes.
5. Have fun!

Nutrition: Calories: 242. **Fat:** 19 g. **Carbs:** 3 g. **Fiber:** 0 g. **Sugar:** 0 g. **Protein:** 13 g.

394. French Toast With Baked Bananas (Recipe)

Preparation Time: 10 minutes
Cooking Time: 60 minutes
Servings: 8
Ingredients:
Sugar glaze with bananas:

- ½ cup (115 g) butter
- ¾ cup (150 g) brown sugar
- 1 tsp. cinnamon
- 1 tsp. extract of vanilla
- 5 bananas, peeled and chopped into slices

Customization:

- 8 large eggs
- ⅓ (150 g) cup brown sugar
- ¼ tsp. nutmeg
- 1 tsp. cinnamon
- 2 tsp. extract from vanilla
- 1 cup (240 mL) heavy cream
- 1 cup (240 mL) milk
- 1 French loaf, sliced into cubes of 1 inch (2 ½ cm)

Garnish:

- To taste, with powdered sugar

Directions:

1. Preheat oven to (180° C) (350° F)
2. Over the medium-high fire, melt the butter and mix in the brown sugar, cinnamon, and vanilla. Bring the sliced bananas to a boil, then reduce to low heat.
3. Whisk together 8 eggs, powdered sugar, cinnamon, nutmeg, vanilla, heavy cream, and milk in a big mixing cup.
4. Gently stir in the cubes of French bread until they have absorbed much of the oil.
5. Bread should be halfway filled into a greased 9x13 inch (23x33 cm) baking dish. Drizzle the sugar glaze and over the banana.
6. Preheat oven to 350° F and bake for 45 to 50 minutes, or until golden brown and crisp around the sides and end. (Due to differences in ovens, times and temperatures can vary.)
1. Sprinkle powdered sugar before serving.
2. Have fun!

Nutrition: Calories: 604. **Fat:** 32 g. **Carbs:** 71 g. **Fiber:** 3 g. **Sugar:** 42 g. **Protein:** 15 g.

395. Bananas & Chocolate Bread Pudding

Preparation Time: 10 minutes
Cooking Time: 60 minutes
Servings: 6
Ingredients:

- 6 slices of stale bread, cut into small cubes
- 4 fully ripe bananas
- 3 eggs
- 1 cup (240 mL) milk
- 1 tsp. cinnamon
- 2 tsp. extract from vanilla
- 1 cup (175 g) cocoa nibs
- Ice cream to increase tasting
- Chocolate syrup to increase tasting
- Whipped cream to increase tasting

Directions:

1. Break the bread up into little cubes on a chopping board. To help dry out the bread, place it on a baking sheet and bake it for 5 minutes at 350° F (175° C).

2. Combine ripe bananas and mush in a big mixing tub.

3. Blend the pounded eggs, milk, cinnamon, and vanilla extract in a mixing pot.

4. Attach the bread and soak it for 5 to 10 minutes until it is well mixed.

5. Add another couple of chocolate chips on top. In a large muffin pan, whisk together all of the ingredients. Preheat oven to 350° F (175° C) and bake for 20 minutes.

6. Cover with chocolate sauce and a scoop of your choice ice cream or whipped cream.

1. Have fun!

Nutrition: Calories: 413. **Fat:** 16 g. **Carbs:** 61 g. **Fiber:** 5 g. **Sugar:** 28 g. **Protein:** 11 g.

396. Lemon Blueberry Cake Recipe

Preparation Time: 15 minutes
Cooking Time: 60 minutes
Servings: 10
Ingredients:

- 2 big eggs
- 1 cup sugar (granulated)
- 1 cup (8 oz.) sour cream
- ½ cup olive oil either veg oil
- 1 tsp. extract of vanilla
- ¼ tsp. salt
- 2 cups flour (all-purpose)
- 2 tsp. baking powder
- 1 medium lemon, split (zest and juice)
- ½ tbsp. corn starch
- 16 oz. new blueberries
- Powdered sugar may be placed on top if needed.

Directions:

1. Cover the bottom of a 9-inch springform pan with parchment paper and lightly butter it. Preheat oven to 375° F. 2 eggs and 1 cup sugar, whisked together at high speed for 5 minutes, or until light and thick.

2. Whisk together 1 cup sour cream, ½ cup oil, 1 tsp. of vanilla, and ¼ tsp. of salt on low speed until well mixed.

3. 2 cups flour + 2 tsp. of baking powder whisked together, then add ⅓ at a time to batter, whisking to mix after each addition (do not overmix). Add 1 tbsp. of lemon juice and ½ tbsp. of lemon zest last.

4. Blueberries should be rinsed and drained thoroughly. Toss blueberries with ½ tbsp. of corn starch and 1 tsp. of lemon juice in a medium mixing cup, stirring until well mixed and no dry white cornstarch remains.

5. Half of the batter should be poured into the prepared springform pan and distributed uniformly. Half of the blueberries should be on top. Spread the remaining batter on top, then scatter the remaining blueberries uniformly over the top, gently pressing them into the batter (about halfway). Bake for 45 to 55 minutes, or until a toothpick inserted in the middle comes out clean (mine took 55 minutes). Allow cake to rest in pan for 15 to 20 minutes before removing ring and cooling until room temperature or just warm. Just before eating, top with powdered sugar.

Nutrition: Calories: 353. **Calories From Fat:** 144. **Fat:** 16 g. **Saturated Fat:** 4 g. **Cholesterol:** 44 mg. **Sodium:** 91 mg. **Potassium:** 222 mg. **Carbs:** 48 g. **Fiber:** 2 g. **Sugar:** 25 g. **Protein:** 4 g. **Vitamin A:** 215IU. **Vitamin C:** 10.3 mg. **Calcium:** 83 mg. **Iron:** 1.7 mg.

Brunch

397. Chipotle-Mojo Shrimp

Preparation Time: 25 minutes
Cooking Time: 60 minutes
Servings: 6
Ingredients:

- 2 garlic heads (approximately 26 cloves), peeled and crushed
- 1 ½ cups extra-virgin olive oil
- Salt kosher
- ¼ cup lemon juice
- 1 seeded and minced chipotle in adobo sauce
- 2-lb. medium shrimp, shelled and deveined but with tails still attached
- Pepper, freshly ground
- Garnish with chopped cilantro
- Wedges of lime, for serving

Directions:

1. Preheat the oven to 325° F. Combine the crushed garlic, olive oil, and a sprinkle of salt in a 4-cup ceramic baking dish. Place the dish on a baking sheet and bake for 30 minutes, or until the garlic is soft and browning. Bake for another 15 minutes, or until the garlic is golden and very juicy, after which add the lime juice. Allow the mixture to cool for a few minutes.
2. In a shallow saucepan, combine the garlic and oil. Mash the garlic with a fork against the side of the pan and whisk in the oil; the sauce will seem to have split. Season with salt and keep the chipotle soft.
3. 2 tsp. of mojo garlicky oil, heated in a big skillet until shimmering Cook, rotating once, until golden and cooked through, about 3 minutes over medium-high heat with half of the shrimp and a generous pinch of salt and pepper. To serve the shrimp, arrange it on a platter. Repeat with the remaining shrimp and 2 tsp. of garlicky oil. Garnish the shrimp with chopped cilantro and more garlic mojo. Pass the leftover garlic mojo at the table with the lime wedges.

Nutrition: Calories: 275. **Fat:** 7 g. **Carbs:** 49 g. **Protein:** 6 g. **Fiber:** 6 g.

398. Antiquated Fashioned Chicken Pie

Preparation Time: 25 minutes
Cooking Time: 1 hour
Servings: 4
Ingredients:
For poaching the chicken:

- 1 onion, tiny
- 1 leek, tiny
- 1 stalk celery
- 1 carrot, tiny
- 4 drumsticks de chicken
- 4 thighs of chicken
- 1 bay leaf
- 1 thyme sprig
- 1.25 liters chicken stock (light) (or water)
- 500g puff pastry block made entirely of butter oven-roasted caramelized onions
- 1 egg yolk, lightly pounded with a few drops of water, to glaze

Pie filling:

- 2 medium carrots, peeled and cutting diagonal direction into 1cm slices
- 2 trimmed medium leeks, sliced into 2cm slices
- 50 g butter
- 50 g pure flour and a little more for dusting
- 2 tbsp. cream (single or double)

Directions:

1. Chop the cabbage, leek, celery, and carrot coarsely. Place the chicken, carrots, a level tsp. of salt, and the bay leaf and thyme in a large skillet. Bring just enough stock to cover the contents to a gentle boil. Remove any scum, lower the fire, cover, and poach the chicken for about 30 minutes, or until the meat is soft when stabbed with a knife and the juices run clear. Allow cooling in the stock for a few minutes.
2. When the chicken is cold enough to treat, strain the stock but hold the vegetables and save the stock (for the sauce). Remove the chicken skin and toss it out. Remove all of the meat from the bones and place it in a 1.2-liter pie dish.
3. Bring 600 mL of the reserved stock to a boil, then add the carrots and bake for an extra added 5 minutes. When the leeks have returned to a boil, cut all of the vegetables with a slotted spoon and add to the chicken.
4. **Tip:** don't be apprehensive about making your own pastry; it'll be well worth your time. You may also use pre-made all-butter puff pastry.
5. To make a roux, melt the butter in a separate pan, stir in the flour, and simmer for a few minutes, stirring continuously. Using a wooden spoon or a balloon brush, stir in a small ladleful of the hot stock. Repeat the process, stirring constantly, until all of the stock has been added. Season with salt then pepper, and stir in the milk, if used. Stir in the sauce after pouring it over the chicken and vegetables. Allow cooling. Heat the oven to 220° C, (Gas 7)
6. Print out the pastry to about ½ cm thick on a floured surface, sufficiently to generously fill the pie dish with an overlap. Butter the dish's edge and cut a strip of pastry 2 ½ cm wide from the rolled-out pastry's outer edge, pressing tightly across the dish's edge. Brush the remainder of the pastry on top with cold water and press down the lip. With a sharp knife, trim away the waste. Decorate the top with leaves or another pattern made

from the pastry trimmings and crimp the edge with a fork. To make the pieces adhere, rub a little water on them.

7. Brush the beaten egg over the pastry. Cook for 45 to 50 minutes or until golden and tender.

Nutrition: Calories: 950. **Fat:** 61 g. **Saturates:** 32 g. **Carbs:** 55 g. **Sugars:** 6 g. **Fiber:** 6 g. **Protein:** 45 g. **Salt:** 0.8 g.

399. Potato-Topped Pie and Creamy Chicken

Preparation Time: 15 minutes
Cooking Time: 1 hour
Servings: 2 servings, double for 4
Ingredients:
- 1 (50 g) pot of soft cheese
- 1 (11g) sachet chicken stock mixture
- 4 potatoes, white
- 1 leek, chopped
- 1 pot (5.5 g) Dijon mustard
- 1 carrot
- 2 x 125 g fillets chicken breast
- 120 g spinach, shredded
- 2 cloves garlic

You'll also need:
- Butter, flour, milk, olive oil, pepper, and salt are all used in this recipe.

Directions:
1. Preheat oven to 220° C, (fan) 200° C (gas 7)
1. Get a kettle to a boil, then cut the potatoes (skins on) into big bite-size chunks.
2. Bring the diced potatoes to a boil in a kettle of plenty of boiling water and a pinch of salt over high heat.
3. Cook until fork-tender, 12 to 15 minutes, then drain and return to the pot to steam dry.
4. Add the chicken breasts to a baking tray with a drizzle of olive oil and a sprinkle of salt and pepper as the potatoes are boiling.
5. Bake for 15 minutes or until the meat is cooked through (no pink meat!), then reboil half a kettle.
6. Cut the leek[s] in half lengthwise, then vigorously wash to clear any grit from between the leaves, then head, back, and finely chop. Carrots should be topped, tails removed, and diced.
7. Heat 15 g [30 g] butter in a big, wide-bottomed pan (preferably nonstick) over medium heat.
8. After the butter has melted, add the minced leek and carrot, along with a pinch of salt, and cook for 5 minutes, or until softened.
9. Peel and finely cut (or grate) the garlic in the meantime.
10. In 250 mL (400 mL) boiling water, dissolve the chicken stock mix and Dijon mustard.
11. Add half of the minced garlic and 1 tbsp. (2 tbsp.) flour to the softened vegetables and boil for 30 seconds.

12. Bring the stock and soft cheese to a boil over high heat, then reduce to low heat and simmer for 3 to 4 minutes, or until thickened.
13. Transmit the cooked chicken to a fresh chopping board and "pull" that apart from two forks.
14. With a knob of butter and a tiny splash of milk, return the drained potatoes to low heat.
15. Mash with a fork until smooth, seasoning with salt and pepper.
16. Blend in the pulled chicken, as well as a good grind of black pepper, until smooth (this is your creamy chicken pie filling.) Place the mashed potatoes on top of the fluffy chicken pie filling in an oven-safe bowl.
17. This is your fluffy chicken potato-topped dessert, which should be baked for 15 to 20 minutes or until bubbling and golden.
18. When the pie is almost finished, melt a knob of butter in a separate big, wide-based pan (preferably nonstick) over medium heat.
19. When the pan is heated, add the shredded kale and the remaining minced garlic, and cook for 3 to 4 minutes, or until the kale is soft but still has a bite (these are your garlicky greens).
20. Serve the garlicky greens with the fluffy chicken potato-topped pie.
21. Have fun!

Nutrition: Calories: 275. **Fat:** 7 g. **Carbs:** 49 g. **Protein:** 6 g. **Fiber:** 6 g.

400. A Recipe of Meatball

Preparation Time: 10 minutes
Cooking Time: 60 minutes
Servings: 4
Ingredients:
- 1 lb. meat (ground) (pork, beef, veal, chicken, turkey, or a combination)
- ½ cup bread crumbs (panko)
- A single egg
- 1 tsp. kosher salt (additional salt as needed)
- To taste, season with black pepper and/or ground cumin, curry powder, chile flakes, garam masala, and other spices.
- Garlic, cabbage, scallions, or shallots, minced
- Parsley, basil, or cilantro, chopped
- Frying oil made from olives (optional)

Directions:
1. Gently combine all ingredients in a big mixing bowl. Make 1 ½-inch ball out of the dough. Place on a baking sheet to cool.
2. Broil for 7 to 10 minutes, or until golden and strong. Alternatively, fry in oil until well-browned all over. Until eating, season with a little more salt.

Nutrition: Calories: 332. **Fat:** 24 g. **Saturated Fat:** 9 g. **Trans Fat:** 1 g. **Monounsaturated Fat:** 10 g.

Polyunsaturated Fat: 1 g. **Carbs:** 6 g. **Dietary Fiber:** 0 g. **Sugars:** 0 g. **Protein:** 22 g. **Sodium:** 311 mg.

401. Deviled Chicken & Honey Chipotle Sauce

Preparation Time: 10 minutes
Cooking Time: 60 minutes
Servings: 4
Ingredients:

- 4 chicken breasts, boneless and skinless
- 1 cup rice (jasmine)
- ½ pound grape tomatoes
- 2 poplins (Plano peppers)
- 2 sliced scallions
- 1 tbsp. Dijon mustard
- 2 tbsp. butter
- 1 ¼ cup panko breadcrumbs
- ¼ cup cilantro sauce
- 4 tsp. honey
- 2 tsp. paste of Chile chipotle
- ¼ cup mayonnaise
- ¼ cup Parmesan cheese, grated
- 1 tbsp. Mexican spice blend (anchor Chile powder, smoked paprika, garlic powder, ground cumin & dried Mexican oregano)
- Salt and pepper

Directions:

1. Get the honey to room temperature by removing it from the refrigerator. Preheat the oven to 450° F and place an oven rack in the upper third. New produce should be washed and dried. Cut the tomatoes in half. Separate the white bottoms and hollow green tops of the scallions by thinly slicing them. Remove the pepper stems and discard them. Remove the ribs and seeds from the peppers, then thinly slice them crosswise. Immediately after treating, thoroughly wash your face. Combine the halved tomatoes, sliced white bottoms of the scallions, and a drizzle of olive oil in a mixing bowl; season to taste with salt and pepper.
2. Using foil, line a sheet pan. Melt the butter in a medium pot over medium heat (or melt in a large bowl in the microwave). Switch to a wide mixing bowl, reserving the pot. Season with salt and pepper after adding the spice blend and mustard. Whisk all together until it's fully smooth. Combine the breadcrumbs and cheese on a large plate and season with salt and pepper. Clean the chicken with paper towels and season it with salt and pepper on both sides. Working one piece at a time, coat the seasoned chicken in the spiced butter (letting excess drip off) and then in the seasoned breadcrumbs (pressing gently to adhere). On a baking sheet, position the breaded chicken.
3. Drizzle some olive oil over the breaded chicken. Set the pan on the oven's top rack. Bake for 19 to 21

minutes or until golden brown and cooked through. Switch off the oven and remove the baking sheet.

4. An instant-read thermometer can read 165° F.
5. Meanwhile, heat 2 tbsp. olive oil on medium-high in the reserved pot (or a medium pot) until hot. Season with salt and pepper and add the sliced peppers. Cook for 2 to 3 minutes, stirring regularly, or until slightly softened. 2 cups water, rice, and a generous pinch of salt (carefully, as the liquid may splatter). To mix, stir all together. On high, bring to a boil. Reduce the heat to low until the water has boiled. Cover and cook for 12 to 14 minutes, or until the water is absorbed and the rice is tender, without stirring. Remove the pan from the heat and use a fork to fluff it up. Stir in the cilantro sauce until it is well mixed. If needed, season with salt and pepper after tasting.
6. Meanwhile, in a mixing bowl, whisk together the mayonnaise, honey (kneading the package before opening), and as much Chile paste as you want, depending on how spicy you want the dish to be; season with salt and pepper. Serve the baked chicken with rice and peppers that have been roasted. Drizzle the sauce over the chicken. Cover with the sliced green tops of the scallions and the dressed tomatoes.
7. Have fun!

Nutrition: Calories: 750. **Total Fat:** 27 g. **Cholesterol:** 155 mg. **Sodium:** 600 mg. **Total Carbs:** 75 g. **Dietary Fiber:** 4 g. **Total Sugars:** 11 g. **Saturated Fat:** 7 g. **Protein:** 49 g. **Calcium:** 110 mg. **Iron:** 2.8 mg. **Potassium:** 1020 mg. **Vitamin A:** 200 mcg. **Vitamin C:** 64 mg. (includes added sugars: 6 g.)

402. Golden Pork Chops

Preparation Time: 15 minutes
Cooking Time: 1 hour
Servings: 6
Ingredients:

- 6 pork chops
- ¼ tsp. seasoned salt
- ¼ tsp. black pepper, freshly ground
- 1 sliced onion
- ½ cup sliced new mushrooms
- 2 cans (10.75 oz.) condensed golden mushroom soup

Directions:

1. Preheat the oven to 375° F (190° C).
2. Pork chops should be rinsed, patted dry, and seasoned with seasoned salt and pepper. Fill a 9x13 inch baking dish halfway with them. Combine the onion, mushrooms, and broth in a separate shallow cup. Combine all of the ingredients in a large mixing bowl and spoon over the chops.
3. Cover and bake for 45 minutes at 375° F (190° C). Bake for another 15 minutes after removing the cover.
4. **Note:** Depending on the thickness of the chops, cooking time can vary.

5. When the internal temperature of pork chops reaches 145° F, they are cooked (63° C).

Nutrition: Calories: 409. **Protein:** 19.4 g. **Carbs:** 8.8 g. **Dietary Fiber:** 0.4 g. **Sugars:** 2.4 g. **Fat:** 32.6 g. **Saturated Fat:** 10.6 g. **Cholesterol:** 79.2 mg. **Vitamin A:** 49IU. **Niacin Equivalents:** 8.5 mg. **Vitamin B6:** 0.4 mg. **Vitamin C:** 2.2 mg. **Foliate:** 9.8 mcg. **Calcium:** 49.7 mg. **Iron:** 2.1 mg. **Magnesium:** 24.3 mg. **Potassium:** 419.4 mg. **Sodium:** 754.4 mg. **Thiamin:** 0.8 mg. **Calories From Fat:** 293.1 g.

403. Baked Lemon & Herb Basa With Cherry Tomatoes

Preparation Time: 10 minutes
Cooking Time: 60 minutes
Servings: for 2 people, double for 4
Ingredients:

- 10 g dill & parsley
- 5.5 g vegetable stock mix
- 1 tsp. oregano, dried
- 3 potatoes, white
- 2 x 100g fillets of Basa
- 1 tsp. basil (dried)
- 50 g lettuce (lamb)
- 250 g tomatoes, cherry
- 3 cloves of garlic
- A single lemon

You'll also need:

- Butter, salt, and olive oil

Directions:

1. Before you get started... Preparing this recipe takes about 5 minutes (or 10 minutes), so get your oven-safe dish and all of your ingredients ready first, then wash your fruits and vegetables.
2. Now, let's get started! Preheat the oven to 220° C (fan)/ 200° C (gas 7). Bring half a kettle to a boil. Cut the potatoes into small parts that are easy to eat. Place them in a big oven-safe bowl.
3. Squash the garlic cloves with the side of a knife (keeping the skins on!) to crush them.
4. Add the crushed garlic, cherry tomatoes, a generous drizzle of olive oil, and a pinch of salt to the dish. Mix all together thoroughly before placing the dish in the oven for the first 35 minutes.
5. Meanwhile, make your herby stock by dissolving the vegetable stock mix in 100mL (150 mL) boiling water and stir in the dried basil and oregano. ½ [1] lemon, cut into slices, and set aside for later. Clear the table, have a cup of tea, or simply relax during this period!
6. Remove the dish from the oven after 35 minutes and pour the herby stock over the potatoes and tomatoes. Add the basa fillets on top. Squeeze the rest of the lemon over the basa fillets and serve with the reserved lemon slices.

7. Return the dish to the oven for another 15 to 20 minutes, or until the fish is finished (this is your baked lemon and herb basa with cherry tomatoes).
8. **Tip:** When your fish turns opaque and flakes quickly, it's over.
9. After washing the lettuce for the lamb, pat it dry with kitchen paper.
10. To eat, toss the potatoes with a few knobs of butter and set them aside to melt.
11. Toss the parsley and dill with the cherry tomatoes on top of the baked lemon & herb basa.
12. Place the dish in the table's middle, ready to be shared.
13. Drizzle some olive oil over the lamb's lettuce and serve it alongside.
8. Have fun!

Nutrition: Energy: 1142 kJ. **Fat:** 3.1 g. (of which saturates 1.2 g.) **Salt:** 0.95 g. **Carbs:** 39.5 g. (of which sugars 7.3 g.) **Fiber:** 6.9 g. **Protein:** 23.6 g.

404. Baked Sausage With Peppers Onions and Potatoes

Preparation Time: 20 minutes
Cooking Time: 60 minutes
Servings: 8
Ingredients:

- 2 tsp. olive oil (extra virgin)
- 2-pound links of Italian sausage, cut into 2-inch chunks
- ¼ cup extra virgin olive oil
- 4 big peeled and thickly sliced potatoes
- 2 seeded and cut into wedges big green bell peppers
- 2 seeded and cut into wedges big red bell peppers
- 3 onions, peeled and cut into wedges
- ½ cup wine (white)
- ½ cup stock (chicken)
- 1 tsp. Italian spices
- Mix with salt and pepper to taste

Directions:

1. Oven preheated to 400° F (200° C).
2. In a large skillet, heat 2 tsp. of olive oil over medium heat and brown the sausage, stirring occasionally. In a large baking dish, place the cooked sausage.
3. Pour ¼ cup of olive oil into the skillet and cook the potatoes for about 10 minutes, stirring occasionally. Remove the potatoes from the skillet and place them in the baking dish, leaving some oil in the skillet.
4. In a hot skillet, cook and stir the green and red peppers and onions until they begin to soften, about 5 minutes. Vegetables should be piled high in the baking dish.
5. Over the vegetables and sausage, pour the wine and chicken stock, and season with Italian seasoning, salt,

and pepper. Combine the bacon, potatoes, and vegetables in a small mixing bowl.

6.   Cook for 20 to 25 minutes in a preheated oven until hot and bubbling. Serve immediately.

Nutrition: Calories: 539.2. **Protein:** 20.2 g. **Carbs:** 45.8 g. **Dietary Fiber:** 6.7 g. **Sugars:** 7.3 g. **Fat:** 29.8 g. **Saturated Fat:** 8.7 g. **Cholesterol:** 44. 9mg. **Vitamin A:** 1478.2IU. **Niacin Equivalents:** 9.2 mg. **Vitamin B6:** 1.1 mg. **Vitamin C:** 126 mg. **Foliate:** 67.7 mcg. **Calcium:** 62.9 mg. **Iron:** 3.2 mg. **Magnesium:** 73.2 mg. **Potassium:** 1269.3 mg. **Sodium:** 1041 mg. **Thiamin:** 0.7 mg. **Calories from Fat:** 268 g.

405. Healthy Granola

Preparation Time: 5 minutes
Cooking Time: 60 minutes
Servings: 8 cups
Ingredients:

*   4 cups rolled oats, old-fashioned (use certified gluten-free oats for gluten-free granola)
*   1 ½ cup raw nuts and/or seeds (1 cup pecans, ½ cup pipits)
*   1 tsp. fine-grain sea salt (use less if using regular table salt to a ¼ tsp.)
*   ½ tsp. cinnamon powder
*   ½ cup coconut or olive oil, melted
*   ½ cup honey or maple syrup
*   1 tsp. extract de vanilla
*   ⅓ cup dried fruit, chopped if big (I used dried cranberries)
*   ½ cup chocolate chips or coconut flakes* are totally optional extra mix-ins.

Directions:

1.   Preheat the oven to 350° F and line a wide-rimmed baking sheet with parchment paper.
2.   Combine the oats, nuts and/or seeds, salt, and cinnamon in a big mixing bowl. To combine the ingredients, stir them together.
3.   Combine the oil, maple syrup and/or honey, and vanilla extract in a mixing bowl. Mix until all of the oats and nuts are finely covered. Pour the granola into the prepared pan and spread it out evenly with a wide spoon.
4.   Bake for about 21 to 24 minutes, stirring halfway through (for extra-clumpy granola, press the stirred granola down with your spatula to create a more even layer). When the granola cools, it will crisp up even more.
5.   Before eating, let the granola cool fully (at least 45 minutes). Lastly, sprinkle the dried fruit on top (and
6.   Optional chocolate chips, if using). If you want big chunks of granola, break it up with your hands, or stir it around with a spoon if you don't want it to be too clumpy.
7.   Keep the granola in an airtight jar at room temperature for 1 to 2 weeks, or freeze it in a packed bag

in the freezer for up to 3 months. Since the dried fruit will solidify if left out too long, bring it to room temperature for 5 to 10 minutes before serving.

Nutrition: Calories: 234. **Total Fat:** 11.7 g. **Saturated Fat:** 6.3 g. **Sodium:** 134.4 mg. **Polyunsaturated Fat:** 1.6 g. **Monounsaturated Fat:** 3.1 g.

406. Cake With Sour Cream and Coffee

Preparation Time: 15 minutes
Cooking Time: 1 hour
Servings: 12
Ingredients:
Cake:

*   ½ (113 g) cup unsalted butter at room temperature
*   1 ¼ (260 g) cup sugar
*   2 large eggs
*   1 ½ (188 g) cup flour
*   1 ½ tsp. baking powder
*   ½ tsp. baking soda
*   ½ tsp. salt
*   ¼ (300 g) cups sour cream
*   1 ¼ tsp. vanilla extract

Topping:

*   ½ (104 g) cup sugar
*   2 tsp. flour (all-purpose)
*   1 tbsp. cinnamon
*   ⅓ cup (70 g) pecans or walnuts, chopped

Directions:

1.   To make the butter and sugar light or fluffy, combine them together until light and fluffy. Beat the eggs one by one, beating well after each addition.
2.   Sift together flour, baking powder, baking soda, and salt in a separate cup. Alternate adding the flour mixture, sour cream, and vanilla to the butter mixture on low speed until just mixed. Do not overmix the ingredients. Pour the batter into the baking pan that has been prepared.
3.   To make the topping, combine the sugar, cinnamon, flour, and nuts in a small mixing bowl.
4.   Bake for 30 to 35 minutes, or until a cake tester comes out clean. Allow cooling before serving.

Nutrition: Calories: 347. **Fat:** 18 g. **Saturated Fat:** 8 g. **Trans-Fat:** 0 g. **Monounsaturated Fat:** 6 g. **Polyunsaturated Fat:** 2 g. **Polyunsaturated:** 2 g. **Sodium:** 220 mL. **Carbs:** 45 g. **Dietary Fiber:** 1 g. 31 **Sugars:** 4 g. **Protein:** 45 g. **Carbs:** 1 g. **Dietary Fiber:** 31 g. **Sugars:** 4 g. **Protein:** 45 g. **Dietary Fiber:** 31 g.

Appetizers, Snacks, and Bun

407. Beet Chips

Preparation Time: 25 minutes
Cooking Time: 60 minutes
Servings: 8
Ingredients:

- 12 beets
- 2 tsp. sea salt
- ½ cup olive oil

Directions:

1. Turn on the oven, set the temperature to 300° F, and then select the oven cooking method.
2. Meanwhile, scrub the beets, remove the top, and then cut beets into thin slices, about $\frac{1}{16}$ inch thin.
3. Take a large bowl, place the beet slices in it, season with salt, drizzle with oil and then toss until coated.
4. Let the beet slices rest for 20 minutes, toss again, drain the liquid, and then spread the beet slices on the oven basket in a single layer.
5. Cook the beet slices for 60 minutes until crisp and golden, turning halfway and when done, cool the chips completely and then serve.

Nutrition: Calories: 172. **Fat:** 14 g. **Carbs:** 12 g. **Protein:** 2 g. **Fiber:** 3 g.

408. Baked Avocados With Strawberry Salsa

Preparation Time: 10 minutes
Cooking Time: 60 minutes
Servings: 4
Ingredients:

- 3 avocados
- Olive oil
- 1 cup strawberries
- 2 scallions
- 2 tbsp. goat cheese crumbles
- 2 tbsp. fresh basil
- 1 tbsp. balsamic vinegar

Directions:

1. Start by stemming and quartering the strawberries and thinly slice the basil and scallions.
2. Preheat oven to 400° F.
3. Cut avocados in half lengthwise and remove the pit.
4. Lay avocados on a baking sheet flesh side up and brush with olive oil.
5. Bake avocados for 8 minutes.
6. While avocados bake, mix all other ingredients in a medium bowl.
7. Add strawberry salsa to each avocado slice and return to the oven for another 3 minutes.
8. Serve warm.

Nutrition: Calories: 474. **Sodium:** 173 mg. **Dietary Fiber:** 60 g. **Total Fat:** 42.9 g. **Total Carbs:** 22.1 g. **Protein:** 7.3 g.

409. Baked Eggs With Marinara and Parmesan

Preparation Time: 10 minutes
Cooking Time: 60 minutes
Servings: 4
Ingredients:

- 8 eggs
- 1 cup marinara sauce
- ¼ cup whipping cream
- ¼ cup parmesan cheese
- Salt and pepper
- Chives for garnish

Directions:

1. Start by greasing 4 ramekins.
2. Preheat oven to 400° F.
3. Pour ¼ cup of marinara into each ramekin.
4. Crack 2 eggs into each ramekin.
5. Top eggs with 1 tbsp. each of whipping cream and parmesan.
6. Sprinkle with salt and pepper and bake for 15 minutes.
7. While eggs bake, chop chives.
8. Remove ramekins from the oven, top with chives, and serve with toast.

Nutrition: Calories: 250. **Sodium:** 519 mg. **Dietary Fiber:** 1.6 g. **Total Fat:** 15.9 g. **Total Carbs:** 10.0 g. **Protein:** 17.1 g.

410. Easy & Quick Bread Pudding

Preparation Time: 10 minutes
Cooking Time: 60 minutes
Servings: 12
Ingredients:

- 1 loaf bread
- 2 cups evaporated milk
- 1 cup condensed milk
- 1 cup raisins

Directions:

1. Start by preheating the oven to 400° F.
2. Pour evaporated milk into a pan.
3. Add bread and mash together with hands.
4. Add condensed milk.
5. Add in raisins and stir.
6. Bake for 40 minutes, then allow cooling before cutting.

Nutrition: Calories: 329. **Sodium:** 475 mg. **Dietary Fiber:** 1.8 g. **Total Fat:** 7.4 g. **Total Carbs:** 57.2 g. **Protein:** 9.7 g.

411. Twice-Baked Sweet Potato With Coconut

Preparation Time: 30 minutes

Cooking Time: 60 minutes
Servings: 8
Ingredients:

- 4 medium sweet potatoes
- ½ cup coconut milk
- 1 tbsp. maple syrup
- 1 tsp. minced fresh ginger root
- 1 tsp. adobo sauce
- ½ tsp. salt
- ¼ cup chopped pecans
- ¼ cup flaked coconut

Directions:
1. Scrub sweet potatoes and pierce with a fork, then microwave for 10 minutes.
2. Cut each potato down the center lengthwise, scoop out the insides into a bowl, and keep the shells.
3. Preheat the oven to 350° F. In a bowl, mash the potato with coconut milk, then stir in the adobo, salt, syrup, and ginger.
4. Spoon the mixture back into the shells.
5. Place on a baking sheet and top with pecans and coconut.
6. Bake for 25 minutes.
Nutrition: Calories: 185. **Sodium:** 173 mg. **Dietary Fiber:** 3.2 g. **Total Fat:** 15.2 g. **Total Carbs:** 12.4 g. **Protein:** 2.4 g.

412. Zucchini Lasagna Toasts
Preparation Time: 15 minutes
Cooking Time: 60 minutes
Servings: 4
Ingredients:

- Bread
- 1 medium zucchini
- 1 clove garlic
- 1 tbsp. olive oil
- 4 ripe plum tomatoes
- Salt and pepper to taste
- 1 cup ricotta cheese
- ¼ cup freshly grated Romano cheese
- 4 oz. fresh mozzarella cheese

Directions:
1. Start by preheating the oven to 450° F. Toast bread for 10 minutes.
2. Combine oil, garlic, and zucchini in a microwave-safe bowl—microwave on high for 4 minutes.
3. Add tomatoes, salt, and pepper to the bowl and microwave for another 3 minutes.
4. In a separate bowl, mix ricotta and Romano with salt and pepper.
5. Spread ricotta mixture on each bread slice, then top with tomato mixture.

6. Place mozzarella over each slice and place it on a baking sheet.
7. Bake for 10 minutes.
Nutrition: Calories: 318. **Sodium:** 506 mg. **Dietary Fiber:** 2.2 g. **Total Fat:** 18.1 g. **Total Carbs:** 17.9 g. **Protein:** 22.9 g.

413. Mushroom Onion Strudel
Preparation Time: 20 minutes
Cooking Time: 60 minutes
Servings: 4 to 6
Ingredients:

- 12 sheets phyllo dough
- 3 tbsp. olive oil
- 1 egg
- 1-lb. mushrooms
- 1 medium onion
- 3 tbsp. butter
- 1 tbsp. dry sherry
- 1 tbsp. all-purpose flour
- Leaves from 1 sprig of thyme
- 6 tbsp. freshly grated parmesan
- Salt and pepper to taste

Directions:
1. Start by preheating the oven to 400° F.
2. Line a baking sheet with parchment paper.
3. Pour oil into a skillet on medium heat and sauté mushrooms and onions for about 7 minutes.
4. Add sherry and cook for another 3 minutes.
5. Mix in the flour, thyme salt, and pepper and remove from heat.
6. Melt butter in a small sauté pan.
7. Brush one-half of the phyllo sheet lengthwise with butter.
8. Fold the unbuttered side over the buttered side and smooth out any wrinkles or bubbles.
9. Again, brush one-half of the phyllo with butter, and fold the unbuttered side over it again. You'll end up with one long column.
10. Place one spoonful of mushroom filling at the end of the column and sprinkle parmesan on top.
11. Fold one corner of the phyllo over the filling to create a triangle shape and keep folding over triangles until you reach the other end of the column (like folding a flag).
12. Beat the egg and brush it over the strudel triangle. Repeat for as many strudels as you can safely fit on a baking sheet and bake for 15 minutes.
Nutrition: Calories: 312. **Sodium:** 376 mg. **Dietary Fiber:** 2.0 g. **Total Fat:** 19.2 g. **Total Carbs:** 25.9 g. **Protein:** 11.1 g.

414. Nacho Avocado Toast
Preparation Time: 10 minutes
Cooking Time: 60 minutes

Servings: 2
Ingredients:
- 2 slices whole-grain bread
- 3 tbsp. black bean & cilantro spread
- 3 tbsp. guacamole
- ½ cup baby spinach
- ¼ small red onion
- ¼ cup frozen sweet corn
- ¼ cup plant-based nacho cheese sauce

Directions:
1. Mince spinach and onion.
2. Put corn in a strainer and run hot water over it for a minute to thaw.
3. Place toast on a baking sheet and spread with bean and cilantro spread.
4. Spread guacamole over the bean spread, and sprinkle spinach, onion, and corn over the top.
5. Toast for 4 minutes or until toast reaches the desired level of crispiness.
6. While the bread toasts, warm cheese sauce in the microwave, or a heat-safe bowl on top of the oven.
7. Drizzle sauce over toast and serve.

Nutrition: Calories: 117. Sodium: 221 mg. Dietary Fiber: 3.6 g. Total Fat: 4.2 g. Total Carbs: 18.8 g. Protein: 4.2 g.

415. Parmesan Green Onion Hash Brown Cups

Preparation Time: 10 minutes
Cooking Time: 60 minutes
Servings: 6
Ingredients:
- 1 (20-oz.) bag hash browns, shredded
- 3 green onions
- ½ cup grated parmesan cheese
- 1 tsp. kosher salt
- ½ tsp. black pepper
- 2 tbsp. olive oil

Directions:
1. Start by chopping green onions.
2. Preheat oven to 350° F.
3. Combine potatoes, cheese, onion, salt, and pepper in a large bowl.
4. Drizzle olive oil over potato mixture and toss with a fork.
5. Grease a muffin tin and spoon mixture into the tin.
6. Pack mixture into each cup by pushing it down with the rounded side of the spoon.
7. Bake for 1 hour, 15 minutes.

Nutrition: Calories: 325. Sodium: 805 mg. Dietary Fiber: 3.3 g. Total Fat: 18.7 g. Total Carbs: 34.2 g. Protein: 6.2 g.

416. Simply Delicious Garlic Kale Chips

Preparation Time: 5 minutes
Cooking Time: 60 minutes
Servings: 2
Ingredients:
- 4 cups kale
- 1 tbsp. olive oil
- ¼ tsp. pepper
- ¼ tsp. garlic powder
- Salt to taste

Directions:
1. Start by preheating the oven to 350° F.
2. Tear kale into 1-inch pieces and place in a bowl.
3. Add oil, pepper, garlic powder, and salt, and toss until kale is well coated.
4. Bake for 10 minutes.

Nutrition: Calories: 128. Sodium: 136 mg. Dietary Fiber: 2.1 g. Total Fat: 7.0 g. Total Carbs: 14.4 g. Protein: 4.1 g.

417. Wholesome Pita Chips

Preparation Time: 5 minutes
Cooking Time: 60 minutes
Servings: 1
Ingredients:
- 1 regular whole wheat pita
- 1 tsp. olive oil
- Salt to taste

Directions:
1. Start by preheating the oven to 375° F.
2. Brush both sides of the pita with oil and sprinkle with salt.
3. Cut pita into 6 wedges.
4. Place wedges on an ungreased baking sheet and bake for 8 minutes.

Nutrition: Calories: 210. Sodium: 496 mg. Dietary Fiber: 4.7 g. Total Fat: 6.3 g. Total Carbs: 35.2 g. Protein: 6.3 g.

418. Tomato Whole Grain Grilled Cheese Bites

Preparation Time: 2 minutes
Cooking Time: 60 minutes
Servings: 1
Ingredients:
- 4 slices tomato
- 2 whole-grain crackers
- 1-oz. cheddar cheese
- Salt to taste

Directions:
1. Start by preheating the oven broiler on high.
2. Place crackers on a cookie sheet.
3. Add tomatoes to crackers and sprinkle with salt.

4.	Top with cheese and broil until cheese is fully melted.

Nutrition: Calories: 165. **Sodium:** 402 mg. **Dietary Fiber:** 0.8 g. **Total Fat:** 11.5 g. **Total Carbs:** 7.6 g. **Protein:** 8.2 g.

Vegetables

419. Brown Rice, Spinach and Tofu Frittata

Preparation Time: 5 minutes
Cooking Time: 60 minutes
Servings: 4
Ingredients:

- ½ cup baby spinach, chopped
- ½ cup kale, chopped
- ½ onion, chopped
- ½ tsp. turmeric
- 1 ¾ cups brown rice, cooked
- 1 flax egg (1 tbsp. flaxseed meal + 3 tbsp. cold water)
- 1 package firm tofu
- 1 tbsp. olive oil
- 1 yellow pepper, chopped
- 2 tbsp. soy sauce
- 2 tsp. arrowroot powder
- 2 tsp. Dijon mustard
- ⅔ cup almond milk
- 3 big mushrooms, chopped
- 3 tbsp. nutritional yeast
- 4 cloves garlic, crushed
- 4 spring onions, chopped
- A handful of basil leaves, chopped

Directions:
1. Preheat the air fryer oven to 375° F. Grease a pan that will fit inside the air fryer oven.
2. Prepare the frittata crust by mixing the brown rice and flax egg. Press the rice onto the baking dish until you form a crust. Brush with a little oil and cook for 10 minutes.
3. Meanwhile, heat olive oil in a skillet over medium flame and sauté the garlic and onions for 2 minutes.
4. Add the pepper and mushroom and continue stirring for 3 minutes.
5. Stir in the kale, spinach, spring onions, and basil. Remove from the pan and set aside.
6. In a food processor, pulse together the tofu, mustard, turmeric, soy sauce, nutritional yeast, vegan milk, and arrowroot powder. Pour in a mixing bowl and stir in the sautéed vegetables.
7. Pour the vegan frittata mixture over the rice crust and cook in the air fryer oven for 40 minutes.

Nutrition: Calories: 226. **Fat:** 8.05 g. **Protein:** 10.6 g.

420. Cinnamon Apple Granola Recipe

Preparation Time: 15 minutes
Cooking Time: 1 hour
Servings: 4

Ingredients:

- ⅓ cup honey
- ¼ cup light brown sugar
- 2 tbsp. pure maple syrup
- ¼ cup unsweetened apple sauce
- ¾ cup melted coconut oil
- 1 tbsp. apple pie spice
- ½ tsp each cinnamon and kosher salt
- 4 cups old fashioned rolled oats
- ¾ cups walnuts, chopped
- ½ cup pecans, chopped
- 1 cup dried apple chips

Directions:
1. Preheat the oven to 250° F. Spray a sheet pan with nonstick cook spray and line it with aluminum foil. Place aside.
2. Whisk together the honey, brown sugar, maple syrup, apple sauce, oil, apple pie spice, cinnamon, and salt in a small mixing bowl.
3. Combine the oats, walnuts, and pecans in a medium mixing bowl. Place in a thin layer on a large baking sheet (use two pans if necessary).
4. Stirring once halfway through, bake for 1 hour or until the granola is golden brown and toasted.
5. Do not stir after taking from the oven! The granola will still be damp. Allow the granola to cool for 15 to 20 minutes on the counter. Toss in the apple chips to mix.
6. For up to 1 week, keep in an airtight container at room temperature.

Nutrition: Calories: 533. **Carbs:** 52 g. **Protein:** 8 g. **Fat:** 34 g. **Saturated Fat:** 18 g. **Sodium:** 151 mg. **Potassium:** 271 mg. **Fiber:** 5 g. **Sugar:** 22 g. **Vitamin C:** 0.3 mg. **Calcium:** 48 mg. **Iron:** 2.5 mg.

421. Cabbage Wedges Roasted

Preparation Time: 10 minutes
Cooking Time: 60 minutes
Servings: 4
Ingredients:

- 1 medium green cabbage
- Salt and ground black pepper
- Olive oil for drizzling
- 3 tbsp. sherry vinegar
- 1 tsp. Dijon mustard
- Grated parmesan cheese for garnishing
- 4 tbsp. olive oil

Directions:
1. Preheat the convection oven to 425° F.
2. Cut cabbage into a similar size of eight wedges—place wedges on a baking tray lined with baking paper. Drizzle olive oil on each side of cabbage and sprinkle salt

and fresh ground pepper on top and mix lightly with your hands to coat.

3. Roast in the convection oven until it turns brown on the upper side for around 20 to 25 minutes.

4. Meanwhile, take a bowl and whisk the sherry vinegar with Dijon mustard, then add the 3 tbsp. of olive oil and mix well until creamy mixture forms.

5. When cabbage is roasted. Transfer wedges onto a plate and drizzle the vinegar topping and sprinkle with grated parmesan and serve.

Nutrition: Calories: 182. **Fat:** 14.4 g. **Protein:** 3 g. **Carbs:** 13.4 g.

422. Dijon Crispy Smashed Potato

Preparation Time: 10 minutes
Cooking Time: 60 minutes
Servings: 6
Ingredients:

- 24 oz. baby potatoes red
- 3 cloves of minced garlic
- 2 tsp. honey
- 2 tbsp. Dijon mustard
- ½ tsp. dried thyme
- 1 tbsp. whole-grain Dijon mustard
- ½ tsp. dried rosemary
- Salt and ground black pepper to taste
- Olive oil

Directions:

1. Preheat the convection oven to 400° F. Coat a baking sheet with baking spray.

2. Boil potatoes and drain water.

3. In a small-sized mixing bowl, whisk Dijon mustard, olive oil, whole grain mustard, honey, garlic, rosemary, and thyme, and season with salt and pepper and mix.

4. Place potatoes onto a coated baking tray. Carefully smash the potatoes to flatten but still should remain in one piece with a potato masher. Brush all potatoes with a mustard mixture.

5. Bake potatoes for 18 to 20 minutes in a convection oven until they turn golden and crispy. Serve warm.

Nutrition: Calories: 135.7. **Fat:** 4.7 g. **Protein:** 2.3 g. **Carbs:** 21.7 g.

423. Vegetable Cheesy Casserole

Preparation Time: 10 minutes
Cooking Time: 60 minutes
Servings: 4
Ingredients:

- ½ lb. frozen green beans
- 4 oz. crispy French's onions(divided)
- ½ lb. frozen cauliflower and broccoli mixture
- 2 cups cheddar cheese shredded(divided)
- 1 can of cream of mushroom soup

- ¼ cup milk or water
- ½ tsp. garlic powder

Directions:

1. Preheat the convection oven to 325° F. Cook green beans, cauliflower, and broccoli according to your package directions until they become crispy.

2. In a medium-sized mixing bowl, mix broccoli, green beans, cauliflower, cream of mushroom soup, garlic powder,1 ½ cups of cheese, milk, and half of the crispy onions. Pour the mixture into a casserole dish and spread the remaining cheese on the top.

3. Bake in a preheated convection oven for around 30 minutes, spread the remaining crispy onions on top, and bake for another 10 minutes.

Nutrition: Calories: 513. **Fat:** 35 g. **Protein:** 21 g. **Carbs:** 29 g.

424. Roasted Brown Sugar Rutabaga

Preparation Time: 5 minutes
Cooking Time: 60 minutes
Servings: 4
Ingredients:

- 3 lb. rutabaga
- 2 tbsp. brown sugar
- 1 tbsp. olive oil
- 2 tbsp. butter
- ½ tsp. thyme
- Salt and pepper to taste

Directions:

1. Preheat the convection oven to 400° F. Peel rutabaga skin and cut into 1-inch cubes. Mix with olive oil, salt, thyme, and pepper.

2. Spread coated rutabaga onto a large-sized roasting pan and roast in convection for 45 to 50 minutes or until they become tender and golden.

3. Take out the pan from the convection oven, spread brown sugar and butter over rutabaga, mix for coating, and roast for more than 5 minutes.

4. Serve hot and enjoy.

Nutrition: Calories: 513. **Fat:** 35 g. **Protein:** 21 g. **Carbs:** 29 g.

425. Classic Italian Parmesan Eggplant

Preparation Time: 15 minutes
Cooking Time: 60 minutes
Servings: 8
Ingredients:

- 1 ½-2 lb. eggplant sliced (cut into ¼-inch slices)
- 4 eggs
- 26 oz. readymade pasta sauce
- 2 cups breadcrumbs
- 16 oz. shredded mozzarella cheese

- ½ cup flour
- ½ cup shredded parmesan cheese
- ¼ cup chopped fresh parsley or basil
- ⅓ cup shredded parmesan cheese
- ½ tsp. basil
- 1 lemon zest
- ½ tsp. garlic powder

Directions:

1. Preheat the convection oven to 400° F. Arrange two baking sheets with parchment paper and keep them aside.
2. Cut eggplant slices with ¼-inch thickness. And coat with salt and let stand for 20 minutes.
3. In a bowl, whisk together eggs. In another mixing bowl, add the flour, and in the third mixing bowl, mix parmesan, breadcrumbs, lemon zest, basil, and garlic powder and keep all 3 bowls aside.
4. Now rinse salted eggplant under cold water and pat dry eggplant with a kitchen towel.
5. Coat all slices of eggplant one by one, first in the flour, then in egg, and lastly in the breadcrumb mixture. Transfer all the eggplant slices to a prepared baking sheet—spray eggplants with cooking spray.
6. Bake in a preheated convection oven for 10 minutes, then remove the eggplant baking sheet from the oven and lower the temperature to 350° F.
7. Spread a layer of pasta sauce in the bottom of a 9x13 baking dish, then a layer of ⅓ of the eggplant slices, herbs, parmesan cheese, and mozzarella cheese. Repeat the procedure of layers finishing with cheese on top.
8. Bake for 25 to 30 and serve warm.

Nutrition: Calories: 339. **Fat:** 2 g. **Protein:** 31 g. **Carbs:** 39 g.

Poultry

426. Turkey Breast

Preparation Time: 5 minutes
Cooking Time: 60 minutes
Servings: 6
Ingredients:

- 4 lb. turkey breasts
- 2 tsp. salt
- 1 tbsp. olive oil

Rub:

- ½ tsp. paprika
- 1 tsp. dried thyme
- ½ tsp. dried oregano
- 2 tbsp. butter, unsalted

Directions:

1. Turn on the oven, set the temperature to 350° F, and then select the oven cooking method.
2. Meanwhile, prepare the turkey and for this, place all the ingredients for the rub in a small bowl and then stir until mixed.
3. Spread the rub gently under the skin of the turkey breast, rub ½ tbsp. oil, season with salt, and then rub remaining oil over the skin side.
4. Place chicken in the oven tray and then cook for 30 minutes per side until cooked.
5. When done, let the chicken rest for 10 minutes, cut it into pieces, and then serve.

Nutrition: Calories: 361.2. **Fat:** 11.1 g. **Carbs:** 0.2 g. **Protein:** 65.2 g. **Fiber:** 0 g.

427. Herb Roasted Turkey

Preparation Time: 5 minutes
Cooking Time: 1 hour
Servings: 12
Ingredients:

- 14-lb. whole turkey, cleaned
- 4 cloves of garlic, peeled, sliced
- 1 tbsp. salt
- 1 tsp. ground black pepper
- 6 tbsp. butter, cut into slices
- Olive oil as needed
- ½ cup chicken broth

Directions:

1. Turn on the oven, set the temperature to 400° F, and then select the oven cooking method.
2. Meanwhile, prepare the turkey and for this, place slices of garlic and butter under the skin and breast of the turkey, brush with oil, and then season with salt and black pepper.
3. Place the turkey breast-side down in the baking pan, pour ½ cup broth over the prepared turkey, and then cook for 2 hours until done, basting the broth every 30 minutes.
4. Flip the turkey, baste with the broth and then continue cooking for 1 hour.
5. When done, let the turkey rest for 20 minutes, carve it into pieces, and then serve.

Nutrition: Calories: 669. **Fat:** 29 g. **Carbs:** 6 g. **Protein:** 91 g. **Fiber:** 1 g.

428. Sweet and Sour Chicken

Preparation Time: 25 minutes
Cooking Time: 1 hour
Servings: 6
Ingredients:

- 2 ½-lb. chicken breasts, boneless and skinless
- A pinch of salt and pepper
- 1 cup cornstarch
- 3 finely pounded eggs
- ¼ cup palm oil
- 1 cup sugar
- 6 tbsp. ketchup
- ¼ cup apple cider vinegar
- 1 ½ tbsp. soya sauce
- 1 ½ tsp. powdered garlic

Directions:

1. Chop the chicken into small bits. To taste, season with salt and pepper.
2. Preheat the oven to 325° F (180° C).
3. Combine the cornstarch and water in a shallow dish. Crack the shells in a separate dish. In a big skillet, heat the oil over medium-high heat. Dredge the chicken in cornstarch and then in the egg, working in batches. Cook in the hot oil until golden brown on all sides. You don't have to cook the chicken all the way through; just brown the outside to get a crispy crust. Transfer the chicken to a 913-inch baking dish and repeat for the rest of the chicken.
4. Combine the sugar, ketchup, cider vinegar, soy sauce, and garlic powder in a mixing cup. Pour the sauce over the chicken and serve.
5. Preheat the oven to 350° F and bake the chicken for 1 hour, stirring after 15 minutes. Serve over rice that has been cooked.

Notes:

1. This recipe was adapted from Mel's Kitchen Cafe.
2. Nutritional data is given as a guideline only. Counts may be affected by different brands and materials. The dietary information included can only be seen as a guideline. Rice for serving is not used in the nutritional counts.

Nutrition: Calories: 528. **Sugar:** 36 g. **Sodium:** 1316 mg. **Fat:** 17 g. **Saturated Fat:** 3 g. **Unsaturated Fat:** 11 g. **Trans Fat:** 0 g. **Carbs:** 58 g. **Fiber:** 0 g. **Protein:** 42 g. **Cholesterol:** 185 mg.

429. Juicy Chicken Drumsticks

Preparation Time: 10 minutes
Cooking Time: 60 minutes
Servings: 6
Ingredients:

- 6 chicken legs
- ¼ cup soy sauce
- 2 tbsp. olive oil
- ½ tsp. paprika
- ½ tsp. oregano
- 1 ½ tsp. onion powder
- 1 tsp. garlic powder
- ½ tsp. pepper
- ½ tsp. salt

Directions:
1. Preheat the oven to 375° F.
2. Add chicken legs and remaining ingredients into the zip-lock bag, seal bag, shake well, and place it in the refrigerator for 1 hour.
3. Place rack onto a baking tray, then arrange marinated chicken legs onto the rack. Insert into the oven.
4. Bake for 45 minutes.
5. Serve and enjoy.

Nutrition: Calories: 315. **Fat:** 20.1 g. **Carbs:** 1.9 g. **Sugar:** 0.5 g. **Protein:** 30.5 g. **Cholesterol:** 105 mg.

430. Crispy Chicken Wings

Preparation Time: 10 minutes
Cooking Time: 60 minutes
Servings: 6
Ingredients:

- 2 lbs. chicken wings
- 1 tbsp. baking powder
- 1 tsp. Italian seasoning
- 1 tsp. smoked paprika
- 1 tsp. garlic powder
- ¼ tsp. pepper
- 1 tsp. salt

Directions:
1. Preheat the oven to 425° F.
2. Add chicken wings and remaining ingredients into the mixing bowl and toss well.
3. Place rack onto a baking tray, then arrange chicken wings onto the rack. Insert into the oven.
4. Bake for 30 minutes.
5. Turn chicken wings and bake for 20 minutes more.
6. Serve and enjoy.

Nutrition: Calories: 295. **Fat:** 11.5 g. **Carbs:** 1.9 g. **Sugar:** 0.2 g. **Protein:** 43.9 g. **Cholesterol:** 135 mg.

431. Lemon Pepper Chicken Wings

Preparation Time: 10 minutes
Cooking Time: 60 minutes

Servings: 6
Ingredients:

- 1 ½ lb. chicken wings
- 3 tbsp. olive oil
- 2 tbsp. honey
- ½ lemon juice
- ½ tsp. pepper
- 6 tbsp. butter, melted
- Pepper
- Salt

Directions:
1. Preheat the oven to 425° F.
2. Brush chicken wings with oil and season with pepper and salt.
3. Place rack onto a baking tray, then arrange chicken wings onto the rack. Insert into the oven.
4. Bake for 25 minutes.
5. In a small bowl, mix honey, lemon juice, pepper, and butter.
6. Brush chicken wings with honey mixture and serve.

Nutrition: Calories: 399. **Fat:** 26.9 g. **Carbs:** 5.9 g. **Sugar:** 5.8 g. **Protein:** 33 g. **Cholesterol:** 131 mg.

432. Spicy Chicken Sandwiches With Roasted Garlic Sauce

Preparation Time: 15 minutes
Cooking Time: 60 minutes
Servings: 4
Ingredients:

- 5 or 6 large garlic cloves
- 3 tbsp. extra-virgin olive oil, divided
- 2 (8- to 10-oz.) boneless, skinless chicken breasts
- 1 tsp. kosher salt, divided
- 1 cup all-purpose flour
- 1 tsp. Cajun or Creole seasoning
- 2 large eggs
- ½ tsp. hot sauce
- 2 cups panko bread crumbs
- ⅓ cup mayonnaise
- 4 ciabatta rolls or other sturdy buns split in half
- Lettuce and tomato slices, for serving (optional)

Directions:
1. Select Convection Roast and preheat the oven to 400° F. Set a rack in a sheet pan.
2. Put the garlic cloves on a piece of aluminum foil and drizzle with 1 tbsp. of oil. Place in the oven while it preheats.
3. Place the chicken breasts on a cutting board and cut each one in half parallel to the board so that you have four flat fillets. Place a piece of plastic wrap over the chicken pieces and use a rolling pin or small skillet to

gently pound them to an even thickness of about ½ inch. Season the chicken on both sides with ½ tsp of salt.

4. In a shallow bowl, mix the flour, remaining ½ tsp. of salt, and the Cajun seasoning. In another bowl, whisk together the eggs and hot sauce. Combine the panko and the remaining 2 tbsp. of oil in another bowl.

5. Lightly dredge both sides of the chicken pieces in the seasoned flour, then dip them in the egg wash to coat completely, letting the excess drip off. Finally, dredge the chicken in the panko. Carefully place the breaded chicken pieces on the prepared rack.

6. Roast the chicken for 7 to 8 minutes, then carefully turn the pieces over. Return the pan to the oven and roast for another 5 to 6 minutes, until the chicken is no longer pink in the center. Let the chicken rest while you make the sauce. Put the mayonnaise in a small bowl. Remove the packet of garlic from the oven and smash it before adding it to the mayonnaise. Smash the garlic and stir to combine.

7. Divide the sauce among the bun bottoms and top each with a piece of chicken. Add lettuce and tomato slices (if using) and close the buns.

Simple swap: If you're not a garlic fan, mix the mayonnaise with a tsp. of Dijon mustard instead.

Nutrition: Calories: 284. **Total Fat:** 7.9 g. **Saturated Fat:** 1.4 g. **Cholesterol:** 36 mg. **Sodium:** 704 mg. **Total Carbs:** 46 g. **Fiber:** 3.6 g. **Sugar:** 5.5 g. **Protein:** 17.9 g.

433. Crispy Garlic Chicken Thighs With Potatoes and Carrots

Preparation Time: 10 minutes
Cooking Time: 60 minutes
Servings: 4
Ingredients:

- ¼ cup olive oil
- 2 lb. bone-in, skin-on chicken thighs
- 1 ½ tsp. kosher salt, divided
- 1 small lemon
- 20 garlic cloves (about ½ cup)
- 12 oz. small red potatoes (about 2 inches in diameter), quartered
- 2 large carrots, peeled and cut into 1-inch pieces
- 1/3 cup low-sodium chicken broth
- ½ tsp. freshly ground black pepper

Directions:

1. Select the Convection Roast option and preheat the oven to 425° F. Coat a sheet pan with the oil and place it in the oven while it preheats.

2. Salt the chicken thighs on both sides with ¾ tsp. of salt.

3. When the oven is heated, remove the sheet pan and place the chicken thighs skin-side down on it. Roast the chicken for 10 minutes.

4. Meanwhile, cut the ends off the lemon and use a mandoline or knife to slice it very thin. Cut the slices in half and remove any seeds.

5. Transfer the chicken thighs to a cutting board or plate. Put the garlic cloves, carrots, and potatoes on the sheet pan and sprinkle with the remaining ¾ tsp. of salt. Toss to coat with the oil, then move the vegetables to the outer edges of the pan. Arrange the lemon slices in the center of the pan in 2 or 3 layers and place the chicken thighs on top of them, skin-side up.

6. Roast for 30 to 35 minutes until the chicken registers 175° F, and the carrots and potatoes are golden brown and crisp.

7. Transfer the chicken, carrots, and potatoes to a platter. Add the chicken broth and pepper to the sheet pan and mix with the chicken juices, smashing the garlic slightly as you stir. Pour the sauce around the chicken and vegetables and serve.

Nutrition: Calories: 284. **Total Fat:** 7.9 g. **Saturated Fat:** 1.4 g. **Cholesterol:** 36 mg. **Sodium:** 704 mg. **Total Carbs:** 46 g. **Fiber:** 3.6 g. **Sugar:** 5.5 g. **Protein:** 17.9 g.

434. Teriyaki Chicken With Snow Peas

Preparation Time: 40 minutes
Cooking Time: 60 minutes
Servings: 4
Ingredients:

- ½ cup tamari or other gluten-free soy sauce
- 3 tbsp. honey
- 1 tbsp. rice vinegar
- 1 tbsp. rice wine or dry sherry
- 2 tsp. minced fresh ginger
- 2 garlic cloves, minced
- 1 ½ lb. boneless, skinless chicken thighs
- 2 tsp. toasted sesame oil
- 8 to 12 oz. snow peas

Directions:

1. Select the Convection Roast option and preheat the oven to 400° F.

2. In a small bowl, whisk together the tamari, honey, vinegar, rice wine, ginger, and garlic until the honey is dissolved. Set aside 2 tbsp. of the marinade and pour the rest into a zip-top bag. Put the chicken thighs in the bag and seal, squeezing as much air out as possible. Squish the chicken around to coat it completely, then let the chicken marinate for 30 minutes, turning the bag every 10 minutes.

3. Put the snow peas on a sheet pan and toss with the reserved marinade and the oil. Move the peas to the outer edges of the pan.

4. Arrange the chicken in a single layer in the center of the pan.

5.   Roast the chicken and peas for 8 minutes. Remove from the oven. Turn the chicken over and stir the peas. Roast for another 10 minutes, or until the chicken is browning in spots and the peas are tender.

Nutrition: Calories: 284. **Total Fat:** 7.9 g. **Saturated Fat:** 1.4 g. **Cholesterol:** 36 mg. **Sodium:** 704 mg. **Total Carbs:** 46 g. **Fiber:** 3.6 g. **Sugar:** 5.5 g. **Protein:** 17.9 g.

435. Adobo-Style Chicken and Rice

Preparation Time: 10 minutes
Cooking Time: 60 minutes
Servings: 4
Ingredients:

- ½ cup white vinegar
- ¼ cup tamari or other gluten-free soy sauce
- 6 garlic cloves, lightly smashed
- 1 tsp. coarsely ground black pepper
- 2 dried bay leaves
- 2 lb. boneless, skinless chicken thighs
- 1 cup long-grain white rice
- 1 ¼ cups water
- ½ cup low-sodium chicken broth

Directions:

1.   In a Dutch oven or other oven-safe pot, combine the vinegar, tamari, garlic, pepper, and bay leaves. Add the chicken, cover, and marinate in the refrigerator for 1 to 3 hours.

2.   Select the "Convection Roast" option and preheat the oven to 350° F.

3.   Add the rice, water, and broth to the pot with the chicken, lifting the chicken pieces so the rice sinks to the bottom. Place the pot over medium heat and bring the liquid to a simmer.

4.   Cover the pot and place it in the oven. Bake for 20 minutes, then stir. The rice should be barely tender, with some liquid remaining in the pot. Return the pot to the oven uncovered, and bake for another 10 minutes until the rice is tender. The chicken is done (cut into the thickest part to be sure no pink remains). Remove the bay leaves and garlic.

5.   Spoon the rice onto plates and top with the chicken.

6.   **Helpful Hack:** If you use boiling water, you can skip heating the dish on the stovetop.

Nutrition: Calories: 284. **Total Fat:** 7.9 g. **Saturated Fat:** 1.4 g. **Cholesterol:** 36 mg. **Sodium:** 704 mg. **Total Carbs:** 46 g. **Fiber:** 3.6 g. **Sugar:** 5.5 g. **Protein:** 17.9 g.

436. Chicken Tenders With Spinach-Artichoke Gratin

Preparation Time: 10 minutes
Cooking Time: 60 minutes
Servings: 4
Ingredients:

- 1 ½ lb. chicken tenders
- 1 tsp. kosher salt, divided
- 2 tbsp. unsalted butter
- 1 small onion, chopped
- 3 garlic cloves, minced
- 1 pound baby spinach
- 1 (14-oz.) can of artichoke hearts, drained
- ½ cup heavy (whipping) cream
- 4 oz. cream cheese, softened
- ¼ cup grated Parmesan cheese
- 1 cup shredded mozzarella cheese

Directions:

1.   Select the "Convection Roast" option and preheat the oven to 350° F.

2.   Sprinkle the chicken with ½ tsp. of salt and set aside.

3.   In a large cast-iron or other oven-safe skillets, melt the butter over medium heat. When the butter is foaming, add the onion, sprinkle with the remaining ½ tsp. of salt, and cook, stirring, for 1 to 2 minutes, until the onion starts to soften. Add the garlic and stir for about 30 seconds. Add the spinach in large handfuls, stirring to wilt. Add the artichoke hearts, stirring them into the spinach. Add the heavy cream and cream cheese and cook until the cream cheese has melted into the vegetables. Stir in the Parmesan.

4.   Pat the chicken dry and place the fillets in a single layer on top of the spinach mixture. Top with the mozzarella cheese.

5.   Put the skillet in the oven and bake for 35 to 40 minutes, or until cheese is lightly browned on top and the mixture is bubbling.

6.   Let cool for 5 to 10 minutes, then serve.

7.   **Helpful Hack:** A chicken "tender" is a breast meat piece that runs along a boned breast half. If you can't find them, just cut boneless, skinless breasts into 1-inch-thick strips.

8.   **Even Easier:** Use frozen spinach, thawed and well-drained, in place of the fresh spinach.

Nutrition: Calories: 284. **Total Fat:** 7.9 g. **Saturated Fat:** 1.4 g. **Cholesterol:** 36 mg. **Total Carbs:** 46 g. **Fiber:** 3.6 g. **Sugar:** 5.5 g. **Protein:** 17.9 g.

Beef

437. Beefy Steak Topped With Chimichurri Sauce

Preparation Time: 5 minutes
Cooking Time: 60 minutes
Servings: 6
Ingredients:

- 1 cup commercial chimichurri
- 3 lb. steak
- Salt and pepper to taste

Directions:

1. Place all ingredients in a Ziploc bag and marinate in the fridge for 2 hours.
2. Preheat the air fryer to 390° F.
3. Place the grill pan accessory in the air fryer.
4. Grill the skirt steak for 20 minutes per batch.
5. Flip the steak every 10 minutes for even grilling.

Nutrition: **Calories:** 507. **Fat:** 27 g. **Protein:** 63 g.

438. Garlic-Cumin and Orange Juice Marinated Steak

Preparation Time: 6 minutes
Cooking Time: 60 minutes
Servings: 4
Ingredients:

- ¼ cup orange juice
- 1 tsp. ground cumin
- 2 lb. skirt steak, trimmed from excess fat
- 2 tbsp. lime juice
- 2 tbsp. olive oil
- 4 cloves of garlic, minced
- Salt and pepper to taste

Directions:

1. Place all ingredients in a mixing bowl and allow to marinate in the fridge for at least 2 hours
2. Preheat the air fryer oven to 390° F.
3. Place the grill pan accessory in the air fryer.
4. Grill for 15 minutes per batch and flip the beef every 8 minutes for even grilling.
5. Meanwhile, pour the marinade on a saucepan and allow to simmer for 10 minutes or until the sauce thickens.
6. Slice the beef and pour over the sauce.

Nutrition: **Calories:** 568. **Fat:** 34.7 g. **Protein:** 59.1 g. **Sugar:** 1 g.

439. Sauce Glazed Meatloaf

Preparation Time: 10 minutes
Cooking Time: 60 minutes
Servings: 4
Ingredients:

- 1 lb. ground beef
- ½ onion chopped
- 1 egg
- 1 ½ garlic clove, minced
- 1 ½ tbsp. ketchup
- 1 ½ tbsp. fresh parsley, chopped
- ¼ cup breadcrumbs
- 2 tbsp. milk
- Salt to taste
- 1 ½ tsp. herb seasoning
- ¼ tsp. black pepper
- ½ tsp. ground paprika

Glaze:

- ¾ cup ketchup
- 1 ½ tsp. white vinegar
- 2 ½ tbsp. brown sugar
- 1 tsp. garlic powder
- ½ tsp. onion powder
- ¼ tsp. ground black pepper
- ¼ tsp. salt

Directions:

1. Thoroughly mix ground beef with egg, onion, garlic, crumbs, and all the ingredients in a bowl.
2. Grease a meatloaf pan with oil or butter and spread the minced beef in the pan.
3. Press the Power button of the oven and turn the dial to select the Bake mode.
4. Press the Time button and again turn the dial to set the cooking time to 40 minutes.
5. Now push the Temp button and rotate the dial to set the temperature at 375° F.
6. Once preheated, place the beef baking pan in the oven and close its lid.
7. Meanwhile, prepare the glaze by whisking its ingredients in a saucepan.
8. Stir cook for 5 minutes until it thickens.
9. Brush this glaze over the meatloaf and bake it again for 15 minutes.
10. Slice and serve.

Nutrition: Calories: 134. **Total Fat:** 4.7 g. **Saturated Fat:** 0.6 g. **Cholesterol:** 124 mg. **Sodium:** 1 mg. **Total Carbs:** 54.1 g. **Fiber:** 7 g. **Sugar:** 3.3 g. **Protein:** 26.2 g.

440. Zucchini Beef Meatloaf

Preparation Time: 10 minutes
Cooking Time: 60 minutes
Servings: 8
Ingredients:

- 2 lbs. ground beef
- 1 cup zucchini, shredded
- 2 eggs
- 3 garlic cloves minced
- 3 tbsp. Worcestershire sauce
- 3 tbsp. fresh parsley, chopped
- ¾ cup Panko breadcrumbs
- ⅓ cup beef broth

- Salt to taste
- ¼ tsp. ground black pepper
- ½ tsp. ground paprika
- ¾ tsp onion
- 1 tbsp oil (or 2 tbsp butter)

Directions:

1. Thoroughly mix ground beef with egg, zucchini, onion, garlic, crumbs, and all the ingredients in a bowl.
2. Grease a meatloaf pan with oil or butter and spread the minced beef in the pan.
3. Press the "Power Button" of the oven and turn the dial to select the "Bake" mode.
4. Press the Time button and again turn the dial to set the cooking time to 40 minutes.
5. Now push the Temp button and rotate the dial to set the temperature at 375° F.
6. Once preheated, place the beef baking pan in the oven and close its lid.
7. Slice and serve.

Nutrition: Calories: 387. **Total Fat:** 6 g. **Saturated Fat:** 9.9 g. **Cholesterol:** 41 mg. **Sodium:** 154 mg. **Total Carbs:** 37.4 g. **Fiber:** 2.9 g. **Sugar:** 15.3 g. **Protein:** 14.6 g.

441. Carrot Beef Cake

Preparation Time: 10 minutes
Cooking Time: 60 minutes
Servings: 10
Ingredients:

- 3 eggs, beaten
- ½ cup almond milk
- 1-oz. onion soup mix
- 1 cup dry bread crumbs
- 2 cups shredded carrots
- 2 lb. lean ground beef
- ½-lb. ground pork
- 2 tbsp oil

Directions:

1. Thoroughly mix ground beef with carrots and all other ingredients in a bowl.
2. Grease a meatloaf pan with oil or butter and spread the minced beef in the pan.
3. Press the Power Button of the oven and turn the dial to select the Bake mode.
4. Press the Time button and again turn the dial to set the cooking time to 60 minutes.
5. Now push the Temp button and rotate the dial to set the temperature at 350° F.
6. Once preheated, place the beef baking pan in the oven and close its lid.
7. Slice and serve.

Nutrition: Calories: 212. **Total Fat:** 11.8 g. **Saturated Fat:** 2.2 g. **Cholesterol:** 23 mg. **Sodium:** 321 mg. **Total**

Carbs: 14.6 g. **Dietary Fiber:** 4.4 g. **Sugar:** 8 g. **Protein:** 17.3 g.

442. Crumbly Oat Meatloaf

Preparation Time: 10 minutes
Cooking Time: 60 minutes
Servings: 8
Ingredients:

- 2 lb. ground beef
- 1 cup salsa
- ¾ cup Quaker oats
- ½ cup chopped onion
- 1 large egg, beaten
- 1 tbsp. Worcestershire sauce
- Salt and black pepper to taste

Directions:

1. Thoroughly mix ground beef with salsa, oats, onion, egg, and all the ingredients in a bowl.
2. Grease a meatloaf pan with oil or butter and spread the minced beef in the pan.
3. Press the Power Button of the oven and turn the dial to select the Bake mode.
4. Press the Time button and again turn the dial to set the cooking time to 60 minutes.
5. Now push the Temp button and rotate the dial to set the temperature at 350° F.
6. Once preheated, place the beef baking pan in the oven and close its lid.
7. Slice and serve.

Nutrition: Calories: 412. **Total Fat:** 24.8 g. **Saturated Fat:** 12.4 g. **Cholesterol:** 3 mg. **Sodium:** 132 mg. **Total Carbs:** 43.8 g. **Dietary Fiber:** 3.9 g. **Sugar:** 2.5 g. **Protein:** 18.9 g.

443. Creole Beef Meatloaf

Preparation Time: 10 minutes
Cooking Time: 60 minutes
Servings: 6
Ingredients:

- 1 lb. ground beef
- ½ tbsp. butter
- 1 red bell pepper diced
- ⅓ cup red onion diced
- ⅓ cup cilantro diced
- ⅓ cup zucchini diced
- 1 tbsp. creole seasoning
- ½ tsp. turmeric
- ½ tsp. cumin
- ½ tsp. coriander
- 2 garlic cloves minced
- Salt and black pepper to taste

Directions:

1. Mix the beef mince with all the meatball ingredients in a bowl.

2. Make small meatballs out of this mixture and place them in the air fryer basket.

3. Press the Power Button of the oven and turn the dial to select the Air Fry mode.

4. Press the Time button and again turn the dial to set the cooking time to 15 minutes.

5. Now push the Temp button and rotate the dial to set the temperature at 370° F.

6. Once preheated, place the basket in the oven and close its lid.

7. Slice and serve warm.

Nutrition: Calories: 331. **Total Fat:** 2.5 g. **Saturated Fat:** 0.5 g. **Cholesterol:** 35 mg. **Sodium:** 595 mg. **Total Carbs:** 69 g. **Fiber:** 12.2 g. **Sugar:** 12.5 g. **Protein:** 26.7 g.

444. Healthy Mama Meatloaf

Preparation Time: 10 minutes
Cooking Time: 60 minutes
Servings: 8
Ingredients:

- 1 tbsp. olive oil
- 1 green bell pepper, diced
- ½ cup diced sweet onion
- ½ tsp. minced garlic
- 1-lb. ground beef
- 1 cup whole wheat bread crumbs
- 2 large eggs
- ¾ cup shredded carrot
- ¾ cup shredded zucchini
- Salt and ground black pepper to taste
- ¼ cup ketchup, or to taste

Directions:

1. Thoroughly mix ground beef with egg, onion, garlic, crumbs, and all the ingredients in a bowl.

2. Grease a meatloaf pan with oil or butter and spread the minced beef in the pan.

3. Press the Power Button of the oven and turn the dial to select the Bake mode.

4. Press the Time button and again turn the dial to set the cooking time to 40 minutes.

5. Now push the Temp button and rotate the dial to set the temperature at 375° F.

6. Once preheated, place the beef baking pan in the oven and close its lid.

7. Slice and serve.

Nutrition: Calories: 322. **Total Fat:** 11.8 g. **Saturated Fat:** 2.2 g. **Cholesterol:** 56 mg. **Sodium:** 321 mg. **Total Carbs:** 14.6 g. **Dietary Fiber:** 4.4 g. **Sugar:** 8 g. **Protein:** 17.3 g.

445. Beef Short Ribs

Preparation Time: 10 minutes
Cooking Time: 60 minutes
Servings: 4

Ingredients:

- 1 ²/₃ lbs. short ribs
- Salt and black pepper, to taste
- 1 tsp. grated garlic
- ½ tsp. salt
- 1 tsp. cumin seeds
- ¼ cup panko crumbs
- 1 tsp. ground cumin
- 1 tsp. avocado oil
- ½ tsp. orange zest
- 1 egg, beaten

Directions:

1. Place the beef ribs in a baking tray and pour the whisked egg on top.

2. Whisk the rest of the crusting ingredients in a bowl and spread over the beef.

3. Press the Power Button of the oven and turn the dial to select the Air Fry mode.

4. Press the Time button and again turn the dial to set the cooking time to 35 minutes.

5. Now push the Temp button and rotate the dial to set the temperature at 350° F.

6. Once preheated, place the beef baking tray in the oven and close its lid.

7. Serve warm.

Nutrition: Calories: 267. **Total Fat:** 15.4 g. **Saturated Fat:** 4.2 g. **Cholesterol:** 168 mg. **Sodium:** 203 mg. **Total Carbs:** 58.5 g. **Sugar:** 1.1 g. **Fiber:** 4 g.

446. Basic Meatloaf

Preparation Time: 10 minutes
Cooking Time: 60 minutes
Servings: 8
Ingredients:

- 2 lbs. ground beef
- 1 shallot, chopped
- 2 eggs
- 3 garlic cloves minced
- 3 tbsp. tomato sauce
- 3 tbsp. parsleys, chopped
- ¾ cup Panko breadcrumbs
- 1/3 cup milk
- 1 ½ tsp. salt or to taste
- 1 ½ tsp. Italian seasoning
- ¼ tsp. ground black pepper
- ½ tsp. ground paprika

Directions:

1. Thoroughly mix ground beef with egg, onion, garlic, crumbs, and all the ingredients in a bowl.

2. Grease a meatloaf pan with oil or butter and spread the minced beef in the pan.

3. Press the Power button of the oven and turn the dial to select the Bake mode.

4.   Press the Time button and again turn the dial to set the cooking time to 40 minutes.

5.   Now push the Temp button and rotate the dial to set the temperature at 375° F.

6.   Once preheated, place the beef baking pan in the oven and close its lid.

7.   Slice and serve.

Nutrition: Calories: 284. **Total Fat:** 7.9 g. **Saturated Fat:** 1.4 g. **Cholesterol:** 36 mg. **Sodium:** 704 mg. **Total Carbs:** 46 g. **Fiber:** 3.6 g. **Sugar:** 5.5 g. **Protein:** 17.9 g.

Lamb

447. Armenian-Style Lamb and Beef Pizza

Preparation Time: 20 minutes
Cooking Time: 60 minutes
Servings: 8
Ingredients:

- 1 lb. ground lamb
- 8 (6 inches) flour tortillas
- 1 lb. ground beef
- 1 can (6 oz.) of tomato paste
- 2 tbsp. dry red wine
- 1 sliced onion
- 2 diced and seeded jalapeno peppers
- 2 tbsp. harissa chili paste
- 1 tbsp. ground sumac
- ¼ cup fresh parsley minced
- 1 lemon wedges
- ¼ tsp. salt
- Cooking spray
- ½ tsp. ground cinnamon
- ¼ tsp. pepper

Directions:
1. Preheat the convection oven broiler.
2. Cook lamb and beef with onion and crumble them in a large-sized skillet on medium-high heat until meat changes its color for around 8 to 10 minutes.
3. Add in all other ingredients except tortillas and lemon wedges to the meat mixture and cook. Keep stirring in between until completely blended. Remove from stove.
4. One by one, coat both sides of tortillas with cooking spray and arrange on a baking sheet. Broil in a convection oven 3 to 4 inches away from heat until crispy 1 minute per side. Top up broiled tortillas with meat mixture and side with lemon wedges upon serving.
Nutrition: Calories: 568. **Fat:** 34.7 g. **Protein:** 59.1 g. **Sugar:** 1 g.

448. Classic Lamb Gratin

Preparation Time: 30 minutes
Cooking Time: 1 hour
Servings: 8
Ingredients:

- 3 large thinly sliced potatoes
- 1 lb. ground lamb
- 2 cups milk
- 2 cups fresh sliced mushrooms
- 1 (1 oz.) package of dry onion soup mix
- 2 diced carrots
- 1 cup sharp cheddar cheese shredded
- 1 diced onion
- 1 cup Havarti cheese shredded
- 2 tbsp. all-purpose flour
- 1 clove of minced garlic
- 2 tbsp. butter
- Salt and black pepper (to taste)
- 1 beaten egg

Directions:
1. Preheat the convection oven to 375° F.
2. On medium-high heat in a large-sized skillet, cook lamb; mix in onions, garlic, and carrots. Continue cooking and keep stirring until lamb is crumbly and browned about 6 to 8 minutes. Fold in soup mix into the lamb mixture; remove from stove.
3. On medium heat, melt butter in a medium-sized saucepan. Whisk flour in the heated butter, add 1 tbsp. at a time, make sure no lumps remain. Put milk into butter mixture keep whisking; until the mixture thickens. Switch off the heat and remove the saucepan from the stove. Fold in Havarti cheese and cheddar cheese into milk mixture until cheeses meltdown.
4. Place a small amount of cheese sauce mixture into a beaten egg in a small mixing bowl; whisk well and pour the egg into the cheese sauce mixture and fold.
5. In the bottom of the greased casserole dish, place sliced potatoes, sprinkle with pepper and salt. Spread $\frac{1}{3}$ of the cheese sauce on the potatoes layer evenly. On top of the cheese, layer spread lamb mixture evenly. Again, spread the remaining potatoes layer on top of the lamb mixture and season with pepper and salt. Pour with remaining cheese over the top sauce. Cover baking dish with lid.
6. Bake for around 60 minutes in the preheated convection oven. After 60 minutes, remove the cover and bake for another 30 minutes until gratin turns golden brown from the top.
Nutrition: Calories: 435. **Fat:** 23 g. **Protein:** 23.2 g. **Carbs:** 35.1 g.

449. Tasty Lamb Meatballs Baked

Preparation Time: 20 minutes
Cooking Time: 60 minutes
Servings: 21 meatballs
Ingredients:

- ¼ cup yogurt
- 1 lb. ground lamb
- ¼ cup raisins
- 2 slices of bread, split into small pieces
- 1 clove of minced garlic
- ⅛ tsp. ground black pepper
- ¼ tsp. dried basil
- ¼ cup fresh cilantro
- ⅛ tsp. salt
- ¼ tsp. dried oregano

Directions:

1.   Preheat the convection oven at 350° F.
2.   Combine bread, lamb, raisins, yogurt, garlic, oregano, salt, basil, cilantro, and pepper and mix together in a medium-sized bowl. Make 1-inch balls out of the mixture (mixture will make 21 meatballs).
3.   Arrange meatballs on a greased baking sheet and bake for around 20 minutes in the preheated convection oven.

Nutrition: Calories: 298. **Fat:** 16.1 g. **Protein:** 21.6 g. **Carbs:** 16.1 g.

450. Delicious Lamb Stuffed Peppers

Preparation Time: 20 minutes
Cooking Time: 1 hour
Servings: 6
Ingredients:
- 8 oz. ground lamb
- 1 chopped onion
- 6 green bell peppers medium
- 1 cup rice cooked
- 1 cup feta cheese crumbled
- 1 cup cold water
- 2 tbsp. fresh dill chopped
- 1 tbsp. olive oil
- 1 cup tomato sauce
- 1 tbsp. lemon juice
- ½ tsp. ground black pepper
- 1 tsp. white sugar
- ½ tsp. ground allspice
- 1 garlic clove minced
- ¾ tsp. salt

Directions:
1.   Preheat the convection oven at 350° F.
2.   On medium heat, heat the oil in a large-sized skillet and add onion; cook for 4 to 5 minutes until translucent. Mix in garlic and cook for another 1 minute.
3.   Cut the tops of bell peppers and discard seeds. Arrange bell peppers in 9x12 inches baking dish.
4.   Combine cooked onion mixture, salt, allspice, dill, and pepper, in a large-sized bowl. Mix lamb, rice, and fold feta cheese in the mixture. Stuff bell peppers with the prepared mixture.
5.   Mix in water with tomato sauce, sugar, and lemon juice. Spread half over the bell peppers and half on the bottom of a baking dish, and cover the dish with heavy-duty foil.
6.   Bake in the preheated convection oven for around 45 minutes, remove foil and bake for another 15 minutes. Top up with more sauce if required.

Nutrition: Calories: 273. **Fat:** 16.8 g. **Protein:** 12.4 g. **Carbs:** 19.3 g.

451. Baked Lamb Moroccan Kebabs

Preparation Time: 15 minutes
Cooking Time: 60 minutes
Servings: 6
Ingredients:
- 5 oz. goat cheese
- 2 lb. ground lamb
- 1 chopped red onion
- 1 cup raisins
- ⅓ cup mayonnaise
- 2 tbsp. fresh cilantro chopped
- ½ tsp. ground cumin
- Ground black pepper to taste
- ¾ tbsp. cayenne pepper
- Salt to taste
- 2 cloves of chopped garlic
- ½ tsp. ground coriander

Directions:
1.   Preheat the convection oven at 350° F.
2.   Mix together raisins, lamb, mayonnaise, red onion, goat cheese, cayenne pepper, cumin, cilantro, salt, coriander, garlic, and black pepper in a medium-sized bowl. Distribute mixture into 6 equal parts and press on the skewers.
3.   Place skewers on a baking sheet and cook in the preheated convection oven for around 30 to 40 minutes or more until kebabs are browned and completely cooked. In the end, broil for 1 to 2 minutes in the convection oven.

Nutrition: Calories: 554. **Fat:** 37.6 g. **Protein:** 32.2 g. **Carbs:** 22.7 g.

Pork

452. Curry Pork Roast in Coconut Sauce

Preparation Time: 10 minutes
Cooking Time: 60 minutes
Servings: 6
Ingredients:

- ½ tsp. curry powder
- ½ tsp. ground turmeric powder
- 1 can unsweetened coconut milk
- 1 tbsp. sugar
- 2 tbsp. fish sauce
- 2 tbsp. soy sauce
- 3 pounds pork shoulder
- Salt and pepper to taste

Directions:
1.   Place all ingredients in a bowl and allow the meat to marinate in the fridge for at least 2 hours.
2.   Preheat the air fryer to 390° F.
3.   Place the grill pan accessory in the air fryer.
4.   Grill the meat for 20 minutes making sure to flip the pork every 10 minutes for even grilling and cook in batches.
5.   Meanwhile, pour the marinade in a saucepan and allow to simmer for 10 minutes until the sauce thickens.
6.   Baste the pork with the sauce before serving.
Nutrition: Calories: 688. **Fat:** 52 g. **Protein:** 17 g.

453. Roasted Pork Tenderloin

Preparation Time: 5 minutes
Cooking Time: 1 hour
Servings: 4
Ingredients:

- 1 (3-lb.) pork tenderloin
- 2 tbsp. extra-virgin olive oil
- 2 garlic cloves, minced
- 1 tsp. dried basil
- 1 tsp. dried oregano
- 1 tsp. dried thyme
- Salt
- Pepper

Directions:
1.   Drizzle the pork tenderloin with olive oil.
2.   Rub the garlic, basil, oregano, thyme, and salt and pepper to taste all over the tenderloin.
3.   Pour into the oven rack/basket. Place the rack on the middle shelf of the Air fryer oven. Set temperature to 350° F, and set time to 45 minutes. Use a meat thermometer to test for doneness
4.   Open the air fryer and flip the pork tenderloin. Cook for an additional 15 minutes.
5.   Remove the cooked pork from the air fryer and allow it to rest for 10 minutes before cutting.

Nutrition: Calories: 283. **Fat:** 10 g. **Protein:** 48 g.

454. Asian Pork Chops

Preparation Time: 2 hours 10 minutes
Cooking Time: 60 minutes
Servings: 4
Ingredients:

- ½ cup hoisin sauce
- 3 tbsp. cider vinegar
- 1 tbsp. Asian sweet chili sauce
- ¼ tsp. garlic powder
- 4 (½-inch-thick) boneless pork chops
- 1 tsp. salt
- ½ tsp. pepper

Directions:
1.   Stir together hoisin, chili sauce, garlic powder, and vinegar in a large mixing bowl. Separate ¼ cup of this mixture, then add pork chops to the bowl and marinate in the fridge for 2 hours. Remove the pork chops and place them on a plate. Sprinkle each side of the pork chop evenly with salt and pepper.
2.   Pour into the oven rack/basket. Place the rack on the middle shelf of the Air fryer oven. Set temperature to 360° F, and set time to 14 minutes. Cook for 14 minutes, flipping halfway through. Brush with reserved marinade and serve.
Nutrition: Calories: 338. **Fat:** 21 g. **Protein:** 19 g. **Fiber:** 1 g.

455. Bolognaise Sauce

Preparation Time: 5 minutes
Cooking Time: 60 minutes
Servings: 2
Ingredients:

- 13 oz ground beef
- 1 carrot
- 1 stalk of celery
- 10 oz diced tomatoes
- ½ onion
- Salt and pepper to taste
- Oven-safe bowl

Directions:
1.   Preheat the air fryer oven to 390° F.
2.   Finely dice the carrot, celery, and onions. Place into the oven-safe bowl along with the ground beef and combine well.
3.   Place the bowl into the air fryer oven tray and cook for 12 minutes until browned.
4.   Pour the diced tomatoes into the bowl and replace them in the air fryer.
5.   Season with salt and pepper, then cook for another 18 minutes.
6.   Serve over cooked pasta or freeze for later use.
Nutrition: Calories: 617. **Protein:** 56.49 g. **Fat:** 28.53 g. **Carbs:** 39.46 g.

456. Breaded Spam Steaks

Preparation Time: 5 minutes
Cooking Time: 60 minutes
Servings: 2
Ingredients:

- 12 oz. can luncheon meat
- 1 cup all-purpose flour
- 2 eggs, beaten
- 2 cups Italian seasoned breadcrumbs

Directions:
1. Preheat the air fryer oven to 380° F.
2. Cut the luncheon meat into ¼-inch slices.
3. Gently press the luncheon meat slices into the flour to coat and shake off the excess flour. Dip into the beaten egg, then press into breadcrumbs.
4. Place the battered slices into the air fryer tray and cook for 3 to 5 minutes until golden brown.
5. Serve with chili or tomato sauce.

Nutrition: Calories: 315. **Protein:** 45.77 g. **Fat:** 54.27 g. **Carbs:** 132.92 g.

457. Air Fryer Burgers

Preparation Time: 5 minutes
Cooking Time: 60 minutes
Servings: 4
Ingredients:

- 1-lb. lean ground beef
- 1 tsp. dried parsley
- ½ tsp. dried oregano
- ½ tsp. pepper
- ½ tsp. salt
- ½ tsp. onion powder
- ½ tsp. garlic powder
- Few drops of liquid smoke
- 1 tsp. Worcestershire sauce

Directions:
1. Ensure your air fryer oven is preheated to 350° F.
2. Mix all seasonings together till combined.
3. Place beef in a bowl and add seasonings. Mix well, but do not overmix.
4. Make 4 patties from the mixture and using your thumb, make an indent in the center of each patty.
5. Add patties to the air fryer basket.
6. Set temperature to 350° F, and set time to 10 minutes, and cook 10 minutes. No need to turn.

Nutrition: Calories: 148. **Fat:** 5 g. **Protein:** 24 g. **Sugar:** 1 g.

458. Cheese-Stuffed Meatballs

Preparation Time: 10 minutes
Cooking Time: 60 minutes
Servings: 4
Ingredients:

- ⅓ cup soft bread crumbs
- 3 tbsp. milk
- 1 tbsp. ketchup
- 1 egg
- ½ tsp. dried marjoram
- Pinch salt
- Freshly ground black pepper
- 1 pound 95 percent lean ground beef
- 20 ½-inch cubes of cheese
- Olive oil for misting

Directions:
1. In a large bowl, combine the bread crumbs, milk, ketchup, egg, marjoram, salt, and pepper, and mix well. Add the ground beef and mix gently but thoroughly with your hands. Form the mixture into 20 meatballs. Shape each meatball around a cheese cube. Mist the meatballs with olive oil and put them into the air fryer oven basket.
2. Bake for 10 to 13 minutes or until the meatballs register 165° F on a meat thermometer.

Nutrition: Calories: 393. **Fat:** 17 g. **Protein:** 50 g. **Fiber:** 0 g.

459. Homemade Pork Ratatouille

Preparation Time: 10 minutes
Cooking Time: 60 minutes
Servings: 4
Ingredients:

- 4 pork sausages

For ratatouille:

- 1 red pepper, chopped
- 2 zucchinis, chopped
- 1 eggplant, chopped
- 1 medium red onion, chopped
- 1 tbsp. olive oil
- 1-oz. butterbean, drained
- 15 oz. tomatoes, chopped
- 1 tbsp. balsamic vinegar
- 2 garlic cloves, minced
- 1 red chili, chopped

Directions:
1. Mix red pepper, eggplant, olive oil, onion, and zucchinis and add to a baking pan. Roast for 20 minutes on Bake function at 390° F. Lower temperatures to 350° F.
2. Place a saucepan over medium heat and add in the vegetables and the remaining ratatouille ingredients. Mix well and bring to a boil. Let the mixture simmer for 10 minutes; season.
3. Add sausages to the frying basket and fit in the baking tray; cook for 10 minutes, select Air Fry mode at 350° F. Serve the sausages with ratatouille.

Nutrition: Calories: 284. **Total Fat:** 7.9 g. **Saturated Fat:** 1.4 g. **Cholesterol:** 36 mg. **Total Carbs:** 46 g. **Fiber:** 3.6 g. **Sugar:** 5.5 g. **Protein:** 17.9 g.

460. Sweet Marinaded Pork Chops

Preparation Time: 10 minutes
Cooking Time: 60 minutes
Servings: 4
Ingredients:

- 3 pork chops, ½-inch thick
- Salt and black pepper to taste to season
- 1 tbsp. maple syrup
- 1 ½ tbsp. minced garlic
- 3 tbsp. mustard

Directions:
1.   In a bowl, add maple syrup, garlic, mustard, salt, and pepper; mix well.
2.   Add in the pork and toss to coat. Slide out the basket and place the chops inside. Fit in the baking tray and cook in your oven at 350° F for 6 minutes under the Air Fry mode.
3.   Flip the chops with a spatula and cook further for 6 minutes. Once ready, remove them to a platter and serve with steamed asparagus.

Nutrition: Calories: 284. **Total Fat:** 7.9 g. **Cholesterol:** 36 mg. **Total Carbs:** 46 g. **Fiber:** 3.6 g. **Sugar:** 5.5 g. **Protein:** 17.9 g.

461. Beef Rolls With Pesto & Spinach

Preparation Time: 10 minutes
Cooking Time: 60 minutes
Servings: 4
Ingredients:

- 2 lb. beef steaks, sliced
- Salt and black pepper to taste
- 3 tbsp. pesto
- 6 slices mozzarella cheese
- ¾ cup spinach, chopped
- 3 oz. bell pepper, deseeded and sliced

Directions:
1.   Top the meat with pesto, mozzarella cheese, spinach, and bell pepper.
2.   Roll up the slices and secure them using a toothpick. Season with salt and pepper.
3.   Place the slices in the basket and fit in the baking tray; cook for 15 minutes under Air Fry mode at 400° F, turning once. Serve immediately!

Nutrition: Calories: 284. **Total Fat:** 7.9 g. **Saturated Fat:** 1.4 g. **Cholesterol:** 36 mg. **Total Carbs:** 46 g. **Fiber:** 3.6 g. **Sugar:** 5.5 g.

462. Savory Pulled Pork With Cheddar & Bacon

Preparation Time: 10 minutes
Cooking Time: 60 minutes
Servings: 2
Ingredients:

- 1 pork steak
- 1 tsp. steak seasoning
- Salt and black pepper to taste
- 5 thick bacon slices, chopped
- 1 cup grated cheddar cheese
- ½ tbsp. Worcestershire sauce
- 2 bread buns, halved

Directions:
1.   Preheat oven on Bake function to 380° F. Place the pork steak in the baking pan and season with pepper, salt, and steak seasoning. Cook for 20 to 22 minutes, turning once. Remove the steak onto a chopping board and, using two forks, shred it into pieces. Return to the baking pan.
2.   Place the bacon in a skillet over medium heat and cook for 5 minutes until crispy. Add the bacon to the pork pan and stir. Mix in Worcestershire sauce, cheddar cheese, salt, and pepper.
3.   Place the pan again in the oven and cook for 4 minutes. Slide-out, stir with a spoon, and cook further for 1 minute. Spoon the meat into the halved buns and serve with tomato dip.

Nutrition: Calories: 284. **Total Fat:** 7.9 g. **Saturated Fat:** 1.4 g. **Cholesterol:** 36 mg. **Total Carbs:** 46 g. **Fiber:** 3.6 g. **Sugar:** 5.5 g. **Protein:** 17.9 g.

463. Italian-Style Pork Chops

Preparation Time: 10 minutes
Cooking Time: 60 minutes
Servings: 4
Ingredients:

- 4 pork chops, sliced
- 2 tbsp. olive oil
- Salt and black pepper to taste
- 1 whole egg, beaten
- 1 cup breadcrumbs
- 1 tsp. Italian herbs

Directions:
1.   In a bowl, place olive oil, salt, Italian herbs, and pepper and mix well. Stir in the pork, cover, and let it marinate for 15 minutes. Place the beaten egg on a plate. On a separate plate, add the breadcrumbs
2.   Preheat oven under Air Fry mode to 400° F. Dip the pork in the egg and then into the breadcrumbs. Place in the cooking basket and fit in the baking tray; cook for 20 minutes, shaking once. Serve warm.

Nutrition: Calories: 284. **Saturated Fat:** 1.4 g. **Cholesterol:** 36 mg. **Total Carbs:** 46 g. **Fiber:** 3.6 g. **Sugar:** 5.5 g. **Protein:** 17.9 g.

Fish

464. Crispy Air Fryer Fish

Preparation Time: 10 minutes
Cooking Time: 60 minutes
Servings: 4
Ingredients:

- 4 to 6 whiting fish fillets sliced
- Fuel to smear
- Marine salt
- ¾ cup very good cornflour
- ¼ cup rice
- 2 tsp. old bay
- 1 ½ tsp. salt
- 1 tsp. paprika
- ½ tsp. garlic powder
- ½ tsp. black pepper
- Your favorite tuna seasoning

Directions:

1. Blend ingredients for fish seasoning in a Ziplock bag and shake. Place into the side. Instead, you can use your fish seasoning.
2. Rinse and pat dry your fish fillets with paper towels. They will appear to be wet.
3. Place fish fillets in a Ziplock bag and shake till fillets are fully coated with seasoning.
4. Place fillets on a baking rack allowing any extra flour to fall off.
5. Grease your basket's base and position that the fillets from the bowl—Cook filets at 400° F for 10 minutes.
6. Open the basket and then spray the fish onto the side facing upward. Before spinning, ensure that the fish is fully covered. Flip and cook the other hand for 7 minutes. Remove fish and work.

Nutrition: Calories: 267. **Total Fat:** 15.4 g. **Saturated Fat:** 4.2 g. **Cholesterol:** 168 mg. **Sodium:** 203 mg. **Total Carbs:** 58.5 g. **Sugar:** 1.1 g. **Fiber:** 4 g.

465. Air Fryer Garlic Shrimp Easy Shrimp

Preparation Time: 10 minutes
Cooking Time: 60 minutes
Servings: 4
Ingredients:

- 1 lb. raw shrimp, peeled deveined,
- Jojoba spray or wax to paint shrimp
- ¼ tsp. garlic powder
- Salt, to taste
- Black pepper, to taste
- Lemon wedges
- Minced parsley or chili peppers (optional)

Directions:

1. In a bowl, toss the fish with the oil. Add garlic powder, pepper, and salt and toss to coat the fish evenly.
2. Add shrimp to the basket in one layer.
3. Air fry at 400° F for approximately 10 to 14 minutes, lightly shaking and turning halfway, based on shrimp's size.
4. Transfer fish to bowl, squeeze lemon juice on top. Sprinkle chili or parsley peppers and serve hot.

Nutrition: Calories: 267. **Total Fat:** 15.4 g. **Saturated Fat:** 4.2 g. **Cholesterol:** 168 mg. **Sodium:** 203 mg. **Total Carbs:** 58.5 g. **Sugar:** 1.1 g. **Fiber:** 4 g.

466. Air Fryer Tuna Patties

Preparation Time: 10 minutes
Cooking Time: 60 minutes
Servings: 2
Ingredients:

- 2 can of tuna in water
- 2 tsp. Dijon Mustard
- ½ cup Panko breadcrumbs
- 1 tbsp. lemon juice
- 2 tbsp. chopped parsley
- 2 eggs
- 3 tsp. olive oil
- Tabasco sauce, pepper, and salt to taste

Directions:

1. Drain the bulk of the liquid in the canned tuna. Mix the bread crumbs, lemon juice, and parsley in a dish. Insert some Tabasco to add flavor.
2. When the mix seems a little dry, add a tbsp. of olive oil and combine
3. Add the egg and then mix. Add pepper and salt to taste
4. On a sheet of baking paper, spoon the tuna mixture into patties.
5. To keep the patties in contour, refrigerate for one hour or 2 (or instantly, if possible).
6. Preheat the oven to 360° F.
7. Set the patties and cook for 10 minutes. If you'd like them to be crunchier, bring the patties in and get additional 5 minutes.

Nutrition: Calories: 267. **Total Fat:** 15.4 g. **Saturated Fat:** 4.2 g. **Cholesterol:** 168 mg. **Sodium:** 203 mg. **Total Carbs:** 58.5 g. **Sugar:** 1.1 g. **Fiber:** 4 g.

467. Tilapia on Your Air Fryer

Preparation Time: 10 minutes
Cooking Time: 60 minutes
Servings: 2
Ingredients:

- 2 can 3 Tilapia Fillets
- 1 tbsp. coconut oil
- Your choice of seasoning to taste (optional)

Directions:

1. Preheat your oven to 400° F

2. Brush the Tilapia fillets using the oil, providing a good even coating
3. Insert the seasoning you have selected, sprinkle around
4. Spritz the basket with nonstop cooking spray
5. Set the Tilapia from the basket
6. Place the air fryer mode for 8 minutes, slide the basket, and twist the fish halfway through. When the time is completed, check the fish is cooked through (some fryers may need around 12 minutes).

Nutrition: Calories: 267. **Total Fat:** 15.4 g. **Saturated Fat:** 4.2 g. **Cholesterol:** 168 mg. **Sodium:** 203 mg. **Total Carbs:** 58.5 g. **Sugar:** 1.1 g. **Fiber:** 4 g.

468. Air Fried Salmon

Preparation Time: 10 minutes
Cooking Time: 60 minutes
Servings: 4
Ingredients:

- 500 g salmon
- ½ tsp. garlic powder
- ½ tsp. paprika
- ½ tsp. kosher salt

Directions:
1. Preheat the oven to 280° F
2. Mix the salt and spices, and scatter over the salmon.
3. Place the salmon, skin side down in the jar, and cook for 10 minutes. Correct the time based on your taste.
4. Remove and function!

Nutrition: Calories: 284. **Total Fat:** 7.9 g. **Saturated Fat:** 1.4 g. **Cholesterol:** 36 mg. **Sodium:** 704 mg. **Total Carbs:** 46 g. **Fiber:** 3.6 g. **Sugar:** 5.5 g. **Protein:** 17.9 g.

469. Clams Oreganata

Preparation Time: 10 minutes
Cooking Time: 60 minutes
Servings: 4
Ingredients:

- 1 cup unseasoned breadcrumbs
- ¼ cup Parmesan cheese, grated
- ¼ cup parsley, chopped
- 1 tsp. dried oregano
- 3 tsp. garlic, minced
- 4 tbsp. butter, melted
- 2 dozen clams, shucked

- 1 slice lemon wedges
- 1 tbsp. lemon zest
- 1 tsp. peppermint

Directions:
1. In a skillet, combine the breadcrumbs, Parmesan, parsley, peppermint, garlic, lemon zest, and melted butter. Mix to make crumbs.
2. Put a heaping tbsp. of the crumb mixture on the exposed clams. Fill out the cake fit, having a cup of sea salt—Nestle the clams from the salt and cook at 400° F for 3 minutes. Garnish with fresh parsley and lemon wedges.

Nutrition: Calories: 284. **Total Fat:** 7.9 g. **Saturated Fat:** 1.4 g. **Cholesterol:** 36 mg. **Sodium:** 704 mg. **Total Carbs:** 46 g. **Fiber:** 3.6 g. **Sugar:** 5.5 g. **Protein:** 17.9 g.

470. Air-Fryer Fish and Fries

Preparation Time: 10 minutes
Cooking Time: 60 minutes
Servings: 4
Ingredients:

- 1 lb. sausage (about 2 medium)
- 2 tbsp. olive oil
- ¼ tsp. pepper
- ¼ tsp. salt
- 1/ 2 lb. potatoes cut lengthwise into ½-in. -thick pieces

Fish:

- ⅓ cup all-purpose flour
- ¼ tsp. pepper
- 1 large egg
- 2 tbsp. water
- ⅔ cup crushed cornflakes
- 1 tbsp. grated Parmesan cheese
- ⅛ tsp. cayenne pepper
- ¼ tsp. salt
- 1 lb. haddock or cod fillets
- Tartar sauce, discretionary

Directions:
1. Preheat oven to 400° F. Peel and cut potatoes lengthwise into ½-in. -thick pieces; cut pieces into ½-in. -thick rods.
2. In a large bowl, toss potatoes with oil, salt, and pepper. As required, working in batches, put potatoes in one layer in the basket; cook till just tender, 5 to 10 minutes Toss potatoes in basket redistribute; continue to cook till lightly browned and crispy 5 to 10 minutes more.
3. Meanwhile, in a bowl, combine flour and pepper. In another shallow bowl, then whisk the egg. In a third bowl, then throw cornflakes with cayenne and cheese. Sprinkle fish with salt; dip into flour mixture to coat both sides; shake off excess. Dip in egg mixture, then in the cornflake mixture, patting to assist coating in adhering.

4. Eliminate chips out of the basket; keep heat. Place fish in one layer in a fryer basket. Cook until fish is lightly browned and just starting to flake easily with a fork, turning halfway through cooking, 8 to 10 minutes. Don't overcook. Return chips to basket to warm through. Drink immediately. If desired, serve with tartar sauce.

Nutrition: Calories: 284. **Total Fat:** 7.9 g. **Saturated Fat:** 1.4 g. **Cholesterol:** 36 mg. **Sodium:** 704 mg. **Total Carbs:** 46 g. **Fiber:** 3.6 g. **Sugar:** 5.5 g. **Protein:** 17.9 g.

471. One Basket Fish & Chips

Preparation Time: 10 minutes
Cooking Time: 60 minutes
Servings: 4
Ingredients:

- 200 g white fish filet (tilapia, cod, pollack)
- 30 g tortilla chips
- 1 egg
- 300 g (red) potatoes
- 1 tbsp vegetable oil
- 1 tbsp. lemon juice
- Salt and pepper

Directions:
1. Preheat your oven to 350° F.
2. Cut the fish into four equal portions; this process ensures that they cook. Rub the lemon juice, salt, and pepper. Allow the fish to break for 5 minutes.
3. Using a food processor, blitz that the tortilla chips into very fine pieces. From the food processor and move the floor, tortilla chips into a plate.
4. Whisk the egg in a bowl.
5. Now dip each fish slice into the egg by one and roll the pieces of fish throughout the flour tortilla chips, so they are thoroughly covered.
6. Sterile, then cut the potatoes into thin strips.
7. Scrub the potato pieces in water for 30 minutes.
8. Drain them and pat dry, then coat them with acrylic.
9. Add a separator from the fryer basket. Put the potato strips on both sides along with the bits of fish on the opposite
10. Set the timer to 12 minutes and then stir fry until golden brown

Nutrition: Calories: 284. **Total Fat:** 7.9 g. **Saturated Fat:** 1.4 g. **Cholesterol:** 36 mg. **Sodium:** 704 mg. **Total Carbs:** 46 g. **Fiber:** 3.6 g. **Sugar:** 5.5 g. **Protein:** 17.9 g.

472. Air Fryer Lobster Tail

Preparation Time: 10 minutes
Cooking Time: 60 minutes
Servings: 4
Ingredients:

- 4 lobster tails
- 2 tbsp. melted butter
- ½ tsp. salt

- 1 tsp. pepper

Directions:
1. Preheat your oven to 380° F.
2. Cut the freshwater lobster through the tail segment. The casing can be extremely sharp. Split and pull the casing.
3. Brush your lobster tails together with melted butter, pepper, and salt.
4. Lay the buttery lobster tails at the fryer basket and fry for 380° F for 4 minutes. Insert the remaining melted butter, and fry for 2 minutes.

Nutrition: Calories: 284. **Total Fat:** 7.9 g. **Saturated Fat:** 1.4 g. **Cholesterol:** 36 mg. **Sodium:** 704 mg. **Total Carbs:** 46 g. **Fiber:** 3.6 g. **Sugar:** 5.5 g. **Protein:** 17.9 g.

473. Lemon Pepper Dill Fish

Preparation Time: 5 minutes
Cooking Time: 60 minutes
Servings: 4
Ingredients:

- 1 lb. haddock fillets
- ½ cup butter
- Dried dill weed to taste
- lemon pepper to taste
- 3 tbsp. fresh lemon juice

Directions:
1. Place fish fillets in a microwave-safe dish. Cut butter into pieces and place all over fish. Sprinkle with dill weed and lemon pepper. Drizzle fresh lemon juice all over the fish.
2. Cover and cook on high for 3 to 5 minutes or until the fish turns white.

Nutrition: Calories: 305. **Total Fat:** 23.8 g. **Cholesterol:** 125 mg. **Sodium:** 233 mg. **Total Carbs:** 1 g. **Protein:** 21.7 g.

Seafood

474. Cheesy Crabmeat Dip

Preparation Time: 10 minutes
Cooking Time: 60 minutes
Servings: 8
Ingredients:

- 1 cup shredded white cheddar cheese
- 1 cup meatless spaghetti sauce
- 1 package of softened cream cheese (8 oz.)
- 1 can of drained and flaked crabmeat (6 oz.)
- 2 tbsp. Worcestershire sauce
- ½ tsp. salt
- 2 tbsp. Old Bay® Seasoning
- 1 tsp. ground black pepper

Directions:
1. Preheat the convection oven at 325° F.
2. In the bottom layer of the baking dish spread the spaghetti sauce evenly.
3. Mix the cream cheese, crabmeat, and cheddar cheese. Season with Worcestershire sauce, old bay, salt, and pepper. Spread over the spaghetti sauce layer evenly.
4. Bake for around 40 minutes in a preheated convection oven. Serve straight away with crackers or baguettes.

Nutrition: Calories: 210. **Fat:** 15.7 g. **Protein:** 10.7 g. **Carbs:** 6.7 g.

475. Simple Crab Tart With Avocado

Preparation Time: 20 minutes
Cooking Time: 60 minutes
Servings: 8
Ingredients:

- 375 g pack of ready-rolled puff pastry
- 24 peeled raw king prawns
- 400 g of fresh white crabmeat
- 3 sliced small ripe avocados
- 2 tbsp. crème Fraiche
- Unsalted butter knob
- 1 tbsp. mayonnaise heaped
- ½ lime juice
- Pinch of cayenne pepper
- A handful of chopped fresh dill

Directions:
1. Preheat the convection oven at 375° F. Unroll and spread the pastry on a non-stick baking sheet, flatten using your hands, and prick holes all over the pastry with a fork. Bake for around 15 to 18 minutes in a preheated oven.
2. Once done, remove from the convection oven, let it cool down for 10 minutes and cut into 8 equal squares. Keep them aside.

3. Mix together mayonnaise and crab meat, crème Fraiche, lime juice, cayenne pepper, and chopped dill. Set them aside.
4. In a frying pan, heat butter over medium-high heat and cook prawns until pink in color and slightly golden, cooked well and, set them aside.
5. Divide the sliced avocados evenly between the 8 pastry squares, then top up with a spoon full of the crab mixture and 3 prawns. Sprinkle with dill and serve.

Nutrition: Calories: 372. **Fat:** 25.5 g. **Protein:** 18.6 g. **Carbs:** 18.3 g.

476. Shrimp and Crabmeat Enchiladas

Preparation Time: 20 minutes
Cooking Time: 60 minutes
Servings: 6
Ingredients:

- ¼ lb. peeled and chopped shrimp
- 1 cup half-and-half cream
- ½ lb. fresh crabmeat
- 1 chopped onion
- 6 flour tortillas (10 inches)
- ½ cup sour cream
- 8 oz. Colby cheese
- ¼ cup melted butter
- 1 tbsp. butter
- ½ tsp. garlic salt
- 1 ½ tsp. dried parsley

Directions:
1. Preheat the convection oven at 325° F.
2. Cook onion in one tbsp. of butter in a large-sized skillet until it softens. Remove the skillet from the stove and add in crabmeat and shrimp. Mix half of the shredded cheese into the seafood. Spoon a mixture into each tortilla and roll the tortillas up to cover the mixture. Transfer the rolled tortillas to a 9x13 inch baking pan.
3. On medium heat, in a saucepan, combine sour cream, half and half cream, parsley, ¼ cup of butter, and garlic salt, mix. Pour prepared sauce on enchiladas and top up with remaining cheese.
4. Bake for around 30 minutes in a preheated oven and serve.

Nutrition: Calories: 607. **Fat:** 36.5 g. **Protein:** 26.8 g. **Carbs:** 42.6 g.

477. Delicious Seafood Gratin

Preparation Time: 15 minutes
Cooking Time: 60 minutes
Servings: 8
Ingredients:

- 1 lb. rinsed and drained bay or sea scallops
- 2 cups shredded provolone cheese
- 1 lb. peeled fresh shrimp

- 1 lb. crab meat cooked
- ½ cup Parmesan cheese grated
- 1 can of drained button mushrooms (4 oz.)
- 2 cups hot chicken broth
- ½ cup white wine
- 3 tbsp. shallots chopped
- 2 tbsp. fresh parsley chopped
- 3 tbsp. butter
- 2 tbsp. olive oil
- 2 tbsp. all-purpose flour

Directions:
1. Preheat the convection oven at 375° F. Greased 8 smalls baking dishes with butter.
2. On medium-high heat, in a large-sized skillet, heat olive oil and cook scallops and shrimp until they are firmed, for 5 minutes.
3. Melt butter in a medium-sized saucepan over medium heat. Mix in flour and slowly add chicken broth and turn the heat to high keep stirring until thickened. Add in mushrooms, shallots, and wine; keep cooking for 5 to 10 minutes.
4. Spread scallops, crab, and shrimp in the bottom of greased dishes. Pour the sauce over seafood and top up with cheese.
5. Bake in a preheated convection oven for about 12 to 15 minutes.
6. Upon serving, sprinkle with parsley.
Nutrition: Calories: 397. **Fat:** 19.8 g. **Protein:** 44.4 g. **Carbs:** 4.2 g.

478. Crab Filled Crescent Cups
Preparation Time: 15 minutes
Cooking Time: 60 minutes
Servings: 18 crescent cups
Ingredients:
- 4 oz. softened cream cheese
- ½ cup mozzarella and ⅓ cup(divided)
- 1 can of Pillsbury Crescent rolls
- ¼ cup mayonnaise
- 1 can of crabmeat (6 oz.)
- 1 ½ tsp. lemon juice
- 1 finely sliced green onion
- ½ tsp. Worcestershire sauce
- 1 clove of minced garlic

Directions:
1. Preheat the convection oven at 350° F.
2. Combine mayonnaise, cream cheese, Worcestershire sauce, lemon juice, garlic, ½ cup of mozzarella, and green onion. Fold in the crab meat and set them aside.
3. Unfold crescent rolls, spread, and cut into 18 even squares.

4. Arrange crescent squares in a muffin pan and press the rolls into the cups. Distribute filling between cups. Sprinkle with the remaining ⅓ cup of cheese.
5. Bake for 12 to 14 minutes in a convection oven and cool for some time before serving.
Nutrition: Calories: 568. **Fat:** 34.7 g. **Protein:** 59.1 g. **Sugar:** 1 g.

479. Tasty Seafood Stuffed Peppers
Preparation Time: 15 minutes
Cooking Time: 60 minutes
Servings: 8
Ingredients:
- 4 Cubanelle peppers (hollowed out and cut in half)
- 1 tilapia fillet (bite-size pieces)
- 8 oz. cheddar cheese shredded
- 8 oz. Monterey Jack cheese shredded
- 4 oz. small bay scallops
- 1 lb. peeled and diced medium shrimp (uncooked)
- 2 cups white rice cooked
- 1 cup tomato cocktail
- 1 small diced onion
- 1 tbsp. lemon juice
- 3 tbsp. olive oil
- 1 tbsp. seafood seasoning
- 10 chopped basil leaves
- 3 cloves of minced garlic

Directions:
1. Preheat the convection oven at 325° F. On medium-high heat in a pan, heat oil, add garlic and onion, and cook for 3 minutes. Add in tilapia, bay scallops, and shrimp, cook for 4 to 5 minutes until they are halfway done. Mix in tomato cocktail, seafood seasoning, lemon juice, rice, and basil, and cook for 5 minutes more.
2. Remove from stove; mix in Monterey jack cheese. Spoon prepared mixture into peppers and place in a non-stick baking sheet, cover with heavy-duty foil and bake for around 20 minutes in a preheated convection oven. After 20 minutes, remove foil and sprinkle the top of peppers with cheddar. Bake for additional 5 minutes or until cheese melts down.
Nutrition: Calories: 411. **Fat:** 24.1 g. **Protein:** 31.4 g. **Carbs:** 16.3 g.

Breads

480. Family Banana Nut Bread

Preparation Time: 15 minutes
Cooking Time: 1 hour
Servings: 10
Ingredients:

- 8 oz. cream cheese, softened
- 1 cup white sugar
- ½ cup butter
- 2 eggs, beaten
- 2 ripe bananas, mashed
- 2-¼ cups all-purpose flour
- 2 tbsp. baking soda
- 1-½ tbsp. baking powder
- 1 cup walnuts, chopped

Directions:
1.   Beat cream cheese, sugar, butter, eggs, and mashed banana in a mixing bowl until well mixed and smooth.
2.   Stir with flour, baking soda, baking powder, and walnuts until well combined. Pour the batter on a greased loaf pan.
3.   Slide the pizza rack on shelf position 5 and place the loaf pan on top.
4.   Select the bake setting on the oven and set the temperature at 350° F for 75 minutes. Press starts
5.   Let the bread cool for 10 minutes before serving.
Nutrition: Calories: 449. **Carbs:** 49.3 g. **Fat:** 26 g. **Protein:** 8 g.

481. Peaches and Cream Bread

Preparation Time: 10 minutes
Cooking Time: 60 minutes
Servings: 8
Ingredients:

- ¾ cup canned peaches, drained and chopped
- ⅓ cup heavy whipping cream, at 80° F to 90° F
- 1 egg, at room temperature
- 1 tbsp. melted butter cooled
- 2 ¼ tbsp. sugar
- 1 ⅛ tsp. salt
- ⅓ tsp. ground cinnamon
- ⅛ tsp. ground nutmeg
- ⅓ cup whole-wheat flour
- 2 ⅔ cups white bread flour
- 1 ⅙ tsp. bread machine or instant yeast

Directions:
1.   Place the ingredients in your Hamilton Beach bread machine.
2.   Select the Bake cycle. Program the machine for Whitbread, select light or medium crust, and press Start.

3.   When the loaf is done, eliminate the bucket from the machine.
4.   Let the loaf cool for 5 minutes.
5.   Shake the bucket to eliminate the loaf, and place it out onto a rack to cool.
Nutrition: Calories: 277. **Cholesterol:** 9 g. **Carbs:** 48.4 g. **Dietary Fiber:** 1.9 g. **Sugars:** 3.3 g. **Protein:** 9.4 g.

482. Healthy Spelt Bread

Preparation Time: 15 minutes
Cooking Time: 60 minutes
Servings: 10 slices
Ingredients:

- 1 ¼ cups milk
- 2 tbsp. sugar
- 2 tbsp. olive oil
- 1 tsp. salt
- 4 cups spelt flour
- 2 ½ tsp. yeast

Directions:
1.   Add all ingredients according to the bread machine manufacturer instructions into the bread machine.
2.   Select basic bread setting then select light/medium crust and start. Once the loaf is done, remove the loaf pan from the machine.
3.   Allow it to cool for 10 minutes. Slice and serve.
Nutrition: Calories: 223. **Carbs:** 40.3 g. **Fat:** 4.5 g. **Protein:** 9.2 g.

483. Chia Seed Bread

Preparation Time: 10 minutes
Cooking Time: 60 minutes
Servings: 16 slices
Ingredients:

- ½ tsp. xanthan gum
- ½ cup butter
- 2 tbsp. coconut oil
- 1 tbsp. baking powder
- 3 tbsp. sesame seeds
- 2 tbsp. chia seeds
- ½ tsp. salt
- ¼ cup sunflower seeds
- 2 cups almond flour
- 7 eggs

Directions:
1.   Preheat the oven to 350° F.
2.   Beat eggs in a bowl on high for 1 to 2 minutes.
3.   Beat in the xanthan gum and combine coconut oil and melted butter into eggs, beating continuously.
4.   Set aside the sesame seeds, but add the rest of the ingredients.
5.   Line a loaf pan with baking paper and place the mixture in it. Top the mixture with sesame seeds.

6. Bake in the oven until a toothpick inserted comes out clean, about 35 to 40 minutes.
Nutrition: Calories: 405. **Fat:** 37 g. **Carbs:** 4 g. **Protein:** 14 g.

484. Iranian Flatbread
Preparation Time: 3 hours 15 minutes
Cooking Time: 60 minutes
Servings: 6
Ingredients:
- 4 cups almond flour
- 2 ½ cups warm water
- 1 tbsp. instant yeast
- 12 tsp. sesame seeds
- Salt to taste

Directions:
1. In a bowl, add 1 tbsp. yeast to ½ cup warm water. Let stand for 5 minutes to activate.
2. Add salt and 1 cup water. Let stand for 10 minutes more.
3. Add flour 1 cup at a time, and then add the remaining water.
4. Knead the dough and then shape into a ball and let stand for 3 hours covered.
5. Preheat the oven to 480° F.
6. With a rolling pin, roll out the dough and divide it into 6 balls. Roll each ball into ½ inch thick rounds.
7. Line a baking sheet with parchment paper and place the rolled rounds on it. With a finger, make a small hole in the middle and add 2 tsp. sesame seeds in each hole.
8. Bake for 3 to 4 minutes and then flip over and bake for 2 minutes more.
Nutrition: Calories: 26. **Fat:** 1 g. **Carbs:** 3.5 g. **Protein:** 1 g.

485. Bread De Soul
Preparation Time: 10 minutes
Cooking Time: 60 minutes
Servings: 16
Ingredients:
- ¼ tsp. cream of tartar
- 2 ½ tsp. baking powder
- 1 tsp. xanthan gum
- ⅓ tsp. baking soda
- ½ tsp. salt
- 1 ⅔ cup unflavored whey protein
- ¼ cup olive oil
- ¼ cup heavy whipping cream or half and half
- 2 drops of sweet leaf stevia
- 4 eggs
- ¼ cup butter
- 12 oz. softened cream cheese

Directions:

1. Preheat the oven to 325° F.
2. In a bowl, microwave cream cheese and butter for 1 minute.
3. Remove and blend well with a hand mixer.
4. Add olive oil, eggs, heavy cream, and a few drops of sweetener and blend well.
5. Blend together the dry ingredients in a separate bowl.
6. Combine the dry ingredients with the wet ingredients and mix with a spoon. Don't use a hand blender to avoid whipping it too much.
7. Grease a bread pan and pour the mixture into the pan.
8. Bake in the oven until golden brown, about 45 minutes.
9. Cool and serve.
Nutrition: Calories: 200. **Fat:** 15.2 g. **Carbs:** 1.8 g. **Protein:** 10 g.

486. Coconut Flour Almond Bread
Preparation Time: 10 minutes
Cooking Time: 60 minutes
Servings: 4
Ingredients:
- 1 tbsp. butter, melted
- 1 tbsp. coconut oil, melted
- 6 eggs
- 1 tsp. baking soda
- 2 tbsp. ground flaxseed
- 1 ½ tbsp. psyllium husk powder
- 5 tbsp. coconut flour
- 1 ½ cup almond flour

Directions:
1. Preheat the oven to 400° F.
2. Mix the eggs in a bowl for a few minutes.
3. Add in the butter and coconut oil and mix once more for 1 minute.
4. Add the almond flour, coconut flour, baking soda, psyllium husk, and ground flaxseed to the mixture. Let sit for 15 minutes.
5. Lightly grease the loaf pan with coconut oil. Pour the mixture into the pan.
6. Place in the oven and bake until a toothpick inserted in it comes out dry, about 25 minutes.
Nutrition: Calories: 475. **Fat:** 38 g. **Carbs:** 7 g. **Protein:** 19 g.

487. Keto Cloud Bread Cheese
Preparation Time: 5 minutes
Cooking Time: 60 minutes
Servings: 12
Ingredients:
Cream cheese filling:
- 1 egg yolk
- ½ tsp. vanilla stevia drops for filling

- 8 oz. softened cream cheese
- Base egg dough
- ½ tsp. cream of tartar
- 1 tbsp. coconut flour
- ¼ cup unflavored whey protein
- 3 oz. softened cream cheese
- ¼ tsp. vanilla stevia drops for dough
- 4 eggs, separated

Directions:
1. Preheat the oven to 325° F.
2. Line two baking sheets with parchment paper.
3. In a bowl, stir the 8 oz. cream cheese, stevia, and egg yolk.
4. Transfer to the pastry bag.
5. In another bowl, separate egg yolks from whites.
6. Add 3 oz. cream cheese, yolks, stevia, whey protein, and coconut flour. Mix until smooth.
1. Whip cream of tartar with the egg whites until stiff peaks form.
2. Fold in the yolk/cream cheese mixture into the beaten whites.
3. Spoon batter onto each baking sheet, 6 mounds on each. Press each mound to flatten a bit.
4. Add cream cheese filling in the middle of each batter.
5. Bake for 30 minutes at 325° F.

Nutrition: Calories: 120. **Fat:** 10.7 g. **Carbs:** 1.1 g. **Protein:** 5.4 g.

488. Blueberry Bread Loaf

Preparation Time: 20 minutes
Cooking Time: 60 minutes
Servings: 12
Ingredients:
Bread dough:
- 10 tbsp. coconut flour
- 9 tbsp. melted butter
- ⅔ cup granulates swerve sweetener
- 1 ½ tsp. baking powder
- 2 tbsp. heavy whipping cream
- 1 ½ tsp. vanilla extract
- ½ tsp. cinnamon
- 2 tbsp. sour cream
- 6 large eggs
- ½ tsp. salt
- ¾ cup blueberries

Topping:
- 1 tbsp. heavy whipping cream
- 2 tbsp. confectioner swerve sweetener
- 1 tsp. melted butter
- ⅛ tsp. vanilla extract
- ¼ tsp. lemon zest

Directions:

1. Preheat the oven to 350° F and line a loaf pan with baking paper.
2. In a bowl, mix granulated swerve, heavy whipping cream, eggs, and baking powder.
3. Once combined, add the butter, vanilla extract, salt, cinnamon, and sour cream. Then add the coconut flour to the batter.
4. Pour a layer of about ½ inch of dough into the bread pan. Place ¼ cup of blueberries on top of the dough. Keep repeating until the dough and blueberry layers are complete.
5. Bake for 65 to 75 minutes.
6. Meanwhile, in a bowl, beat the vanilla extract, butter, heavy whipping cream, lemon zest, and confectioner swerve. Mix until creamy.
7. Cool the bread once baked. Then drizzle the icing topping on the bread.
8. Slice and serve.

Nutrition: Calories: 155. **Fat:** 13 g. **Carbs:** 4 g. **Protein:** 3 g.

489. Cauliflower Bread Loaf

Preparation Time: 1 hour 10 minutes
Cooking Time: 60 minutes
Servings: 10
Ingredients:
Bread dough:
- 1 ¼ cups almond flour
- 3 cups rice cauliflower
- 1 tbsp. baking powder
- 6 tbsp. olive oil
- 6 large eggs, separated
- 1 tsp salt

Optional flavorings:
- Dried or fresh herbs
- Shredded parmesan or cheddar cheese
- Garlic powder or minced garlic

Directions:
1. Preheat the oven to 350° F. Line a bread loaf with baking paper.
2. Place cauliflower into the small pot to steam until it becomes tender. Place it to the side.
3. Cream the whites of the eggs in a food processor for 4 minutes. Set to the side.
4. In a bowl, whisk the egg yolks, and almond flour until mixed well. Next, add the baking powder, oil, and salt and mix until smooth.
5. Remove excess fluid from the cooled cauliflower with a paper towel.
6. Stir in the dried cauliflower and mix well. Add the flavoring ingredients.
7. In small amounts, fold the egg white mixture into the mixture until fluffy. Don't overbeat.
8. Transfer the dough into the bread loaf pan.

9. Bake in the oven for 45 minutes. Test with a knife.

10. Cool, slice, and serve.

Nutrition: Calories: 155. **Fat:** 13 g. **Carbs:** 4 g. **Protein:** 3 g.

490. Quick Low-Carb Bread Loaf

Preparation Time: 45 minutes
Cooking Time: 60 minutes
Servings: 16
Ingredients:

- $^2/_3$ cup coconut flour
- ½ cup butter, melted
- 3 tbsp. coconut oil, melted
- 1 $^1/_3$ cup almond flour
- ½ tsp. xanthan gum
- 1 tsp. baking powder
- 6 large eggs
- ½ tsp. salt

Directions:

1. Preheat the oven to 350° F. Cover the bread loaf pan with baking paper.

2. Beat the eggs until creamy.

3. Add in the coconut flour and almond flour, mixing them for 1 minute. Next, add the xanthan gum, coconut oil, baking powder, butter, and salt and mix them until the dough turns thick.

4. Put the completed dough into the prepared line of the bread loaf pan.

5. Place in oven and bake for 40 to 45 minutes. Check with a knife.

6. Slice and serve.

Nutrition: Calories: 174. **Fat:** 15 g. **Carbs:** 5 g. **Protein:** 5 g.

Pizza

491. Ortolana Pizza

Preparation Time: 30 minutes
Cooking Time: 60 minutes
Servings: 4
Ingredients:

- 1 yellow pepper
- Pepper to taste
- 1 tbsp. dried oregano
- 200 g mozzarella
- 50 g black olives
- 1 aubergine
- 3 tbsp. extra virgin olive oil
- 2 courgettes
- Salt to taste
- 400 g bread dough
- 30 g caper in salt
- 200 g tomato puree

Directions:

1.   Start by cleaning the courgettes and aubergine. Peel and cut them into slices about half a centimeter thick lengthwise and allow them to grill under a grill in the oven or a cast iron.

2.   Peel the peppers and put them in the prongs of a fork one at a time. Cut them into strips after peeling them and toast them on the flame.

3.   In boiling water, blanch the tomato, allow it to dry, then peel it and cut it into strips. Cut into strips the grilled aubergine. Use oil to grease a round pizza pan.

4.   On the bottom, spread the bread dough and use your fingers to flatten it, and with the fork prongs, prick it here and there.

5.   In a bowl, put all vegetables with a pinch of salt, tsp. of oil, ½ tsp. oregano and a pinch of pepper and allow them to steep for 10 minutes.

6.   Spread the vegetables over pasta and sprinkle them with basil strips and diced mozzarella. Use the remaining oil to sprinkle.

Nutrition: Calories: 463. **Protein:** 26.5 g. **Fat:** 11.61 g. **Carbs:** 65.62 g.

492. Napoletana Pizza

Preparation Time: 30 minutes
Cooking Time: 60 minutes
Servings: 4
Ingredients:

- 600 g water
- 7 g dry brewer's yeast
- 60 g extra virgin olive oil
- 20 g salt
- 1 kg 0 flour
- 20 g salt

To season:

- 24 caper fruits
- 16 fillets anchovies in oil
- Extra virgin olive oil
- 700 g tomato sauce
- 10 g oregano
- Black pepper to taste
- 20 g salt

Directions:

1.   To make the Napoletana pizza, begin by pouring the flour into a mixer bowl. Add 100 mL of water and yeast and then use a hook mounted at medium-low speed to operate the planetary mixer.

2.   Continue by adding a little water at a time and make sure you wait till the previous dose is well absorbed by the flour. When you have added at least ¾ of water, keep kneading after adding salt. Always keep adding the rest of the water flush and allow it to work until you get a homogeneous and smooth mixture.

3.   Gradually add the oil at this point and remove the dough from the planetary mixer once the oil has absorbed completely and use your hands to shape it until you form a ball. Put it in a bowl that is lightly greased.

4.   Use a clean cloth or a cling film to cover and allow it to rise in the oven while lights are on. Hold on until the dough has doubled in its size but better if tripled and continue with the pizza preparation.

5.   Transfer the dough to the pastry board once it rises and divide it into 4 equal parts. Do this for each of the balls. Let it stand for 30 minutes after covering it with a clean tea towel.

6.   Use a drizzle of oil to lightly grease four 30 cm diameter pizza pans and put the dough ball in the center of the pan. Begin squeezing from the center outwards if necessary, pulling the sides slightly. If the dough tends to return to its original shape or it's too elastic, put aside the pizza that you spread and begin rolling another one, leaving the previous one to rest. Try spreading the dough over the whole surface of the tray.

7.   In a large bowl, pour in the tomato sauce and season with oil, pepper, salt, and oregano. On the pizza base, pour a generous ladle of tomato sauce and spread it in a circular motion leaving only a boarder of 1.5 cm but covering almost the entire area. Set the caper fruits aside after cutting them in half.

8.   You can now do the seasoning with caper fruits cut into half, a drizzle of oil, and anchovies. Allow the pizza that has been stuffed to rest for 10 minutes and use a static oven to bake for 20 minutes at 210° F.

9.   Serve the Napoletana pizza as soon as you remove it from the oven.

Nutrition: Calories: 163. **Protein:** 31.41 g. **Fat:** 9.24 g. **Carbs:** 228.92 g.

493. Tuna and Onions Pizza

Preparation Time: 1 hr. 30 minutes

Cooking Time: 20 minutes
Servings: 4
Ingredients:
- 1 batch of pizza dough
- 400 ml – 13.5 oz. tomato puree
- 2 tbsp extra virgin olive oil
- 1 tbsp oregano
- Salt to taste
- 350 grams – 12.5 oz. bocconcini or fresh mozzarella (half sliced and half shredded)
- 2 x185 grams – 6.5 oz. cans of tuna under oil, drained and crumbled
- 1 onion thinly sliced
- 1 tbsp. Extra virgin olive oil
- 1 tsp. Basil

Directions:
1. Make the pizza dough as per this recipe and keep it to rise.
2. While the dough rests, prepare the toppings: slice and shred the mozzarella.
3. Prepare the tomato base by mixing the tomato purée with the extra virgin olive oil, oregano and salt to taste.
4. When the pizza dough is ready, divide it in 4 smaller balls and roll them with a rolling pin into 4 circles approximately 0.5 cm – ¼ inch thick.
5. Now spread the tomato base on the pizza and bake in a preheated fan forced oven at 180°C – 355°F for 15 minutes.
6. Take them out of the oven and put the mozzarella, tuna and sliced onion on the top. Put back in the oven for 5 minutes to let the cheese melt.
7. When ready, take the pizza out of the oven and drizzle with some extra virgin olive oil.
8. Decorate with fresh basil leaves, cut and enjoy warm!

Nutrition: Calories: 188. **Protein:** 64.45 g. **Fat:** 18.32 g. **Carbs:** 187.02 g.

494. Marinara Pizza

Preparation Time: 30 minutes
Cooking Time: 60 minutes
Servings: 4
Ingredients:
- 7 g dry brewer's yeast
- 600 g water
- 1 kg 00 flour
- 60 g extra virgin olive oil
- 20 g salt

Dressing:
- 4 garlic cloves
- 700 g tomato sauce
- 20 g dry oregano

- Black pepper to taste
- Salt to taste

Directions:
1. To make the marinara pizza, begin by pouring the flour into a mixer bowl. Add 100 mL of water and yeast and then use a hook mounted at medium-low speed to operate the planetary mixer.
2. Continue by adding a little water at a time and make sure you wait till the previous dose is well absorbed by the flour. When you have added at least ¾ of water, keep kneading after adding salt. Always keep adding the rest of the water flush and allow it to work until you get a homogeneous and smooth mixture.
3. Gradually add the oil at this point and remove the dough from the planetary mixer once the oil has absorbed completely and use your hands to shape it until you form a ball. Put it in a bowl that is lightly greased.
4. Use a clean cloth or a cling film to cover and allow it to rise in the oven while lights are on. Hold on until the dough has doubled in its size but better if tripled and continue with the pizza preparation.
5. Transfer the dough to the pastry board once it rises and divide it into 4 equal parts. Do this for each of the balls. Let it stand for 30 minutes after covering it with a clean tea towel.
6. Use a drizzle of oil to lightly grease four 30 cm diameter pizza pans and put the dough ball in the center of the pan. Begin squeezing from the center outwards if necessary, pulling the sides slightly. If the dough tends to return to its original shape or it's too elastic, put aside the pizza that you spread and begin rolling another one, leaving the previous one to rest. Try spreading the dough over the surface of the tray.
7. In a large bowl, pour in the tomato sauce and season with oil, pepper, salt, and oregano. On the pizza base, pour a generous ladle of tomato sauce and spread it in a circular motion leaving only a boarder of 1.5 cm but covering almost the entire area.
8. Cut the garlic into half after peeling it and remove the core then cut into thin slices. Season with a drizzle of oil, garlic, and oregano.
9. All the pizza has been stuffed to rest for 10 minutes and then bake in a static oven at 210° F or in a fan oven for 15 minutes.
10. You can now remove the marinara pizza from the oven and serve it hot.

Nutrition: Calories: 174. **Protein:** 31.83 g. **Fat:** 9.36 g. **Carbs:** 231.63 g.

Cake

495. Moist and Tasty Basic Chocolate Cake

Preparation Time: 10 minutes
Cooking Time: 60 minutes
Servings: 12
Ingredients:

- 1 ¾ cups flour
- 1 cup hot boiling water
- 2 cups sugar
- ¾ cup cocoa powder
- 1 cup milk
- 2 eggs
- ½ cup vegetable oil
- 2 tsp. baking soda
- 1 tsp. vanilla extract
- 1 ½ tsp. baking powder
- ½ tsp. salt

Directions:
1. Preheat the convection oven at 325° F.
2. Combine flour, cocoa, baking powder, salt, sugar, and baking soda in a large-sized bowl.
3. Mix in eggs, oil, vanilla, and milk to dry ingredients mixture and mix with an electric beater on medium speed for 2 minutes. Gently add in hot boiling water mix until fully incorporated.
4. Spread batter into 3x8 inches greased and floured round cake pan and bake in the preheated convection oven for 25 to 35 minutes. Cool for some time before slicing. Serve with your favorite frosting and drizzle with a topping of your choice.
Nutrition: Calories: 248. **Fat:** 10 g. **Protein:** 2 g. **Carbs:** 39 g.

496. Easy and Delicious Gingerbread Cake

Preparation Time: 15 minutes
Cooking Time: 60 minutes
Servings: 16 slices
Ingredients:

- 2 cups all-purpose flour
- 1 cup sugar
- 1 cup hot boiling water
- 1 cup vegetable oil
- 1 cup molasses
- 2 tbsp. warm water
- 3 eggs
- 2 tsp. baking soda
- 1 ½ tsp. cinnamon
- 1 ½ tsp. ginger
- 1 tsp. cloves

Directions:

1. Preheat the convection oven at 325° F.
2. Add sugar, molasses, spices, eggs, and oil and mix with a hand mixer until fully combined. Mix in flour gradually.
3. Combine together 2 tbsp. of water and baking soda. Mix into the batter and whisk well. Add hot boiling water and mix until fully incorporated.
4. Shift the batter into a 9x13 inches grease cake pan line with baking paper and spread evenly.
5. Bake for around 35 to 45 minutes in the preheated convection oven. Allow to cool completely and pipe whipped cream over the cake while serving.
Nutrition: Calories: 177. **Fat:** 3 g. **Protein:** 3 g. **Carbs:** 35 g.

497. Classic Banana Chocolate Cake

Preparation Time: 15 minutes
Cooking Time: 60 minutes
Servings: 8
Ingredients:

- 1 ½ cups flour
- ½ cup chocolate chips mini
- 4 mashed bananas
- ½ cup cocoa powder
- ½ cup butter at room temperature
- ¼ cup brown sugar
- 2 eggs
- 1 tsp. baking soda
- ½ cup white sugar
- ½ tsp. baking powder

Directions:
1. Preheat the convection oven at 325° F.
2. Whisk together sugars and butter until creamy. Mix in the eggs and mashed bananas.
3. In a large-sized bowl, combine cocoa powder, flour, baking powder, and baking soda.
4. Mix in the chocolate chips and flour mixture to the banana mixture and whisk until completely combined.
5. Spread the batter into 9 inches greased and floured round cake pan.
6. Bake for around 25 to 30 minutes in the preheated convection oven
Nutrition: Calories: 391. **Fat:** 16 g. **Protein:** 6 g. **Carbs:** 60 g.

498. Lemon and Ricotta Cheese Dessert Cake

Preparation Time: 10 minutes
Cooking Time: 60 minutes
Servings: 8
Ingredients:

- 1 cup ricotta cheese
- 1 cupcake flour

- ¼ cup milk
- ½ cup softened butter
- 3 eggs
- ¾ cup white sugar
- Zest and juice of 1 large lemon
- 2 tsp. baking powder
- 1 tsp. vanilla extract

Directions:

1. Preheat the convection oven at 300° F.
2. Combine flour and baking powder together in a small-sized bowl.
3. In a large-sized bowl, beat softened butter and sugar together using an electric beater. Mix in vanilla and eggs one at a time beat until completely combined. Put the lemon zest, ricotta cheese, and lemon juice into the mixture and beat for 2 to 3 minutes on medium speed. Pour in milk and beat the mixture on low speed just to combine everything.
4. Spread batter into round 8 inches greased and lined springform pan.
5. Bake in the preheated convection oven for around 45 to 50 minutes; keep checking when a cake is baking, so it doesn't get burnt.

Nutrition: Calories: 314. **Fat:** 16 g. **Protein:** 7.6 g. **Carbs:** 36.6 g.

499. Tasty and Moist Red Velvet Cheesecake

Preparation Time: 15 minutes

Cooking Time: 60 minutes

Servings: 12

Ingredients:

Red velvet:

- ½ cup vegetable oil
- 1 box of red velvet cake mix
- ⅓ cup milk
- 1 egg

Cheesecake (no-bake):

- 1 ½ cups heavy cream
- 12 oz. cream cheese
- 1 tsp. vanilla
- 1 ½ cups powdered sugar

Topping/decorating:

- Whipped cream
- Raspberries

Directions:

1. Preheat the convection oven at 350° F. Take 10 inches springform pan and grease the bottom and sides of the pan with cooking spray.
2. Add egg, oil, dry cake mixes, and milk and mix using an electric beater on medium speed for 2 minutes.
3. Pour the batter into the greased pan and bake in the preheated convection oven for around 20 to 25 minutes or check by inserting a wooden skewer or knife in the center if it comes out dry cake is done.
4. Whisk together powdered sugar, cream cheese, and vanilla using an electric beater until smooth and fluffy. Mix in heavy cream and keep beating until the mixture is thick.
5. To loosen the cake, run a knife around the edges of the cake. Pour cheesecake mixture all over the cooled red velvet cake evenly. Cover with plastic wrap and keep in the refrigerator for at least 4 hours or overnight.
6. While serving, spread whipped cream on top of the cake and evenly layer out with cake knife place raspberries on top of the cream, slice and enjoy!

Nutrition: Calories: 499. **Fat:** 36 g. **Protein:** 5 g. **Carbs:** 44 g.

Cookies

500. Biscuit Mini-Batch

Preparation Time: 15 minutes
Cooking Time: 60 minutes
Servings: 8
Ingredients:

- 1 cup flour
- 1 tsp. baking powder
- 1 tbsp. butter, melted
- ½ cup milk

Directions:

1. Pre-heat toaster oven to 425° F.
2. Mix the flour and baking powder.
3. Work in melted butter.
4. Add milk and mix into a soft dough.
5. Drop 6 biscuits onto a small baking sheet that will fit into your toaster oven.
6. Bake for 8 to 12 minutes or until done.
7. Pay careful attention to the doneness because toaster ovens aren't as reliable in their temperature control as full-size ovens.

Nutrition: Calories: 187. **Total Fat:** 9.1 g. **Saturated Fat:** 5.6 g. **Cholesterol:** 24 mg. **Sodium:** 144 mg. **Total Carbs:** 22.6 g. **Fiber:** 0.8 g. **Sugar:** 1.7 g. **Protein:** 3.7 g.

501. Carrot Cake Cookies

Preparation Time: 30 minutes
Cooking Time: 60 minutes
Servings: 24
Ingredients:

- ¼ cup brown sugar
- ¼ cup vegetable oil
- ½ tsp. baking soda
- ¼ cup applesauce or fruit puree
- ¼ tsp. nutmeg
- 1 egg
- ½ tsp. vanilla
- ½ cup flour
- ½ cup wheat flour
- ½ tsp. baking powder
- A dash of salt
- ½ tsp. ground cinnamon
- ¼ tsp. ground ginger
- 1 cup old-fashioned rolled oats
- ¾ cup grated carrots
- ½ cup raisins or golden raisins

Directions:

1. In a large mixing bowl, combine sugar, oil, applesauce, egg, and vanilla.
2. In another bowl, mix all dry ingredients. Then, add dry ingredients to wet ingredients. Mix till blended. Toss in carrots and raisins.

3. Drop by teaspoonful onto a silicone baking ring or parchment-lined cookie sheet.
4. Place on 1-inch rack and cook at 300° F (Level 8) for 12 to 14 minutes or until golden brown.

Nutrition: Calories: 252. **Carbs:** 20 g. **Total Fat:** 7 g. **Protein:** 3 g.

502. Homemade Oreos

Preparation Time: 15 minutes
Cooking Time: 60 minutes
Servings: 9
Ingredients:

- 1 crescent sheet roll
- 9 Oreo cookies

Directions:

1. Place the sheet of crescent roll dough onto a flat surface and unroll it.
2. With a knife, cut the dough into 9 even squares.
3. Wrap each cookie in 1 dough square completely.
4. Arrange the Oreos onto a cooking tray.
5. Arrange the drip pan in the bottom of the oven cooking chamber.
6. Select Air Fry mode and then adjust the temperature to 360° F.
7. Set the timer for 4 minutes and press the "Start."
8. When the display shows Add Food, insert the cooking tray in the center position.
9. When the display shows Turn Food, turn the Oreos.
10. When cooking time is complete, remove the tray from the oven
11. Serve warm.

Nutrition: Calories: 137. **Total Fat:** 6.4 g. **Saturated Fat:** 2.2 g. **Cholesterol:** 0 mg. **Sodium:** 237 mg. **Total Carbs:** 17.1 g. **Fiber:** 0.3 g. **Sugar:** 6.8 g. **Protein:** 2.3 g.

503. Brown Cookies

Preparation Time: 1 hour
Cooking Time: 60 minutes
Servings: 3 dozen
Ingredients:

- 12 oz. semi-sweet chocolate chips
- ½ tsp. salt
- ¼ tsp. baking soda
- ⅓ cup unsweetened baking cocoa
- 1 ⅓ cups flour
- 3 eggs
- 1 tsp. vanilla
- 1 tbsp. water
- 1 ½ tsp. packed brown sugar

Directions:

1. Preheat your oven to a temperature of 375° F.
2. Mix the eggs, vanilla, water, salt, baking soda, cocoa, and flour, and beat it in the medium setting until they become thoroughly mixed.

3.   Add the chocolate chips while in a low setting. Put 3 tbsp. of dough on the ungreased baking sheets. Bake gently for 10 minutes. Never overcook.

Nutrition: Calories: 145. **Carbs:** 3.6 g. **Protein:** 2.1 g. **Fat:** 13.6 g.

504. Peanut Butter Chocolate Chip Oatmeal Cookies

Preparation Time: 1 hour
Cooking Time: 60 minutes
Servings: 8
Ingredients:

- ¾ cup crunchy peanut butter
- 1 cup butter, softened
- 1 cup white sugar
- 1 cup packed brown sugar
- 2 eggs
- 1 tsp. vanilla extract
- 2 cups all-purpose flour
- 1 tsp. baking soda
- 1 tsp. salt
- 2 cups old fashioned oats
- 6 oz. semi-sweet chocolate chips

Directions:

1.   In a microwave-safe bowl, heat the crunchy peanut butter on low heat until just melted. Set aside to cool slightly.
2.   In a medium bowl or stand mixer, cream together the butter, white sugar, and brown sugar. Beat in the eggs one at a time, then add in the vanilla and peanut butter.
3.   Combine flour, baking soda, and salt; stir into the creamed mixture. Mix in oats and chocolate chips. Cover, and chill dough for at least one hour, or freeze it to bake later.
4.   Preheat oven to 350° F/325° F for convection. Line cookie sheets with parchment paper. Roll 2 tbsp. of dough into balls, and place 2 inches apart on cookie sheets.
5.   Bake for 8 to 10 minutes in a preheated oven. Allow cookies to cool on a baking sheet for 5 minutes before transferring to a wire rack to cool completely.

Nutrition: Calories: 145. **Carbs:** 3.6 g. **Protein:** 2.1 g. **Fat:** 13.6 g.

505. Microwave Eggless Cookies

Preparation Time: 10 minutes
Cooking Time: 60 minutes
Servings: 2
Ingredients:

- 1 ½ cups flour
- ¼ cup milk
- 1 tsp. vinegar
- 1 cup butter
- ½ cup sugar, powdered
- 1 tsp. vanilla essence

Directions:

1.   Mix flour, milk, vinegar, butter, sugar, and vanilla together.
2.   Mix the flour to make a smooth dough.
3.   Make 24 small balls and flatten them with a fork.
4.   Place six at a time on a microwave baking tray or lightly greased greaseproof paper and cook at 100 percent for 1 ½ to 2 ¼ minutes, depending on the cookies' size.
5.   Give the tray a half-turn halfway through the cooking time.
6.   Allow cooling on a wire rack.
7.   Repeat with the remaining mixture.
8.   Switch on the grill also according to your oven's manual

Nutrition: Calories: 145. **Carbs:** 3.6 g. **Protein:** 2.1 g. **Fat:** 13.6 g.

506. Salted Chocolate Chip Cookies

Preparation Time: 10 minutes
Cooking Time: 60 minutes
Servings: 18 cookies
Ingredients:

- ½ cup unsalted butter, at room temperature
- 2 tbsp. granulated sugar
- 2 tbsp. turbinado sugar
- ¾ cup plus 2 tbsp. packed dark brown sugar
- 1 egg, at room temperature
- 1 tsp. vanilla extract (although I usually add an extra tsp.)
- 1¾ cups all-purpose flour
- ½ tsp. kosher salt
- ¾ tsp. baking soda
- 6 oz. bittersweet chocolate, cut into roughly ½ inch chunks
- Flaky salt, such as Maldon, for finishing

Directions:

1.   In a medium bowl, cream the butter and the sugars together with an electric mixer, set on medium speed, until light in color and texture. You will see the difference in the butter/sugar mixture after 3 to 5 minutes. Scrape down the sides of the bowl with a rubber spatula as needed. Add the egg and vanilla and mix well to combine.
2.   In a medium bowl, whisk the flour, baking soda, and salt to combine. Add to the mixing bowl in 3 to 4 additions. Mix until streaks still run through the dough, then add the chocolate and mix everything until it just comes together.
3.   At this point, if you'd like a more caramel taste, refrigerate the dough for 24 hours to let the flavors fully develop. It also improves the texture of these cookies.
4.   When you are ready to bake, start by lining your CSO tray with parchment. You will be able to fit about 5

cookies on it (2-1-2 in a row). Set your CSO baking rack in the middle of the oven. No need to preheat the CSO.

5.　　Use a ¼ cup ice cream scoop to scoop out my cookie dough, although you can use a tablespoon to measure the cookie dough. After scooping, flatten the cookies slightly, then sprinkle a little Maldon Flaky sea salt on top. Now you are ready to pop the cookies into the CSO. Turn your dial to Bake Steam, set the temperature at 325° F and the time for 9 minutes, then press start. If you need another minute or two at the end of baking time, you can add it, using the same temperature setting but changing the time to 1 or 2 minutes.

6.　　Let the cookies cool on the rack for 5 minutes, then transfer to a wire rack to finish cooling. These cookies are best eaten within a day or two of baking.

Nutrition: Calories: 145. **Carbs:** 3.6 g. **Protein:** 2.1 g. **Fat:** 13.6 g.

507. Melt in Your Mouth Peanut Butter Cookies

Preparation Time: 10 minutes
Cooking Time: 60 minutes
Servings: 36
Ingredients:

- 1 cup shortening
- 1 cup white sugar
- 1 cup packed brown sugar
- 1 cup peanut butter
- 2 eggs
- 2 tbsp. water
- 2 ½ cups sifted all-purpose flour
- 1 tsp. baking soda
- 1 tsp. salt

Directions:

1.　　Preheat oven to 375° F (190° C).

2.　　Beat the shortening with the sugars and the peanut butter until well mixed. Beat in the egg and the water.

3.　　Gradually beat in the flour, baking soda, and salt. Form cookies on an ungreased baking sheet with a cookie press or roll into balls and smash flat with a floured fork or fingers.

4.　　Bake at 375° F (190° C) for 12 minutes or more until done, usually when the puffed-up cookie has lowered down to level. Before then, it is chewier.

5.　　For High Altitude, omit the water and add eggs last, mixing well but not beating them at sea level. Raise the temperature to 390° F (200° C). Or use a convection oven at 312° F (155° C) for 15 min works even better.

Nutrition: Calories: 173. **Protein:** 3.1 g. **Carbs:** 19.6 g. **Fat:** 9.7 g. **Cholesterol:** 10.3 mg. **Sodium:** 138.2 mg.

508. Oatmeal Raisin Cookie (Soft & Chewy)

Preparation Time: 10 minutes

Cooking Time: 60 minutes
Servings: 18
Ingredients:

- 1 ½ cups raisins or sultanas
- 1 ¼ cups plain flour
- ½ tsp. salt
- 1/2 tsp. baking powder
- 1 tsp. ground cinnamon
- 225 g unsalted butter, softened
- 1 cup brown sugar, packed
- ¾ cup white sugar (caster sugar OK too)
- 2 large eggs (50 to 55 g each), at room temperature
- 3 cups rolled oats, not instant

Directions:

1.　　Adjust oven racks to the middle and low position, ensuring you have 4"/10 cm between each rack.

2.　　Preheat oven to 180° C/350° F (standard ovens) or 160° C/325° F (fan forced / convection)

3.　　Butter 2 large baking trays, or line with parchment/baking paper.

4.　　**Optional:** Soak raisins in boiled water for 10 minutes. Drain, then pat dry. (This makes them plumper).

5.　　Sift flour, salt, baking powder, and cinnamon into a bowl.

6.　　Using a stand mixer or electric mixer, beat butter until creamy. Then beat in sugar until fluffy (about 2 to 3 minutes).

7.　　Beat in eggs one at a time until incorporated.

8.　　Use a wooden spoon to stir the flour mixture in.

9.　　Stir in oats and raisins—this requires a bit of effort!

10.　　Form 2"/5 cm balls (16 to 20) and place onto baking trays 4"/10 cm apart.

11.　　Bake for 11 minutes. Then swap the trays between the shelves and turn the trays around. Bake for a further 11 to 14 minutes, or until cookies are golden on the edges and lightly golden on the surface.

12.　　Cool on the trays for 5 minutes before transferring to a cooling rack. Cool for 30 minutes before serving.

Nutrition: Calories: 145. **Carbs:** 3.6 g. **Protein:** 2.1 g. **Fat:** 13.6 g.

Dessert

509. Cinnamon Apple Tart

Preparation Time: 10 minutes
Cooking Time: 60 minutes
Servings: 1
Ingredients:

- 2 tsp. light brown sugar
- ½ tsp. ground cinnamon
- 1 (6-inch) flour tortilla
- 1 tbsp. unsalted butter
- ½ honey crisp apple
- Salt to taste

Directions:
1. Melt butter and slice apples into $\frac{1}{8}$-inch-thick slices.
2. Mix cinnamon and sugar.
3. Brush the tortilla with butter and sprinkle with half the sugar and cinnamon.
4. Toast in the toaster oven until tortilla crisps, about 3 minutes.
5. Arrange the apple slices in a circle around the tortilla.
6. Return to toaster oven and toast for another 10 minutes.
7. Sprinkle with salt to taste.
Nutrition: Calories: 227. **Sodium:** 250 mg. **Dietary Fiber:** 4.3 g. **Total Fat:** 12.4 g. **Total Carbs:** 30.1 g. **Protein:** 1.8 g.

510. Blackberry Peach Cobbler

Preparation Time: 25 minutes
Cooking Time: 60 minutes
Servings: 12
Ingredients:

- 1-½ cups sliced peaches
- 1 cup blackberries
- 3 tbsp. coconut sugar
- 1-½ tsp. cinnamon
- 2-½ cups dry oats
- 1 egg
- ½ cup unsweetened applesauce
- ¾ cup almond milk
- ½ cup chopped walnuts
- 1 tbsp. coconut oil, melted
- ½ tsp. cinnamon

Directions:
1. Start by preheating the toaster oven to 350° F.
2. Combine peaches, berries, sugar, and 1 tsp. cinnamon in a medium saucepan over medium heat. Simmer for about 20 minutes, stirring regularly.
3. While the peach mixture cooks beat an egg in a large bowl, then mix in applesauce and milk.
4. In a separate bowl, add egg mixture to the oats.
5. Pour oats mixture into a greased baking pan and top with peach mixture.
6. Combine coconut oil, walnuts, coconut sugar, and ½ tsp. cinnamon, and pour over the pan.
7. Bake for 30 minutes
Nutrition: Calories: 176. **Sodium:** 9 mg. **Dietary Fiber:** 3.7 g. **Total Fat:** 9.4 g. **Total Carbs:** 20.6 g. **Protein:** 4.7 g.

511. Blueberry Cream Cheese Croissant Puff

Preparation Time: 30 minutes
Cooking Time: 60 minutes
Servings: 10
Ingredients:

- 3 large croissants
- 1 cup fresh or frozen blueberries
- 1 package (8-oz.) cream cheese
- $\frac{2}{3}$ cup sugar
- 2 eggs
- 1 tsp. vanilla
- 1 cup milk

Directions:
1. Start by preheating the toaster oven to 350° F.
2. Tear up croissants into 2-inch chunks and place them in a square pan.
3. Sprinkle blueberries over croissant chunks.
4. In a medium bowl, combine cream cheese, sugar, eggs, and vanilla.
5. Slowly add milk, mixing as you add.
6. Pour cream cheese mixture over croissants and let stand for 20 minutes.
7. Bake for 40 minutes.
Nutrition: Calories: 140. **Sodium:** 97 mg. **Dietary Fiber:** 0.5 g. **Total Fat:** 5.8 g. **Total Carbs:** 20.0 g. **Protein:** 3.2 g.

512. Peanut Butter and Jelly Bars

Preparation Time: 10 minutes
Cooking Time: 60 minutes
Servings: 8
Ingredients:

- ½ cup whole wheat pastry flour
- ½ tsp. baking powder
- ¼ tsp. salt
- 1 small banana

- ¼ cup smooth peanut butter
- 3 tbsp. real maple syrup
- 2 tsp. melted coconut oil
- ½ tsp. pure vanilla extract
- 2 tbsp. chopped raw shelled peanuts
- 2 tbsp. raspberry preserves

Directions:

1. Start by preheating the toaster oven to 350° F.
2. Mash the banana.
3. Mix banana, syrup, oil, peanut butter, and vanilla in a bowl until thoroughly combined.
4. In a separate large bowl, add flour, salt, and baking powder and combine using a fork.
5. Create a hole in the flour mix and pour in the banana mix.
6. Sprinkle with nuts and stir for 2 minutes.
7. Pour batter into a bread loaf pan lined with parchment paper. Drop ½ teaspoonfuls of raspberry preserves over batter.
8. Bake for 20 minutes.
9. Allow to cool, then transfer using the parchment paper and cut.

Nutrition: Calories: 143. **Sodium:** 78 mg. **Dietary Fiber:** 1.8 g. **Total Fat:** 6.5 g. **Total Carbs:** 19.0 g. **Protein:** 3.5 g.

513. Cinnamon Pear Oatmeal Crisp

Preparation Time: 10 minutes
Cooking Time: 60 minutes
Servings: 1
Ingredients:

- 1 cup pears, peeled and thinly sliced
- 2 tbsp. rolled oats
- 1 tbsp. whole wheat pastry flour
- 1 tbsp. brown sugar
- 1 tbsp. butter
- ½ tsp. cinnamon
- Freshly grated nutmeg to taste

Directions:

1. Preheat toaster oven to 375° F.
2. Place pears in an oven-safe dish.
3. In a separate bowl, mix all other ingredients and pour on top of pears.
4. Bake for 25 minutes.

Nutrition: Calories: 300. **Sodium:** 87 mg. **Dietary Fiber:** 7.4 g. **Total Fat:** 12.7 g. **Total Carbs:** 46.9 g. **Protein:** 2.9 g.

More Than 60 Minutes

514. Roasted Vegetable Salad

Preparation Time: 5 minutes
Cooking Time: 85 minutes
Servings: 4
Ingredients:

- 3 eggplants
- 1 tbsp. olive oil
- 3 medium zucchinis
- 1 tbsp. olive oil
- 4 large tomatoes, cut them into eighths
- 4 cups one shaped pasta
- 2 peppers of any color
- 1 cup sliced tomatoes cut into small cubes
- 2 tsp. salt substitute
- 8 tbsp. grated parmesan cheese
- ½ cup Italian dressing
- Leaves of fresh basil

Directions:

1. Wash your eggplant and slice it off then discard the green end. Make sure not to peel.
2. Slice your eggplant into ½ inch thick rounds.
3. Pour 1tbsp. of olive oil on the eggplant round.
4. Put the eggplants in the basket of the air fryer and then toss them in the air fryer oven. Cook the eggplants for 40 minutes. Set the heat to 360° F
5. Meanwhile, wash your zucchini and slice it then discard the green end. But do not peel it.
6. Slice the zucchini into thick rounds of ½ inch each.
7. In the basket of the Air Fryer, toss your ingredients
8. Add 1 tbsp. of olive oil.
9. Cook the zucchini for 25 minutes on the heat of 360° F and when the time is offset it aside.
10. Wash and cut the tomatoes.
11. Arrange your tomatoes in the basket of the air fryer. Set the timer to 30 minutes. Set the heat to 350° F
12. When the time is off, cook your pasta according to the pasta guiding directions, empty it into a colander. Run the cold water on it and wash it and drain the pasta and put it aside.
13. Meanwhile, wash and chop your peppers and place them in a bow
14. Wash and thinly slice your cherry tomatoes and add them to the bowl. Add your roasted veggies.
15. Add the pasta, a pinch of salt, the topping dressing, add the basil and the parmesan, and toss everything together. Set the ingredients together in the refrigerator, and let them chill

16. Serve your salad and enjoy it.
Nutrition: Calories: 496. **Protein:** 12.98 g. **Fat:** 17.95 g. **Carbs:** 77.81 g.

515. Baked Okra and Tomato Delight

Preparation Time: 10 minutes
Cooking Time: 1 hour and 30 minutes
Servings: 4
Ingredients:

- ½ cup lime beans, frozen
- 4 tomatoes, chopped
- 8 oz. okra, fresh and washed, stemmed, sliced into ½-inch-thick slices
- 1 onion, sliced into rings
- ½ sweet pepper, seeded and sliced thin
- Pinch of crushed red pepper
- Salt to taste

Directions:

1. Preheat oven to 350° F in Bake mode.
2. Cook lime beans in water accordingly and drain them, take a 2-quarter casserole tin.
3. Add all listed ingredients to the dish and cover with foil; bake for 45 minutes.
4. Uncover the dish, stir well and bake for 35 minutes more.
5. Give it a final stir, serve, and enjoy!
Nutrition: Calories: 55. **Protein:** 3 g. **Fat:** 0 g. **Carbs:** 12 g.

516. Morning Quinoa Bread

Preparation Time: 10 minutes
Cooking Time: 1 hour and 30 minutes
Servings: 4
Ingredients:

- 1 and ¾ cups uncooked quinoa, soaked and overnight, rinsed
- ¼ cup sesame seeds
- ½ tsp. baking soda
- ¼ tsp. salt
- ¼ cup olive oil
- ½ cup sparkling water
- 1 tbsp. fresh lemon juice

Directions:

- Preheat oven to 300° F in Air Fry mode
- Line loaf pan with parchment paper
- Take a food processor and add all ingredients, pulse well
- Transfer into the pan and transfer pan to cooking basket
- Cook for 30 to 40 minutes until a toothpick comes clean
- Remove pan from fryer and keep in the cooling rack, let it cool

- Serve and enjoy!

Nutrition: Calories: 140. **Protein:** 14 g. **Fat:** 7 g. **Carbs:** 16 g.

517. Zucchini & Coconut Bread

Preparation Time: 15 minutes
Cooking Time: 3 hours
Servings: 10
Ingredients:

- 2 ½ cups zucchini, shredded
- ½ tsp. salt
- 1 ⅓ cups almond flour
- ⅔ cup coconut, shredded
- 2 tsp. ground cinnamon
- ½ tsp. ground ginger
- ¼ tsp. ground nutmeg
- 3 large organic eggs
- ¼ cup butter, melted
- ¼ cup water
- ½ tsp. organic vanilla extract
- ½ cup walnuts, chopped
- 1 tsp. baking powder
- 1 tbsp Erythritol

Directions:

1. Arrange a large sieve in a sink.
2. Place the zucchini in a sieve and sprinkle with salt. Set aside to drain for about 1 hour.
3. With your hands, squeeze out the moisture from zucchini.
4. In a large bowl, add the almond flour, coconut, Erythritol, baking powder, and spices and mix well.
5. Add the zucchini, eggs, coconut oil, water, and vanilla extract and mix until well combined.
6. Fold in the walnuts.
7. At the bottom of a greased oven, place the mixture.
8. Close the oven with a crisping lid and select Slow Cooker.
9. Set on Low for 2 ½ to 3 hours.
10. Press Start/Stop to begin cooking.
11. Keep the bread inside for about 5 to 10 minutes.
12. Carefully remove the bread from the pot and place it onto a wire rack to cool completely before slicing.
13. Cut the bread into desired-sized slices and serve.

Nutrition: Calories: 145. **Carbs:** 3.6 g. **Protein:** 2.1 g. **Fat:** 13.6 g.

518. Carrot Bread

Preparation Time: 15 minutes
Cooking Time: 3 hours
Servings: 12
Ingredients:

- 1 cup almond flour
- ⅓ cup coconut flour
- 1 ½ tsp. organic baking powder
- 1 tsp. ground cinnamon
- ¼ tsp. ground cloves
- ¼ tsp. ground nutmeg
- ¼ tsp. salt
- 1 cup Erythritol
- ⅓ cup coconut oil, softened
- 3 organic eggs
- 1 tsp. organic vanilla extract
- ½ tsp. organic almond extract
- 2 cups plus 2 tbsp. carrots, peeled and shredded

Directions:

1. In a bowl, add the flours, baking powder, baking soda, spices, and salt and mix well.
2. In another large bowl, add the Erythritol, coconut oil, eggs, and both extracts and beat until well combined.
3. Add the flour mixture and mix until just combined.
4. Fold in the carrots.
5. Place the mixture into a greased 8x4-inch silicone bread pan.
6. Arrange a Reversible Rack in the pot of the oven.
7. Place the pan over the Reversible Rack.
8. Close the oven with a crisping lid and select Slow Cooker.
9. Set on Low for 3 hours.
10. Press Start/Stop to begin cooking.
11. Place the bread pan onto a wire rack for about 5 to 10 minutes.
12. Carefully remove the bread from the pan and place it onto the wire rack to cool completely before slicing.
13. Cut the bread into desired-sized slices and serve.

Nutrition: Calories: 145. **Carbs:** 3.6 g. **Protein:** 2.1 g. **Fat:** 13.6 g.

519. Garlic Herb Butter Roast Chicken

Preparation Time: 10 minutes
Cooking Time: 1 hour and 25 minutes
Servings: 4
Ingredients:

- 4 lb. whole chicken, cleaned, rinsed
- 2 tbsp. minced garlic
- 1 medium head of garlic, peeled, cut in half crosswise
- 2 tbsp. chopped parsley
- 3 sprigs of rosemary
- 1 lemon, cut in half
- 2 tsp. salt
- 2 tsp. ground black pepper
- ¼ cup unsalted butter, melted

- 3 tbsp. olive oil

Directions:
1. Turn on the oven, set the temperature to 430° F, and then select the oven cooking method.
2. Meanwhile, juice half of the lemon and then drizzle with butter and oil over the chicken, inside the cavity, and under the skin.
3. Season the chicken with salt and black pepper, and then sprinkle with parsley.
4. Rub the garlic over the chicken, then stuff rosemary and garlic head into the chicken cavity, squeeze the other lemon half, and tie the chicken legs with the kitchen twine.
5. Arrange the chicken on the baking pan, roast it for 1 hour and 20 minutes, baste it with juice, turn on the broiler and then broil the chicken for 3 minutes until golden brown.
6. When done, cover the chicken with foil, let it stand for 10 minutes, and then carve it into pieces.
7. Serve straight away.

Nutrition: Calories: 510. **Fat:** 31 g. **Carbs:** 4 g. **Protein:** 71 g. **Fiber:** 1 g.

520. BBQ Chicken

Preparation Time: 3 hours and 5 minutes
Cooking Time: 1 hour and 30 minutes
Servings: 6
Ingredients:
- 1 whole chicken, about 4 pounds

Marinade:
- 3 tbsp. minced garlic
- 2 tsp. onion powder
- 1 tbsp. five-spice powder
- 1/3 cup sesame oil
- 1 cup soy sauce

Directions:
1. Place all the ingredients for the marinade in a medium bowl and then whisk until combined.
2. Take a large zip-lock bag, place the chicken, and pour the prepared marinade into it.
3. Seal the bag, turn it upside down to coat the chicken, and then marinate it for 3 hours in the refrigerator.
4. Meanwhile, turn on the oven, set the temperature to 350° F, and then select the oven cooking method.
5. Then place the chicken on the rotisserie and cook for 1 hour and 30 minutes until the internal temperature reaches 185° F.
6. When done, let the chicken rest for 10 minutes, cut it into pieces, and then serve.

Nutrition: Calories: 143. **Fat:** 12 g. **Carbs:** 4 g. **Protein:** 4 g. **Fiber:** 1 g.

521. Beef Brisket Recipe from Texas

Preparation Time: 15 minutes
Cooking Time: 1 hour and 30 minutes
Servings: 8
Ingredients:
- 1 ½ cup beef stock
- 1 bay leaf
- 1 tbsp. garlic powder
- 1 tbsp. onion powder
- 2 lb. beef brisket, trimmed
- 2 tbsp. chili powder
- 2 tsp. dry mustard
- 4 tbsp. olive oil
- Salt and pepper to taste

Directions:
1. Preheat the air fryer oven for 5 minutes. Place all ingredients in a deep baking dish that will fit in the air fryer.
2. Bake for 1 hour and 30 minutes at 400° F.
3. Stir the beef every after 30 minutes to soak in the sauce.

Nutrition: Calories: 306. **Fat:** 24.1 g. **Protein:** 18.3 g.

522. Cumin-Paprika Rubbed Beef Brisket

Preparation Time: 5 minutes
Cooking Time: 2 hours
Servings: 12
Ingredients:
- ¼ tsp. cayenne pepper
- 1 ½ tbsp. paprika
- 1 tsp. garlic powder
- 1 tsp. ground cumin
- 1 tsp. onion powder
- 2 tsp. dry mustard
- 2 tsp. ground black pepper
- 2 tsp. salt
- 5 lb. brisket roast
- 5 tbsp. olive oil

Directions:
1. Place all ingredients in a Ziploc bag and allow to marinate in the fridge for at least 2 hours.
2. Preheat the air fryer oven for 5 minutes.
3. Place the meat in a baking dish that will fit in the air fryer.
4. Place in the air fryer and cook for 2 hours at 350° F.

Nutrition: Calories: 269. **Fat:** 12.8 g. **Protein:** 35.6 g. **Fiber:** 2 g.

523. Lasagna Bolognese

Preparation Time: 20 minutes

Cooking Time: 4 hours and 30 minutes
Servings: 8
Ingredients:
Bolognese sauce:
- 2 oz. diced pancetta, finely chopped
- 1 medium Spanish onion or yellow onion, finely chopped
- 1 rib celery, finely chopped
- 1 carrot, finely chopped
- 4 tbsp. unsalted butter
- 11 oz. ground beef
- 4 oz. ground pork
- 4 oz. ground Italian sausage
- 1 clove, freshly ground
- Dash freshly ground cinnamon
- 1 tsp. freshly ground black pepper
- 2 lb. tomatoes, peeled and chopped, or 1 (28-oz.) can whole peeled tomatoes
- 1 cup whole milk
- ½ tsp. sea salt

Béchamel sauce:
- 2 cups whole milk
- ¼ cup unsalted butter
- ¼ cup all-purpose flour

Lasagna:
- About 16 sheets lasagna noodles (De Cecco brand recommended), enough to make 4 layers in a 13 x 9-inch baking pan with the noodles overlapping each other a little bit.
- 1 cup freshly grated Parmesan cheese

Directions:
Make the soffritto:
1. Combine pancetta, onion, celery, and carrot in a sauté pan with butter and cook over medium heat until the onion turns pale gold.

Add other ingredients:
1. Add the beef, pork, and sausage to the soffritto and increase the heat to high. Cook until browned. Sprinkle with the ground clove, cinnamon, and pepper.

Add the tomatoes:
1. Stir in the tomatoes and bring to a simmer. Reduce the heat to medium. Cook over medium heat for 15 minutes. If you are using whole canned tomatoes, break them up as you add them to the sauce.
2. Add milk and simmer:
3. Add the milk, season with sea salt, then turn down the heat and let simmer for 2 ½ hours. Stir at least every 20 minutes. Whenever the sauce simmers down to the point that it is sticking to the bottom of the pan, just add ¼ cup of water and scrape up the browned bits from the bottom and continue to cook.

Make the béchamel sauce:

Make the roux:
1. Heat the milk until almost boiling in a heavy-bottomed saucepan.
2. In a separate pan melt the unsalted butter with the flour over low heat. Stir rapidly with a spoon. Cook this for 1 minute and then remove from the heat. (See Wikipedia on Béchamel Sauce for more information on this sauce.)

Add half the milk to the roux:
3. Slowly add half the hot milk to your butter and flour mixture. During this process stir constantly.
4. Add remaining milk and thicken the sauce.
5. Return the milk, butter, flour mixture to low heat until the sauce begins to thicken. Add the remaining milk slowly while stirring working it into the thickened sauce. Continue to stir until it comes to a boil.
6. Season, then stir.
7. Season with some sea salt, and continue stirring until the right consistency has developed. If any lumps form, beat them out rapidly with a whisk until they dissolve. Remove from heat.

Prepare the lasagna:
1. Cook the lasagna noodles.
2. Preheat oven to 375° F. Cook the lasagna according to instructions. About 8 minutes in 6 quarts of boiling salted water. Drain, rinse with cold water.
3. Lay the individual lasagna noodles out on kitchen towels, not touching, so they do not stick together while you layer the casserole.

Layer the lasagna:
1. Spread a little olive oil around the inside of a 13x9-inch baking pan. Make sure your baking pan is non-reactive (pyrex or stainless steel). Do not use an aluminum pan as it will react with the acidity of the sauce and ruin the flavor.
2. Put a layer of lasagna noodles down first. Layer on a third of the Bolognese sauce, then a third of the bechamel sauce.
3. Sprinkle with grated Parmesan. Repeat two more times. Top with a final layer of noodles and sprinkle with grated Parmesan.

Bake:
1. Tent the casserole with aluminum foil. Put lasagna into the middle rack of a pre-heated 375° F oven. Bake for 20 to 30 minutes, until the top, begins to get lightly browned.
2. Remove from oven and let cool 5 to 10 minutes before serving.

Nutrition: Calories: 680. **Fat:** 37 g. **Carbs:** 54 g. **Protein:** 33 g.

Conclusion

Imagine the possibilities that now await you with this newfound knowledge. With any luck, this post will have opened your eyes to the benefits of using a convection oven for cooking and will have given you plenty of new ideas for dishes to make.

A convection oven is an appliance that cooks food by circulating hot air throughout it, which can cut down on your cooking time, energy consumption, and sometimes even clean-up! That means it can be used in all sorts of ways to enhance your cooking experience. It's undeniably one of the most versatile kitchen appliances out there.

Surely, by now you've realized that convection ovens are much more than conventional devices only suited for baking bread and roasting meat. Rather, you can use them to cook almost anything, from tasty pies and cakes to delicate pastries and risotto.

Convection ovens are different from gas, electric, or ceramic ovens because they use circulating hot air to cook food. They're designed to evenly distribute hot air throughout a certain space, resulting in an oven that cooks better and faster than conventional methods. This is because the apparatus's circulation of hot air ensures that heat is evenly distributed throughout an item or dish.

You can find convection ovens in a variety of sizes and ranges in the market. They're often outfitted with digital displays and convenience features such as digital controls, timers, and clocks to help you get the best result from your cooking endeavors.

If you've done some research and read some reviews and still feel like you need more information before making a decision about which convection oven to purchase, here are some things to keep in mind:

- **Cabinet Style:** built-in models offer style and space-saving convenience because they fit into your home's cabinets.

- **Heating Element:** standing models are freestanding and can be placed on a counter or tabletop surfaces. The heating element of a convection oven is designed to rapidly circulate hot air throughout the unit's interior in order to cook food with the most efficiency.

- **Material:** choosing between an exposed-element and concealed-element convection oven is largely a matter of personal preference, but exposed-element models tend to be more popular in the marketplace today. Convection ovens come with black, white, and stainless-steel finishes; white and stainless steel are by far the most common.

- **Maintenance:** these finishes are all high-grade materials that make baking and cooking more aesthetically pleasing. Maintenance: In order to extend the life of your convection oven, ensure that you clean it after each use.

- **Technology:** it's also a good idea to keep the handles and knobs clear of debris to ensure that they don't end up clogging or affecting the circulation of hot air.

Convection ovens come with a choice of speed and temperature settings, as well as a number of features that make cooking easier and more efficient.

- **Consumption:** using a convection oven can reduce your cooking time by as much as 50%. Like any modern-day appliance, a convection oven will require a certain level of energy to function.

Please note that the power consumption of the unit will vary depending on what you are cooking and at what temperature. As a result, it's a good idea to study this information before purchasing a unit with the goal of lowering your energy cost. This recipe book is for anyone who wants to learn how to cook using modern convection ovens. In this comprehensive guide, you'll learn not only how to use convection ovens

Made in the USA
Monee, IL
28 January 2022

90053669R00116